Who Rules South Africa?

Martin Plaut and Paul Holden

Biteback Publishing

First published in Great Britain in 2012 by
Biteback Publishing Ltd
Westminster Tower
3 Albert Embankment
London SE1 7SP
Copyright © Martin Plaut and Paul Holden 2012

First published in South Africa in 2012 by Jonathan Ball Publishers

ISBN 978-1-84954-408-5

10 9 8 7 6 5 4 3 2 1

A CIP catalogue record for this book is available from the British Library.

Set in Sabon MT Pro by Triple M Design

Printed and bound in Great Britain by
CPI Group (UK) Ltd, Croydon CR0 4YY

Contents

Abbreviations and Acronyms

ADS	African Defence Systems
AFASA	African Farmers' Association of South Africa
ALFA	Advanced Light Fighter Trainer
ANC	African National Congress
ANCYL	ANC Youth League
BEE	Black Economic Empowerment
Cope	Congress of the People
Cosatu	Congress of South African Trade Unions
CPSA	Communist Party of South Africa
CSVR	Centre for the Study of Violence and Reconciliation
DA	Democratic Alliance
DCN	Direction des Constructions Navales (France)
DIIGSA	Defence Industry Interest Group of South Africa
DIPCI	Directorate for Priority Crime Investigation
DIS	Department of Security and Intelligence (ANC)
DSO	Directorate of Special Operations (aka the Scorpions)
FBS	Futuristic Business Solutions
Fosatu	Federation of South African Trade Unions
GEAR	Growth, Employment and Redistribution strategy
GFC	German Frigate Consortium
GSC	German Submarine Consortium

ICU	Industrial and Commercial Workers Union
Idasa	Institute for Democracy in South Africa
IRIS	Incident Registration System
JSC	Judicial Services Commission
LDPHS	Local Democracy, Peace and Human Security
LIFT	Lead-In Fighter Trainer
LRAD	Land Redistribution for Agricultural Development programme
MDC	Movement for Democratic Change (Zimbabwe)
MK	Umkhonto we Sizwe
Nail	New African Investments Limited
NAT	Department of National Intelligence and Security (ANC)
NDPP	National Director of Public Prosecutions
NDR	National Democratic Revolution
NEC	National Executive Committee (ANC)
NP	National Party
NPA	National Prosecuting Authority
NUM	National Union of Mineworkers
Numsa	National Union of Metalworkers of South Africa
PAC	Pan Africanist Congress
PSC	Public Service Commission
R2K	Right2Know
RDP	Reconstruction and Development Programme
SAAF	South African Air Force
SABC	South African Broadcasting Corporation
SACP	South African Communist Party
Sactu	South African Congress of Trade Unions
SADF	South African Defence Force
Sanco	South African National Civic Organisation
SANDF	South African National Defence Force
Scopa	Standing Committee on Public Accounts
SIU	Special Investigating Unit
SOMO	State Oil Marketing Organization (Iraq)
TAC	Treatment Action Campaign
TAU SA	Transvaal Agricultural Union
UDF	United Democratic Front

Introduction

Martin Plaut and Paul Holden

South Africa's air of a well-governed liberal democracy is beguiling. To tourists and businesspeople spilling out of its sparkling new airports and gliding away on smooth highways, everything exudes confidence and prosperity. Men and women go about their daily business untroubled by the wars and rebellions that so disfigure the rest of the continent.

Why then the unease that pervades so much of South African debate? Change has arrived, apartheid has been abolished and the country has moved on to happier times. More than two decades after Nelson Mandela's release, however, South Africa is still a troubled nation. Racism, no longer so overt, still plagues relations between its peoples. A sea of poverty and unemployment laps around the fortresses of wealth and privilege. The small, but growing, black elite that has gained a foothold on the ladder of advantage appears on the whole little concerned by the plight of the majority. A sense of fear and distrust pervades luxury shopping malls and tin shack informal settlements alike.

A R100-million wave of festivities will deliver the ruling African National Congress (ANC) at Mangaung (Bloemfontein) for the party's centenary conference in December 2012, but senior party officials have been confessing since as early as October 2009 that the party is wracked by internal conflict.[1] According to a cable released by Wikileaks, the ANC's Gauteng spokesman, Dumisa Ntuli, told a US diplomat that the party was deeply divided not only between supporters of President

Jacob Zuma and former President Thabo Mbeki, but 'along multiple other lines': 'There are die-hard Zuma supporters, the pro-labour people, the Communists, the pro-Mbeki people and no one speaks for the same things.' Another leaked cable has the ANC Treasurer, Mathews Phosa, telling the Americans: 'Everyone talks about 2012.' According to him, the next five-yearly party conference would be 'worse than Polokwane' in 2007, when Zuma and his allies ousted Thabo Mbeki, convulsing the political system.

It is obvious that South Africa's future holds another bruising contest of political heavyweights in 2012, although it remains unclear as to which parties will emerge victorious and whether it will be a first-round knock-out or a decision on points. That is not to say that the pundits are blind to the basic contours of what may emerge, or to the advantages and disadvantages of all sides. The ANC Youth League and its allies, would-be king-makers, have all the speed and unpredictability of a rookie heavyweight, devastating in short bursts and at close range, but they have been dealt a stiff uppercut with the disciplining of Youth League President Julius Malema. Their likely opponent, a motley semi-leftist spy-heavy grouping around Zuma, may move slowly but has extensive reach, experience and the proven stamina to go the long rounds – and, if worst comes to worst, the referee in its pocket. To further balance the scales, both fighters will have remarkably similar men (and women) in their corners – different typologies of the Black Economic Empowerment (BEE) millionaire – and both will bus in supporters from provincial heartlands to sway the emotions of the judges. Organised labour will most likely shake their heads over what has happened to the nobility of the sport and bemoan the paucity of fighting talent.

An accurate prediction of the victor, and the length and impact of the reign, depends on a simple question: who rules South Africa? This book attempts an answer, although the simplicity of the query does not guarantee a straightforward reply. Part of the complexity is owing to the slipperiness of the concept of power itself. Power is amorphous; often invisible or disguised; relevant or 'activated' in certain contexts and meaningless in others; differentiated by type (economic, political, cultural, social or a combination of these); and, most importantly, diffuse. In a complex and contested country like South Africa, locating its holders is even more difficult. A formal democracy suggests a democratic distribution of power, when, in fact, power is most frequently wielded outside democratic structures – and, more recently, in defiance of them. The country is no simple top-down African dictatorship, with clear lines of authority from the president to the citizen.

In addition, it is difficult, if nigh on impossible, to interrogate who rules South Africa without understanding a related corollary: how power is held and what has been done with it. Without understanding how the use of power in different contexts can strengthen, contour or dissipate power in those self-same contexts, we can only arrive at a partial grasp of the complexity of South African power politics. Power is not static, nor is it timeless, something that would be missed if we did not try to grasp how the wielding of power, in itself, changes the balance of power.

We will not attempt to provide a simplistic summary of our eventual conclusion here. The complexity of South Africa, in any event, prevents a simplistic answer to our guiding question. Instead, we have decided to describe key developments that have dominated South Africa over the last decade and a half, using these as routes by which we can navigate the vexed questions we are posing. These are dealt with in four broad sections on what we feel are the dominant themes that have emerged in post-apartheid South Africa.

The first section – Best Friends, Worst Enemies – provides a brief history of South African politics (at the national level) and, most importantly, an examination of the alliance between the ANC, the South African Communist Party (SACP) and the Congress of South African Trade Unions (Cosatu). The narrative extends from the mid-1950s, when this alliance first formed, and extends to the present day. What is key, here, is the realisation that the Alliance is the centre of political power in the New South Africa, operating sometimes mysteriously and secretly, its power held and wielded outside the formal structure of the state.

The second section – Oversight, Corruption and the Consolidation of Executive Power – looks at the state of South Africa's democratic institutions. It uses two massive scandals – the Arms Deal and the abuse of the secret services – to illustrate the extent to which the democratic limits on the political power of the ANC and its executive have been swept aside, leaving many aspects of the checks and balances of the new democratic order in tatters, ineffective and subservient. This section also examines the role of those institutions and bodies that have, so far, resisted the depredations of the ANC's drive for consolidated power: the judiciary, the independent (read: non-SABC) media and civil society. It should be noted, however, that the independence of each group and their successes in constraining executive power according to constitutional imperatives have generated fresh discord between them and the ANC executive; hence, over the last two years at least, a sustained campaign to pilot laws and measures that would bring them to heel.

The third section – The Way In: Money, Money, Money – is partially a continuation of the section above (at least, it cross-pollinates, as both this and the previous section have to deal with the power of corruption and the corruption of power). It looks at the way in which money – economic power – has impacted on the state and has guided some of the ANC's more questionable policy drives.

Next, we look at the policy of Black Economic Empowerment, and how it has created new, immensely influential political players and new, powerful tensions within the Alliance. Here, what is notable in our argument is a frequently ignored point: that BEE has created a number of billionaires with holdings that appear on closer inspection to be little more than paper. This has driven new developments, in particular the re-emergence of nationalisation as a political programme, conceived in populist terms but, in reality, driven by the need to bail out the emerging 'patriotic bourgeoisie'.

This section ends with a look at how the ANC has overcome one of its own largest obstacles to the unquestioned rule of the party – access to funding. What is clear, from our examination, is that the ANC has, by means that offend corruption investigators and political analysts alike, secured a stable and secure source of funds that dwarfs that available to opposition parties. This, perhaps more than any other development, has placed the ANC in a position where it can be confident of ruling for a considerable period of time. That this has reduced the reliance of the ANC on Cosatu and the SACP, and the resources these organisations mobilise, has created its own tensions.

The final section, 'New Centres of Power, New Contests', turns away from the Alliance and the pillars of the state, and considers alternative centres of power and pressures that affect the politics of the country. The governance of the Western Cape – now ruled by the opposition Democratic Alliance (DA) – is described in detail as an insight into why, in one corner of South Africa, the ANC's power has been muted and rejected. A chapter on organised crime opens up the underbelly of South African life and reveals how it interacts with and feeds into much of what we have already described, threatening to embed itself inside the structures of the state.

A chapter on land provides a counterpoint to previous chapters with a description of the impact of politics on the powerless, the most marginalised group in South Africa, the rural poor. And the final chapter, on the failure of service delivery in key areas, points to a newly emerging threat to the status quo. This is the possibility that the thousands of frequently violent community protests over local state failure might coalesce into a widespread popular revolt against the uses and abuses of power in the New South Africa.

Best Friends, Worst Enemies

Chapter 1

The Uneasy Alliance

Martin Plaut

The alliance between the African National Congress, the South African Communist Party and the trade unions in Cosatu is perhaps the most important political force in the country.[1] More influential than Parliament, it is debates within the Alliance, rather than speeches before the legislature, that are the critical impetus within South Africa today. The fact that the ANC sees its members of Parliament as primarily representatives of the party, rather than of the electorate, has a lot to do with this. There are no constituencies with their own MP to hold to account. The proportional representation system means that MPs are answerable only to their parties, which decide where they will be on the all-important, career-defining party lists.

The 1994 code of conduct for ANC MPs specifically states that: 'All elected members shall be under the constitutional authority of the highest decision-making bodies of the ANC, and decisions and policies of the highest ANC organs shall take precedence over all other structures, including ANC structures in Parliament and government.'[2] The code of conduct further forbids any 'attempt to make use of the parliamentary structures to undermine organisational decisions and policies'. This has undermined the centrality of Parliament. Hardly surprising that ANC MPs are frequently absent during debates. Their chief whip can only bemoan the 'empty benches' and complain that this will 'erode the image and integrity of this institution and betray the trust that the people placed in us'.[3]

Hardly a day goes by without a reference to the Alliance, yet little is really known about just how it operates. Even its origins remain obscure. With no founding document and no written constitution, it is nonetheless the beating heart of South African politics.

The Alliance's objective is to realise what is termed the 'National Democratic Revolution' (NDR). Its initial aim was to eradicate apartheid, but its ultimate goal was much wider. The SACP quotes from the Green Book drawn up by the ANC in 1979, to lay out the aims of the Alliance:[4]

> The aims of our national democratic revolution will only be fully realised with the construction of a social order in which all the historic consequences of national oppression and its foundation, economic exploitation, will be liquidated, ensuring the achievement of real national liberation and social emancipation. An uninterrupted advance towards this ultimate goal will only be assured if within the alignment of revolutionary forces struggling to win the aims of our national democratic revolution, the dominant role is played by the oppressed working people.

The communists then outline just how they believe the relationship between their party and the ANC should develop: 'The Party had also understood that the main organisational vehicle to achieve the goals of these shared political perspectives beyond just the NDR, was the Alliance, primarily between the ANC and the SACP.' They point to the fact that during their years underground the relationship between the ANC and the SACP 'evolved into a deeper relationship and conscious collaboration between communists' inside both the ANC and its military wing, Umkhonto we Sizwe, 'with communists occupying prominent and leading positions in the latter two formations'.[5] The party's aim was and continues to be a close, at times symbiotic relationship, with SACP members holding key positions within the ANC while retaining their positions in their own organisation.

The third element of the Alliance is the trade union movement. The unions, which developed during the first half of the twentieth century, came under the shadow of the ANC and the SACP during the 1950s. As we shall show, the non-racial unions, members of the South African Congress of Trade Unions (Sactu) were drawn into a relationship with the ANC and the communists, which gradually sapped their ability to represent the organised black working class. When the unions re-emerged in the 1970s they were determined to retain their independence, and continue to jealously guard their rights, even while working with their political allies.

Although the Alliance is vital to South African political life, the way in which it functions is less than transparent. It operates largely in private and seldom publishes details of its debates, even if many of its key decisions are soon leaked to the public. While the organisations that constitute the Alliance have public faces and work openly in civil society, the same cannot be said of the body that binds them together. Discussions within the Alliance are perhaps too sensitive to conduct in the open, since it is here that the horse-trading takes place that is the real substance of politics.

One report on the Tripartite Alliance Summit of 1997 (three years after the first post-apartheid general election) gave a fascinating glimpse into its workings.[6] It spoke of the national secretariats of the three organisations meeting on a 'fairly regular basis (in theory fortnightly) throughout the last three and a quarter years'. But it went on to say that such meetings 'often lack a capacity to carry through decisions, reflecting organisational weaknesses within the respective formations. The meetings are often focused on immediate interventions, and on crisis management.' National officials of the ANC, SACP and the unions also met 'relatively frequently'. There had been five meetings of the executive of the Alliance before September 1997. It was resolved that they would in future be more frequent, 'around 3 per year'. This may have been accepted, but certainly in recent years meetings have not been held at this frequency, leaving the SACP and Cosatu to grumble about the ANC's apparent lack of interest in convening Alliance summits.

In recent years the Alliance has become increasingly dysfunctional. Since by its very nature it embodies the stresses and strains of South

African society, encapsulating the divergent interests of its constituent elements, Alliance members find themselves both operating within and fighting against the state. Key members like union leader Zwelinzima Vavi work with Alliance colleagues while keeping up a blistering attack on them. How else does one explain his warning that: 'If the broad liberation movement does not act decisively, we are heading rapidly in the direction of a full-blown predator state, in which a powerful, corrupt and demagogic elite of political hyenas will increasingly control the state as a vehicle for self-enrichment.'[7]

In its current form the Alliance officially came into being on 9 May 1990,[8] but its origins go far further back in time. In his speech to the ANC rally marking the party's centenary on 8 January 2012, Jacob Zuma traced its roots to the 1920s:[9]

> The movement prides itself on having a strong historical relationship with the working class. The South African Communist Party was formed in 1921 and had engaged itself in issues affecting workers and the working class. Already then, the seeds of a unique Alliance were germinating when the ANC and the Communist Party of South Africa resolved to work together in 1929. Meanwhile, the relationship with the trade union movement can be traced back to the first major trade union of Africans, the Industrial Workers Union, which was formed in Bloemfontein in 1920 and also through the South African Congress of Trade Unions (Sactu), and later the Congress of South African Trade Unions (Cosatu).

Roots of the relationship

The ANC was founded in 1912, and the Communist Party of South Africa in 1921. The trade unions can trace their origins even further back in time.

The first recorded strike was on the docks in Cape Town in 1854, but it was the discovery of diamonds in 1867 and gold in 1886 that led to the development of mining and with it the first unions. In 1891 the 'Knights of Labour' was formed to fight for the rights of workers, declaring 'perpetual war and opposition to the encroachment of monopoly and organized capital'.[10] But these were unions established specifically to fight for the rights of white workers. They opposed black and Chinese labour being brought onto the mines to undercut their wages. This confrontation came to a climax with the Rand Revolt of 1922, when the gold price collapsed and 10 000 white miners feared retrenchment. Under the notorious banner, 'Workers of the World Fight and Unite for a White South Africa,' they took on the state. Prime Minister Jan Smuts ordered out the military, and broke the strike by force of planes, tanks and machine guns. Around 250 strikers died, 5 000 were arrested and four executed.[11]

Black workers had begun to organise in the aftermath of the First World War. Clements Kadalie founded the Industrial and Commercial Workers Union (ICU) in 1919, and by 1927 had 100 000 members.[12] The Communist Party, which had earlier concentrated on working with white unions and rejected the ANC as dominated by 'instruments of the ruling class', decided in the mid-1920s to turn to black labour.[13] The Party worked closely with Kadalie until communists concerned by corruption in the union demanded to look at the books. In December 1926 the ICU passed a resolution that no member of the ICU should be a Party member. Many of its best organisers, forced to choose between the Party and the union, chose the communists. Wracked by splits and robbed of some of its leading cadres, the ICU soon declined.

The 1920s and 1930s were, internationally, among the most traumatic and complex periods of the twentieth century. The mass unemployment and inflation that accompanied the Depression saw the rise of fascism in Germany and Italy. The Soviet Union, which had encouraged international revolution through the Communist International, reversed its position, forcing communist parties around the world to subjugate their own revolutions to the defence of the socialist motherland.

In February 1927 a meeting of the League against Imperialism was held in Brussels. The ANC delegation included a future president, Josiah Tshangana Gumede. Addressing the meeting on the conditions of servitude in which most of his countrymen lived, Gumede made what has become a famous remark:

> I am not a Communist, but we find that the Communist Party
> are the only people who are with us in spirit and we are watch-
> ing them ... There are two forces working today, imperialism
> and a workers' republic in Russia. We hear little of it. We hear
> much against it. I would point out that I wish to learn more
> and more of it. We shall have to put these two on a scale and
> see which would be the best to ally with.[14]

Gumede went on to visit Moscow and to praise what he found. This
visit is still warmly recalled by the ANC. President Jacob Zuma recently
referred to his address, saying: 'The alliance between the ANC, workers
and the communist party has been a subject of analysis and debate over
many years ... This organisation has never shied away from the workers. If you see us being in alliance with Cosatu it is not something we
decided recently. It is an old tradition.'[15]

For South African communists the late 1920s were a period of deep
division, with the left of the party attempting to resist Moscow's imposition of a theory that revolution in South African would only be
achieved in stages.[16] This turn to the right by the Soviets forced communist parties around the world to adopt similar positions. Pure class
struggle was abandoned, and the South African communists obediently
embraced the view that the country would first have to end colonial rule
and establish a 'Native Republic' before attempting the overthrow of
the capitalist order and bringing about a socialist society.[17] Arcane as
this debate may be, the 'stages of revolution' theory was to throw a long
shadow across South African history, and the current leadership of the
ANC still use 'National Democratic Revolution' to refer to the present
situation.

It was during the Second World War that the black trade union movement really took off. The ANC, which had previously taken only a
passing interest in labour, launched a mineworkers' union in 1941. The
following year the Council of Non-European Trade Unions was formed,
with Dan Tloome, a communist and an ANC member, as its vice-pres-
ident. With many white workers away on war service the unions had
industrial muscle. Although strikes were illegal, they won real wage increases. Unionisation grew rapidly, and by the end of the war there were

119 unions with a total membership of 158 000,[18] with both the ANC
and the communists vying for control of the union movement.[19]

This was a critical period. The ANC had no more than 5 000 members.[20] Its leadership was of the old school: respectful, Christian and
gentlemanly. Younger members, among them Anton Lembede, were fed
up with their modest petitions to the government. In 1944 they founded
the Congress Youth League, whose manifesto described the party's elders
as 'a body of gentlemen with clean hands'. Nelson Mandela was among
the first members of the Youth League and was elected onto its executive. At first he, like others, was critical of the links with the Communist
Party, despite the fact that there had been some overlapping membership
of the ANC and the Party since the 1920s.[21] When Ruth First wrote to
the Youth League to invite them to join the Progressive Youth Council –
a Communist Party front – the League wrote back saying: 'We fear there
is a yawning gap between your party or philosophic outlook and ours.
We are devoting our energies to the preparation for the greatest national
struggle of all time, the struggle for national liberation.'[22]

This hostility did not last. In 1946 the mineworkers took industrial
action, bringing the mines to a halt and 76 000 workers out on strike
for a week. Mandela visited the mines with the communist leader,
JB Marks.[23] Lembede's death in 1947 left the way open for a more con-
ciliatory attitude between the two organisations. This was also a period in which the Communist Party was one of the few organisations to
genuinely embrace a non-racial culture. Multiracial dances organised
by the party as a recruitment drive were an important meeting point for
people of all races.[24]

This kind of social interaction was important in forming the thinking
of young ANC members, including Nelson Mandela. In 1943 he became
a student at the University of the Witwatersrand, meeting for the first
time men and women like Joe Slovo, Ruth First, George Bizos and Ismail
Meer, all members of the left.[25] It was no time for sectarian rivalries:
many ANC members moved to the left. Nelson Mandela was among
them and – according to recent research by Stephen Ellis – became a
member of the Communist Party himself in the late 1950s or 1960.[26]

Afrikaner nationalism was on the rise and in 1948 the National Party
claimed electoral victory. Apartheid was to become the official policy

of the land, building on decades of racism and sweeping away the few electoral rights black, Coloured and Indian citizens had enjoyed. The Nationalists' election pamphlet on race relations put it simply: 'The fundamental guiding principle of National Party policy is preserving and safeguarding the White race.'[27]

The Communist Party was the first organisation to be attacked as the government brought in an array of laws to suppress dissent. The Suppression of Communism Act, passed on 26 June 1950, not only banned the party but made the propagation of communist ideology illegal. The Communist Party of South Africa dissolved itself, and after a spate of detentions most of its 1 500 members went underground or kept their membership secret, while they became members of other organisations. Some went into exile, notably to London, where in time they were to provide the backbone of the Anti-Apartheid Movement. It was only in 1953 that the party was re-formed, this time known as the South African Communist Party.[28]

Banning the communists produced exactly the opposite effect to that which the government had intended. It cemented the relationship with the ANC, with party members throwing themselves into ANC activities and building the existing black trade unions. 'Before 1950 there was the feeling that there were two camps; some belong to one, some to the other,' the future ANC leader Oliver Tambo later recalled. 'But after 1950 we were all together and when we discussed politics we never thought of the differences in our philosophies. We were equals deciding what to do.'[29]

This process, building on links that went back to earlier times, grew gradually. It started with an emergency conference in Johannesburg in May 1950, convened by Walter Sisulu of the ANC, to try to halt the expected banning of the communists. In attendance were the African National Congress, African People's Organisation, South African Indian Congress, Communist Party of South Africa and Transvaal Council of Non-European Trade Unions. Rusty Bernstein of the Communist Party described the significance of the occasion:[30]

> At the meeting hatchets were buried ... A unified council of war was set up to run a joint campaign – something the

movement had been previously unable to do. The government had created the first all-inclusive alliance against its own policies. There is little reference to that meeting in the histories, yet there – unnoticed – the foundation stone was laid for the ANC coalition that would come to dominate the next decades of South African liberation politics.

The Defiance Campaign brought 10 000 volunteers onto the streets offering themselves for arrest as they broke unjust and racist laws. In November 1952 a public meeting was again held in Johannesburg, under the auspices of the ANC and the South African Indian Congress. Whites were urged by Oliver Tambo to join an organisation that could work with the other Congresses. This was a critical development. After all, the ANC had been born as an African nationalist organisation, which did not admit other ethnic groups. Some of its leading members, like Moses Kotane, had been communists, but this moment marked the ANC's decision to formally reach out to organisations representing South Africa's diverse peoples. It was a step that was finally to lead to the ANC's decision to admit whites (and other ethnic groups) as full members taken at the Morogoro conference of April 1969.[31]

A year later, drawing on the Springbok legion, a left-wing organisation of ex-servicemen who had fought during the Second World War, the Congress of Democrats was founded. They included former communists as well as other members of the left.[32] In March 1954 these organisations were joined by a fourth – the South African Coloured People's Organisation, later the Coloured People's Congress. The activities of the alliance were coordinated by a National Consultative Committee consisting of representatives of each of its component organisations.[33]

Then, in 1955, the Freedom Charter was signed, pledging to work towards the establishment of a non-racial nation. The ANC increased in strength, taking its membership to around 100 000.[34]

While the ANC launched its protest campaigns, the Communist Party had been working with the union movement. In 1955 'progressives' in the union movement broke with the Trade Union Congress of South Africa (which had refused to admit African unions) to form the South African Congress of Trade Unions, Sactu.[35] With 19 affiliates, it claimed a membership of 20 000. From the first it adopted an openly political stance, rejecting what Lenin would have called a mere 'trade union' consciousness. The organisation's first annual conference in 1956 stated:

> Sactu is conscious of the fact that the organising of the mass of workers for higher wages, better conditions of life and labour is inextricably bound up with a determined struggle for political rights and liberation from all oppressive laws and practices. It follows that a mere struggle for the economic rights of all workers without participation in the general struggle for political emancipation would condemn the Trade Union movement to uselessness and to a betrayal of the interests of the workers.[36]

The government's response to the opposition of the ANC and its associates was repression. In 1956 it charged 156 people with treason, among them Nelson Mandela. Ben Turok, another treason trialist, pinpoints this as the moment when the Alliance was formed. He recalls how people of all races came together in 1956:[37]

> … we met together as the Treason Trial accused. This sent out a wonderful message across the country that all races who believed in democracy could unite in the Congress Alliance. Such unity across racial lines was formalised in the joint executives of the Congress Alliance…So the Congress Alliance came together in the joint executives with ten delegates each from the ANC, the Indian Congress and the Coloured People's Organisation, and even ten delegates from the (white) Congress of Democrats and from the Congress of Trade Unions – always under the leadership of Chief Luthuli.

The movement was now complete. The Congress Alliance brought four pro-ANC political organisations together with trade unions that opposed apartheid. Turok says that because of the intense repression during this period it was almost impossible for the full Alliance executive of 50 delegates to hold meetings, although some did take place.[38] Instead, a secretariat was formed in 1958, with Turok as its administrative secretary.[39] Walter Sisulu of the ANC led this critical body, which consisted of one representative from each of its constituent organisations. The secretariat met every day. 'Our job was to co-ordinate the positions of the different organisations,' Turok recalls.[40]

Exactly what happened next remains a matter of some controversy. Stephen Friedman argues that while the unions initially prospered and grew, they came under the direction of the ANC, whose members were launched on a series of actions designed to confront the government. Perhaps the best known protests were the strikes (known as 'stay aways') in 1957 and 1958, originally called around the issue of a living wage, with the slogan 'One Pound a Day'. The ANC, Friedman believes, took over the campaigns' planning and running.[41]

The campaigns were not a success. Only around one in ten African workers supported the strike of 1958 in Johannesburg, although larger numbers came out in Port Elizabeth. The ANC called off the action after just one day, without consulting Sactu.[42] Friedman concludes:

> Congress leaders did not value a workers movement as an end in itself: where unions acted in support of worker goals, as in 1957, they were indifferent. They valued the unions' ability to mobilise workers, but insisted that they do this to serve the Congress movement's goals: it was the Congresses' job to choose the issues and make the tactical decisions – the unions' task was to rally workers behind them. Because Sactu's leaders believed workers would only achieve their goals if the Congresses achieved theirs, they accepted these terms.[43]

This assessment has been hotly contested by the ANC and those aligned to it. Some argue quite the opposite – that the links with the Congress Alliance helped Sactu grow, and that by 1959 it had 46 000 members and 35 affiliates.[44] Indeed, it is suggested that the unions had a powerful and lasting impact on the ANC.

As we shall see later in this chapter, this controversy was not forgotten. What is clear is that the unions and the wider ANC alliance came up against the brick wall of government oppression. The key date was 21

March 1960. A march was called by the ANC's rival – the Pan Africanist Congress (PAC) – to the police station at the township of Sharpeville, outside Vereeniging. It was in protest against the introduction of the notorious 'passes' for African women. These documents already dominated the lives of African men, restricting their movement and residence to narrowly prescribed areas of South Africa. When 20 000 men and women came to protest outside the police station in Sharpeville, the 150 police stationed there panicked and opened fire. At least 69 were killed, including eight women and ten children. Some 200 were injured. The government reacted with savage repression. In April 1960 the ANC and PAC were banned and a state of emergency was imposed. Thousands were rounded up and imprisoned.

In the wake of Sharpeville there were attempts to form a united front against the increasingly repressive apartheid government. In December 1960, 36 African leaders, including representatives of the PAC and the Liberal Party, assembled at a Consultative Conference in Orlando.[45] The conference was disrupted by the police, but this was not the chief reason why attempts to bring a wider opposition body into being floundered. The Liberals and the Pan Africanists accused the ANC and communists of manipulating events. As Jordan Ngubane, a Liberal Party member, recalled, the ANC and communists met in secret to set the agenda of meetings. They provided, he said, 'an invisible hand that moved events towards its own goal'.

This impression is reinforced by the tight, clandestine manner in which the Congress Alliance's secretariat operated. The key individuals representing the five organisations went into hiding, living underground in safe houses. It was, says Turok, the secretariat which took the key decisions during this period, meeting every day. 'We worked like crazy,' he recalls. 'Because of the security situation you needed a small ginger group who could act, and that was our job. So we led. I am not ashamed to say that.'[46]

Interviewed by a British television journalist, Brian Widlake, from hiding in May 1961, Nelson Mandela famously described the ANC's reaction to the events that Sharpeville unleashed:[47]

> There are many people who feel that the reaction of the government to our stay at home – ordering a general mobilisation,

arming the white community, arresting ten thousands of
Africans – this show of force throughout the country, notwithstanding our clear declaration that this campaign is being run
on peaceful and non-violent lines, close a chapter as far as our
methods of political struggle are concerned. There are many
people who feel that it is useless and futile for us to continue
talking peace and non-violence against a government whose
reply is only savage attacks on an unarmed and defenceless
people. And I think the time has come for us to consider, in
the light of our experiences in this stay at home, whether the
methods which we have applied so far are adequate.

For many years this was one of the few glimpses the outside world had
of the ANC's now legendary leader – replayed endlessly as his 27 years
in jail ticked by. But the decision to turn to armed struggle was not as
straightforward as this stark but clearly carefully worded statement
would make it appear.

Exactly when the decision was taken to turn to armed struggle, illegality and underground resistance is something of a mystery. Raymond
Suttner, himself a member of the ANC underground, suggests the key
date was 1953, when a decision was taken in secret at the ANC annual
conference to draw up a plan – later known as the M-Plan or Mandela
Plan – to 'enable the movement to operate underground in the likely
event that it would be banned by the Nationalist government'. [48]

The SACP decided to create an armed force at a conference in
December 1960, after discussions with the Chinese Communist Party
and a meeting with Chairman Mao Zedong.[49] The journalist Howard
Barrell reports that the piece of paper bearing the decision was burned
in front of the delegates and crushed into fine powder.[50] The ANC apparently took a little longer to take the decision. Barrell goes on to
quote Joe Modise, the man who later led the ANC's military wing,
Umkhonto we Sizwe (MK), as saying that a meeting took place in early
1961 at which all the movements associated with the ANC – including
the communists and the unions – decided to launch the armed struggle.[51] Stephen Ellis believes that the decision was, in fact, taken by the
Communist Party and then adopted by the ANC, concluding that 'it is

clear that the Party took the decision first and then influenced the ANC, with Mandela playing a prominent intermediary role'.[52]

However the decision was taken, there is little doubt about the date on which the first attack took place. On 15 December 1961 a pass office in Durban and an electricity pylon were targeted. The campaign had been meant to begin the following day, but spotting that officials at the pass office were drunk, the MK leadership in Natal decided to strike. The following day there were ten more attacks in Port Elizabeth and Johannesburg.

Trade unionists were to continue to play a key role in many future military actions. But members of Sactu had a particularly difficult role in the years ahead, since they operated openly as well as covertly. Their organisation was not banned, and although individuals were arrested and the movement was subjected to intense repression, they could still function as trade unions. Eric Mtshali, a Durban trade unionist, recalls this double existence: 'The Party's big task ... was doing ANC work, [supporting] the ANC branches, using our experience to build the ANC underground, also using Sactu, because Sactu was not banned and the leadership of Sactu were mainly Communists in almost all provinces.'[53]

Crushed and then reborn

By the early 1960s the cast of South African politics for most of the next decade was set. The ANC and SACP had gone into exile, their futures now intimately linked. They decided to maintain separate representations in exile, leaving the other political elements of the Congress Alliance to gradually wither and die.[54]

The Alliance attempted to maintain an underground presence in South Africa, but to little effect. The ANC would spend years attempting to gather its strength in Africa, with limited assistance from the newly independent African states. It was left relying on its Communist Party links to gain arms and training from East Germany and the Soviet Union. At the same time, with the help of established SACP exiles and the wider Anti-Apartheid Movement, the ANC would gradually gain leverage in the corridors of power in Western Europe, the United States and the United Nations.

The National Party government had unleashed its security forces and – at least until the early 1970s – was able to rule South Africa almost un-opposed. The unions representing black workers, although unbanned, were eroded by arrests and repression and reduced to a tiny rump. Sactu, operating from London, cultivated its links with union movements around the world, on both sides of the Iron Curtain.

In the 1970s, two events were to change the course of South African history. Both were as unforeseen by the government as they were by the ANC and its allies. Both were to pose major challenges to the regime and its opponents. These critical moments of resistance were the Durban strikes of 1973, which re-ignited the flame of trade unionism, and the Soweto uprising of 1976, which re-established the tradition of popular resistance. The organisations they were to produce – Cosatu and, in the 1980s, the United Democratic Front (UDF) – were, in the end, to play the major roles in eliminating apartheid. This is not to underestimate the work of the ANC or the wider Alliance, but the ousting of the South African regime was mainly the result of resistance on the streets and in the townships. This, together with international pressure in the form of sanctions and disinvestment promoted by the ANC and Oliver Tambo in particular, fatally undermined the regime. Despite the sacrifices of many thousands of brave men and women, it was not an ANC army that marched into Pretoria. Instead, it was negotiations, rather than armed struggle, that ended centuries of white rule.

The Durban strikes – rolling industrial action that spread across the city in January 1973 – came like a bolt from the blue. From brickworks to textile plants, workers downed tools. Crowds of workers gathered in fields outside their firms. Refusing to elect leaders who could be arrested by the police or harassed by management, they shouted their demands for an improvement in their crushingly low levels of pay. It was a crude but effective tactic. In three months, 61 000 workers went out on strike, more than the total for the previous eight years.[55]

Rebuilding the black trade union movement was a slow and painful process. Some activists were drawn from white trade unions. Others were former members of Sactu. Sympathetic white university students and intellectuals filled some of the leadership roles. The response from London and Lusaka was less than enthusiastic. The ANC and Sactu judged that the emerging trade unions would only legitimise South Africa's repressive government by making it appear more liberal than it really was. In a paper published in June 1977, John Gaetsewe, Sactu General Secretary, argued that:

> ... there are ultimately only two options open to legal African trade unions: either advance, taking up political as well as economic questions, and eventually being crushed or driven underground; or for the leadership to become co-opted and the trade unions emasculated – tools in the hands of the employers and (white) registered unions.... Repression of trade union activity means that in the long term, meaningful advances can only be made on an underground basis.[56]

Sactu went out of its way to mobilise its resources, particularly in Britain, the headquarters of the Anti-Apartheid Movement, to ensure that its viewpoint prevailed. That South Africa was an openly fascist state in which no open, organised dissent would be tolerated was a position reiterated as late as 1982: 'Sactu was forced underground. And there is nothing to suggest that the apartheid regime will ever tolerate a strong, progressive and open trade union movement for very long. It would be a mistake to act on this basis.'[57]

Certainly there were many reverses. Union members were jailed and harassed and organisers were killed. Despite this, the unions continued to grow in strength. In April 1979 at a church seminary at Hammanskraal, the Federation of South African Trade Unions (Fosatu) was born. It brought together 12 unions, representing 45 000 members, committed to a non-racial trade union movement controlled and directed by its members.[58]

The union movement was still tiny and fragile, with only 20 000 fully paid-up members, but it was beginning to drive a wedge into the rock face of government oppression. A month later the government released a report recommending the recognition of the right of African workers to form and belong to trade unions. This apparently small step may have appeared an insignificant sop designed to ameliorate black anger and international criticism of poverty-level wages, but it was to mark the moment that opposition began loosening the National Party's hold on power. The 1979 legislation gave black Africans full industrial citizenship; the same collective bargaining rights as white workers. A process of disenfranchisement that had begun in the Cape Province with the Franchise and Ballot Act of 1892, raising the franchise qualifications from £25 to £75 to the disadvantage of Africans, Coloureds and poor whites, was beginning to be reversed.[59]

The unions that formed Fosatu were characterised not just by a non-racial perspective, but also by a determination to root the union movement firmly in the workplace. Memories of how the ANC and the Communist Party had attempted to use the union movement as a battering ram in the 1950s lingered on. While by no means hostile to the ANC, there was a feeling that a certain distance was required from the movement, if the unions were to truly represent their membership. As the eminent scholar of industrial relations, Professor Eddie Webster, put it: 'The "shop-floor" unions that first emerged in 1973 eschewed political action outside production. They believed it was important to avoid the path taken by Sactu in the 1960s.'[60] As a result Fosatu adopted a deliberate strategy of first building economic muscle before becoming involved in community and political issues.

Unsurprisingly, Sactu reacted negatively to what was perceived to be a direct challenge to its existence. As the most authoritative study of this issue concluded:

> There seems little doubt that Sactu feared Fosatu as a potential rival. Precisely because Fosatu embodied the principles of non-racial, industrial trade unionism, and had united unions from a diversity of regions, it could not be decried. Yet, Fosatu's early insistence that political engagement would divert energies from the factories, that unions could not work with political groups without endangering their independence, accorded ill with Sactu's conception of political unionism. Further, Sactu worried that Fosatu might lead workers up a blind alley of reformism.[61]

In fact, Sactu feared that it would be outflanked and displaced on the left. This was a constant concern of Sactu and the communists. Norma Kitson fell out with the Anti-Apartheid Movement when she began a non-stop picket outside the South African embassy in London, calling for better conditions for her unionist husband, David Kitson, who was in prison in South Africa. She vividly recalled the pressures the Communist Party put on her, memorably describing the London communists as the 'Chevra Kadisha' – Hebrew for a Burial Society:[62]

> If anyone starts any activity that is not under their control they 'bury them' – immobilise them, or manoeuvre them out of the solidarity movement.... There are many of us who don't recognise the Chevra as communists although that is what they call themselves. The Chevra holds sway over the London ANC, and have influence over the Anti-Apartheid movement and David's trade union, TASS. They're a very small, powerful group over here – mainly middle class whites who left South Africa before the going got very tough.

It was in exile that some of the most vociferous debates took place. During heated exchanges that surfaced at the Anti-Apartheid annual general meetings in 1981 and 1982, the question of trade union solidarity between unions in Britain and South Africa was vigorously debated. Finally, in the April 1982 edition of Sactu's journal, *Workers Unity*, an article appeared entitled 'Direct links stinks'. It argued that visits by British trade unionists to South Africa undermined real trade union activity. Perhaps most tellingly, it attacked these links as an attempt to bypass what it termed 'the people's revolutionary organisations, the ANC (SA) and Sactu'.

This perspective had a direct impact on the ability of the newly emerging unions to build their international relations. Mike Murphy represented the South African unions in Britain in the late 1970s as they fought for recognition from multinational companies. He went to see Sactu, meeting John Gaetsewe. Despite amicable discussions, there was intense pressure on him to fall in behind the Sactu line. When he refused to do so, and went on to arrange for shop stewards from British Leyland

in Coventry and from a plant in Scotland to visit South Africa, he had
to face a campaign by both Sactu and the Anti-Apartheid Movement to
halt the visits.[63]

These attempts to isolate Fosatu unions had only limited success, and
gradually the international labour movement came to see their South
African counterparts as legitimate partners. Despite this, as late as
December 1983, the mineworkers' leader, Cyril Ramaphosa, was still
having to resist demands by Sactu that funds donated by the British
National Union of Miners to its South African counterparts should be
channelled through its offices.[64]

Within South Africa, the unions were well aware of the pressures
upon them to toe the line. But knowing what had taken place during the
1950s, they were determined to assert their independence. This perspective was most clearly articulated by the then General Secretary of Fosatu,
Joe Foster, when he delivered the key address at the Federation's annual
conference in April 1982. The union movement was just three years old
at the time, but it had grown five-fold since it was founded, from around
20 000 workers to over 100 000.[65] What the delegates heard was a speech
that ranks among the most important statements of principle delivered
to a South African labour movement. Although Joe Foster read it, the
speech reflected the work of many people. Its authors have never been
revealed, but the hand of Alec Erwin – Fosatu's first General Secretary,
and later South African Minister of Trade and Industry – was almost
certainly among them.

The speech, entitled 'The workers' struggle – where does Fosatu
stand?' – charted a political course for the movement. It attempted to
define how workers, as a class, should situate themselves in the struggles that lay ahead. In so doing it looked beyond the end of apartheid
to the form of society that would emerge a decade later, once the ANC
took power. These were ambitious goals, and the speech deserves to be
remembered for that reason alone. But its significance goes beyond this,
and can best be judged by the response that it evoked. Not to put too
fine a point on it, the ANC and SACP panicked. They realised that they
were being outflanked on the left, and that they would have to reassert
their assumed role as the natural leadership of South Africa's oppressed.

It is not hard to see why their reaction was so extreme. The speech, which was then adopted as Fosatu policy, challenged their most cherished beliefs. It provided a brief tour of South African history in which it asserted that there had never been a workin-class movement in South Africa (a direct repudiation of the SACP's position), and that the ANC engaged in 'populist' and 'opportunistic' politics to bolster its position in exile and had failed to support the international labour struggle (such as that of Solidarity in Poland) because of its links with the Soviet Union. Finally, and most tellingly, there was the prediction that because the ANC was a populist mass movement, it would in the end go the way of all other anti-colonial movements in Africa and turn on its own working-class supporters. The speech concluded:[66]

> It is, therefore, essential that workers must strive to build their own powerful and effective organisation even whilst they are part of the wider popular struggle. This organisation is necessary to protect worker interests and to ensure that the popular movement is not hijacked by elements who will in the end have no option but to turn against their worker supporters.

While carefully not repudiating the ANC, the Fosatu statement spelt out the movement's limitations, and demanded action to ensure the protection of workers' interests. As one workers' leader put it: 'Of course we want Mandela to be Prime Minister, but we must make sure that when he is, workers control him.'[67] The powerful critique also held out the implicit threat that Fosatu could be the launch pad from which a workers' party would be formed, possibly on the lines of the Workers Party in Brazil.

The reply was provided by *African Communist*, the theoretical journal of the SACP, frequently used as the mouthpiece of the Alliance. The union federation was labelled as 'syndicalist' and accused of attempting to substitute itself for the Communist Party as the party of the working class. The language was intemperate. 'Dare Fosatu ignore this? And dare it ignore the confusion and division it will sow in the ranks of the working class if it sets up a new "workers movement" in competition with or alongside the still living Communist Party?'[68]

The ANC did more than issue angry denunciations. It mobilised its forces inside and outside the country to ensure that it not only won the unions to its cause, but also aligned them to its political perspective. It is important to recall that this was a period of intense conflict in the country, with black communities engaged in fierce opposition to apartheid. This led to the formation of the United Democratic Front in 1983, to unite their resistance. In the circumstances, Fosatu's position began to look increasingly isolated. For its part, the ANC was determined to change the stance of the unions. Within four years the party had managed to exert enough political muscle and persuasion to get the South African union movement to transform itself into the Congress of South African Trade Unions, adopting the Congress label as an indication that its loyalty was to the Congress Alliance. On 30 November 1985, beneath a banner proclaiming: 'Workers of the World Unite!' the movement was launched. Seven hundred and sixty delegates from 33 unions attended, representing 460 000 workers.[69]

Elijah Barayi was elected Cosatu President and the hall rang to his impassioned words. 'You must all know that a lion has been born ... To the South African government I say: Your time is over ... We do not apologise for being black. We are proud of it. As from today Mandela and all political prisoners should be released.'[70]

Just eight days after the formation of Cosatu, the new General Secretary of the organisation, Jay Naidoo, went to Harare, ostensibly for a conference of the World Council of Churches. On 9 December, a statement announced that during the conference Naidoo had met members of the ANC and Sactu for informal talks.[71] In his autobiography Naidoo gives few clues as to the discussions that must have taken place inside Cosatu before the meeting went ahead. 'It was our first public function after Barayi's speech and everyone was very interested in Cosatu,' he explains. 'I also knew I would meet with senior comrades from the ANC and I needed their support to implement the resolution on building strong national industrial unions and political unity.'[72]

Naidoo admits that his action caused some disquiet within the union movement. The new federation had agreed on adopting a more political line, but there were still those within its ranks who were wary of the ANC's embrace. 'There was considerable conflict about this in the federation and some people were asking: "Are Naidoo and Barayi taking

Cosatu into the ANC camp?" But I had made sure that the office bearers, then in the major unions were behind me.'[73]

The Cosatu central executive committee held a meeting in February and resolved that it would be independent of all political organisations, but work with all progressive organisations fighting oppression. It agreed to send a fact-finding delegation to meet the ANC to discuss policy and clarify the goals of each organisation. Jay Naidoo, supported by his deputy, Sydney Mufamadi, and the NUM General Secretary, Cyril Ramaphosa, met the ANC in Lusaka on 5 and 6 March 1986. The ANC had assembled its key players. Its President, Oliver Tambo, led the delegation. He was supported by Thabo Mbeki, Chris Hani of Umkhonto we Sizwe and Mac Maharaj, from the political department. In attendance, too, was John Nkadimeng, General Secretary of Sactu. Apart from Tambo, all were also members of the SACP Central Committee.[74] Only Nkadimeng had a trade union background. Naidoo, Mufamadi and Ramaphosa were therefore not negotiating with their trade union counterparts, but with the political heavyweights in the Alliance.

At the end of this critical meeting a carefully worded communiqué was issued, signed by the ANC, Cosatu and Sactu.[75] They concluded that: 'lasting solutions can only emerge from the national liberation movement, headed by the ANC, and the entire democratic forces of our country, of which Cosatu is an important and integral part'. The communiqué committed Cosatu to mobilise the workers in this struggle, 'both as an independent organisation and as an essential component of the democratic forces of our country'. Sactu and Cosatu were reported to have agreed that 'there was no contradiction whatsoever arising from their separate existence'.

Those opposed to these developments could do little more than complain that Naidoo had acted without a mandate in taking this position.[76] The metalworkers' union issued a paper arguing that the Cosatu leadership 'should not have agreed to Cosatu struggling under the leadership of the ANC'. Rather, the unions 'should have made it clear that Cosatu … would struggle together with other progressive organisations, but independently, under its own leadership'.[77] Jan Theron, then General Secretary of the Food and Allied Workers Union, recalls that there was no consultation prior to this momentous meeting. 'The decision was not discussed with the affiliates [of Cosatu],' he says; 'the leadership just did it.'[78] At the same time, he is philosophical about the way it took place. He believes the South African government would have done all it could to prevent the meeting, if news of what was planned had leaked out. 'I remember asking the question myself [about the lack of consultation] and the answer was that it would not have been possible. It would have been stopped ... there could have been detentions to prevent such a meeting.'

These concerns were, in reality, quibbles after the event. The 'workerists' among the union activists (as they were labelled at the time) had been outmanoeuvred by the ANC and its 'populist' supporters. On the political front at least, the unions accepted that they would, in future, be led by the ANC. During the next 18 months the apartheid government went on the offensive to try to contain the growing revolt in the black community. Political differences within Cosatu were put to one side in the face of this onslaught.[79]

The community takes to the streets

Back to the 1970s, and while these events were taking place in the factories, mines and workshops, in the townships and villages communities were also on the move. The first, and best known, incident took place in Soweto. When the Department of Education issued a decree that from 1 January 1975 Afrikaans was to become a language of instruction in schools, the situation was already volatile.[80] Students objected to being taught in the language of their oppressors. Many teachers themselves could not speak Afrikaans, but were now required to teach their subjects in it. June 16, 1976 was the start of what became known as the Soweto uprising. High school students took to the streets, demanding a better education. Police responded with teargas and ammunition. The photograph of the body of Hector Petersen, cradled in Mbuyisa Makhubo's arms after being shot, his sister, Antoinette Sithole, running beside them, is the iconic image of the time.

The student revolt of 1976 was repressed, but it had two enduring impacts. Firstly, it led to tens of thousands of young, militant Africans fleeing across the border. This revitalised the liberation movements, with the ANC the greatest beneficiary, although dealing with these new recruits was to prove a headache for an organisation that had become accustomed to operating more as a clandestine clique than a mass movement. Secondly, it lit a flame of popular resistance inside the county that could not be extinguished. In Soweto, groups of students met with old ANC activists like Joe Gqabi, to discuss the way forward.[81]

Although troops and the police entered the townships; although tear gas and live ammunition were used against protests; although activists were arrested, tortured and killed; the genie was out of the bottle. The long years of uncontested white rule were at an end. The murder of Black Consciousness leader Steve Biko, who was beaten to death in police custody in September 1977, only fuelled the resistance.

By 1983, community organisations around the country had gained sufficient confidence to believe that a new form of organisation was required. On 7 January the *Cape Times* published an interview with the chaplain of students of the University of the Western Cape, Allan Boesak, in which he said he believed a 'united front' was likely to be formed. By chance, issuing the ANC's annual statement the following day, Oliver Tambo called for a 'strong mass democratic organisation'.[82]

Boesak's call, almost an aside, as he later put it, fell on fertile ground. On 20 August 1983, around 1 000 delegates and 500 observers from over 500 organisations came together at the Rocklands Community Centre in Mitchell's Plain, on the outskirts of Cape Town. They founded the UDF, which was to lead the internal confrontation with the government until the unbanning of the ANC in 1990.

Although many of the organisations attending the meeting were supportive of the ANC, others were not. Some unions chose to support the UDF, including some affiliated to the Council of Unions of South Africa, which had a Black Consciousness ideology. But those unions led by Fosatu decided not to join. Memories of past mistakes lay behind this initial reluctance to support the UDF. 'We had discussed whether or not Fosatu would attend the launch of the UDF,' recalls Jay Naidoo.

'The response was very negative. Fosatu even convened a series of seminars ostensibly to discuss the launch but designed to discourage any link with the UDF. Part of this was the experience of how repression had undermined Sactu as an organisation because the leadership had been so intertwined with the political movements of the time.'[83]

Behind the scenes, there were intense discussions. The Fosatu General Secretary, Joe Foster, said that since a portion of the union's membership did not support the UDF, it would be divisive to join. Dave Lewis, General Secretary of the General Workers Union, argued that democratic working-class organisations could not submit their membership to political decisions taken by a loose coalition like the UDF, whose own structures could not ensure democratic accountability.[84]

This sceptical attitude towards the UDF did not last. Jay Naidoo points to a community boycott of Simba chips in September 1984 in support of the workforce, which had been sacked during a strike, as being a key turning point in the relationship between the unions and the community. 'The consumer driven boycott was a first for a Fosatu affiliate and we had to argue for these within the structures. The Simba boycott was victorious and everyone was reinstated.'[85] It was, he says, 'a turning point in Fosatu politics. It convinced many that we could succeed in a difficult balancing act: maintaining the integrity of our organisation and building the leadership at the point of production; but at the same time driving that organisation into alliances with like-minded bodies. For me it was not only impossible but undesirable to separate the struggle for rights on the factory floor from the broader struggle for freedom in the country.'[86]

This was, indeed, a critical moment. Although the independence of the unions would continue to be maintained, they would now gradually fall in behind the wider political demands. As the clashes on the streets intensified, and particularly after the formation of Cosatu in November 1985, the unions lent their weight to the attacks on the apartheid government.

Towards a wider movement

In many ways this development was inevitable. It would have been un-thinkable for adults to remain aloof from the activities of their own children; impossible for workers to stand aside as their own homes were surrounded by the security forces. By day they might be shop stewards, but by night many union activists were leaders of their own communi-ties. While the leaders of the ANC called for South Africa to be made 'ungovernable', it was in the townships and the villages that this was being realised.

As the conflict intensified during the 1980s, the distance and suspicion between the union movement and the ANC receded as the two sides came to trust one another and to recognise that each had something to contribute to the fight against apartheid. For example, in February 1988, after the UDF had been effectively banned, with many of its leading members restricted in what they could do, it was the union movement that stepped into the void. 'It was Cosatu and its affiliated unions, tak-ing advantage of their relatively limited restrictions, which played the leading role in the debate over how to maintain the momentum of the struggle, and in particular how the struggle should be broadened.'[87]

When Nelson Mandela walked free from Pollsmoor prison on 11 February 1990, he had his wife, Winnie, to his left. To his right was the leader of the mineworkers' union, Cyril Ramaphosa. Ramaphosa went on to become the key ANC negotiator with the National Party in talks to write a new constitution; he became ANC Secretary-General in 1991. Together with Joe Slovo, of the newly unbanned SACP, Ramaphosa was a formidable force, extracting the maximum concessions from the white government. The unity between the ANC, the communists and the re-established union movement appeared unshakeable.[88] From the halting and uncertain relations of the 1950s, the Alliance had weathered the arid years of exile to re-emerge triumphant as the leading force within the country, dominating government and intellectual life.

Yet the constituent parts of the Alliance brought with them the marks of their past. The ANC had its inheritance as an African nationalist party, which had only embraced non-racialism during the hard years of the Defiance Campaign and the treason trial of the 1950s. For the SACP, there was the revolutionary rhetoric associated with the ideology of a National Democratic Revolution as a first step towards a socialist future. And for the trade unions of Cosatu there was an emphasis on independence and democratic accountability to their members that arose from the distrust engendered by their experiences during the 1950s and 1970s. As the years slipped by, these divergent viewpoints were to shape debates and disagreements within the Alliance.

Chapter 2

From De Klerk to Zuma: The Long, Hard Road of Post-Apartheid Politics

Martin Plaut

The second session of the ninth Parliament of the Republic of South Africa opened on 2 February 1990. As President FW de Klerk walked into the Parliament buildings, he turned to his wife Marike, saying, 'After today South Africa will never be the same again.'[1] He was right, for the speech he gave transformed the political landscape. Addressing Parliament, the President spoke of 'the growing realisation by an increasing number of South Africans that only a negotiated understanding among the representative leaders of the entire population can ensure lasting peace.' If the road of drastic change were not followed, he warned:

> The alternative is escalating violence, tension and conflict, which is unacceptable and in nobody's interest. The well-being of all in this country is linked inextricably to the ability of the leaders to come to terms with one another on a new dispensation. No-one can escape this simple truth.[2]

Before he sat down, De Klerk had announced the unbanning of not just the ANC, but also the PAC, the SACP and a host of other organisations.

He had lifted the state of emergency and announced that political prisoners would be freed. Just nine days later, Nelson Mandela walked out of Victor Verster prison a free man, for the first time in 27 years. Ahead lay the difficult negotiations that finally resulted in ANC victory in the first fully democratic elections South Africa had ever held, on 27 April 1994.

Today this transformation appears inevitable, but it did not seem so at the time. The hand that the ANC held, although enormously strong, contained within it weaknesses that have since become apparent. Nelson Mandela had to restructure a country disfigured by centuries of racism. He enjoyed massive goodwill, but there was also considerable underlying resistance. His new administration had to deal with numerous obstacles, including an obdurate civil service and a hostile military and police without any prior experience of serving a democratic government.

Within just a few years, a series of problems within the ANC-led Alliance had come to the fore. Serious divisions had emerged, particularly over economic policy. At first they appeared to be little more than grumblings between partners, but soon they were revealed as something much more serious. Once Mandela handed the presidency on to Thabo Mbeki in June 1999, the rifts within the ANC deepened. So too did the differences between the party and its allies. These divisions were to lead to some of the most serious conflicts in government ever experienced in South Africa. They finally resulted in the ousting of Thabo Mbeki and his replacement by Jacob Zuma as leader of both the party and the country. In the process, the factions employed almost all non-violent means at their disposal, including the dark forces of the intelligence community. It was a conflict that was to transform firm friends into bitter rivals.

At the root of these difficulties lay the weakness of the ANC. Although the party had come to power with the immense goodwill of the majority of South Africans, it was far less powerful than many assumed. Many of the levers of power were beyond its grasp – notably economic power, which continued to lie in the hands of white business. The business community, aided by pressure from institutions like the IMF and World Bank as well as international financiers, twisted the arm of the new government. The men who had run South Africa for decades also embarked on a process designed to incorporate senior members of the

ANC. Radical economic policies were dropped in favour of more conventional macro-economic prescriptions. The party's old links with the left began to unravel, putting immense strains on the Alliance.

The end of white rule

A great deal has been written about the end of apartheid. This is not the place to rehash the details of the complex and lengthy negotiations that produced a non-racial constitution and the inauguration of Nelson Mandela as President in May 1994. A brief sketch of the circumstances in which these changes took place will probably be useful, however, since they were the most significant in the country's history.

Though the vision of Hendrik Verwoerd and his plan for a 'separate but equal' society built on racial divisions were in ruins, victory was qualified by the circumstances in which it was won. To the end, President FW de Klerk retained the support of the key institutions of white power. These included the white electorate, the army, the security services and the business community. As a result the National Party government managed to strike a deal that retained considerable elements of white privilege. But the support that De Klerk enjoyed was not unquestioning, reflecting the growth in strength and confidence of the Anti-Apartheid Movement over the years.

Black workers, whose unions had been broken in the 1960s, had painfully re-built them in the 1970s and 1980s; they were a growing force in the land. Sanctions had hit the economy and made life increasingly difficult for white business. International lending had become more expensive as pension funds and banks found it increasingly embarrassing to hold South African debt. Capital was flowing out of the country at the rate of $2 billion a year.[3] The military no longer ruled supreme across southern Africa. At the battles of Cuito Cuanavale in Angola in 1987 and 1988, the South African army was held at bay by Angolan and Cuban forces. The military had discovered the limits of its power. But above all, the resilience of black youth, in the townships across South Africa itself, remained unbroken. The country had not, as the ANC had hoped, become 'ungovernable', but white rule was no longer uncontested. An increasing number of young white men were becoming fed up with month after month in the army, fighting their own countrymen and women in remote corners of the region, or in the streets of the cities they had grown up in.

The military learnt important lessons from neighbouring Rhodesia, where Prime Minister Ian Smith hung grimly on to the end. As the former head of the Defence Force, General Constand Viljoen, put it: 'In 1980, when the final collapse took place, I had some Rhodesian officers on a staff course at the army college, and I asked them to analyse for me the mistakes made by the Rhodesian security forces and the government ... Mr. Smith eventually settled for much less than he could have got if he had settled earlier ... I presented that paper to government and I said, "Now, there you have it. There are the lessons that you can learn from Rhodesia. Please apply those lessons in South Africa."'[4]

The need to learn from these mistakes was clear to the security services. In the early 1980s they decided that the fight to retain white rule could not be sustained indefinitely. Apartheid had to be brought to an end.[5] Their view – as portrayed by Dr Niel Barnard, former head of the National Intelligence Service – was that talks had to be opened with Nelson Mandela. This was authorised by President Botha, but, said Barnard, not even government ministers could be informed: 'I told PW Botha, "the moment you inform Cabinet, there is at least one member who is genetically incapable of keeping information like that to himself".'[6] So when FW de Klerk succeeded Botha in August 1989, he was told for the first time about the three years of secret negotiations with the ANC. These included dozens of clandestine meetings with Mandela. Barnard says the newly elected President was shocked but took the revelation in his stride.

Some senior members of the military were deeply opposed to the change of policy. Under domestic and international pressure, De Klerk headed them off through a series of measures. In 1991 he demoted his hard-line Minister of Police, Adriaan Vlok, and sacked his Minister of Defence, Magnus Malan.[7] Further action was to follow to halt the network of agents run by the security services to bolster the state, known as the 'third force'. In what De Klerk later described as the most difficult decision of his career, he fired 23 senior officers on 19

December 1992, in an event that became known as the 'Night of the Generals'.[8] A shiver ran through the military and, for a moment, they considered rebellion, but the President's action defused the crisis and the moment passed.

What this indicated was one of the strengths of the Afrikaners' position in the early 1990s. The state they had created was not just authoritarian in its treatment of the majority population, but of the minority white community as well. The leaders of the Afrikaner nation, with channels of influence through their churches and other organisations, some of them secret societies like the Broederbond, were capable of taking momentous decisions knowing that most of their people would fall in behind them. There had always been bitter feuds and divisions within Afrikaner society, but in the end most people were willing to be led. Despite sections of the English-speaking whites opposing apartheid, only a small percentage did much more than talk disparagingly about the government round the dinner table. The majority of whites were grudgingly willing to follow their government, giving De Klerk the latitude to make the deal that he did.

At the same time, international events had, in De Klerk's view, moved in his favour. The collapse of the Soviet Union undermined the influence the SACP had over the ANC.[9] The relationship between the ANC and the communists did not collapse, but the white government's fear that a Communist Party laden with Soviet weaponry and Moscow gold might dictate terms to a Mandela government had clearly faded.

For its part, the ANC was not in a powerful military position. Its troops, despite spending years in training in Africa and the Soviet bloc, never inflicted a military defeat on Pretoria. As the ANC Secretary-General, Alfred Nzo, admitted in 1989, 'we do not have the capacity to intensify the armed struggle in any meaningful way'.[10] At the same time, the ANC enjoyed support abroad, as well as at home. Oliver Tambo's painstaking efforts over many years had built an extraordinary degree of international backing. The adulation the party received from the majority of South Africans was evidence of the ANC's popularity inside the country. This was shown by the tumultuous welcome given to Mandela and Tambo when they first appeared in public. It was underlined in the first truly democratic election, which the ANC won with 62.65 per cent of the vote.

Yet popularity and political support were not enough. Many forms of influence still eluded the ANC's grasp. Of these, the security forces were among the most immediate concerns. They were still largely in white hands, despite fighters of Umkhonto we Sizwe gradually being brought home and integrated into the military, police and intelligence. This was a lengthy and tricky process. After 1994 there were 'heated exchanges' at the highest level between the political leadership, led by the Minister of Defence, Joe Modise, and the Chief of the National Defence Force, a position held until 1998 by General George Meiring.[11] Despite this, progress was made in integrating the former guerrilla force into the formal military structures. By late 1998, 16 per cent of the uniformed troops were former ANC fighters, while seven of the 41 generals were drawn from the ranks of the ANC or its rival, the Pan Africanist Congress.[12]

At the same time, there were many former fighters who did not find new professions in the Defence Force. Years later this still produces smouldering resentment. There has been anger among ex-combatants from a variety of military backgrounds at the way in which the demobilisation process was handled. Many found themselves destitute, with few skills to offer prospective employers. Some turned to crime,[13] while others believed a fresh round of fighting might erupt. Arms caches stored by the mainly Zulu Inkatha Freedom Party to resist the ANC were still being uncovered at the Ulundi Legislative Assembly as late as July 2004.[14]

Apartheid spies were also civil servants, with jobs protected by sunset clauses in their contracts, which meant they were kept on for five years after the 1994 election. Melding together the intelligence operatives of the former white regime with their counterparts from the ANC produced what has been colourfully described as a 'mixed marriage from hell'.[15]

Strategies of incorporation

If security was a problem, the critical weakness of the ANC was that it had no stake in the economy. Nor did it have the experience needed to run the mines, farms and factories that are the backbone of the country.

Their position was in stark contrast to the situation that prevailed in 1948 when Afrikaner nationalism came to power. The origins of Afrikaner economic power can be traced back to the period after the First World War, when first the Cape newspaper, *Die Burger*, was founded and then a mutual aid society – Helpmekaar – was formed. Around 500 people each donated what was at the time the huge sum of £100 to bring this about.[16] From these early developments came a range of life assurance companies and banks, including Sanlam and Volkskas. By 1948 the Afrikaners were still largely a nation of farmers, shopkeepers, priests and employees, but they also held a considerable stake in the economy. They owned more than 13 000 enterprises (up from 3 700 a decade earlier) employing 121 000 people and accounting for 11 per cent of the non-agricultural economy.[17]

This included a stake in mining, but it was tiny – just one per cent of the sector. Since South Africa's mines were the power-house of the economy, this was a critical deficiency, but it was about to change. In the wake of the Sharpeville massacre, foreign funding flowed out of the country. The Afrikaans-run insurance firm, Sanlam, made the most of the opportunity and bought heavily into industry at rock-bottom prices. Then, in 1963, the giant Anglo American Corporation, guided by the ever-canny Harry Oppenheimer, ensured that a subsidiary of Sanlam obtained a major stake in mining. Federale Mynbou took control of the General Mining and Finance Corporation (later named Gencor after its incorporation with Union Corporation).[18]

It was during this period that staunch proponents of a brand of Afrikaner national socialism within the Broederbond – including the secret society's then leader, JF Klopper, and Nico Diederichs, the Minister of Finance – dropped their opposition to 'English' capital. They became the darlings of the Chamber of Mines when the creation of Gencor was accepted as a pay-off for not nationalising the other 'English' mines.[19] This was an extraordinary coup for the English-speaking elite.

Afrikaner antipathy towards big business and the rule of the mine magnates abated and then disappeared. As a 'Concerned Afrikaner' wrote in 1965, 'the next step will be to build up and portray the men of Mynbou as being the real leaders of the Afrikaners and as representing forces of "moderation" and "progress". Other Afrikaner financial leaders will be encouraged to follow suit, and each time a new Oppenheimer-Afrikaans deal is closed, there will be less and less criticism, to the point of disappearing altogether.'[20]

It was not the last time that such a 'deal' was cut by the men who ran South Africa's mines.

When the ANC came to power in 1994 it was clear that a similar arrangement was required to extend the narrow circle of wealth and power – hitherto exclusively white – to make room for the newly powerful. As before, the aim was to incorporate the emerging rulers. The policy that was used to achieve this was 'Black Economic Empowerment', or BEE for short.

Moeletsi Mbeki, businessman, journalist and the sceptical brother of former President Thabo Mbeki, believes this key ANC policy was not dreamed up by the ANC at all. 'This could not be further from the truth,' Mbeki argues. 'BEE was, in fact, invented by South Africa's economic oligarchs, that handful of white businessmen and their families who control the commanding heights of the country's economy, that is mining and its associated chemical and engineering industries and finance.'[21] He believes the policy was adopted well before the ANC came to power.

Mbeki explains that Sanlam, a cornerstone of Afrikaner capital, helped create the flagship black empowerment company, New African Investments Limited (Nail) – led by Nthato Motlana, Nelson Mandela's former doctor – in 1992. This was two years before the ANC assumed office. Others followed, including Real African Investment Limited, sponsored by the Anglo American Corporation.

'The objective of BEE,' Mbeki suggests, 'was to co-opt leaders of the black resistance movement by literally buying them off with what looked like a transfer to them of massive assets at no cost. To the oligarchs, of course, these assets were small change.'[22] This version of events is by no means universally accepted, since there were groups, like the Black Management Forum, that had pressed for a greater role for black business since their formation in 1976. Morakile Shuenyane, a spokesman for the Forum, was quoted in 1988 as saying: 'At one time black managers in South Africa were little more than token blacks in white business.

Now it is the responsibility of black management to play a role model with the intention of melting white attitudes.'[23]

Whatever the origins of the ANC policy, there was a determination to widen the share of black business. Perhaps the emblematic deal of the post-apartheid era was the sale of JCI – Johannesburg Consolidated Investments – one of the country's most venerable mining houses. 'Johnnies' had been founded in 1888 by the legendary mining tycoon, Barney Barnato, who had the foresight to buy all the land that was needed to build the city of Johannesburg, having already made a fortune from Kimberley diamonds. In 1996, with the ANC in power, Johnnies was sold to a consortium led by Mzi Khumalo, who thus came to own South Africa's fourth largest gold producer, becoming the first black person to take control of a mining house. The *Sunday Times* pithily explained the significance of the deal:

> [Khumalo's] first real opportunity came when Anglo American found it expedient to go along with the official economic re-structuring policies. In much the same way as, almost 40 years beforehand, an Anglo led by Harry Oppenheimer had facilitated Afrikaner capital's acquisition of General Mining, by the late '90s it was time to turn over something to black capital. That was to be the mining rump of Johannesburg Consolidated Investments (JCI), shorn of its core diamond and platinum interests, and Khumalo emerged as the favoured buyer of 35%.[24]

Khumalo and Motlana were not alone; soon others in the leadership of the ANC and the wider Alliance followed in their footsteps. The ANC former Secretary-General and NUM leader, Cyril Ramaphosa, went on to make a fortune in business. So did the former Black Consciousness activist and ANC guerrilla fighter, Tokyo Sexwale.[25] Both managed to straddle the worlds of politics and finance. Ramaphosa retained his position on the ANC National Executive (NEC), while Sexwale had interests in diamond mining and oil, via Mvelaphanda Holdings, as well as serving as Minister of Human Settlements. By August 2011, about three quarters of Cabinet's 35 members were found to have financial interests outside their main occupations.[26] So did 59 per cent of the country's 400 members of Parliament.

The firebrands of the union movement and the heroes of the township resistance had put on suits and ties and adopted a new lifestyle. Like the Afrikaner elite before them, these members of the ANC had become, in essence, the 'Mynbou men' of their era.

The new deal

What took place in the years following the end of apartheid was no white plot or right-wing conspiracy. It was a simple survival strategy by business, determined to bind a segment of the newly emerging black elite to the existing structures of wealth and influence. Room was made at the top table for a restricted section of black society, who were only too willing to be wooed. At the same time, little more than crumbs from the top table fell to the majority of the population. Indeed, South Africa is today a more unequal society than it was at the end of apartheid, as the trade union movement tartly pointed out.[27]

The post-apartheid deal had placed political power in black hands while economic control remained with whites. The economist Stephen Gelb, who helped the ANC develop economic policies during its first years in office, describes rather more elegantly the pressures surrounding the redistribution of economic power:

> These imperatives underpinned what I have called an 'implicit bargain' or accommodation between white big business and the ANC, involving the ANC committing to macroeconomic stability and international openness, and business agreeing to participate in 'capital reform' to modify the racial structure of asset ownership, which would come to be called 'black economic empowerment' (BEE). The broad outlines of this accommodation emerged in 1990, and policy planning and implementation of trade and financial liberalisation began well before the 1994 elections.[28]

Once this deal had been struck, a further development took place in the mid-1990s that set the seal on the country's mid-term future. This was the demobilisation of the civic organisations that had opposed the apartheid government during the previous decade. The UDF had fought valiantly against apartheid from inside South Africa during the 1980s, while the ANC was banned. Ten years later it was drained of its senior leadership by the party that it had supported. This was perhaps inevitable; a necessary part of the re-establishment of the ANC as the senior organisation inside the country.

The leadership was drawn into party structures and took on the ANC mantle that the UDF had worn, first covertly and then openly, in the preceding years.[29] When a UDF member complained that the ANC was poaching its staff, he was told that 'the UDF should always remember that the ANC needs the best cadres to re-establish itself'.[30] There may have been little alternative, but the loss of the leaders of the civic organisations – especially grassroots organisations inside the townships – was painful and led to some bitterness.

By the mid-1990s the alliance between the ANC, the unions and the SACP had emerged in better shape than might have been anticipated just ten years earlier. The ANC was established as the government of the country. It had by its side both of the allies that had supported it during the years of exile and conflict. Yet tensions remained. Much has been made of the differences between the 'insiders', the leadership that had emerged inside the country during the 1980s, and the 'exiles', the formal leadership of the ANC, as represented by Oliver Tambo, who had lived all those years outside the country. While this was real and can be seen in the battle for position by individuals at all levels of the organisation, it does not represent what was perhaps the most serious division: the ideological divide.

During the long years outside of South Africa the exiles had endured years of loneliness, hardship and the ever-present danger of infiltration by agents of apartheid. They had come to wear a tough outer shell. This, combined with the traditions of Marxism-Leninism that they learned in the Soviet Union and East Germany, drove them to adopt habits of secrecy and autocracy. Worse still, these circumstances seemed to have led to some ANC members developing a ruthlessness and brutality that at times resulted in the torture and death of some of its most loyal comrades.[31] By contrast, the trade unions and the civic societies, as represented by the UDF, had necessarily interacted with a much broader constituency. While they had adopted secret ways of working under a repressive state, they had nonetheless developed a democratic culture of consultation and open debate that was the lifeblood of their movements.

The cultures of the exiles and the insiders were poles apart.

In organisational terms, the UDF bequeathed to the ANC a political culture of internal debate and self-criticism. This was a tradition which the UDF had inherited from the ANC from the 1950s, both which had appeared to have weakened within the ANC amidst the conditions of exile and guerrilla warfare. Some ANC leaders returning to the country seemed to be taken aback by the demands for consultation and the spirited criticism made at regional and national levels.[32]

By the late 1990s the ANC had taken control of South Africa's political destiny, yet still had only a limited hold on power. The economy remained largely beyond its grasp, even though some senior members of the party and their allies were now beginning to enjoy the advantages of wealth. The vast majority of ANC supporters remained as poor as they ever had been, even though the restrictions on movement and ownership imposed during apartheid had been lifted. The unions, mostly clustered around Cosatu, were beginning to detect that the interests of their members were no longer automatically aligned with those of the ANC.

It's the economy, stupid[33]

The ANC had sketched out its economic policy while in exile in London. After De Klerk lifted the ban on the party, released Nelson Mandela and entered into talks on a new constitution, it became imperative that the direction of policy should be spelled out with greater clarity. According to Alan Hirsch, one of Mandela's senior economic advisers, this process began at a meeting in 1991 at the Swiss ski resort of Davos. Mandela had been invited to speak to the World Economic Forum's annual gathering of international investors and bankers and had to make plain the

ANC's economic outlook. But the material he had been provided with would have sent shudders through the gathering.

> The original draft of the speech had left space for a section on the ANC's economic policies, which was to be prepared by an ANC-allied economist in the United Kingdom. When the insert arrived from London it was included in the draft speech. However, when Mandela and his economic advisers read the section they found that it was fashioned in a traditional social-ist style, virtually calling for the nationalisation of the com-manding heights of the economy. Tito Mboweni, 31 years old, one of Mandela's key aides and an economist, had to redraft the economic section in great haste. [34]

Mboweni, who went on to become Governor of the Reserve Bank, re-wrote the speech. Plans for a socialist economy were replaced with statements 'carefully written, harmless and mildly reassuring for the collected band of plutocrats and international financial bureaucrats'.[35]

Returning to the snows of Davos the following year, Mandela made plain the ANC's move away from the socialist economic policies em-bodied in one of its key documents, the Freedom Charter of 1955. He assured the gathering of his party's support for a mixed economy. In the speech Mandela promised that the ANC would 'address such questions as security of investments and the right to repatriate earnings, realistic exchange rates, the rate of inflation, and the fiscus'.[36]

International investors breathed a collective sigh of relief, but these were not the policies the left in the ANC and its Alliance partners had hoped for. There were soon rumblings of discontent. Relations between the ANC, SACP and the unions were about to enter a downward trajec-tory brought about by disagreements over the economic direction of the country. As so often in South Africa, the dispute centred around two key policies best known by their acronyms – RDP (or Reconstruction and Development Programme) versus GEAR (Growth, Employment and Redistribution strategy).

The RDP programme had been drawn up by the left prior to the first post-apartheid elections in 1994, with many ideas coming from the trade union movement. The Macro Economic Research Group was particularly involved in this work.[37] The ANC fought the election on the RDP platform.[38] It was an enormously ambitious agenda, promising to right the wrongs of apartheid and to cater for every sector of society. Many of the promises were at least partially redeemed.[39] Houses sprang up across the country where once there had only been shacks. Between 1994 and the start of 2001 over 1.1 million cheap houses eligible for government subsidies had been built, accommodating 5 million of the estimated 12.5 million South Africans without proper housing. Electricity, water, and sanitation were provided, and there were new schools and clinics.

The former trade union leader, Jay Naidoo, says he was called in by President Mandela to lead the programme. 'We have a big task ahead,' he was told. 'You have been driving the Reconstruction and Development Programme from my ANC office. We went to our people with that as our Manifesto and now I want it to be the centre of all our government programmes.'[40] Naidoo was appointed Minister without Portfolio in the Presidency, responsible for delivering this promise, a position he relished.

Naidoo set about his new task with considerable energy, but his hopes were soon dashed. On 28 March 1996, less than two years after it was opened, the office of the Reconstruction and Development Programme was closed down. The man Naidoo blamed for this reverse was Thabo Mbeki, Prime Minister under Nelson Mandela's presidency, and in many ways the real driving force in the administration. Mbeki believed that the RDP was badly flawed. In his account of what took place, Naidoo recalls that Mbeki believed that its plans were simply unaffordable. He saw the RDP office as approving spending without concern, driving a hole in government's carefully constructed budgets and frightening off potential international investors.

At least as important, Naidoo suggests, were the links the RDP was trying to make with civil society. He had attempted to bring the participative culture of the UDF into government, making contact with organisations in civil service to try to drive official policy. This was anathema to Mbeki, a man steeped in what Naidoo describes as the trench warfare of liberation movements, who had little time for this kind of democratic involvement. 'There was a natural suspicion of anything that resembled

a civil society organisation, particularly a trade union movement enter-
ing the terrain of liberation political movements.'[41] In Mbeki's view, says
Naidoo, the ANC, and the ANC alone, should run government.

For the left, closing down the RDP extinguished hopes that the government would rule in the interests of the poor. In Naidoo's view, halting
the programme also caused serious damage to the Tripartite Alliance. 'It
was no longer the driving force of change,' he concluded.

Others go further and suggest that Mbeki always intended to move
away from the participatory politics the unions and the civic organisations had developed during the 1980s. They point to a paper he drew
up prior to the ANC's National Conference in December 1994,[42] which
took a long, hard look at the politics of South Africa, inside and outside the Alliance. It was a scathing attack on the left and what Mbeki
believed was its destructive influence on government. It contains this
monumental sentence predicting that an attempt would be made to destroy the Alliance by:

❏ Encouraging the SACP to publicly project itself as the 'left
  conscience' which would fight for the loyalty of the ANC in
  the cause of the working people, against an ANC leadership which is inclined to over-compromise with the forces
  of bourgeois reformism;

❏ Inciting the SACP to use its independent structures as a
  Party to carry out such a campaign while also encouraging the members of the SACP within the ANC to form
  themselves into an organised faction to pursue the same
  objective;

❏ Encouraging the constitution of an ultra-left political formation which would, itself, challenge the policies and revolutionary credentials of the SACP, to force the latter to
  intensify its offensive to 'rectify the line' within the ANC;

❏ Encouraging Cosatu and its affiliates to project the pursuit
  of political and socio-economic objectives different from
  those that the ANC has set itself as a governing party;

❏ Encouraging Cosatu to exploit the fact of the democratic transition and the place of the ANC in government to

interpret this to mean that the ANC has an obligation to 'its electorate', namely the African working class, to support it in all its demands or face denunciation as a traitor;

❑ On these bases, to encourage the launching of a major and sustained mass campaign, which, while addressing various legitimate worker demands would, at the same time, pose the spectre of ungovernability;

❑ And otherwise, encouraging the unions to be suspicious of the intentions of the 'ANC in government' on the basis that the latter is likely to act in a manner intended to appease the domestic and international business world and multilateral financial institutions.

Clearly Mbeki was deeply distrustful of what he considered to be the destructive influences of the left within the movement, and determined to prevent them having more than a token influence on government. Mark Gevisser, his perceptive and sympathetic biographer, gives a complex and nuanced account of why Mbeki broke with the left.[43] This portrays the RDP as a Keynesian wish list, dreamt up by a group of London-based exiles, supported by left-wing economists. It was, in the view of Mbeki and his closest associates (including the Finance Minister, Trevor Manuel, and his deputy, Alec Erwin) a programme that would drive the South African economy into the mire. They believed it would bankrupt the country, leaving it in the hands of the IMF and World Bank. The outside world, still nervous of the ANC's socialist rhetoric in exile, was not prepared to give the new government the benefit of the doubt.

With foreign currency leaving the country and the rand on the slide, the authorities had to rein in the left. A new economic strategy, GEAR, was therefore drawn up, re-establishing liberal market economics and the discipline of the Treasury. In May 1996 Trevor Manuel took the new strategy to Cabinet, allowing only limited consultation with the ANC's allies. As Gevisser put it, 'the risk was too high that the Congress of South African Trade Unions (Cosatu) might leak the document or voice its opposition publicly prior to its release, forcing compromise and exacerbating the worry, among potential investors, that the communist tail still wagged the

ANC dog.'[44] The policy was made public in June, with Mbeki reportedly turning on his critics with a dismissive: 'Call me a Thatcherite!'

The left, at first stunned into silence, reacted with fury. 'Something has gone terribly wrong in South Africa if a document such as [GEAR] could be put on the table,' thundered the head of Cosatu, Mbhazima Shilowa.[45] These fulminations were in vain: in 1998 President Mandela – no longer leader of the party, though still a major force within the Alliance – waded into the debate, telling an SACP Congress that that the character and content of its criticism of GEAR (and by inference, the ANC government) was unacceptable.[46]

At the same meeting, Thabo Mbeki, who had become ANC President in 1997, went even further. He castigated the left for suggesting that the ANC had surrendered to the IMF and the forces of international capital. In a blistering critique, Mbeki focused on a discussion document circulated by the SACP that contained this statement: 'The most serious strategic threat to the National Democratic Revolution is the attempt by capital to stabilise a new, "deracialised" capitalist ruling bloc, under the mantle of the ANC itself.'[47] For Mbeki, any suggestion that the ANC was selling out its programme or its constituency to placate international capital was little short of treason. Drawing on what he called the 'full authority of the leadership and membership of the African National Congress', he warned that no organisation would be allowed to build itself by 'scavenging on the carcass of a savaged ANC'.

From bad to worse

Thabo Mbeki won his battle with the left. GEAR became official government policy, but the cost was high and relations between the government and the left appeared to be close to rock bottom. To his critics, Mbeki had moved the ANC to the right, but worse was to follow. He then gradually undermined the checks and balances on him by his party and his government. The centralisation of power and silencing of debate became a central tenet of his administration.

What began as a difference of opinion over economic policy was to leave a lasting bitterness and to undermine key institutions, including the judiciary and the security services. At its heart was the apparent willingness of supporters of President Mbeki to deploy the forces of the party and the state against his political enemies.

A report by a conservative American think-tank, the Rand Corporation, drawn up in 2005, long after the events, explained just how serious the politicisation of the security services had been:[48]

> A series of scandals involving the South African intelligence services in the mid-to-late 1990s demonstrated that, whilst the legislative framework seemed impressive on paper, it was far from thoroughly effective on the ground. Despite the 1994 Intelligence Services Act, which obliges each service's Director-General to ensure 'no action is carried out that could give rise to any reasonable suspicion that the agency or service is concerned in furthering, protecting or undermining the interests of any section of the population or any political party or organisation', it became increasingly worrying that the intelligence community was being politicised by:
>
> ❑ the placement of ANC loyalists in key positions within the intelligence services, as well as those within the services wishing to meet the anticipated expectations of the political leadership.
> ❑ the failure to ensure the integration of former rival intelligence personnel into the NIA and the emergence of factionalism along old opposing lines within the services.
> ❑ the development of parallel intelligence structures of political purposes due to a lack of trust in the national intelligence functions.

There was a belief within the ANC at this time that its hold on power was fragile and continuously under threat, both from within South Africa and from abroad. A memoir by Barry Gilder, a former ANC intelligence officer who served as South Africa's Coordinator for Intelligence from 2005 until he retired in October 2007, portrays the country as constantly under attack from its enemies. Gilder maintains that the new government had to cope with pressures from all sides as it attempted to transform a society scarred by centuries of racism and the legacy of apartheid.[49] The ANC in general, and Thabo Mbeki in particular, emerge as deeply distrustful of all around them. Mbeki trusted only a narrow circle of supporters, most of whom had been with him for many years, and saw all critics as a threat that had to be rooted out. This goes some way towards explaining how Mbeki managed to so alienate many within his own party.

A most revealing symptom of the developing disease came in April 2001, when three of the ANC's most senior figures, the party's former Secretary-General, Cyril Ramaphosa, Tokyo Sexwale and Mathews Phosa, were accused of plotting to depose the President. All three denied the charges and were finally exonerated (see Chapter 5 on the uses and abuses of intelligence for further details), but the ramifications of these allegations of treason were felt beyond the three named men. Mark Gevisser suggests that this event marks the moment in which Mbeki fell out with his Deputy President, Jacob Zuma, whom he had accused of being implicated in the 'plot'.[50] Zuma issued a press release protesting his loyalty, but relations between the two men were becoming distinctly frosty.

The dark arts of the intelligence services

The rupture between Mbeki and Zuma was to have a devastating impact on relations within the Alliance (see Chapter 5). As the differences between the two men deepened it became apparent that the President's supporters were prepared to use the agencies of the state to marginalise and then remove Zuma from power. However, Jacob Zuma had resources of his own, acquired as head of ANC intelligence during his years in exile, and he mobilised these as the crisis grew.

For South Africans this was a dark episode, notwithstanding public warnings from members of the Alliance. During the outcry over the alleged plot against Mbeki, the unions gave the President this advice: 'Cosatu cautions against any attempt by state organs, including the police, to involve themselves in legitimate internal political contests: such action is both unconstitutional and, in effect, illegal.'[51] It was timely advice, but was ignored by all concerned.

The past intruded too sharply into the present: once under pressure, ANC leaders called on the skills they had learnt in exile. Lauren Hutton, who led a lengthy study for the Institute of Strategic Studies, concluded that although President Mbeki had called on members of the intelligence community to remain politically non-partisan, other pressures drove them in the opposite direction:

> ... one should remember that the current intelligence community is the product of the amalgamation of a Soviet trained liberation struggle intelligence capacity and an undemocratic, highly centralised, militarised and illegitimate apartheid intelligence structure. Both the ANC and the apartheid state used intelligence (intelligence here meaning the gathering and use of information to undermine and score advantage over one's enemy) as a critical lever. This functional approach to intelligence as a tool to score advantage over domestic enemies remains characteristic of the intelligence domain and relates heavily to the manner in which the role of intelligence is conceived in South Africa, the lack of national consensus and participation in defining this role and the continuing relevance of the need for a domestic political intelligence capacity.[52]

There may be another way to understand this rupture, which goes back to events that occurred during the dying days of apartheid. In 2001 the investigative magazine, *Noseweek*, suggested that a split between what they called the 'Vula Boys' and 'Thabo's Boys' really lay at the heart of differences between the Zuma and Mbeki camps.[53]

> The Vula Boys are the collection of communists and (mostly Natal) ANC intelligence operatives who set up Operation Vula, the secret pre-1990 programme to develop the leadership and financial networks inside SA needed to launch a violent revolution. Vula was controversial because it was secret

even inside the ANC: the wider ANC leadership – including Thabo Mbeki – knew nothing about it. (Treason? The Vula Boys would later claim their scheme had been sanctioned by party president Oliver Thambo, which sounds convenient, because, by then, he was too ill to confirm or deny this.) That gap between the groups appears to have persisted.

Operation Vula had been led by Mac Maharaj, a minister under Mandela, but later fired by Mbeki. Today he is President Zuma's spokesman. Vula personnel also included Siphiwe Nyanda (who went on to become chief of the Defence Force), Moe Shaik (demoted by Mbeki but promoted to head of the National Intelligence Agency under Zuma) and Pravin Gordhan (Minister of Finance under Zuma). It was a powerful force at the time, but Vula's aims were diametrically opposed to those of Thabo Mbeki, who was then attempting to open negotiations with President De Klerk. If *Noseweek* is correct, then the differences between these groups smouldered on, just waiting for an appropriate moment to ignite.[54]

Constructing a case against Zuma

In 2000 the investigation unit of the South African Police, the Directorate of Special Operations (better known as the Scorpions) began building a case against Zuma's close confidant and financial adviser, Schabir Shaik, for his involvement in the Arms Deal. Quite why they chose to investigate Shaik's part in the deal is unclear, since there were many others who had a more direct role in the procurement of the weapons systems. After all, when the deal was signed, Zuma was no more than a provincial ANC leader, running the party's affairs in KwaZulu-Natal.

Shaik was accused of acting as an intermediary between Jacob Zuma and the French arms company, Thales.[55] The state claimed that he extracted large sums of money as well as a promise of R500 000 a year for his client from the company.[56]

Unlike many who had faced Mbeki's wrath, Zuma didn't crumble.

Instead, he decided to fight his former ally.[57] The Mbeki camp didn't take the challenge lying down, and soon there were extensive leaks to the media about Zuma's alleged corruption. Hardly a week went by without some aspect of Zuma's life being splashed across the papers. On 23 August 2003, Bulelani Ngcuka, the Director of Public Prosecutions, held a press conference during which he announced that Shaik was to be charged with corruption. He went on to say that 'whilst there is a *prima facie* case of corruption against the Deputy President [Zuma] our prospects of success are not strong enough. That means that we are not sure if we have a winnable case.'[58]

Zuma complained that this left him in legal limbo, since it meant that his name had been tarnished without the case against him ever having been taken to court. (Not that he was in any rush to have the evidence brought before a judge. Zuma's lawyers worked assiduously, then and in the years to come, using every legal avenue to prevent a trial from ever taking place.)

However, Jacob Zuma was an assiduous cultivator of relationships within the ANC and had built a reputation for looking after those who were answerable to him. He had not risen through the ranks of the party without making friends and allies of his own. Out of the blue, Bulelani Ngcuka was accused of being an apartheid spy, known by the codename RS452,[59] and in due course it was revealed that the source of the information for this extraordinary revelation was none other than Schabir Shaik's brother, Moe Shaik, who had served under Jacob Zuma when he was head of ANC intelligence.[60] South African spies, past and present, appeared to be actively briefing against each other.

In the event, Bulelani Ngcuka was cleared by an official enquiry, a major setback for the Zuma camp. Another was soon to follow. On 2 June 2005, Schabir Shaik was found guilty on two counts of corruption and one of fraud. The judge – in a 165-page ruling – found that there was what he described as 'overwhelming' evidence of a corrupt relationship between Shaik and Zuma.

Shaik was sentenced to 15 years in jail. The Supreme Court of Appeal tartly rejected his claim that his relationship with Zuma was no more than friendship:

We find a wealth of evidence to show that the friendship, which
we accept exists, was persistently and aggressively exploited
by Mr Shaik for his own and his group's business advantage.
In particular there were four occasions revealed by the prosecution evidence in which interventions by Mr Zuma at Mr
Shaik's instance advanced, or were aimed at advancing, Mr
Shaik's commercial interests. The most important one concerned the Defence Force's arms procurement program. Mr
Zuma's efforts contributed to Mr Shaik acquiring a material
interest in a highly lucrative contract to supply the armaments
for the Navy's new corvettes. The evidence also showed that
when the payments were made Mr Shaik was in no position
to afford them without substantial borrowings and Mr Zuma
had no realistic prospect of repayment.[61]

Where had this left Jacob Zuma? At the end of Shaik's appeal process,
the Constitutional Court – the highest in the land – ruled that Shaik had
benefited from the payments because of Zuma's involvement. As Justice
Kate O'Regan ruled, 'I have found that the benefits of the shareholding
and the dividends did result from Mr Zuma's interventions on behalf of
the appellants.'[62]

Despite this, Zuma's popularity remained undiminished within both
the party and the wider Alliance. A poll found that 80 per cent of ANC
voters thought he was doing a good job and just under half believed
that the charges of corruption were the work of his enemies.[63] Zuma
continued to be greeted at Alliance events as a hero. Despite this, on 13
June 2005, Thabo Mbeki sacked Zuma as Deputy President. 'I've come
to the conclusion that the circumstances dictate that in the interests of
the honorable deputy president, the government and our young democratic system ... It will be best to release honorable Jacob Zuma from his
responsibilities as deputy president of the republic and member of the
cabinet,' he told a joint session of Parliament.

Inside the ANC, many greeted the decision with outrage. There were
cries of *Phansi ngo Mbeki! Phambili ngo Zuma!* (down with Mbeki, up
with Zuma!) at an ANC rally. It was becoming evident that while Jacob
Zuma was losing the legal contest, he was winning the support of his party.

At this point a fresh problem surfaced which looked as if it might over-whelm his campaign. In November 2005 a member of the police leaked a report to the media indicating that Zuma had been accused of rape. In a country in which rape is at epidemic proportions, with one man in four admitting that he has engaged in this crime, the allegation was even more damaging to Zuma's reputation than the allegation of corruption.

A 31-year-old woman, a family friend, came forward to press charges against Zuma, alleging that he had raped her at his Johannesburg home. She said he had entered the bedroom in which she was sleeping, saying that he wanted to 'tuck her in'. What followed, she alleged, was rape. In the trial Zuma denied the charge. When asked about having unprotected sex with a woman whom he knew to be HIV positive, he declared fa-mously that after having had unprotected sex, he had gone on to take a shower. Zuma later said he knew taking a shower didn't give protection against Aids, 'but I'd never imagined I'd have to give detailed explana-tions about my activities in the bedroom and bathroom. I was flustered and said what came into my head.'[64]

The case divided the nation and divided the ANC. Women in the movement were outraged that a leader could possibly have behaved in this way, while some of Zuma's supporters used sexist chants and taunts against their opponents. In the end Zuma was found not guilty. His sup-porters were jubilant, but continued to query the role of the secret ser-vices in framing the case.

It turned out that the woman (who had made previous allegations of rape against other men) had phoned Ronnie Kasrils, the Minister of Intelligence, before she reported the crime to the police.[65] It also tran-spired that her sister worked in the Intelligence Ministry. Kasrils main-tained that she was no more than a family friend and the fact that he was Minister was a mere coincidence.

When the trial verdict was finally delivered, Zuma spoke to his jubi-lant supporters from outside the court. He castigated the media for hav-ing pre-judged him. Speaking in Zulu, he said: 'They insulted me and called me names.' He then added darkly: 'Others were not doing it on their own but were sent by some people somewhere.'[66]

Those 'others' were about to launch another assault, and once more it came in the form of a leak to the media. The leaked report contained emails allegedly indicating that Zuma had secured funding from Angola and Libya to launch a coup against Mbeki, using ANC veterans (see Chapter 5). Marked 'Top Secret' and known as the 'Browse Mole Report', the document was sent to Cosatu on 7 May 2007. The unions immediately made the matter public and sent the document to the government. The whole issue was finally turned over to a parliamentary committee for investigation.

The Joint Standing Committee on Intelligence published its findings in November 2007.[67] The Browse Mole report was described as 'extremely inflammatory' and 'very dangerous' for South Africa's national interests. The committee rejected the information in the emails, which it found had been prepared by the Scorpions. It appeared that the security services were once more becoming embroiled in internal party politics. The Browse Mole episode appeared to be an attempt to frame Zuma by elements in the state's security services. If so, the revelations backfired. As we shall see, Jacob Zuma's political career was finally saved by the very report that was apparently designed to destroy him.

The fight for the presidency

The stage was now set for the final act of this drama. By 2007 Mbeki and Zuma were at daggers drawn, marshalling their supporters for a showdown at the ANC conference to be held in the Limpopo Province capital, Polokwane, in December. By this time Zuma was backed by a range of groups so angered by Mbeki that they were determined to remove him. Everything from the President's imperial style of government to his disregard for the views of the other parties in the Alliance was held against him. Thabo Mbeki's economic policies were anathema not just to the left in the ANC, but also to other organisations within the ANC family, the Women's League and the Youth League.[68]

For his part, Thabo Mbeki was still pressing to have a third term as President of the ANC, even if he had to stand down as President of South Africa. Those who backed Mbeki, including the ANC Chairman, Mosiuoa 'Terror' Lekota, were having trouble making themselves heard at party rallies, which were increasingly dominated by supporters wearing T-shirts emblazoned with '100 per cent', beneath a photograph of Jacob Zuma.

By the time the 4 000 ANC delegates arrived at Polokwane, the writing was on the wall. Yet Mbeki still assumed he could win, and less than half an hour before the outcome of the vote he said as much to some of his closest aides. Mbeki was deluding himself – the party's verdict was unambiguous. Zuma took 2 329 votes to 1 505 for Mbeki.[69] The President looked stunned when he walked onto the stage to listen to the public announcement. Always the consummate politician, Zuma graciously paid tribute to his rival, describing Mbeki as a 'friend and a brother'. It was not only the President who was swept away by this tide of opposition; so too were all his allies in the ANC leadership. It was an emphatic victory for Zuma and those who had supported him through the torment of the preceding years.

Yet there was one final twist to come in this complex saga. Ten days after Zuma was elected ANC President he was charged, once more, in connection with the Arms Deal. The National Prosecuting Authority (NPA) produced fresh allegations that included money laundering, racketeering and tax evasion. The response from ANC members was one of utter fury. Almost all sections of the party united to denounce the new charges, with the Youth League proclaiming extravagantly that they were prepared to 'die for Zuma'.

The ANC was determined that the courts would not be used to eliminate its newly elected leader and began to apply pressure on the judiciary. Intimidating demonstrations were held outside the courts in which the case was to be heard. Zuma's supporters at the highest level also started questioning the independence of the judiciary. ANC Secretary-General Gwede Mantashe spoke out, appearing to accuse the Constitutional Court of being part of what he described as a 'counter-revolutionary conspiracy'. So concerned was the KwaZulu-Natal Judge President, Vuka Tshabalala, that he called on the ANC not to try to intimidate the courts.[70] 'We must prevent a situation where our courts and judges are politicised,' he pleaded.

The deteriorating political climate prompted two of South Africa's most respected legal figures to speak out. Former Chief Justice Arthur

Chaskalson and advocate George Bizos, both of whom had served on Nelson Mandela's defence team in the 1960s, issued a statement expressing concern about the debate around the Zuma trial. They appealed to political leaders to tone down the rhetoric, saying that 'putting pressure on the courts by making allegations of partiality, uttering threats of massive demonstrations, and expressing opinions in intemperate language, are harmful to the judicial process, to our constitutional order and to our country's reputation'.[71]

These warnings appear to have carried little weight in the increasingly febrile atmosphere, even inside the judiciary. In March 2008 the Judge President of the Cape, John Hlophe, is alleged to have approached two members of the Constitutional Court, Justice Bess Nkabinde and Acting Justice Christopher Jafta. What allegedly took place rocked the South African system of justice. For Hlophe is reported to have asked them to decide a pending appeal in favour of Zuma. 'You are our last hope,' he is said to have told them.[72]

These allegations were strongly contested by Hlophe. However, the Chief Justice of South Africa, Pius Langa, was sufficiently concerned to draft a formal complaint against Hlophe, which was signed by all eleven members of the Constitutional Court. The matter went before the Judicial Services Commission (JSC), which oversees the judiciary. Its members include the Chief Justice of the Constitutional Court, the President of the Supreme Court of Appeal and the Minister of Justice. It is a widely representative body, but in the end divisions within the Commission meant that the process ran into the sand. The JSC's disciplinary committee decided by a majority ruling at the end of August 2009 that it was not going to continue with the investigation into the Constitutional Court's complaint against Justice Hlophe.

The result shocked the legal community. In the view of David Unterhalter, Professor of Law at the University of the Witwatersrand, it weakened the judicial system.[73] '[We] are left only with damaged institutions,' he wrote –

> The JSC divided against itself. With a majority decision using flimsy reasoning to avoid proper adjudication, and a minority decision that reasoned, rightly, that disputes of fact required

a formal hearing that will never happen, the Constitutional Court is left badly bruised. It claimed that there was improper interference by Hlophe and the majority of the JSC found its complaint so wanting as not to require a formal hearing. And Hlophe, far from getting the vindication of thorough adjudication, is chastised for his conduct and must now try to lead his division, tainted but not to the point of gross misconduct. It is hard to imagine a worse outcome.

The matter did not end there, since the Premier of the Western Cape, Helen Zille, took the matter to court, arguing that the disciplinary committee had not been properly constituted. Zille argued that as premier of the province in which the High Court judge sat, she was constitutionally required to have been included on the disciplinary committee. The Appeal Court ruled in her favour, re-opening the issue, which the JSC will have to reconsider.[74] This ruling was strengthened when the Constitutional Court ruled in favour of the legal rights group, Freedom Under Law, which had challenged the procedural issues that had been holding up the case.[75]

Those close to Jacob Zuma believed his ascent to the presidency of the ANC would allow him to finally put the Arms Deal allegations behind him. According to a confidential dispatch later leaked, on 25 July 2008, Moe Shaik met the US embassy's Political Officer, who in turn briefed the Americans that: 'President Jacob Zuma has entered into secret talks with the National Prosecuting Authority (NPA) about the corruption charges pending against Zuma ... the ANC President hoped to convince the NPA to "view the facts in a different light" and exercise their "prosecutorial discretion" to withdraw the corruption charges. Zuma does not want to become national president in 2009 with charges hanging over him, Shaik stressed.'[76] Commenting on the discussions, the US ambassador to Pretoria, Eric Bost, wrote that this might have been wishful thinking on Shaik's part, but that it was 'possible that the NPA believes they are better off cutting a deal with Zuma than pushing for a politically-messy trial'.

The Browse Mole Report again

At this point in the saga of Jacob Zuma's rise to power the law intervened once more. On 12 September 2008 Judge Chris Nicholson delivered his verdict on the prosecution's case against Zuma for his alleged involvement in the Arms Deal. Justice Nicholson described the circumstances in which the case had been brought:

> The titanic political struggle between the applicant and the President is no concern of the court unless it impacts on issues to be decided in this application. The rivalry of the applicant and the President is hardly open to question and the polarization of the country into opposing camps before and after Polokwane is well known.[77]

The Judge went on to describe repeated instances of interference in the case by the Minister of Justice and the presidency, saying that he found a continuing 'baleful political influence' on the prosecutor by his political masters.[78] Finally he ruled that the prosecution was invalid and dismissed the charges because of the political influence that had been brought to bear on the case. At the same time, Judge Nicholson stressed that his ruling had no bearing on Zuma's guilt or innocence on the question of corruption.

The Zuma camp was triumphant. The court's finding that the Mbeki administration had interfered in the case was exactly the point that Zuma's lawyers had always argued.

Five days later, the NPA announced it would appeal against the verdict. The ANC believed that Thabo Mbeki, who remained President of South Africa even though he had lost his position as President of the ANC, was behind this decision. Concluding that the President was too dangerous to remain in charge of the country, the NEC forced his resignation. This took place on 24 September 2008. All that was left for President Mbeki was to call his Cabinet ministers, deputies and closest staff together to thank them for their hard work.[79] Then, 'tears streaming' down his face, and defiantly arguing that he had been in the right, Mbeki left the presidency.

One might have assumed that this would be the end of the matter, but it was not. Mbeki, furious that Judge Nicholson had blackened his name, attempted to have the ruling quashed. The matter went to the Supreme Court of Appeal, which in January 2009 overturned the Nicholson judgment, opening the way for Zuma's trial to resume a matter of months before the country went to the polls in the April 2009 general election.

This led to the final twist in this extraordinary drama. It was left to the country's chief prosecutor, Mokotedi Mpshe, to speak to the nation on 6 April 2009. The 90-minute news conference was carried live on national television and radio and the nation hung on his every word. People opened their car doors and turned up their radios so that passers-by could hear the decision being announced. Others watched the announcement on big-screen televisions in coffee bars.

Mpshe began with the following statement: 'I stand before you today to announce the most difficult decision I ever made in my life. It was not an easy task at all.' He then explained why he had, finally, decided to drop the prosecution,[80] revealing that Zuma's lawyers had provided the NPA with fresh evidence. This consisted of taped phone calls between the former head of the Scorpions, Leonard McCarthy, and the former head of the NPA, Bulelani Ngcuka. Mpshe said that the tapes had been authenticated and had shown that McCarthy had decided to prosecute Zuma immediately after the ANC's Polokwane conference as a means of saving President Mbeki. Mpshe said he didn't know whether the recordings had been legally intercepted or were legally in the possession of Zuma's lawyer, Michael Hulley. Nonetheless he had decided to rely on them.

The Prosecuting Authority had contacted the National Intelligence Agency, which confirmed it had itself obtained recordings of 'many of the same conversations' during its investigation of the production and leaking of the Browse Mole Report. This revealed, said Mpshe, an abuse of office.[81] 'Mr McCarthy used the legal process for a purpose other than which the process was designed to serve, i.e. for collateral and illicit purposes. It does not matter that the team acted properly, honestly, fairly and justly throughout. Mr McCarthy's conduct amounts to a serious abuse of process and offends one's sense of justice.' Because of this,

Mpshe had decided that it was 'neither possible nor desirable for the NPA to continue with the prosecution of Mr Zuma'.

So ended the state's case against Jacob Zuma. Those close to the prosecution argue that it would have been simply impossible to continue with the case, since it had been tainted by those seemingly loyal to the Mbeki presidency. The decision did not, however, end the mystery surrounding the tape recordings, who made them and how the Zuma defence team had managed to get hold of them. The best stab at investigating these questions was by the *Mail & Guardian* newspaper,[82] which concluded in April 2009 that the tapes had been given to Zuma's lawyers by the deputy head of the National Intelligence Agency, Arthur Fraser, who wished to ingratiate himself with the man who was about to become the country's President. The agency's spokesman denied this, but the paper said they had evidence of this from three separate sources.

A month later – having done more digging, and following the testimony of the Scorpions' special investigator, Ivor Powell – the *Mail & Guardian's* investigative reporter, Sam Sole, came to a further conclusion.[83] The Browse Mole Report's allegations of an insurrection plot were far fetched, he said. However, they had allowed other facts to be uncovered, in particular the claims of funding from Libya and Angola. In effect, the report had 'inoculated' Zuma against further scrutiny. It also showed that 'the Scorpions were targeting Zuma in areas far beyond the corruption case against him, bolstering claims of a politically motivated investigation'.

It was these taped revelations that finally got Zuma off the state's corruption charge hook, allowing him to become President of South Africa on 9 May 2009. But the damage done to the institutions of the state was immense. As the *Mail & Guardian* concluded in an editorial: 'The very deep and broad politicisation of the intelligence and security services represents one of the most serious, and least understood, threats to our constitutional order ... The story of Powell and the Special Browse "Mole" consolidated report demonstrates how thoroughly the defining political battle of the decade has been fought in the secret world and how completely state institutions have been compromised on both sides.'[84]

Whatever the cost, Jacob Zuma's assumption of the highest office in the land represented a triumph for the Alliance. The ANC, the unions and the SACP had held their nerve and their relationship had survived. They had remained remarkably united during extremely testing times. With the Alliance's support, the ANC had achieved something that no country relishes and almost no African state has ever achieved: the democratic removal of a head of state. No bloodshed was involved and life in South Africa continued as normal. True, the institutions of the state emerged battered and bloodied, but they were still intact. There was a hope that the country might regain its equilibrium after the dark dealings of the Mbeki era.

Chapter 3

Political Hyenas and the Predatory State

Martin Plaut

Zuma's inauguration was a moment of triumph for his allies, but unity did not last. As the SACP later recognised, somewhat ruefully, the anti-Mbeki alliance had been little more than a coalition of convenience:

> The anti-Mbeki coalition quickly unravelled after the 2009 elections. It is clear that the glue that bound us together was not ideology but common disenchantment with the Mbeki-era. It is clear that what the left had identified as a principled opposition towards the way in which the ANC and the Alliance were run, and the need for change, was used as mere rhetoric by some within the ANC to get rid of former President Mbeki.[1]

While this may be clear with hindsight, after their victory at the ANC's conference at Polokwane in December 2007, the left hoped their time had come. They thought that the right wing of the party had been isolated and their own candidates would come to power. Indeed, some of those close to Thabo Mbeki had left the ANC altogether, seeking fresh pastures in the newly formed Congress of the People (Cope). Hence the distress of Zuma's associates when he appointed what was described as a Cabinet of all the talents.

The bane of the left – Trevor Manuel – was appointed as Minister in the Presidency, National Planning Commission. It was Manuel who, as Minister of Finance, had been at the heart of the country's liberal economic policies and a key player in the '1996 class project' so hated by the left.[2] His appointment would lead to a re-emergence of the left–right tensions that had bedevilled the Alliance during the Mbeki years.

Although there is no simple dichotomy within the ANC between these camps, it is possible to identify two poles of attraction, whose membership waxes and wanes over time. The right wing, or populist faction, gathered itself around the Youth League and its president, Julius Malema. He supported and was in turn supported by elements of the new black elite who had used the government's BEE programmes to gain wealth and influence. This is perhaps a little confusing, since Malema has been calling for nationalisation of the land and mines – normally a position associated with the left. The traditional left (the unions and the communists) have been resisting these calls. While this may appear contradictory, the reality is not very complex. A proportion of the new black elite, who received shares in Black Economic Empowerment deals, have found it extremely difficult to repay their loans (see Chapter 8 for further detail).

Highlighting this issue, the SACP attacked those who called for na-tionalisation, Julius Malema included.[3] The party declared that it had warned against the use of state finances to bail out the new rich. It came out strongly against 'diverting billions of rands of public funds to serve the interests of a narrow black (and white) capitalist stratum'. Nor was it just a question of 'bailing-out debt-ridden BEE capital'. According to the SACP, mine union officials had been quietly approached by members of the new black elite, asking: 'why don't you support the nationaliza-tion of the mines? If government takes over the mines they will turn to us to run them.'[4] Turning to the state for nationalisation would relieve the new rich of their crippling debts and enable them to continue to enjoy their newfound wealth.

As for the land issue, as Zimbabwe has demonstrated, cronies of President Mugabe have found ways of winning many of the choic-est farms. No doubt their equivalents in the ANC could see similar opportunities for further entrenching their positions by acquiring land through a policy that was bound to win popular support.

This was all very annoying for the traditional left, which complained that its policies had been hijacked. In June 2006 SACP General Secretary Blade Nzimande accused the right of attempting to re-assert the power it had lost when Mbeki was ousted.[5] In December 2009, the political report to the SACP Special Congress declared that 'emergent class interests' had been attacking the role of the SACP within the ANC. The statement is quoted at some length since it summarises the left's critique of the right:[6]

> ... this anti-communism/anti-SACP tendency has been informed and influenced by ascendancy to state power and prospects of being part of (albeit a compradorial) emergent black sections of the capitalist class. In other words, whilst the anti-communism of the pre 1990 era was informed by a petty bourgeois ideological reaction to communism, the post-1994 anti-communism has been informed by the new emergent class interests accompanied by very real prospects of using state power or accumulated dependent BEE (Black Economic Empowerment) capital to capture our movement. After the political dislocation of the 1996 class project, the new tendency has become more desperate, more brazenly Africanist, but without a coherent ideological outlook. Instead the new tendency is opportunistically using the historical documents and positions of our movement to try and assert its new positions (e.g. an opportunistic use of the clauses of nationalization in the Freedom Charter and the vulgarization of the characterization of our revolution as that seeking to liberate blacks in general and Africans in particular).
>
> Interestingly the seeming desperation of the new tendency is also influenced by the desperate conditions of BEE capital in the light of the current global capitalist crisis and its impact on South Africa. What in fact appears as an articulation of the progressive clauses of the Freedom Charter is immediately betrayed by the naked class interests of trying to use the state

to bail out dependent BEE capital. Ironically, but not surprisingly, the bail out for black capital simultaneously becomes the bail out and strengthening of white domestic capital upon which the former is entirely dependent.

In other words, the SACP accused the right in the ANC, associated with the Youth League, of being seduced by the emerging black capitalist class. It was argued that they were calling for the nationalisation of the mines because of the desperate economic situation in which many BEE firms found themselves (see Chapter 8).

Just how this clash between the left and right inside the Alliance has unfolded since the Polokwane conference will be explored in this chapter. This contest for power comes at a difficult time for the ANC, with two trends emerging. The first is a gradual but consistent decline in popularity, as seen in elections and opinion polls. The second is the growth of organised crime and endemic corruption within local and national government. Many inside the Alliance acknowledge the dangers crime and corruption hold for the movement and the country. At the end of 2010 the Cosatu Central Executive Committee were so concerned they issued a statement declaring that 'if we, as the broad liberation movement, don't act decisively, we are heading rapidly in the direction of a full-blown predator state, in which a powerful, corrupt and demagogic elite of political hyenas increasingly controls the state as a vehicle for accumulation'.[7] A senior government official, who asked not to be named, went on to warn that sections of the leadership are in danger of being 'captured' by organised crime.[8]

Economic and political debates

In September 2009 Trevor Manuel drew up and presented to Parliament a Green Paper proposing a system of planning within which all government decisions could be measured.[9] The left reacted angrily, believing this would leave the SACP and the union's key allies largely toothless, just as they had been under the Mbeki presidency.

Zwelinzima Vavi, the Cosatu General Secretary, roundly rejected the plan. He said that it reflected 'a massive turf battle in Cabinet'. [10] The unions accused Manuel of being determined to sideline Ebrahim Patel, the left-wing Minister of Economic Development. Union leaders expressed concern that Patel would be outflanked by conservatives in the Cabinet, leaving the left without real authority. Patel still had no budget, adding to fears that he could end up in much the same position as Jay Naidoo before him, little more than a 'paper tiger' to be devoured by the right in government, clustered around the Treasury. A congress resolution called for the 'overhaul of the content of the Green Paper on Strategic Planning' and an end to the 'marginalisation of the Alliance and other key ministries in shaping this policy intervention prior to its public release'. [11]

The left were, in effect, demanding that the ANC live up to its promises to include them in government, in the shaping of policy and the preparation of initiatives prior to their presentation to the public. If implemented to the letter, this would lead to a transformation of the administration. Parties that had received no endorsement from the electorate – Cosatu and the SACP – would have privileged access to the levers of power.

The right within the ANC had been on the back foot since Polokwane and the defection of leading members to Cope. They saw the left's demands as an opportunity to draw a line in the sand. In an outspoken attack, Billy Masetlha, a member of the ANC National Executive and a former director of the National Intelligence Agency, drew attention to what he described as the growing dominance of the unions and communists within the ANC. A number of senior ANC leaders had expressed disquiet about the push by the left for a socialist agenda within the ANC, he said. [12]

Masetlha was doing something that few ANC senior members had been prepared to do in recent years – publicly criticising the role of the communists inside the ANC. 'I will have a problem with someone [Blade Nzimande] trying to impose a communist manifesto on the ANC. We fired a lot of [comrades] in the past who wanted to do the same thing,' he said. 'The ANC was not founded on a socialist agenda. Socialism has no space within the ANC.' Masetlha's views received some support, but the ANC officially distanced itself from his remarks. 'The notion that the ANC is under threat from "the push by Cosatu and the SACP for a socialist agenda" is unfounded and regrettable,' it said in a statement.[13]

The left was furious. The Young Communists attacked Masetlha as a 'useful idiot' who worked in the interests of capitalists.[14] The National Union of Metalworkers of South Africa joined the attack, declaring that: 'Comrade Masetlha's assertions fit squarely into the destructive anti-alliance agenda as espoused by the 1996 class project which was partly dislodged by the majority of delegates in Polokwane. He should know that history is littered with names of far greater men and women who have been lost in the dustbin of political history for their anti communist and anti trade unionist agendas.'[15]

It was left to Jacob Zuma to try to pick up the pieces, appealing for unity within his increasingly disunited allies.[16] It was the mission of the Alliance, he said, 'to keep the ANC strong and united so that it can lead the alliance and the country effectively'. The next step in attempts to control the growing row was to call a meeting of Alliance leaders at ANC headquarters on 12 October 2009. Behind closed doors they hammered out a statement reaffirming the ANC's right to lead the movement, while at the same time respecting the right of its partners to express their own views.[17] This ceasefire didn't last.

Renewing the battle

By early 2010 the cracks within the Alliance were widening. This was associated with increasing concern about the corruption and careerism that had become so prevalent within the movement. It was a problem the ANC openly acknowledged, as Secretary-General Gwede Mantashe reported following an NEC meeting held between 15 and 18 January 2010.[18]

Mantashe said that the party had made great strides since the election of 1994, but that '[a]scent to power also impacted negatively on the outlook of the African National Congress'. He spelt out what he meant by quoting from resolutions adopted at the party's Polokwane conference. 'The main weakness that our movement must confront is the "inability to effectively deal with the new tendencies such as social distance, patronage, careerism, corruption and abuse of power. The lack of policy for dealing effectively with the intersection between holding office and business interest is fast corroding the moral authority of our movement in society."'

This erosion of values was associated with a failure to deliver on the promises the ANC had made to improve the lives of its core constituency, the South African poor. A searing indictment was delivered in December 2009 at an SACP Special National Congress, also held in Polokwane. General Secretary Blade Nzimande (who was also the government's Minister of Higher Education and Training) spoke on behalf of the Central Committee. He began his analysis with a blistering attack on the failure of the government to resolve the problems facing ordinary people:[19]

> We need to help our movement and our country understand a major paradox, a cruel irony. Why, after more than 15 years of democracy, after 15 years of many earnest efforts, after 15 years of some real advances ... why do we still live in a society in which the legacy of apartheid appears to be constantly reproduced and even expanded? In 1994 unemployment in SA was at crisis-levels of around 24%. So why, 14 years later towards the middle of last year, after what was heralded as a decade and more of 'unprecedented' growth, and BEFORE the current recession began to hit our economy ... why had we only managed to bring unemployment finally down to roughly the SAME figure of 24%? In 1994 our RDP document estimated that we had a housing shortage of 3 million. Over the past 15 years the state has built 3.1 million low-cost houses for the poor. So why is the housing shortage STILL almost the same as it was back in 1994? Why do we seem to be going around in a circle? Why is our GINI-coefficient, measuring income inequality, still stubbornly amongst the very highest recorded in the world? And why does inequality remain so

dramatically racialised in our country? This Congress must pose these awkward questions.

This is strong stuff indeed. It was remarkable that a senior member of the Alliance – and a government minister to boot – was prepared to make these points quite so bluntly. Nzimande's analysis was accompanied by a similarly withering critique of what he described as the corrupt elements within the ANC who were attempting to capture the movement for their own ends and to 'abuse their political connections for their own private accumulation'. He continued: 'Let us defeat javelin-throwers and "tenderpreneurs". Let us defeat fronters, gobetweens, compradors who parade their blackness only in order to advance their own private interests by doing the bidding of their masters – well-entrenched monopoly capital.'

Late in 2009, reports surfaced suggesting that the right in the ANC, centred on the Youth League, had decided to try to replace Gwede Mantashe with someone more to their liking at the party's next conference in 2012. This was confirmed in January 2010.[20] The attempt to remove Mantashe, who was SACP chairperson as well as ANC Secretary-General, was a clear attack on the left's hold on the ANC. Party leaders reportedly listened in stunned silence as Malema laid into Mantashe, the ANC's third most senior leader after Jacob Zuma and his deputy, Kgalema Motlanthe, and proposed Fikile Mbalula, Deputy Minister of Police and former Youth League president, as his successor.

Mathews Phosa, the ANC Treasurer, briefed the US embassy in Pretoria on these tensions:[21]

Phosa opened the meeting by discussing ongoing tensions within the ruling tripartite alliance – the ANC, South African Communist Party (SACP) and Cosatu trade union federation. He conceded that anti-communism within the ANC is growing and that conflicts have more to do with personalities than issues. He cited the recent debate over nationalization of the country's mines as one example where the debate is about personal ambitions and not whether such a policy would enhance South Africa's economy. He added the feud between Julius

Malema and Jeremy Cronin[22] is not about nationalization or 'bad blood' between the ANCYL President or the SACP Deputy Secretary General.

Rather, Phosa opined the feud is a way for Malema to attack SACP Secretary General Blade Nzimande and SACP National Chairperson Gwede Mantashe. He said, 'They are all talking about 2012. The ANCYL thinks Mantashe is conflicted in his roles as SACP chair and ANC Secretary General.' Phosa relayed a story about a private meeting he attended with Malema and Mantashe in which Malema pointed at the ANC Secretary General and accused him directly of being 'conflicted' because he plays a role in both parties.

The gloves come off

Most of these clashes took place behind closed doors, but as time passed the conflict became increasingly visible. The issue that triggered an outburst of insults was whether to nationalise South Africa's mines. The communists attacked the proposal, suggesting that the timing was wrong. The party's Deputy General Secretary, Jeremy Cronin, wrote a paper opposing the ANC Youth League's proposal.[23] He said that the plan was a typically ill-thought-out suggestion, made on the hoof, and designed to attract attention. Cronin described it as an 'off-the wall sound byte'.

Julius Malema, who was used to being treated with kid gloves, was furious. He replied, describing Cronin's position as openly reactionary.[24] He went on to criticise Cronin (who is white) for siding with white supremacists, and describing him as a 'white messiah'. Communists were stung into action, attacking Malema's remarks as 'disgusting' and 'racist'. Others went further. Cronin himself appeared to apologise, but only made matters worse by saying that he hadn't realised that Malema 'had such a delicate skin'.

The gloves were clearly coming off. Allies who came together to overthrow Thabo Mbeki had clearly fallen out with each other. Until late

2009 these differences could be dismissed as spats, with most of the remarks made off-the-cuff and apparently not representing fundamental divisions. In December 2009 this changed, with carefully prepared statements released at the SACP Congress. Two set-piece speeches laid out in detail the left's attack on the right within the ANC.

Blade Nzimande laid into the Youth League, describing them as playing into the hands of white capitalists, upon whom they were 'entirely dependent'. He went on to attack those in the Youth League who had been courted by white businessmen like the late Brett Kebble, who had arranged his own assassination when his business empire came crashing down about his ears. 'This new tendency has its roots in what we might call 'Kebble-ism' – in which some of the more roguish elements of capital, lumpen-white capitalists, handed out largesse and favours and generally sought to corrupt elements within our movement in order to secure their own personal accumulation agendas,' said Nzimande.

The SACP was now openly attacking Malema and his associates as corrupt politicians whose favours had been bought in exchange for an opulent lifestyle. But there was one final insult to be hurled. Malema and his associates in the Youth League were accused of 'proto-fascism' – the worst insult in the communist lexicon:[25]

> We do not use the term proto-fascist lightly, nor for the moment should we exaggerate it. However, there are worrying tell-tale characteristics that need to be nipped in the bud. They include the demagogic appeal to ordinary people's baser instincts (male chauvinism, paramilitary solutions to social problems, and racialised identity politics).

While Nzimande delivered this lengthy analysis it was left to Gwede Mantashe to spell out the political implications.[26] He insisted that communists were an integral part of the ANC and, as active members, should be accorded full rights. 'Communists in the ANC are not communist members of the ANC, they are members of the ANC,' Mantashe declared.

Confrontation with the Youth League

The scene was set for a showdown. It was in this explosive atmosphere that the ANC delegation arrived at the SACP Congress. Some of the party's most senior members were there, including those associated with the ANC's right wing, including Tokyo Sexwale, Tony Yengeni, Billy Masetlha, and Julius Malema. Despite their political differences, they might have expected a welcome from the gathering, as a delegation from a fraternal party and members of the Tripartite Alliance. Instead they were booed and jeered by the assembled SACP delegates. When Malema walked into the conference hall at the University of Limpopo wearing designer jeans and a Ralph Lauren dress shirt, the delegates started singing *'Asiyifun' i-agenda yamaCapitalists'* (we don't want a capitalist agenda).[27] For Malema, who was accustomed to receiving respect bordering on adulation, this was an extraordinary affront.

When the conference adjourned for lunch, Malema walked up to the stage and confronted Mantashe, who was chairing the meeting, and demanded the right to address the meeting.[28] 'We were insulted in front of the country,' he protested. Mantashe told Malema: 'You are asking for something wrongly,' explaining that he himself was not at the congress as the leader of the ANC but in his capacity as the Chairman of the SACP. There was little that Malema could do but gnash his teeth and bide his time.

The Young Communist League, which had promised to 'meet fire with fire' in defence of the party, dismissed the outburst as the action of a 'drama queen'.[29] Recalling Malema's description of Jeremy Cronin as a 'white messiah', the National Secretary of the young communists, Buti Manamela, told delegates at the conference that those who insulted the SACP and its leaders would be treated accordingly. 'Those who continue to call our leaders racist should never have illusions of receiving red-carpet treatment in this congress,' he said. Soon the humiliation inflicted on Malema was circulating via the electronic media. Seething with anger, Malema and his associates stormed out of the conference. He then sent a chain of text messages to ANC and youth leaders, calling on them to 'defend' the governing party. 'There are no roses in a war, we are called upon to defend the ANC,' his SMS warned.[30] He sent a message to Jeremy Cronin saying: 'If you thought you have taught me a lesson, wait until you see what is coming your direction.'[31] Cronin went on national radio to acknowledge that he had received some threatening SMSs: 'I can't actually believe they are from Julius Malema, but they are signed "Julius Malema". I find it hard to believe that he would send [them].'

Meanwhile, the ANC Youth League branches were circulating messages declaring their support for Malema. The Western Cape branch secretary, Tandi Mahambehlala, said in a statement that the booing invoked 'disgust and disappointment'. 'We call on the SACP to stop convening forums posing as constitutional meetings only to find out they are meant to insult the leadership of the ANC.'[32]

The incident was apparently swept under the carpet, in the best Alliance tradition,[33] but Malema neither forgot nor forgave the insults he had suffered. He appeared more determined than ever to unseat Gwede Mantashe as ANC Secretary-General, removing the most senior communist within the party, at the 2012 ANC Congress. At an NEC meeting in January 2010 he asked: 'Positions are contested in the ANC. Why can't S-G be contested?'[34]

Mid-term blues

The ANC held a National General Council in Durban from 20 to 24 September 2010. The Council is the most high-level meeting the ANC holds between its five-yearly Congresses. It was an important opportunity for all members of the Alliance to re-assess their positions.

The unions – in the form of Cosatu – conducted a lengthy internal debate about their continued relationship with the ANC, which they published.[35] It was a thoughtful discussion of the problems facing the country, and remarkably frank. The paper, subtitled 'The Alliance at a Crossroads – the battle against a predatory elite and political paralysis', is worth quoting at some length as it contains important pointers to the future direction of politics of the ANC's allies.

The paper began by spelling out what the unions saw as the heart of the problem: the corruption paralysing both government and country. This was blamed on the previous Mbeki government, and attacked what was described as the 'perversion of the culture of the movement into one of crass materialism, and self-interest'. The paper concluded that 'the Alliance, and indeed the country, is at a crossroads, and that if we fail to arrest the current trajectory, we face being plunged into a serious crisis'.

The unions warned that unless the ANC tackled these tendencies, South Africa would go the way of the rest of the continent:

> Africa itself, as well as revolutions elsewhere, has seen too many liberation movements with noble ideals, hijacked by corrupt individuals, predatory classes, and foreign interests, for us to close our eyes to that danger now. Our liberation movement, and our struggle, will never be up for sale. It is the working class, and the poorest of the poor, who always end up the worst victims of these failed revolutions. However, while the rich have more resources to cushion themselves, a predator state will ultimately eat away, and consume the whole of society. No one is immune.

Cosatu then set about analysing what exactly that 'predatory state' consisted of, and why South Africa was suffering from it. It talked about the 'systemic creation of a network of patronage and corruption', which meant that soon no one would be able to do business with government without offering a bribe. It also pointed to why corruption flourished, saying that for many ANC members, their access to political patronage was their only route out of poverty. The paper accused the ANC Youth League and its allies among the black business elite (the 'predatory elite') of holding the state to ransom and leaving it paralysed, and of preparing to attack both the ANC Secretary-General – Gwede Mantashe – and Jacob Zuma himself.[36]

To make matters worse, argued the unions, their allies in the SACP had become increasingly silent, even though the party's membership had increased to 109 000. Their presence inside government, as ministers and senior officials, had in Cosatu's view deprived them of the time and energy to take on their opponents on the right of the ANC. 'Increasingly the SACP is unable to play its proper role. It is in danger of becoming more and more invisible, given the full-time role of its office bearers in government and in the ANC.'

The problem for the union movement was what to do about this turn of events. Here the analysis petered out. It renewed its appeal for strengthened campaigns against corruption, while its own analysis showed why these were almost certain to fail. It concluded with a series of questions, pondering whether Cosatu had perhaps misunderstood the nature of politics and society in South Africa. Finally it broached the question of whether it might be better placed if it established an alternative left-wing party of its own:

> Why for 16 years since democracy have we not moved closer towards the ideal which Cosatu resolutions speak to? Do we have the wrong conception of our Alliance – is our insistence on an Alliance programme that will allow all components to drive transformation as a political center under the leadership of the ANC a pipe dream? To what extent are these high Cosatu expectations on how the Alliance should function leading to deep frustrations on our part? Are these expectations on the part of Cosatu unrealistic – do we need another type of Alliance which perhaps will only be limited to Cosatu backing the ANC during elections but not insisting on driving a transformation programme together? The other option would be for Cosatu to align itself with a left party or pro poor/pro working class party and relate to the ANC on ad hoc basis, through e.g. governing coalitions. We need to develop these scenarios further.

This was, of course, not the first time the unions had pondered these questions. The General Secretary of Fosatu, Cosatu's predecessor, had raised much the same issue in 1982. Nearly three decades later, the unions were still at much the same point: still worrying about their relationship with the ANC and tentatively considering whether they should start a party of their own.

'Beating dogs until their owners come out'

Towards the end of 2010, the ANC Youth League had come to the end of a series of deeply divisive regional meetings, leading up to the League's National General Council in August 2010. Malema had managed to retain control of the organisation, but only after a series of bitter battles around the country. These were marked by struggles for power, some of which ended in physical clashes between delegates, while others ended in court cases.

At the General Council Malema laid into the SACP. With typical rhetorical flourishes he spoke out against General Secretary Blade Nzimande, who had expressed concern at faction fighting within the youth body. 'The SACP has failed to take over the youth league. We will never surrender to Blade. He has never been a member, and has no understanding of what the youth league is,' Malema told cheering delegates.[37] 'Their people have been receiving serious lashings in the youth league conferences. As we said before, we will beat the dog [the communists] until the owner [Nzimande] comes out.'

Malema used the occasion to open a new front against his enemies inside the ANC leadership, calling for the party to reflect what he described as a 'generational mix' – code for throwing out the old guard and replacing them with his supporters. He also inflicted sweet revenge on the SACP. Delegates booed the National Secretary of the Young Communist League, Buti Manamela, off the stage. He had barely got through paying respects to the leadership present when delegates started singing.

Emboldened by his successes, Malema went on the attack, warning ANC leaders that they too could be removed at any time.[38] 'You must be careful, you'll be on the streets if you don't respect the power of the masses,' he told the delegates. 'Sometimes power makes you drunk. Leaders should not want to impress those in power, they should rather strive to impress the masses on the ground.' Leaders would come and go, said Malema, but the ANC would remain, and the Youth League wanted to inherit a party that was 'intact'. The jury was still out on President Jacob Zuma's performance: 'You are just starting, Baba,' he warned.

Whatever one might say about Jacob Zuma, he is certainly not 'just starting'. Zuma has been in the ANC since he was a young man. In underestimating him, Malema may have made the mistake that many have made before him. Prior to the ANC's National General Council meeting in Durban, Zuma did what any leader worthy of the title would do: he rallied his troops. He called in favours from the ANC's powerful provincial leaders and laid the ground for the meeting.

The ANC gathers in Durban

By the time Zuma rose to speak to the 2 000 ANC delegates to the National General Council in September 2010, Malema already knew that he was in for a rough ride, and had begun to tone down his rhetoric. The President set out to put his young challenger in his place. 'We have no choice but to reintroduce discipline in the ANC. If we fail to do so, we would be weakening the very fibre and existence of the ANC,' Zuma told the gathering.[39]

In his report to the meeting Zuma dealt at length with the party and its structures. He pointed out that the Youth League and the Women's League were integral elements of the ANC and subject to its discipline. In May 2010 Malema had been convicted of bringing the party into disrepute for claiming that Zuma was worse than former President Thabo Mbeki in his dealings with the Youth League. He had been ordered by the party's disciplinary committee to make a public apology for his conduct, fined R10 000 and ordered to attend anger management classes. 'We have noted some regrettable incidents, particularly relating to the ANC Youth League conferences, which are unacceptable and need to be dealt with,' Zuma reported. 'Juniors,' he told delegates to applause, 'must respect seniors.' Zuma said name-calling among factions and structures of the ANC and the Alliance would also be dealt with. Picking up on points made in pre-conference documents, he said some members were using money to buy their way into party positions, and he condemned the tendency to distribute lists of people to be elected by specific factions.

Most delegates welcomed the speech, and Malema was left licking his wounds, with only his stalwart supporter, Winnie Mandela, to comfort him. The Youth League and its associates lost on a number of counts. Malema himself had been publicly criticised; the League's plans for a 'generational mix' in the top ANC leadership had been rejected. Suggestions that nationalisation of the mines should become ANC policy were kicked into the long grass, with a decision that it would be left for further study by the party. Finally, the ANC passed a report opposing the use of electoral slates, the use of money to buy votes and ill-discipline in general – all practices that took place inside the League.

The veteran political commentator, Allister Sparks, gave this assessment of the conference:[40]

> After all the sturm und drang leading up to the ANC's national general council conference, the meeting itself clarified little. President Jacob Zuma has emerged a little stronger, ANC Youth League leader Julius Malema considerably weaker and the Congress of South African Trade Unions's Zwelinzima Vavi more conflicted. There was no split and there was no healing, except for some temporary bandaging beneath which the deep incompatibilities will continue to fester. As for the critical policy issues that are holding back the country, they remained largely unattended.
>
> So the drift will continue.

Although the Youth League had received a setback, it had not been defeated, and major issues confronting South Africa continued to remain unaddressed. While there were many examples of this, unemployment was perhaps the most obvious. The Department of Labour's first declared objective was 'speeding up economic growth and transforming the economy to create decent work and sustainable livelihoods'.[41] According to the department's own figures, it had trained 636 140 people, yet only managed to find work for 7 008.[42] This was a success rate of just over 1 per cent for a department with a budget of R2 126 372 billion, or more than $300 million. It was failures like this that gave the Youth League space to appeal to the young and dispossessed. Malema's populist rhetoric found a willing audience among young black township residents, who saw the ANC as failing to address their needs.

The political dilemma of the trade unions: Plan 2015 fails

Ever since its inception, one of the key political problems confronting the trade union movement has been its relationship with the ANC. Even before Cosatu's birth, there were those who argued that it was necessary to found a separate working-class party. Time and again, as the unions became fed up with their ANC allies, they looked around to see with whom else they might unite. In 2000, a resolution was tabled at the metalworkers' union calling for the SACP to replace the ANC as leader of the Alliance.[43] It was not passed. A resolution put to the municipal workers' union conference in the same year was adopted, calling for discussions to begin to find an 'alternative to the alliance'.

These rumblings of discontent have not yet been translated into action. In 2003, for example, at the end of the Cosatu congress a statement was issued declaring that despite being fed up with the right-wing drift of politics, the union movement was not about to ditch its allies.[44] Instead the unions pledged themselves to work to implement what was called Plan 2015, hoping that by that year, with a real effort, the unions could transform the situation. This would involve redoubling their efforts to 'defend the progressive and working class bias of the ANC'. Cosatu committed itself to taking on a major political role within the ANC by committing itself to 'swell the ranks of the ANC by calling on its members, shop stewards and leaders to join the ANC *en masse*'.

This determination to transform the ANC rather than leave the Alliance was summed up by the former President of Cosatu, Willie Madisha. 'If I go to heaven,' he said, 'I would not like to be the person explaining to struggle heroes like Chris Hani and Joe Slovo that I was the person responsible for the alliance being broken up.'[45]

Despite this affirmation, the belief that the ANC is the sole organisation within which the union movement should work has gradually weakened. In the run-up to the ANC's National General Council meeting in September 2010, Cosatu issued a paper reviewing the situation since 2003.[46] The statement was remarkably frank. It accepted that Plan 2015 had not achieved its objective of bringing union members into the party. The strategy, it said, 'has failed. At one level Cosatu members haven't joined the ANC in large enough numbers. However, even members of the ANC play a minimal role in defining strategy, and therefore swelling the ranks alone may be ineffective … the organised working class is not the motive force in the ANC at this point.'

From a union perspective, this was all very dispiriting. The strategy the unions had evolved, pursued and nurtured for more than 15 years had run into the sand. While Cosatu was not yet prepared to make a formal break with the ANC, it had considered its options. Unions and their members were no longer prepared to be taken for granted by the ANC as mere voting fodder, only called on for support during elections, and ignored between elections. The Cosatu paper said that its members needed to examine alternative scenarios. Among them was one that called for the establishment of an independent working-class party:[47]

> Walk out of the Alliance and call on the SACP to contest political power or start a new working class Party that would unite labour, SACP, social movements, civil society formations and the leftwing political formations committed to the radical transformation and socialism. Under this scenario Cosatu acts with others to challenge the ANC in power.

This was not endorsed as union policy. Indeed, it may have been no more than a bargaining position. Yet the fact that Cosatu had even been prepared to talk openly in these terms was indicative of the left's deep disillusionment with the ANC government. In part, this reflects a gradual erosion of confidence in the party within the union movement. Loyalty towards the ANC among shop stewards fell from 82 per cent in 1994 to 66 per cent in 2004.[48] The same research indicated that support for an independent working-class party stood at just 6 per cent in 2004.

The unions have not been alone in considering their options in the Alliance. The SACP, so long wedded to the ANC, has also wondered about separation. The party has been deeply critical of the ANC's increasing reliance on the men and women who have used party connections to build their wealth. The communists have repeatedly accused these elements inside the ANC of having a parasitic relationship with white business:[49]

> This emerging class fraction has, typically, not accumulated its own capital through the unleashing of productive processes, but relies on special share deals, 'affirmative action', BEE quotas, fronting, privatisation and trading on its one real piece of 'capital' (access to state power) to establish itself. This compradorism also explains many of the cultural/moral features of this emerging class fraction – its remuneration expectations are aligned with an apartheid-era wage gap, and its life-style aspirations are those of the white capitalist German luxury car, country club and golf-estate. It is not involved in primitive accumulation, so much as primitive consumption.

Why should any left-wing movement associate itself with a party dominated by leaders drawn from this stratum? The answer is simple. The SACP has over the years successfully built its own membership and carved a place in South African society through its relationship with the ANC. It is unlikely to abandon these ties lightly. Despite this, it finds the relationship uncomfortable. Not surprising, then, that even the communists have wondered aloud about their role.[50] 'Is there merit in calling on communist cadres to prioritise the struggle to re-build a mass-based ANC in 2006?' the party asked. 'Or should we rather prioritise consolidating the SACP? While agreeing that these are not necessarily mechanical alternatives what should the Party's medium to longer-term perspective be on electoral participation?' As yet, the SACP has provided no definitive answer to these questions, but they continue to blow in the wind.

The ANC has become accustomed to public grumbling from its allies. Trouble in the Alliance really flares up when the ANC thinks its partners are starting to move beyond speculation. In October 2010 the unions decided to invite a group of more than 50 civil organisations to a conference to discuss a wide range of issues, from corruption to government policy on education. However, Cosatu did not include the ANC or the SACP on the guest list.

In his keynote speech, Cosatu President Sidumu Dlamini delivered some stinging, but not unfamiliar, criticisms of government policy.[51] He pointed out that the end of apartheid in 1994 had not brought the people of South Africa to the promised land and that poverty remained deeply entrenched. Worse still, many in the government were deeply mired in corruption, he said. Dlamini finished his speech with a stirring declaration. He said that in order to counter corruption 'within our organisations, in government and in all spheres of society … we must fight against it to the bitter end and if need be we must all be prepared to lose friends and face the possibility of death in the same way that we were prepared to die when we confronted the apartheid system.'

Zwelinzima Vavi, the federation's General Secretary, was if anything even more scathing, referring to a recent incident in which lavish parties had been held during which sushi was eaten off the bodies of girls dressed only in bikinis:[52]

> It is the sight of these parties where the elite display their wealth often secured in questionable methods that turn my stomach. It is this spitting on the face of the poor and insulting their integrity that makes me sick. Next year this elite will not go out door-to-door to get our people to vote. But soon thereafter they will host victory parties to scavenge on the carcass of our people like the typical hyenas that they are.
>
> Our belief is that if we were to confiscate all the medical aids, that most of us here have; if our cabinet Ministers and MPs were forced to take their children to the public hospitals and be subjected to the same conditions as the poor; if we were to burn their private clinics and hospitals and private schools; if the children of the bosses were to be loaded into unsafe open bakkies to the dysfunctional township schools; if the high walls and electronic wired fences were to be removed; if all were forced to live on R322 a month, as 48% of the population has to do, and if their kids were to die without access

to antiretrovirals, we would have long ago seen more decisive action on many of these fronts.

Our society in many ways is a very sick society. In addition to allowing these massive inequalities and for apartheid to continue in the economy, we are now sitting indifferent when the new elite is on rampage, humiliating the very motive force of our liberation struggle.

While Vavi said explicitly that the conference was not about to launch a political party, he did issue this rallying cry: 'Our goal must be to forge a strong, united movement for change.'

The ANC was having none of it. In less than a week, the conference was the subject of debate at the highest level. The ANC asked why it had not been invited to attend and why the SACP had also been left off the guest list.[53] The party went on to accuse the unions of attempting to lay all the blame for all the failures since 1994 on the ANC. Worse still, the party suggested that some might view the conference as a first step towards what it described as 'regime change'. It went on to accuse Cosatu of initiating steps that had led to the formation of parties independent of liberation movements across the rest of southern Africa:

The fact that some [at the conference] raised the possibility of forming an alternative party, 'the Workers Party', confirms that this is not a new idea, but a recycled idea of weakening, dividing and ultimately dividing the ANC and the alliance. When Cope was formed we raised the consistent efforts made in the region by powerful international forces to weaken the liberation movements.

In the majority of cases, the funding of the divisions of liberation forces is funded by those who supported them originally. This funding is normally directed to organs of civil society with an aim of forming opposition parties. This was the process that preceded the formation of the MDC in Zimbabwe and the MMD in Zambia. The process of getting legitimate individuals from within the liberation movement

informed the support given to Mr Lekota in South Africa and
Mr Hamutenya in Namibia.

Without panicking as accused by the General Secretary of
Cosatu we must be alive to the possibilities of forming blocks
against the liberation movement. The initiative by opposition parties to merge into a strong block against the ANC is
equally informed by the neo-liberal view that liberation movements in the region are too strong.

The ANC has the responsibility of analyzing and understand any initiative that has the potential to divide the liberation forces. The civil society conference can easily be used as
a vehicle that propels individuals with ambitions who understand that individually they cannot go very far. We must therefore continue watching the space. ...The ANC will raise these
issues and the commitment of Cosatu to the Alliance partner-
ship in a meeting that will be called urgently. Whilst we have
not concluded these matters, we none-the-less are appalled by
even reference to some leaders in the ANC as the 'predator
elite' who have shown their back to the plight of the poor.

The union movement was stung into action and immediately replied to
the ANC's statement.[54] While asserting its right to hold any meetings it
wanted to, Cosatu said it was 'shocked' by the party's response and that
there was no suggestion that the conference was a launch pad for an opposition movement. Tempers gradually cooled, but the issue continued
to fester.

Local elections and local politics

The local elections of May 2011 – the most substantial test of public
opinion between general elections – were neither a triumph nor a disaster for the ANC.[55] The party lost ground in most areas across the country
except KwaZulu-Natal, where the decline of the Inkatha Freedom Party
played into the ANC's hands. 'We noted and we are worried about the

downward trend in all the provinces except in KwaZulu-Natal,' Gwede Mantashe told the media.[56] Jacob Zuma fretted about the loss of votes among the country's minorities and called for 'very serious introspection' on the issue.[57] Still, the outcome, with nearly 63 per cent of the vote, was clearly a 'massive victory', as Mantashe claimed. Although the ANC saw declines in its percentage support in six out of eight metros (or conurbations) it could still rely on the majority of the black population for support.

The campaign itself was something of a mess. It began late, was dogged by allegations of unfair practice in the selection of candidates, and required the unions to go door to door to persuade people to come out and vote. Zwelinzima Vavi, despite his searing criticism of the ANC as a party, did all he could to rally the electorate, particularly in Nelson Mandela Bay municipality in the Eastern Cape, where the ANC only scraped home with a 51.9 per cent majority.[58] 'The factor is disillusionment, when a big chunk of the ANC supporters decide to stay at home,' he said.

How powerful is the ANC as a party? It maintains that it has close to a million members, but just how accurate is this figure? Secretary-General Gwede Mantashe told the media that membership had risen by almost 50 per cent since the last conference in 2007.[59] The party's figure for September 2011 was 933 672, compared with 621 000 at the Polokwane conference. In an interview with *The Star* newspaper Mantashe raised concerns about the accuracy of these figures.[60] He pointed out that of the 4 316 branches, only 1 286 'were in good standing during the last audit'. 'This is pointing to the general problem of provinces only taking the need for branches to be in good standing when there are conferences rather than ensuring that this is how the organisation should be,' said Mantashe. He said suspicions of member manipulation were justified because of what he called unfair practices in some provinces as well as the bulk-buying of membership to support certain factions inside the party. 'If we don't confront these problems, our membership will be seen as fake.'

If the membership figures are remotely accurate, why has this leap in numbers taken place? Is it because there is increasing support for the party and its policies in government, or does it indicate that membership of the ANC is perceived as one of the few means the poor have of gaining access to scarce state resources?

At the Polokwane conference the ANC considered this. Gwede Mantashe's lengthy organisational report contained worrying references to the quality of the membership.[61]

A list of 'problems and challenges' facing ANC branches included the scarcity of active members, the lack of unity and cohesion, the rise of 'sectarian practices' and the absence of a strong political consciousness among members.[62] The ANC, perhaps surprisingly for a long-standing member of the major Social Democratic family of parties – the Socialist International – then went on to look to the communist parties of the world for possible solutions. Mantashe quoted Lenin's warning to the 10th Congress of the Communist Party of the Soviet Union in March 1921: '"No profound and popular movement in all history has taken place without its share of filth, without adventurers and rogues, without boastful and noisy elements ... A ruling party inevitably attracts careerists."[63] As a profound and popular movement, which is also a ruling party, the African National Congress, will not be immune from these tendencies.' He went on to report on study tours he had led to China and Cuba, to learn from their parties on a range of issues, including the functioning of the party, the role of political education and the relationship between the 'party and its organs in strategic thinking and providing guidance to state and society'.[64]

This would appear to suggest that the ANC was moving towards a fully fledged Communist Party model, but this is almost certainly not the case. Rather, it showed that the party was struggling with careerists and opportunists in its ranks. It was reaching out to that one 'pure' source of inspiration that had stood by it during its period of exile – communism – to find a means of tackling this scourge.

A much more significant indication of the ANC's character as a party comes in the insightful book by the former editor of the *Mail & Guardian*, Anton Harber, on the township of Diepsloot, outside Johannesburg.[65] This is a settlement that has grown up since the ANC took power and now is home to 200 000 people. Life in the township is rough, violent and poor, but also vibrant, passionate and good-natured. It is impossible to do justice to the complex reality he describes, but some central features stand out which have a bearing on the Alliance.

The ANC is by far and away the most influential organisation. Its councillors run the township and there is a constant jostling for power inside the party, which is one of the few sources of influence over the distribution of state resources. But the ANC does not rule alone. Left-wing organisations like the SACP have a strong representation. Although they are allies, there is a constant tension and bitterness between them. 'The dislike and distrust of each other is visceral … They need to engage with each other, but only with the purpose of wresting control of each other's power base,' observes Harber.[66] 'The divisions run both between and within organisations in the Alliance, and they are personal, bitter and deep.'

Kindiza Ngubeni, a researcher with the Centre for the Study of Violence and Reconciliation, is sceptical about the ANC's real role.[67] 'The ANC is not on the ground,' he says. It is the ANC's allies that are to be found in Diepsloot. They make policy and respond to local needs by putting pressure on the ANC through demonstrations, some of which turn violent. Harber finds a huge disparity in resources available to these allies. So while he meets the ANC leadership in city offices 'complete with assistants and telephones', the left's offices in Diepsloot are dark and empty shacks with nothing more than a few broken chairs and tables for furniture, no electricity and a notable absence of resources.[68] 'The ANC is preoccupied with government projects, and they are most of the people involved in these projects or they are the contractors to do these projects,' explains Ngubeni. Ordinary people are excluded from these benefits, 'that is why they want to rock the government'.[69]

Other political parties have some representation in Diepsloot, with Inkatha and the Democratic Alliance attracting some support. But they are hardly significant forces. The lives of most people are directly affected by the decisions taken in and with the Alliance. It is – says Harber – a constant battle:[70]

> Local political divisions run deep, and at the centre is a battle for control over development projects and the resources made available by the state. Politics in Diepsloot is not at all comradely, it is fractious. The main fissure is between those in state

and party structures – intertwined – who control the available developmental resources and who tend to have state jobs and RDP houses, and those who represent or control the people of the shacks, the unemployed, the marginal of the marginal.

More plots and leadership challenges – can the centre hold?

Even before the first of the May 2011 votes had been cast, news surfaced of yet another plot inside the ANC. This time it contained allegations that a group around Tokyo Sexwale were planning how to replace Jacob Zuma at the next ANC conference in 2012. It was, as Nic Dawes, editor of the *Mail & Guardian*, pointed out, the fourth time such allegations had been made and they had – in his view – 'a depressingly familiar quality'.[71] The treason allegations against Sexwale, Phosa and Ramaphosa (2001), the 'hoax emails' (2005) and the 'Browse Mole' report (2007) all came at critical moments, not long before key ANC conferences. Like all previous incidents, the current plot contained elements of fact and fiction, 'the product of the fixation on conspiracy that is gripping the governing party and the intelligence sector'.

So who was the beneficiary of these plots, real or otherwise? They allowed Zuma to appear as a president under siege and those against him as schemers and manipulators. They cemented the relationship between Zuma and Mantashe, since both appeared to be under attack from the right. With the ANC in turmoil and Malema threatening to organise the defeat of both men, the ANC's elective conference in 2012 had what Talk Radio 702's Stephen Grootes, astute Senior Political Reporter, Eyewitness News, described as the makings of a titanic contest, pitting Sexwale, who has 'shed-loads' of money, against the two arch alliance builders in the party – Zuma and Mantashe. 'It's going to be a wonderful political battle,' Grootes declared with some glee.[72]

It was precisely because so much was at stake that President Zuma could not allow the matter to continue to fester. In November 2011 the ANC finally acted against his critics in the Youth League. Charges were laid and Julius Malema was found guilty of provoking division within the ruling party and of bringing the organisation into disrepute.[73] He was suspended from the ANC for five years and had to vacate his position. In the end, it was rash remarks attacking the government in Botswana, and a threat to send a team to the country to bring about regime change, that were Malema's downfall. But there is little doubt that Zuma could not allow his troublesome challenger to continue to mobilise against him ahead of the 2012 conference. The President acted slowly, but, like the mills of God, in the end he ground exceeding fine.[74]

As Vavi's scathing attacks on the ANC quoted above indicate, the constituency from which the party draws its support is fragmenting. How, indeed, can there be any real coincidence of interests between men who eat sushi off the near-naked bodies of women while swilling the finest whisky, and the poor who make up the majority of the country's population?

This has been recognised by the government, with Trevor Manuel releasing a massive 450-page development plan in November 2011. Its aim was nothing short of transforming the future of the country by 2030, lifting the mass of the population out of poverty. It promised to provide 11 million jobs by that date, to bring down unemployment from 25 per cent to just 6 per cent by promoting labour-intensive industries, making exports more competitive and reinforcing the government's role in economic planning. Gone were the attacks from the unions and the communists on Manuel as a figure of the right, as noted at the start of this chapter. All the left could do was hope that this target would not vanish like so many before it.

It is not difficult to see why. To illustrate the need for action, Manuel talked of a hypothetical young woman called Thandi.[75] 'She was one of 18% of African women who started school in 1999 and matriculated in 2011,' he explained. 'That means 68 000 matriculated out of 1,4m who started school. We might be pleased that 67,5% passed matric but only 30% got university exemption. The chance for an African girl to get into university is 4%,' he said. 'Even with a matric, Thandi's chance of finding a job is only 13%. In other words, her chance of being unemployed in the first year out of school is 87%. Her chance of getting a job in five years is 25%. She might get piece work during her lifetime but she will only break out of poverty when she gets her pension at 60,' said the Minister.

Thandi's life chances are in stark contrast to those of the new elite that now plays such a dominant role in the ANC. They form part of a narrow stratum of the black population that holds a third of all the capital on the Johannesburg Stock Exchange.[76] They have joined the existing white elite and now enjoy a standard of living that most citizens can only watch on television. The ANC has allowed some of its senior leadership to become enmeshed in this web of conspicuous consumption.

As the leading trade unionist in the country, Zwelinzima Vavi issued this warning:[77] 'I have already over and over again pointed out the danger of a ticking bomb, that unless we can do something drastic about the crisis of unemployment, in particular youth unemployment, we risk another 1976 uprising.' There are almost daily protests about service delivery, even though they receive only cursory coverage in the South African media and almost none in the international press. The government has made promises, mended fences, but little has changed.

The issue confronting Vavi and others who share his perspective is the same as it has been for decades: how to deal with the class tensions within the ANC. As trade union leader Joe Foster warned in April 1982, there would come a day when the party would be 'hijacked by elements who will in the end have no option but to turn against their worker supporters'.[78] That day may not be far off; the question for the South African left is how to respond.

As indicated above, the left has toyed with the idea of going its own way and establishing a party of its own. So far this has not happened, and it is not hard to see why this is the case. It would mean a rupture with friends and a tearing apart of relationships. As the events that led to the establishment of Cope after the Polokwane conference showed, this is a terribly difficult process and is certainly not guaranteed to succeed. Many movements, from the Pan Africanist Congress onwards, have attempted to form alternative parties to the ANC. None have really succeeded. Even commentators sympathetic to an alternative left, like Hein Marais, concede that the numerous movements that have grown up in recent years are 'trapped on the margins'.[79]

No wonder the left-wing allies of the ANC hesitate. There is also the question of the loss of power, patronage and influence. How many in leadership positions today would really risk all they have to march down the long and uncertain road of opposition politics? It is not for nothing that the Alliance has held together for all these years, surviving repression, exile and – perhaps most difficult of all – years in government. It is precisely for these reasons that the successful but troubled relationship between the ANC, trade unions and the SACP has endured.

For its part, the ANC knows that some day the split will occur. Hence the party's nervous, angry reaction to Cosatu's conference for civil society in October 2010. As the ANC pointed out, this was the path trodden in Zambia (with the Movement for Multi-Party Democracy, formed in 1991 with support from the unions) and Zimbabwe (where the Movement for Democratic Change was founded in 1999, again with union support.) Indeed, it explains the lukewarm, even hostile, relationship between the ANC and Zimbabwe's Prime Minister, Morgan Tsvangirai. The ANC recalls only too well that he was a mineworkers' leader and Secretary-General of the Zimbabwe Congress of Trade Unions before breaking away from President Mugabe's Zanu-PF to found the MDC.

It may be that it is only once the left forms an alternative political movement that the ANC will finally accept that it is now very similar to other political parties on the continent. The extraordinary vortex of events of the 1950s fused it together with the unions and the communists to form a movement of the left. That momentum helped sustain it through the trauma of exile, but it has run its course. Today the ANC is a ruling party, and its liberation movement credentials no longer suit it. The rhetoric of revolution sits uneasily with the trappings of wealth and power. It has an extraordinary past, but a pedestrian present.

Predicting when the left will leave the ANC to found a new party is a mug's game. Yet it remains the most important question in South African politics. These were the reflections of Stephen Grootes, Senior Political Reporter, Eyewitness News, of Talk Radio 702, in December 2011, with Christmas just around the corner.[80]

Any serious holiday conversation about politics has several questions that keep returning. One is how long the alliance between the ANC, Cosatu and the SACP will survive ... The alliance question is a perennial one because it matters so much. Should the alliance split, our politics would see open public competition, instead of the buying each other off in smoke-filled rooms that happens now. Over the last month, there's been a fundamental change in the answer to this question. And, trust us on this, it matters. The short, snappy, smart-arse answer to the question of when the alliance will split – note the 'if' not 'when' – is when the interests of Cosatu's members are sufficiently divergent from those of the ANC.

For Grootes, the turning point is likely to be defence of the country's hard-won Constitution, which came into force in 1996, guaranteeing fundamental rights, including the freedom of speech. Already key ANC figures have attacked its provisions. Jacob Zuma criticised the judges for interfering in the work of the executive, a position echoed by others in the party. The union movement has made it clear that it will not accept the muzzling of the media by the Secrecy Bill in its current form (or the Protection of State Information Bill, to give it its popular title). As one of the architects of the Constitution, Cyril Ramaphosa, declared in an endorsement of the existing judicial order, 'judges are the champions of the people'.[81]

So is Grootes right – could the unions indeed leave the Alliance in a battle to defend the Constitution? There are simply too many variables in play to make a prediction with any certainty. The future is, invariably, a closed book. How many analysts foresaw the fall of the Berlin wall or the negotiated end of apartheid? What is clear is that the fierce debates inside the Alliance are as alive as ever they have been. This is where the future of the country is shaped. The Alliance remains what it has been since Nelson Mandela assumed the presidency: the critical relationship that drives the politics of South Africa.

Oversight, Corruption and the Consolidation of Executive Power

Chapter 4

The Arms Deal and the Erosion of Parliamentary Power[1]

Paul Holden

Few scandals have dominated South Africa's post-apartheid political landscape like the Arms Deal. As a catch-phrase, it describes the various associated misdeeds, manipulations and miscarriages of justice that have flowed from a decision, in 1999, to purchase a large number of sophisticated items of weaponry, including fighter jets, submarines and warships.

Indeed, it is arguably incorrect to see the Arms Deal as a single event. Rather, it is a series of interlinked scandals orbiting the choices made in 1999, scandals that often uncovered the limitations of the post-1994 political dispensation. By unpacking these scandals – five in total – it is possible to catch a glimpse of a world frequently hidden from view, where *realpolitik* made perfect bedfellows with criminality and the attractions of bountiful lucre. The Arms Deal tells us where power lay for much of the last 15 years, and where it may lie now. In particular, it was both the pre-eminent cause and the ultimate expression of how, only years after the ANC's election in 1994, Parliament was badgered out of fulfilling its role of oversight, becoming a virtual irrelevance in South African political life.

The scandal of origins

The first scandal of the Arms Deal is simple: it is outrageous that it even took place. In the early 1990s, with the ANC's inexorable march to power, there seemed to be little likelihood of major defence acquisitions in the near future. Many baulked at the idea of upgrading and re-equipping a defence force that already exceeded the combined arsenals of nearly the entire Sub-Saharan region,[2] and that had used this military might to engage in human rights abuses at home and amongst the frontline states. Most expected that money would be redirected from the military, already a major recipient of funding during the apartheid period, towards more pressing socio-economic needs.

Such were the fault lines when the military decided to go on the front foot. As early as 1991, the Navy, in particular, started to make a case for the purchase of new frontline fighter frigates, or corvettes. In March 1993, the newly installed Vice Rear-Admiral, Robert Simpson, announced to a well-attended maritime conference that 'the definition and acquisition of a new surface combat ship remains [the Navy's] most urgent priority'.[3] In December 1993, Armscor was forced to admit that it had already put out the contract to tender, and intended to expedite the process.[4] On the shopping list: four corvettes, at a cost of R1.7 billion.

It was a remarkably bold move, considering that the country's first democratic elections were still months away. But, by then, those seeking to push forward large defence purchases already had a friend destined for high office: Joe Modise. The future Minister of Defence had previously served for decades as chief of Umkhonto we Sizwe. He was already notorious, deeply distrusted by many MK rank-and-file, who suspected him of gross corruption,[5] and had frequently been associated with Mbokodo, the exiled ANC's internal security branch, which had engaged in gross human rights abuses against comrades who questioned the strictures of the ANC's conservative military doctrine.[6]

But most importantly, Modise was an unashamed hawk who would take up the cudgels to retain as much of the newly formed South African National Defence Force's cut of the budget as humanly possible. In the same month as Armscor sent out tenders for corvettes, Modise travelled along with Armscor's executive general manager, Tielman de Waal, to Britain as a guest of the Defence Export Services Organisation (DESO),[7] the body that served as the official salesman of British arms exports. Modise's visit could only be seen as a statement of intent, suggesting the political will to drive forward future defence acquisitions. Indeed, in May 1994, only weeks after the ANC's ascent to power, Modise rubber-stamped the decision to put the corvettes contract out to tender. The race to win South Africa's first large defence contract in the post-apartheid era was on.

Over the course of the following year, Modise and representatives of Armscor, itching to justify their position in the new democratic order, went on the offensive to sell the corvette deal. Modise, for one, attempted to sell the need for corvettes despite the country facing no short, medium or long-term threats. Key to this was the idea of the unpredictability of the security environment. 'Many people believe we will never be threatened again,' Modise told assembled MPs in a speech in August 1994. 'Peace is the ideal situation, but ideal situations are difficult to find in the real world ... We need to be properly prepared to counter any form of instability that might affect us.'[8]

Tielman de Waal tried a different approach, arguing that offset programmes associated with the deal would nullify any concerns over economic impact. Offset programmes, which were eventually central to the Arms Deal contracts, are commitments on the part of selling companies to invest in the purchasing country and are intended to literally 'offset' the economic impact of defence spending. Riffing on the guns versus butter debate, De Waal argued that offsets 'ha[ve] added a new dimension to foreign acquisition. Subject to the defence budget and cabinet approval, the acquisition of the corvettes meets convincingly the needs of both the RDP and defence and it is pure butter.'[9]

Civil society and large parts of the ANC were deeply unimpressed by the arguments. Newspaper editors were almost universally opposed to the corvette deal, highlighting that the biggest security problems faced by South Africa stemmed from poverty and unemployment, not ill-defined bogeymen across the border.[10] The unions paused to ponder the deal, wondering about its wisdom at a time of such pressing hardship. The South African Students Congress led a march to Pretoria's Union

Buildings where a simple demand was presented: spend the R1.7 billion, but spend it on a tertiary bursary scheme that would cost the same as four corvettes.[11]

Some of the most vituperative criticism came from within the ANC. During heated debates in Parliament – among the few that occurred before it was neutered – Modise's vision was consistently rubbished. Joe Slovo, newly installed as Minister of Housing, reeled in horror when it was rumoured the corvettes would cost considerably more than R1.7 billion:

> A couple of corvettes in the SA Navy can, in any case, never be much more than symbols. While I appreciate the argument about the discomfort associated with going to sea in a strike-craft designed for use in the placid Mediterranean, I do not see justification for spending what has been reported as R4,6 billion for the corvettes and this at a time when literally millions of people in this country are facing more than simple discomfort, because they are having to deal with the trials and tribulations of living in shacks, in crowded rooms and on the streets of the cities. An amount of R4,6 billion would allow us to provide housing subsidies to 368 000 families – that is, for at least one and a half million people.[12]

Max Sisulu, son of the struggle icon Walter Sisulu, outlined the argument that was made with most force by the doves who were attempting to clip the wings of the hawks:

> There is certainly no external threat to our security. There is, however, an internal threat to our security and that comes from unemployment, poverty and deprivation. That is the enemy that we face, an enemy from within.[13]

Opposition to the corvette deal was vociferous enough to put it on hold. Answering a question in Parliament, Modise announced in August 1995 that it would be halted until the completion of a review of South Africa's defence needs. The outcome, the Defence Review, was finally presented in 1997. While it outlined an ideal force structure consisting of many items that would eventually turn up on the Arms Deal shopping list, it also contained some important caveats. The first, echoing Max Sisulu, was that South Africa's greatest security threat could be found at home:

> The greatest threats to the security of the South African people are socio-economic problems like poverty and unemployment, and high levels of crime and violence ... The government has adopted a narrow, conventional approach to defence. The primary function of the SANDF is defence against external aggression. The other functions are secondary ...[14]

The second caveat was that, although an ideal force model had been presented, the SANDF had to be aware that funds were necessarily limited and that, as a result, the ideal force model would probably not be achievable in the medium term. The third – a last-ditch attempt by doves involved in the process to try and slow down any headlong rush into a shopping spree – was that approval of the Defence Review did not imply approval of all future defence acquisitions to create the ideal force. Each acquisition would need to be approved by Parliament prior to any decision being made. To quote once more from the Defence Review:

> It has become apparent that national priorities and budgetary restrictions place constraints on defence expenditure. This means that the achievement of a sustainable force design of the magnitude envisaged in the Defence Review will not be possible in the short- to medium-term ...
>
> The approval of a force design by the parliamentary defence committee, Cabinet or Parliament does not constitute blanket approval for all implied capital projects or an immutable contract in terms of the exact numbers and types of equipment. At best, it constitutes approval in principle for the maintenance of the specified capabilities at an approximate level ...[15]

Nevertheless, only a few days later, Joe Modise reportedly presented himself to Cabinet with exactly the type of shopping list the Defence

Review argued against. Shortly thereafter a series of tenders was issued to international suppliers and the Arms Deal selection process began in earnest. At no stage was approval ever sought from Parliament: scandalous, considering that the Arms Deal would be the largest single acquisition for close to 15 years.

Why the Arms Deal was pursued with such vigour despite massive opposition has vexed commentators since the decision was made. Within Cabinet, the deal was viewed with a great deal of scepticism. In particular, it was widely reported that Trevor Manuel and Maria Ramos, then Deputy Director-General in the Department of Finance, were dead-set against the deal on economic grounds. Indeed, throughout the Arms Deal selection process, the Department of Finance attempted to limit the scale, extent and, most importantly, the cost of the deal. It was one of only a few times in the years following the ANC's election in 1994 that Finance was so widely disregarded and sidelined.

Why Thabo Mbeki pursued the Deal is also somewhat unclear. He was then Deputy President, but effectively ran the country from at least 1997 onwards, taking over from a tiring Nelson Mandela for the last two years of the latter's presidency. Some have posited that the Arms Deal formed part of his vision of a modern force at the helm of the African Renaissance: a statement that African countries could also purchase, maintain and use ultra-modern defence equipment in the pursuit of humanist goals. More pragmatically, Mbeki's biographer Mark Gevisser has noted that Mbeki owed much to Joe Modise for his support during the bruising battle for the deputy presidency of the ANC against Cyril Ramaphosa and, at an earlier stage, Chris Hani.[16] The Arms Deal may, at some level, have been payback for the support that pushed Mbeki into the forefront of South African politics for the better part of a decade.

Another key development was taking place in the run-up to the Arms Deal. Substantial numbers of politically connected businessmen, many former MK cadres, had started to set up shop as brokers in the defence industry. All of the companies had a similar structure: almost zero capacity to undertake defence logistics or production or any serious business, but bountiful political connectivity. And all of them would benefit substantially from the Arms Deal.

Joe Modise spearheaded developments. In 1995, he entered into business with the Russian entrepreneur Mark Voloshin, taking up a director's position in a company by the name of Marvotech.[17] Also on the board was Foreign Minister Alfred Nzo, a close confidant in exile.[18] Marvotech placed itself in a particular niche, offering Russian technology to upgrade the Cheetah aircraft already in the possession of the SANDF.[19] It was a win-win proposition: if the Arms Deal did not take place, Marvotech would help the SANDF upgrade its existing fleet. If the Arms Deal did take place, Marvotech would still be called upon to upgrade the Cheetahs in preparation for their resale to other countries. Indeed, once the Arms Deal was complete, Marvotech, along with a number of other politically connected companies, was hired to upgrade the Cheetahs for sale to Ecuador.

Other members of the broader Marvol company structure, or what the *Mail & Guardian* would later call Modise's 'greasy brotherhood', included Llew Swan and Fana Hlongwane. Swan was appointed by Modise to the board of Armscor in 1998, and was a key player during the Arms Deal selection process, sitting on most of the most powerful bodies in the chain of command. Hlongwane, ex-MK commander and Modise's friend and political adviser, featured through a subsidiary company, Liselo. Appointed by Modise to the board of Denel in 1998, he was later fingered by numerous investigations as the largest recipient of allegedly corrupt money in the entire Arms Deal.

Other members of the 'greasy brotherhood' (although not on the board of Marvol or Marvotech) included two men who owed their positions to Modise, Armscor chairperson Ron Haywood, and Denel head Major-General Ian Deetlefs, who would help wrangle a supremely curious deal involving a company called Conlog that would have benefited Modise handsomely if it had not been exposed; and arms industry businessman Tony Ellingford, who was later alleged to have entered into a potentially corrupt consultancy agreement with one of the eventual Arms Deal suppliers.[20] The greasy brotherhood would become involved in machinations that would see all of them, including Modise, attempt to benefit from the selection of British Aerospace as a supplier company in the Arms Deal.[21]

Modise was also the patron of the Defence Industry Interest Group of South Africa (DIIGSA), a collection of black-owned businesses that were trying to break into the industry.[22] Notable amongst DIIGSA's members was Futuristic Business Solutions (FBS), which was established soon after the installation of the ANC in government. FBS was headed by Lambert Moloi, a relative of Joe Modise and a former MK commander; Tshepo Molai, another relative of Modise's; and Yusuf Mohammed, who would later turn up as a director at Cell-C, the company given the licence to be South Africa's third mobile phone operator.[23] FBS was the company that arguably benefited most from the Arms Deal: it is estimated that, once the Deal was concluded, FBS had received 70 subcontracts valued at R750 million and overseen logistics valued in the billions.[24]

FBS was also in business with the company that would steal many of the Arms Deal headlines: African Defence Systems (ADS). ADS was jointly owned by the French arms giant Thomson-CSF (later Thales), FBS and Schabir Shaik's Nkobi group of companies.[25] Shaik was, as we have described, exceptionally close to Jacob Zuma, serving as his financial adviser, and would later be sentenced to over a decade in jail for his 'mutually beneficial symbiosis' (read: generally corrupt relationship) with Zuma, which included securing his services to get a slice of the Arms Deal.[26] Shaik's other key connections were familial: Chief of Acquisitions during the Arms Deal was none other than his brother, Shamin 'Chippy' Shaik, while another brother, Moe, is a former chief of South Africa's secret services. Importantly, Shaik was also a key funder of the ANC in KwaZulu-Natal, raising suspicions that a portion of the money he earned from the Arms Deal was intended for party use.

Thus, the Arms Deal was announced in the teeth of massive opposition from civil society and large portions of the ANC, a parliamentary injunction (the Defence Review) that attempted to put the brakes on any potential major arms deal without parliamentary approval, and the distaste of the financial cluster in government. It was a remarkable admission of where power really lay in government – and a foretaste of a number of occasions on which Parliament would be disregarded when it came to matters the executive considered important. During the 1995 fight-back against acquiring the corvettes, Parliament had provided some insight into how politics would work if it remained an independent check on executive power; by 1997, such power seemed to have evaporated.

More prosaically, it was clear who did *not* rule South Africa when it came to issues that mattered most to a small clique of politician-businessmen: civil society, Parliament, and anti-militarist doves.

The scandal of conduct

In late 1997, the Arms Deal started in earnest. International weapons manufacturers were asked to submit proposals for supplying the various types of equipment required by the South African government. In December 1999, the winning bidders and the contents of the deal had been announced. It was a remarkably complete shopping list, restocking key strike craft of both the Navy and the Air Force. In total, South Africa purchased:

- ❑ 26 Gripen fighter jets from a joint British and Swedish BAe/ SAAB team;
- ❑ 24 Hawk trainer jets from BAe;
- ❑ 30 light utility helicopters from the Italian supplier Agusta;
- ❑ 4 corvettes from the German Frigate Consortium (headed by ThyssenKrupp with a combat suite provided by Thomson-CSF and ADS);
- ❑ 3 submarines from the German Submarine Consortium (headed by Ferrostaal).[27]

At least four of the five contracts were later discovered to have been substantially fudged, fiddled and finessed.

The most notorious manipulations occurred in the selection of the Hawk and Gripen jets. South Africa had long used a three-tier structure for its Air Force fighter squadrons. On the first tier was the Astra Pilatus trainer, a sort of training-wheels entry-level plane that pilots would start with. The second was the Impala MKI or MKII, which was used to train pilots in super-fast flight. The third was the operational fighter – the jet actually used in combat situations. This tier was occupied at the time by 50 or so Cheetah supersonic jets.[28]

In the mid-nineties the Air Force believed it only needed to replace the second tier of Impala training jets. This was because the Astra Pilatus had only recently been acquired (despite considerable tub-thumping about sanctions busting at the time) and the Cheetah aircraft were due to remain operational until 2012 (even longer if they were given a relatively inexpensive mid-life upgrade that improved engine performance). In order to get the biggest bang for their buck, the Air Force decided that they would acquire a dual-use jet to replace the Impala – a jet that could act both as a trainer and as a fighter. It was a system designed to maximise combat efficiency and act as a palliative to worries about the longevity of the Cheetah.[29]

Unfortunately for British Aerospace, this structure meant that it would be excluded from the Arms Deal. At the time, BAe had offered its Gripen supersonic fighter (produced along with Sweden's SAAB) and its Hawk trainer jet. Neither fitted the bill: both were purely designed for one function (training or fighting) and could thus not begin to compete with other dual-use offers. In 1996, while the SAAF was comparing different potential offers, both the Hawk and the Gripen were duly rejected. The Hawk was considered 'high cost' and unsuitable for 'SAAF operational requirement[s]', while the Gripen was simply 'unaffordable'.[30]

In 1997, after receiving all the various proposals from suppliers, the SAAF decided that even replacing the Impala system was too expensive. Instead, it was decided to drop the middle training tier. The first-tier Astra Pilatus was confirmed as sufficient to train pilots to move on to combat jets. The new system would thus consist of only two tiers: the Astra trainers on the first tier and a second tier populated by a pure fighter – known in technical parlance as the Advanced Light Fighter Trainer, or ALFA. While the Gripen could now be entered as a contender, BAe's Hawk was totally out of the running.[31]

Enter Joe Modise. In October 1997 the SAAF Command Council met to discuss the matter. On the strict instructions of Modise, the whole system was rejigged once more and a three-tier system was re-adopted.[32] The difference was that the middle tier would not be populated by a fighter-trainer combo jet. Instead, the middle tier would be stocked with a jet whose only function was to train pilots to move onto the combat jets, also known as a Lead-In Fighter Trainer (LIFT). It was a ludicrous decision, unnecessarily increasing costs and providing less combat strength than the original three-tier system. Unsurprisingly, given Modise's contacts, the decision benefited BAe most of all: it could now submit the Hawk to fill the middle tier and the Gripen to fit the third tier. It was as if the SAAF's entire force structure was adapted around BAe's offerings, rather than the other way round.[33]

After the three-tier decision had been made, the selection process began in earnest. When it came to the combat fighter (or ALFA), the Gripen made it onto a final shortlist of three contenders. But it appeared to be dead in the water. In terms of cost and technical ability, the Gripen was ranked last behind offers from France's Dassault and Germany's Daimler-Benz. Where it triumphed, however, was in its financing proposals. During the selection process, offers were evaluated according to three criteria, each counting 33 per cent towards a final normalised score. The financing proposals – the structure of the loans to be granted to South Africa to finance the deal – counted for a full 33 per cent. When financing proposals were requested, only BAe/SAAB submitted details, meaning that both the German and French offers were given a score of zero. It was enough to push the Gripen – the most expensive item purchased in the Arms Deal – into first place.

Whether this was above-board is far from clear. Minutes from the meetings where the Gripen was given the final nod of approval claimed that Dassault and Daimler-Benz had failed to submit their financing proposals 'notwithstanding repeated requests'. When the Auditor-General later reviewed the matter, he could find no evidence that the two losing bidders had been repeatedly contacted over the matter. The Department of Finance, too, could find no records of these requests ever being drafted, sent out or received. Needless to say, it is incredibly hard to believe that gigantic European weapons manufacturers would neglect to provide such key information for a deal valued in the billions. The Gripens were also the most expensive item purchased in the Arms Deal: a decision made despite the fact that there was 'no competitive financial evaluation',[34] according to South Africa's Auditor-General.

Detailing the tortuous process of decisions that propelled the Hawk to first place would take too much space here and is dealt with in detail elsewhere.[35] One decision, however, gives a flavour of the type of decision making it took. Arguably the biggest problem faced by the Hawk was its cost – it was substantially more expensive than the Italian Aeromacchi MB339FD jet, which was preferred by the SAAF. To resolve this, Joe Modise convened a meeting on 30 April 1998 at which he argued that the SAAF needed to adopt a 'visionary approach', as the selection of the Hawk could have led to major investment in South Africa's defence industry.[36] Modise thus argued for a second evaluation, this time excluding cost from the criteria[37] – a remarkable request considering that the LIFT was the second most expensive item bought in the Arms Deal. Soon after, General Pierre Steyn, the highly respected Secretary of Defence, resigned from his position, protesting that he would 'have to account for the costs to Parliament, which I couldn't do'.[38]

Other contracts were similarly manipulated. In selecting the corvette, for example, a number of decisions were made that materially benefited the eventual winner, the German Frigate Consortium (and Thomson-CSF/ADS as providers of the combat suite. The scale of these manipulations cannot be addressed here; suffice to say that even the Joint Investigation Report, widely seen as having been heavily edited in order to facilitate a cover-up of misdeeds in the Arms Deal, found that a competing bidder, Bazan, was the only one that should truly have been considered for the contract, having 'complied with all critical minimum criteria in respect of technical and DIP evaluation ... obtained the highest military value and DIP scores ... provided the highest percentage of DIP and NIP in relation to the contract price [and] offered the lowest bid of the four bidders.'

The selection of the German Submarine Consortium (GSC) as the preferred bidder to supply submarines to the Navy was equally questionable. When the paperwork was reviewed by the Auditor-General, it pointed to a number of decisions that benefited GSC alone, and other decisions that actively prejudiced the other bidders.

Perhaps the most notable decision was to allow GSC to enter the bid in the first place. Much as with GFC, the GSC's bid failed to include the requisite details for its defence-related offsets package. When the matter was referred to Armscor's legal services, their response was clear: 'GSC has failed to meet the essential requirements of the DIP ... The DIP requirements are very specific and GSC's bid is tantamount to an

undertaking of intent.'[39] While it is unclear exactly who made the decision, what is known is that this legal advice was entirely disregarded:
GSC would be allowed to continue with its bid, despite being the only
supplier that failed to submit this information.[40]

This was only one of a number of sleights of hand. Indeed, just how
extensively these various manipulations and oversights benefited GSC
was made clear when the office of the Auditor-General decided to conduct their own selection, correcting errors and re-running scores. They
found that, if all the various areas they had uncovered had been cor-
rected, GSC would have come third out of four bidders, beaten by Italy's
Fincantieri and France's DCN.[41]

The scandal of corruption

The range and extent of problems in the selection process was such that
the excuse of mere managerial inefficiency would have been laughable.
These errors, oversights and direct interventions suggested to many that
the whole process had been rigged to ensure a set of predetermined suppliers emerged victorious. Central to this process was corruption, the
wholesale bribery of significant figures in the selection team and, most
importantly, a coterie of politically connected individuals.

By far the most extensive allegations have centred on British Aerospace
and a set of figures orbiting around Joe Modise. Modise had, by 1997,
set himself up in business in such a way as to ensure his own enrichment
if BAe emerged victorious in the selection process. Along with his con-
fidants Major General Ian Deetleefs and Armscor chief Ron Haywood,
he acquired shares in a company by the name of Conlog, via a series
of trusts.[42] Importantly, Conlog was part of BAe's offset plans: if BAe
won, it had promised to invest substantially in Conlog's business, linking it up with Sweden's ABB in a major deal. Later, BAe claimed that the
Conlog deal was cancelled when it found out about Modise's involvement.[43] But, until at least September 1999 (long after Modise's interventions had ensured BAe's victories), Conlog was listed as part of BAe's
offset commitments.[44] Soon after Modise retired from service in 1999, he

was appointed to the board of Conlog, giving effusive interviews about the wonders of the business world.[45]

Those who investigated Modise's dealings around the Arms Deal were convinced that he had received huge sums of money from various contractors. Andrew Feinstein, who, as we shall see under 'The scandal of oversight' below, was part of a major parliamentary investigation into the Arms Deal, recalled visiting the offices of criminal investigators overseeing the Arms Deal investigation. One investigator took Feinstein (and Gavin Woods, his colleague in the investigation) aside and showed them a 'series of bank statements, signed letters, deposit and withdrawal slips.' The investigator was certain:

> 'This,' said the investigator, 'is a substantial part of the paper trail linking money from a number of successful bidders to Joe Modise.'
>
> 'How much of the trail is outstanding?' Gavin asked.
>
> 'Not much. With the resources and legal powers of the investigating team upstairs, we will complete it in a couple of weeks.'[46]

In 2008, news broke that international detectives based in the UK – the Serious Fraud Office (SFO) – had uncovered a major network of agents employed by British Aerospace to take care of their South African business. In an affidavit submitted in the South African courts during an application for warrants to search the properties of John Bredenkamp and Fana Hlongwane, the SFO described how BAe had developed a secretive system of offshore shells through which payments were made to covert and overt agents in South Africa and abroad.[47] In total, the SFO was able to trace £115m in commission payments from BAe's shell companies to individuals linked to the Arms Deal.[48]

The list of recipients was remarkable. One of largest beneficiaries of the system was the Zimbabwean John Arnold Bredenkamp, who allegedly owned 60 per cent of a company by the name of Kayswell Services. This Virgin Islands registered company received payments totalling £40 million for its services. Why it received such a large sum is uncertain, but it is clear that he has cut a controversial figure. In 2008, the US Treasury

Department seized Bredenkamp's US assets as a result of his relationship with Zimbabwe's Robert Mugabe, simultaneously accusing
Bredenkamp of being 'a well-known Mugabe insider involved in various
business activities, including tobacco trading, gray market arms trading and trafficking, equity investments, oil distribution, tourism, sports
management, and diamond extraction. Through a sophisticated web
of companies, Bredenkamp has financially propped up the [Mugabe]
regime and provided other support to a number of its high-ranking officials.'[49] Bredenkamp has consistently denied allegations and has successfully litigated to have his name removed from European sanctions
lists.[50]

Another agent employed via BAe's extended network was Fana
'Styles' Hlongwane. Soon after the end of apartheid, Modise appointed
Hlongwane as his full-time 'political adviser', a role paid for by the state.
In 1998, he made him a board member of Denel for a brief while. As political adviser, Hlongwane had substantial powers, most notably acting
as a gate-keeper permitting or denying access to Modise. He and his assorted companies are alleged to have received £10 million by September
2003, with a further £9.15 million due to be paid by 2007.[51] In 2011, after a documentary broadcast on Swedish TV that drew heavily on documents supplied by myself and Andrew Feinstein, BAe's partner, SAAB,
admitted that Hlongwane had been paid millions via a company by
the name of South African National Industrial Participation (SANIP).
SANIP was the vehicle by which BAe and SAAB were to manage their
offset investments in South Africa. SAAB claimed that the payments had
been made in secret, without their knowledge, via an employee of BAe.[52]
The Scorpions, in particular, believed that Hlongwane had acted as a
bag man and that it was understood that a large part of the money
transferred to him would be forwarded to other key political and military players.

Evidence of this role, however, was difficult to come by – at least until
the *Mail & Guardian* broke a major story in 2011. According to the
report, Hlongwane had developed a close relationship with SANDF
chief Siphiwe Nyanda. Soon after retiring, Nyanda was offered a position at one of Hlongwane's companies, Ngwane Defence.[53] At the same
time, Hlongwane gave Nyanda a massive home loan to pay for a sizeable

property. By 2009, when Nyanda returned to government as Minister of Communications in Zuma's first Cabinet, he had allegedly only paid back a fraction of the loan.[54] Nevertheless, Hlongwane agreed to cancel the agreement, raising worries that the loan had been merely a sophisticated paper front hiding the fact that Hlongwane had effectively bought Nyanda a sparkling new house.[55]

Proof of the corruption of the corvette contracts, too, was offered when, in 2006, the Hamburg offices of ThyssenKrupp (the lead member of the GFC) were raided by German prosecutors.[56] Shortly thereafter, details emerged of what they were investigating, based on mutual legal assistance requests between Germany and Switzerland[57] – roughly R130 million ($25 million) allegedly paid in bribes by ThyssenKrupp to South African officials.[58] One payment of $23 million was traced to a company named Mallar Inc, registered in Liberia, via which German officials suspected that money had been transferred onwards to South African players.[59] Intriguingly, it was alleged in a stunning *Mail & Guardian* investigation that Mallar Inc was under the effective control of one Tony Georgiades,[60] long alleged to have been a key sanctions-buster during apartheid, helping the NP violate oil embargoes.[61] He was close to FW de Klerk: famously, Georgiades' wife left him to marry De Klerk in the early 1990s.

The additional $3 million was alleged to have been paid to the man at the centre of many Arms Deal decisions: Chippy Shaik. According to Andrew Feinstein, German investigators had seen two sets of confidential minutes emanating from ThyssenKrupp.[62] The first of these allegedly detailed how Chippy Shaik had asked for a bribe; the second confirmed that it had been paid.[63] During conversations with prosecutors in Germany, Feinstein was told that investigators knew where the $3 million had been transferred to, but that the amount remained untouched by Shaik due to fear of prosecution.[64]

The most notorious arrangement that was struck involving the corvette contract was that involving Thomson-CSF, Schabir Shaik and Jacob Zuma. Shaik had established a working relationship with the French defence giant Thomson-CSF from 1995 onwards. To facilitate this, Thomson-CSF established a South African entity by the name of Thomson-CSF (Pty) Limited, based in South Africa, in which both the parent French company and Shaik's Nkobi Holdings (so named after the late treasurer of the ANC, Thomas Nkobi) held shares. Together, Nkobi and Thomson had secured a number of state contracts, including a tender to provide driver's licences to the Department of Transport.[65]

Nkobi expected to benefit greatly if Thomson-CSF won a contract in the Arms Deal, as its South African partner in pursuit of the deal, Altech Defence Systems (now renamed African Defence Systems), had been purchased by Thomson-CSF in 1997. However, to Shaik's immense annoyance, he discovered that Thomson-CSF had not transferred the shares to the joint Thomson-Nkobi South African company: instead, they rested with Thomson-CSF in France. Shaik, it seemed, was going to be cut out of the deal.[66]

Why Thomson suddenly got cold feet over Shaik has been a matter of intense controversy. According to a senior Thomson executive, Pierre Moynot, Thomson was informed that Schabir Shaik was unpopular with leading lights in the ANC, which might prejudice its bid. When Shaik finally faced charges of corruption relating to the Arms Deal, the prosecution submitted a range of documents and letters confirming this. In particular, the prosecutors filed a series of exchanges between Thomson-CSF executives and Barbara Masekela, South Africa's ambassador to France at the time. The letters suggested that, on a number of occasions, Thomson sought to meet with Thabo Mbeki to get his input on the matter. In fact, one letter suggested that the President had met with Thomson executives, although Mbeki claims that he 'cannot recall' any such meeting.

Enter Jacob Zuma. According to the version of events accepted by Judge Squires during Schabir Shaik's corruption trial, Shaik wrote to the head of Thomson-CSF in France, Jean-Paul Perrier, to request a meeting between Thomson and Jacob Zuma. One meeting certainly took place in London in 1998, in which it was claimed that Zuma had merely clarified that Indian South Africans (that is to say, Shaik) were considered acceptable Black Empowerment partners – something Pierre Moynot claimed Thomson was already well aware of.[67] According to the prosecution in the Shaik case, another key meeting took place on 9 July 1998. This time, Chippy Shaik reportedly met with Thomson executives, allegedly claiming that he could 'make things difficult' for

Thomson if they did not cut his brother back into the deal.[68] Finally, on 18 November 1998, Zuma, Schaik and two Thomson executives met in Durban to resolve the matter. Ten per cent of African Defence Systems would be transferred to Nkobi (this rose to 20 per cent when Thomson purchased African Defence Systems outright in 1999).[69] It was an auspicious moment: on that exact same day, Thomson-CSF was announced as the preferred supplier to provide the combat suite on the corvette contract.

The matter did not end there, however. First, while Shaik had secured a slice of the deal, Thomson-CSF still felt it needed a proper Black Empowerment partner. For this, it turned to Futuristic Business Solutions, which similarly received a 20 per cent stake in ADS.[70] As we noted above, Futuristic Business Solutions was heavy on political connectivity, headed by a number of relatives of Joe Modise.[71] Second, there was the matter of the infamous bribe that the court accepted was paid to Jacob Zuma. According to the court's accepted version of events, Zuma met with Shaik and Thomson-CSF executive Alain Thétard on 11 March to conduct a pow-wow.[72] According to an encrypted fax that detailed its outcome, Zuma agreed to help squash any investigation in Thomson-CSF – a real worry for Thomson, as allegations of impropriety had started to spread as early as September 1999.[73] He also agreed to support Thomson in any future government contracts. For his trouble, Zuma was – according to the encrypted fax – to receive R500 000 a year, disguised under the terms of a bogus 'service-provider' agreement between Shaik and Thomson.[74]

Last, but not least, comes the submarine contract. Here, one particular allegation has made the most waves. In August 2008, the *Sunday Times* ran a story claiming that a number of bribes were paid by GSC contractors. In particular, the story claimed that Ferrostaal, the leading member of the GSC consortium, had transferred R30 million to then President Thabo Mbeki.[75] Of this, Mbeki was alleged to have transferred R28 million to the ANC and the remaining R2 million to Jacob Zuma.[76] Unfortunately, corroborating the story has proven difficult. The main source of the allegations was a one-time member of the National Intelligence Agency, Mhleli 'Paul' Madaka.[77] A year prior to the *Sunday Times* story, Madaka had met an unfortunate end when his car careened from a highway off-ramp in a fatal accident. In an ironic twist, Madaka's car ploughed into the business premises of MAN Ferrostaal. Andrew Feinstein has noted that some have questioned whether Madaka's collision was, in fact, an accident: witnesses claimed to see no tyre tracks indicative of an attempt to brake, while reports that he might have been drunk have been undermined by the fact that Madaka was widely known to be teetotal.[78] Needless to say, Thabo Mbeki has furiously denied the allegations,[79] although he has not, despite threats, launched any legal proceedings against the *Sunday Times* for its coverage.

The scandal of oversight

While considerable evidence of mismanagement surrounding the Arms Deal has emerged – and even juicier details of corruption – only the most limited sanctions have ever been levied against individuals and politicians, while additional investigations have ground to a halt. In almost every instance, evidence points to government interference on a grand scale, all with one aim: to ensure a cover-up of epic proportions.

The Arms Deal was subject to suspicions from early on. In November 1998, a full year before full details of the Deal were announced to the public, the Deputy Auditor-General, Shauket Fakie, singled it out as a risky proposition.[80] Initially, Faukie had little success – repeated letters to the Presidency requesting a presidential order for an investigation were stone-walled. The request was only granted in September 1999, after Patricia de Lille, the fiercely outspoken Pan Africanist Congress MP (and now mayor of Cape Town), presented an inflammatory dossier before Parliament that alleged widespread corruption in the deal.[81] Mosiuoa Lekota, then Minister of Defence, quickly wrote to the Auditor-General, approving the request and granting 'access to all documents pertaining to the government-to-government packages for audit purposes'.[82]

Even at this early stage in proceedings, such an unfettered investigation ruffled feathers. Soon after the approval was granted by Lekota, another letter was fired off by one Brigadier-General Keith Snowball, informing Fakie that only the Cabinet sub-committee overseeing the Arms Deal (which included Mbeki, along with Alec Erwin, Trevor Manuel and Stella Sigcau) could give the go-ahead.[83] In other words, Fakie would be required to get approval for his 'terms of reference' from the very Cabinet sub-committee he intended to investigate.[84] The law that required this clearance of the terms of reference was the Defence Special Account Act of 1974, which had been passed by the apartheid government following the imposition of the arms embargo and had served as the legal fig leaf behind which sanctions busting and dirty tricks could hide. The Act allowed the executive to censor any Auditor-General report that was to the 'detriment of the public interest'.[85] That the law remains on South Africa's statute books to this day is a direct affront to democracy.

Fakie was eventually given approval to conduct the investigation, but only via an 'audit steering committee'. The committee included members of the office of the Auditor-General, members of the Arms Deal sub-committee and key members in the procurement process. Two of the latter were Chippy Shaik and Jayendra Naidoo.[86] The former, as we noted above, has been consistently linked to questionable decision-making and corruption in the Arms Deal. The latter, who served as one of the lead negotiators during the latter phase of the Deal, was fired by the Department of Trade and Industry in 2002 after it was discovered that he had received a R55 000 discount on a luxury car sold by an Arms Deal contractor.[87]

Nonetheless, Fakie's investigation unearthed some disturbing findings, detailed in a report in August 2000. In particular, he raised concerns that offset commitments seemed to be flaky and liable to non-delivery. Similarly, the report questioned the wisdom of the selection of the Hawk based on an evaluation that eschewed cost considerations.[88] Importantly, it noted that its findings were only preliminary: further investigation would be necessary to really unpack what was going on.

At the same time, other oversight bodies were also viewing the Arms Deal askance. One such body was the Special Investigating Unit (SIU), then headed by Judge Willem Heath, which had received a number of documents from Arms Deal whistleblower Patricia de Lille.[89] The SIU had wider powers of investigation and, most importantly, the legal right to cancel state contracts if they were found to be irredeemably tainted. Similarly, both the Public Protector's Office and the unit that later became the Scorpions indicated that they had also started preliminary investigations.[90] Like the festering heap it was, the Arms Deal was starting to attract some inquisitive flies.

What posed a real threat to those involved in the Arms Deal was the possibility that the investigations would be coordinated, something that Parliament attempted, but failed, to do. The Auditor-General's 2000 report was received by Parliament's Standing Committee on Public Accounts (Scopa) with great interest. Scopa, which served at the apex of the financial accountability chain in Parliament, oversaw all government expenditure, questioning and corralling where necessary. Andrew Feinstein, an ANC MP who led the ANC contingent on Scopa, and Gavin Woods, an Inkatha Freedom Party MP who acted as chair, worked hard to ensure that the body functioned on a strictly non-partisan basis: a move designed to ensure that the Committee would not be distracted from its essential tasks by political manipulations.

When Feinstein and Woods reviewed the 2000 report, they were immediately motivated to start an investigation. After canvassing opinion amongst Scopa members, it was agreed to call Chippy Shaik and Jayendra Naidoo to testify before Parliament. It was a disaster for Arms Deal defenders. Shaik and Naidoo, under relentless questioning, were forced to admit that the Deal had rocketed in price from its originally stated R30 billion cost to over R43 billion. They also finally acknowledged that the offsets programme, which promised over R100 billion in investment and 65 000 jobs, was of dubious enforceability.[91] Notably, when questioned about his role in overseeing contracts related to his brother, Schabir, Chippy Shaik claimed that he had recused himself from all relevant discussions.[92] Later, an official investigation found that this was far from the truth: not only had he sat in on meetings, but he had actively participated.[93]

As this was unravelling before Parliament, Scopa, in particular Feinstein and Woods, received additional material alleging massive corruption and mismanagement in the Arms Deal. The Committee's report, which slipped through Parliament on a busy day, argued that there was a need for a comprehensive investigation into the Arms Deal, and that Scopa should act as the co-ordinating mechanism to combine the investigations of all those bodies already showing an interest: 'The Auditor-General, the Heath Special Investigating Unit, the Public Protector, the Investigating Directorate of Serious Economic Offences and any other appropriate investigative body should be invited, so that the best combination of skills, legal mandates and resources can be found for such an investigation.'[94]

The report ruffled the feathers of many involved in the Arms Deal. Soon after it was published, the executive went on the offensive. In a remarkable press conference in January 2001, four Cabinet ministers (Alec Erwin, Mosiuoa Lekota, Trevor Manuel and Jeff Radebe) claimed that neither Scopa nor the Auditor-General had fully understood the Arms Deal in all its technical glory:

> [The Cabinet] takes serious issue with the ill-informed conclusions drawn from the Auditor-General's Review and the Scopa Report. These fail to understand the most elementary features of the defence acquisition process. It is our view that the Review and the Report were too cursory to do justice to this matter and have called into question the integrity of government without justification ...
>
> We also find it strange that so many people in our country have been driven into a virtual frenzy by mere allegations of wrongdoing, without a single shred of evidence of actual wrong doing being produced ...[95]

The inclusion of the Heath Special Investigating Unit, in particular, drew the ire of ANC bigwigs, no doubt because of its far-ranging investigative powers and ability to cancel dubious contracts. The independent streak of Willem Heath himself undoubtedly exacerbated concerns. In order to start an official investigation, Heath required a presidential proclamation. He received the most startling response from Thabo Mbeki, by then installed as President. Mbeki claimed that not only did Heath have no evidence, but that his behaviour was incredibly odd: 'you embarked on an unseemly campaign to "tout" for work, with a level of desparation [*sic*] I am still trying to understand'.[96]

To make his point more firmly, Mbeki appeared on TV in a bizarre broadcast in which he questioned the motives of any investigation into the deal. He brandished a set of organograms that he claimed emanated from Heath's unit that linked luminaries such as Mandela to the Deal. In fact, the chart had been drawn up by the editor of *Noseweek* as a thought exercise.[97] In a preview of how he would respond whenever questioned about corruption in the Deal, Mbeki went on to claim that the furore over the Arms Deal was the work of destabilising agent provocateurs:

> Our country and all our people have been subjected to a sus-
> tained campaign that has sought to discredit our Government
> and the country itself by making unfounded and unsubstan-
> tiated allegations of corruption. Among other things, this
> campaign has sought to force us to do illegal things, to break
> important contractual obligations, to accuse major inter-
> national companies of corrupt practice and to damage our
> image globally, arguing that if we did these things, we would,
> inter alia, strengthen international investor confidence in
> South Africa ...
>
> We know that various entities have been hired to sustain the
> campaign to create a negative climate about our country and
> government. I would like to assure you that the campaign will
> not succeed.[98]

Attention was next turned to Scopa. The ANC contingent on Scopa were hauled before the ANC's governance committee, only recently es-tablished to provide 'political leadership' to ANC MPs in Parliament: a not-so-subtle indication that MP independence would not be toler-ated. During the meeting, the ANC members were harangued by senior ANC members, notably Essop Pahad, who pointedly asked the Scopa members: 'Who do you think you are, questioning the integrity of the government, the Ministers and the President?'[99] Under intense politi-cal pressure, the ANC component on Scopa buckled, agreeing to a new Report and a public statement that claimed the 14th Report had not specifically requested Heath's inclusion. Almost immediately thereafter, Feinstein approached the media and disputed the statement, reminding everyone that Scopa had, indeed, demanded Heath's inclusion.

It was the end of Feinstein's ANC career: he was removed as head of the ANC study group and eventually resigned in June 2001.[100] The message was clear. ANC MPs were there at the behest of their superiors and had to follow the party line. Tony Yengeni, then Chief Whip of the ANC in Parliament, explained that 'some people have the notion that the public accounts committee members should act in a non-partisan manner. But, in our system, no ANC member has a free vote.'[101] Shortly thereafter, ANC members on Scopa claimed that they were 'too busy' to continue an Arms Deal investigation.[102] And while Scopa has, since then, held a handful of hearings regarding the Arms Deal, it has issued no judgment and has failed to take any remedial action, despite the mounds of evidence in its possession.

With Scopa neutered, the investigation was left to the 'Three Agencies': the Scorpions, the Auditor-General and the Public Protector. In November 2001 they presented their final report into the Arms Deal, known as the Joint Investigation Report. At 400 pages, it covered a considerable number of wrongdoings. In particular, it fingered Chippy Shaik for his failure to recuse himself from meetings where matters involving African Defence Systems were discussed.[103] It also took issue with Modise's various conflicts of interest, although it tamely found that 'no evidence of impropriety was found' in regard to Modise receiving any inducements to manipulate matters.[104] Most importantly, the Report, despite listing manifold errors and elisions, concluded by clearing the Deal of any wrongdoing. In a passage since frequently quoted by those involved in the Arms Deal, the Report found that:

> No evidence was found of any improper or unlawful conduct by the Government. The irregularities and improprieties referred to in the findings as contained in this report, point to the conduct of certain officials of the government departments involved and cannot, in our view, be ascribed to the President or Ministers involved in their capacity as members of the Ministers' Committee or Cabinet. There are therefore

no grounds to suggest that the Government's contracting position is flawed.[105]

For many, it was a bizarre inclusion, its tone sitting at odds with much
of the content of the Report, which listed many problems in detail. And
many believed that huge sections had been intentionally excised in a
grand cover-up: a claim that was furiously denied by Mbeki himself,
who once again explained that any inference otherwise was motivated
by 'the racist conviction that Africans, who now govern the country, are
mutually prone to corruption, venality and mismanagement'.[106]

By 2005, any argument that the Joint Investigation Report had not
been edited would struggle under the weight of evidence. An Arms
Deal critic, Dr Richard Young, who had lost out to African Defence
Systems for contracts in the Arms Deal due to the extensive manipulation that had allegedly taken place, took the matter to court. In
a groundbreaking judgment, the court ruled that Young should be
handed all drafts of the Joint Investigation Report that had been
drafted prior to its publication, and any pertinent correspondence.
Once the documents were perused, it was clear that massive amounts
of information had been edited out or reworded in curious ways.
The original draft report, for example, was over 800 pages long: the
Joint Investigation Report was half of that length. Correspondence
included in the documents clearly showed that members of Cabinet
(including Mbeki) had been given drafts of the Report before the final report was published,[107] while, in one particular letter, Auditor-
General Fakie outlined to Mbeki under exactly which laws the
President could demand changes.[108]

It is impossible to list all the changes that were made. But one is indicative. As noted above, the Joint Investigation Report concluded that
'no evidence was found of improper or unlawful conduct' in the Arms
Deal. In the original drafts, no such paragraph was included. Indeed, a
key introductory statement (excluded from the final report) explained
why it would have been impossible to make such a bald assertion, in so
doing contradicting the very finding that Arms Deal supporters were so
keen to repeat. The Scorpions, the drafts made clear, had uncovered a
considerable amount of evidence of wrongdoing, but, as the matter was

still under investigation, the evidence gathered could not be included in the Joint Investigation Report – explaining why the Scorpions' contribution to the draft report was a paltry three pages long. Instead of finding no wrongdoing, enough evidence had been gathered to launch a full-fledged criminal investigation into the Arms Deal only a few months prior to the publication of the Joint Investigation Report:

> Numerous allegations of criminal activity were received from various quarters. These allegations were followed up and investigated, some were without any substance and the investigation thereof came to nought, whilst the others that appeared to have any substance are still being pursued …
>
> The [Scorpions] investigation progressed to a stage where on 24 August 2001, the Investigating Director: Directorate of Special Operations instituted an investigation, as opposed to a preparatory investigation, into the suspected commission of offences of fraud and/or corruption in contravention of the Corruption Act, No. 94 of 1992, or the attempted commission of these offences, arising out of the armaments acquisition for the Department of Defence, involving prime bidders/contractors in terms of which certain contracts and/or subcontracts for the supply of armaments were concluded.[109]

It was this very investigation that cast such a long shadow over South African politics for the next decade, generating the cases against Schabir Shaik and Jacob Zuma. The Scorpions, however, had limited success in pursuing the various corruption investigations. And where they were successful, the punishment eventually doled out made a mockery of any sense of justice.

Only two prosecutions were ever successfully mounted flowing from the Arms Deal. The first was the prosecution of Tony Yengeni. During the Arms Deal, Yengeni had served on Parliament's Standing Committee on Defence and subsequently as the ANC's Chief Whip in Parliament. A *Sunday Times* investigation discovered that he had received a considerable discount on a luxury vehicle from a subcontractor in the Arms Deal.[110] After considerable legal wrangling, Yengeni finally entered a plea bargain agreement with the state in 2003, admitting to the lesser charge of fraud (rather than corruption) for failing to inform Parliament of the financial benefit in violation of parliamentary ethics requirements.[111] It was only in 2006, three years after the plea agreement, that Yengeni finally served a derisory amount of jail time after a number of legal appeals.[112]

The other notable prosecution flowing from the Arms Deal was that of Schabir Shaik (discussed above). After going into prison in 2007, Shaik reportedly developed a number of health complications that removed him from his cells and placed him in the relatively luxurious confines of hospital. He spent only 2 years and 4 months of his 15-year sentence in jail before being released on medical parole in March 2009.[113] According to prison authorities, Shaik was in a 'terminal condition': under the terms of South African law, prisoners can be released on compassionate grounds if death is immediately imminent. Three years later, Shaik has shown little sign of shuffling off his mortal coil. Indeed, numerous newspaper reports have alleged that he has been spotted playing golf outside his parole terms, exhibiting few signs of medical distress.[114] And, in March 2011, it was alleged that he had assaulted a man in a dispute over a parking space outside a Durban mosque.[115]

A less reported feature of Shaik's corruption trial has ensured that he remains a wealthy man. When he was found guilty by High Court judge Hilary Squires, a court order was issued whereby R34 million of Shaik's assets that had been corruptly acquired were set aside for seizure by the state. As appeal proceedings progressed (Shaik appealed twice, unsuccessfully, finally reaching the Constitutional Court), the R34 million was placed in an escrow account. While there, it attracted considerable interest: roughly R14 million.[116] To whom the interest belonged was a matter of considerable legal debate between the state and Shaik's counsel, although common perceptions of justice would suggest that the interest on R34 million in criminally acquired money could not possibly be considered the rightful property of the guilty party. Nevertheless, seemingly to avoid interminable legal wrangles, the state agreed to a plea bargain: half of the interest accrued would be returned to Shaik.[117] Of this, R2 million was to cover legal costs, leaving Shaik with a healthy

R5 million: R5 million he would never have seen if he had not engaged in corrupt activity.[118]

The limited number of prosecutions flowing from the Arms Deal has led many to wonder if there wasn't outright political interference to forestall further embarrassment. Initially, these claims were merely rumours, but some evidence has come to light to give them credence. Certainly, the resources that were put into investigations were minuscule enough to suggest a lack of political will. In 2008, the Scorpions, armed with new information from the UK's Serious Fraud Office, launched raids on the business properties of BAe's agents John Bredenkamp and Fana Hlongwane. And while thousands of pages of documents were seized, in addition to computer hard drives and other media, the job of sifting through the material was left to a single investigator who was also responsible for all the other Arms Deal investigations. Leaving a single person to sift through over 4 million pages of seized material could only suggest that political influence had been brought to sway.

Hopes of any meaningful investigation into Arms Deal corruption were seemingly dashed by the disbandment of the Scorpions in late January 2009. Officially, the investigation was transferred to the newly established Directorate for Priority Crime Investigation (DIPCI). In 2010, the head of DIPCI, Anwar Dramat, appeared before Scopa to provide a briefing into the Arms Deal investigation. He confirmed that the unit was investigating R480 million in corruption allegations, but that it would take anywhere between 5 and 10 years to come to completion.[119] Hinting at a lack of political will, he asked Scopa to make an 'executive decision' as to whether it was worth continuing the investigation.[120] Scopa's MPs baulked at the request, pointing out to Dramat the basics of the separation of powers. Nevertheless, shortly thereafter, it was confirmed that the last two active legs of the investigation into the Arms Deal had been closed.[121]

The scandal of consequence

The Arms Deal dominated much of political life of South Africa for over a decade, framing the epic battle between the Mbeki and Zuma factions in the ANC. How the succession battle played out and impacted on democratic governance in the country is dealt with elsewhere. But this meta-narrative of contestation over power in the ANC has obscured some of the subtler consequences of the Arms Deal.

One of the most obvious impacts has been economic. When the Deal was announced, it was set to cost in the region of R30 billion. This figure proved to be a major under-estimate: in 2008, due to currency fluctuations, it was confirmed that the Deal would cost in the region of R47 billion by 2011.[122] This figure excluded the cost of financing the various loans that were granted to pay for the deal, which was estimated by the Auditor-General's office to be in the region of 50 per cent of the contract price.[123] When this is added to the capital cost, the sum escalates to a truly monumental R71 billion. Undoubtedly, spending this much on a largely import-based purchase would have increased the budget deficit at the very time that GEAR was attempting to prevent this. And it has quite obviously diverted funds away from other socio-economic needs, often dwarfing expenditure on other social goods. Between 1999 and 2008, for example, about R20 billion more was spent on the Arms Deal than on state-subsidised low-cost housing and the roll-out of antiretroviral medication combined.[124] If the money had been spent directly on employment, it would have made a major dent: R71 billion could have paid the salaries of over a million maintenance workers for a year, or created 100 000 jobs per year in the same category between 1999 and 2008.[125]

But it is the political impact that will in all likelihood be longest felt. The Arms Deal made it abundantly clear that Parliament and its oversight bodies had only the most limited power to halt or even monitor the activities of the executive. The proportional representation system, in the service of a dominant party that effected political centralism on a grand scale, rendered the idea of independent MPs a figment. At every point in the Arms Deal, Parliament was ignored or actively browbeaten: in pursuing the Deal, the executive bluntly ignored Parliament's request that it approve acquisitions before they were given the go-ahead; when the conduct of the Deal was reviewed by Scopa and other bodies, the executive launched a public attack that could only have undermined confidence in South Africa's primary democratic institution; and when Parliament attempted to deal with the thorny issue of parliamentary ethics and corruption, members were quickly brought into line, harangued, harassed, removed from positions of power and slowly frozen out of the organisation if they failed to sweep their misgivings under the carpet.

Much the same process played out when the country's integral Chapter 9 institutions were called upon to do their duty. These oversight bodies, so named as their creation was stipulated under Chapter 9 of the Constitution, were established as independent mechanisms of accountability and as a check on executive malfeasance. In at least two cases – those of the Auditor-General and the Public Protector – political pressure prevented their operation. The Auditor-General, as noted above, was required to remove large sections from the audit report into the Arms Deal, compelled by legislation that is still enacted despite its threat to democratic practice. The Office of the Public Protector, meanwhile, completely failed to use its powers of investigation to probe the Deal: its contribution to the Joint Investigation Report was a risible 50 pages that betrayed a fundamental miscomprehension of how the Deal was done, no doubt due to the fact that its highly publicised public hearings were cut short as soon as they started touching on sensitive matters. That the Office of the Public Protector acted in much the same way when it was called upon to investigate the Oilgate saga,[126] which deeply implicated the ANC, suggests that the organisation has singularly failed, under constant pressure, to develop any spirit of independent mindedness.

It is entirely possible that these problems, many of which reflect a democratic system creaking under the weight of single party dominance, would have become apparent even if the Arms Deal had not taken place. But it was the Arms Deal that gave them their first expression. The intensity of the publicity surrounding the Deal and its loaded political connotations concertinaed what might otherwise have been a much subtler and less thorough-going erosion of democratic governance: institutions had to be brought in line fast and hard, the blunt instruments of harassment limiting what democratic contestation there might have been if matters had proceeded at a slower pace. This was nowhere more clearly illustrated than when the Scorpions were disbanded despite a stellar record of criminal investigation. Unfortunately, anti-democratic behaviour has a startling ability to beget further anti-democratic attitudes. And when institutions are so thoroughly compromised, political contestation moves outside the confines of accountability and oversight into the murky world of skulduggery and intelligence manipulation.

The Commission of Inquiry

In late 2011, Jacob Zuma took almost everyone by surprise when he announced a formal Commission of Inquiry into the Arms Deal. While the decision has been lauded, with a few qualifications, it is abundantly clear that the President did not appoint the Commission out of respect for good governance and criminal justice. Instead, two primary motives have been suggested.

First, a case brought by the Arms Deal activist Terry Crawford-Browne appeared to be viewed with favour by the Constitutional Court. Crawford-Browne had argued that it was illogical and irrational for Zuma not to appoint a Commission of Inquiry, considering the extent and persistence of allegations of corruption flowing from the Deal. The presiding judges seemed to be leaning towards agreeing with him, which was made clear when the Court moved beyond the legally thorny issues of justiciable action and presidential prerogative and began asking the state to deal with the substance of the corruption allegations presented in Crawford-Browne's founding affidavit. After numerous delays in which the state failed to submit any kind of meaningful response, the impression was created that the state was simply unable to refute the allegations. A victory for Crawford-Browne looked increasingly likely. Deciding to appoint the Commission, and thus ending the litigation in the Constitutional Court, not only saved the government considerable embarrassment, but also prevented the Constitutional Court from having a say in the terms of reference of the inquiry itself. If Zuma appointed the Commission outside of judicial instruction, he would at least retain control over how the Commission was to be staffed and the areas it was allowed to investigate.

The other motive was derived from the internal politics of Zuma's increasingly fractious 'alliance of the angry'. As contests between the Youth League (read: Malema) and Zuma reached fever pitch, the Arms Deal came into play once more. Only three years after unanimously condemning Zuma's prosecution, the League was loudly questioning his role in the Arms Deal, and suggesting that it should be investigated anew. The Arms Deal was Zuma's Achilles' heel, always exposing to attack his commitment to the struggle against corruption. Impossible to ignore the threat of criminal prosecution that could flow from a highly politicised criminal justice system. By appointing the Commission of Inquiry, Zuma was able to head this off at the pass. Vitally, the Commission has been granted a two-year mandate. It will thus only report in 2013 at the earliest, by which time Zuma's most pressing battle, Mangaung in 2012, will be a distant memory, insulating him from the impact of negative findings regarding his conduct, while simultaneously allowing him to clothe himself in the finery befitting the most committed anti-corruption activist.

Whether the Commission of Inquiry will break the pattern of previous Arms Deal investigations by actually reporting on the truth of the matter is yet to be seen. That so many investigations have taken place and, at the same time, been purposefully derailed and hamstrung, does not fill Arms Deal activists with a great deal of confidence in the ability of investigators to probe without fear or favour. But if the Commission of Inquiry does not fulfil its mandate – if it goes the way of other investigations – the credibility of the judiciary who make up its members and the investigators who do its dirty work will be irreparably harmed. Such harm will only favour those whom South Africa should most fear: those whose moral compass long ago lost its bearing.

Chapter 5

Smoke, Mirrors, Emails and Tapes: The Uses and Abuses of Intelligence[1]

Paul Holden

South Africa's news has incontestably dramatic tendencies. Tabloid papers spread the news that *tokoloshe* are making visitations willy-nilly, while the daily grind of multiple car pile-ups and gruesome murder stories occupies the dailies, usually displaced only in the event of a major sporting triumph. Overwhelmed by spectacle, readers and viewers might have expected political commentary to offer some respite, with debate that could be robust, even pointed, but relatively inoculated against the grubby chaos of a country still fractured and traumatised by its apartheid past.

Unfortunately, that was not to be the case. Over the last decade, and especially from the mid-2000s onwards, political coverage has often been dominated by sensational leaks, claims and counter-claims emanating from the country's intelligence services. The driving force was the succession contest between Jacob Zuma and Thabo Mbeki, with their respective intelligence factions using their powers to help or hinder different partisan factions within the ANC. National discourse has become a game of smoke and mirrors facilitated by the abuse of state resources and the politicisation of the security services.

The result has been a frequently staggering abuse of power on the part of both factions and, perhaps most incongruously, a decrease in the certainties one can point to in the political domain. For all the leaks and counter-claims, South African citizens have often been left scratching their heads, uncertain of who did what, when, in what order and for what reason. Uncertainty about the conduct of key political figures has muddied the waters of national politics, making informed debate about the merits (or lack thereof) of various power players increasingly difficult.

Unfortunately, the power conferred by the use and abuse of the intelligence services during the succession debate has meant that there is little political motivation to arrest these developments. Indeed, since Jacob Zuma's ascent to power there have been disturbing signs that a deeply factionalised intelligence service continues to operate for the benefit of various political figures. At the same time, the broader security services have been seen to be motivating for draconian secrecy laws that if enacted will make it almost impossible for investigative journalists or ordinary citizens to hold those in power to account: a crackdown on the free flow of information by those so happy to use disinformation for their own ends.

South Africa's intelligence legacy and the transition to democracy

South Africa's contemporary intelligence woes are not unfamiliar. During apartheid the intelligence agencies associated with the state, as well as that created by the ANC in exile, were frequently associated with gross violations of human rights and partisan politicking. Under the policy of Total Onslaught/Total Strategy, any means were justified in fighting back against the perceived attacks by hostile forces at home and abroad, put into action by the three arms of the intelligence apparatus: the police Security Branch, military intelligence and the civilian National Intelligence Agency.[2]

Each of these units was linked to atrocities on a grand scale. The Security Branch, for instance, notoriously operated out of the top two floors of the dreaded technocratic hub of the SAP, John Vorster Square in Johannesburg. Ferrying suspects to secluded offices by means of a secret elevator, the Security Branch used violent torture and intimidation to interrogate those suspected of supporting the Anti-Apartheid Movement.[3] A number of inmates and suspects were killed in highly suspicious circumstances, either by torture-induced suicide or by 'falling' to their death out of the top story windows. The first of these deaths – that of a one-time student colleague of Thabo Mbeki, Ahmed Timol – took place in 1971; the last – that of Clayton Sithole – occurred 12 days before the release of Nelson Mandela in 1990.[4]

Often the lines between operational activities and intelligence were blurred, as in the creation of the hit squad with the most Orwellian name possible – the Civil Cooperation Bureau. The CCB, created by the Special Forces within the South African Defence Force[5] and driven by such notorious apartheid figures as Magnus Malan,[6] Kat Liebenberg and Eeben Barlow, was responsible for numerous assassinations, including those of the academic David Webster and Swapo activist Anton Lubowski.[7] The unit also made attempts on the lives of other notable figures, including Albie Sachs, Dullah Omar, Father Michael Lapsley and Reverend Frank Chikane.[8] The CCB maintained an intelligence function, which supplied it with the names and locations of suspects in order to make the murder of anti-apartheid activists more focused and direct.[9]

Indeed, as the ISS's intelligence researcher Lauren Hutton notes, all of the apartheid intelligence agencies were deeply involved in the violent suppression of resistance to the regime:

> These services characteristically invaded the privacy of individuals; conducted various forms of surveillance without judicial authorisation; were unaccountable to Parliament; and were involved in political violence, suppression and the manipulation of the domestic political environment.[10]

Although not nearly on the same scale, the ANC's own intelligence structures in exile were similarly guilty of gross human rights violations in their search for 'informers' and spies secretly working for apartheid security forces. [11] It became clear that they were also often used to quell dissent amongst cadres who had many legitimate grievances about the conduct of the political leadership.

This was most clearly shown in the first outbreak of widespread dissent in the ANC in exile in the late 1960s. Led by the fiery Chris Hani, a group of MK soldiers circulated a damning memorandum that attacked a number of features of exile life, including the failure to infiltrate troops back into South Africa and the luxurious lifestyles of some MK leadership, notably Joe Modise. [12]

The response was extreme. The political structures within the ANC called for the dismissal of Hani and his comrades, and a tribunal set up and staffed by five members of the NEC (which had been deeply criticised by the memorandum) expelled them all, only allowing them to be re-admitted in 1969. There were hints that a more sinister plan was being hatched. Lambert Moloi and one General Sijake recalled that 11 freshly dug graves were found on the same Livingstone farm where Hani and co were to be incarcerated in newly built dungeons. [13] According to Hugh Macmillan, a group of MK soldiers also made a midnight visit to the home of Livingstone Mqotsi, where Hani was staying. Hani believed that Mqotsi saved his life when he denied the soldiers entry. [14] Either way, it seemed that elements within the MK were more than willing to use violence against democratic confrontation.

The second outbreak of dissent in the ANC occurred in the early 1980s. Much of it was linked to the same problems experienced by Hani and his colleagues: frustration at a failure to infiltrate cadres back home mixed with a perception that the political leadership was disconnected, and in certain instances, corrupt. [15] What made the situation different was that it occurred against a background of a massive influx of troops into MK as students fled across the border following the Soweto 1976 uprising. [16] The new recruits rubbed many of the old guard up the wrong way, threatening to uproot the political certainties in the organisation. There was also a fear, somewhat justified, that the mass exodus had allowed apartheid security forces to smuggle informers into the ANC to destabilise the organisation. [17]

The ANC's first dedicated intelligence function was created in the early 1970s. The Department of Security and Intelligence (DIS), [18] later renamed the Department of National Intelligence and Security (NAT)[19] was also popularly referred to as *Mbokodo*, meaning grinding stone.[20] From the early 1980s onwards, partially as a result of incidents such as the Black September episode (when water supplying an MK camp was poisoned) and partially as a result of the friction between new and old members of the ANC, Mbokodo drove a brutal process of screening potential informants. Mbokodo's methods veered towards violence, with many of those interviewed complaining of lengthy interrogations bordering on torture.[21] And when cadres were 'found' to be informants – some, such as Pallo Jordan[22] for merely criticising Mbokodo – the punishments were intense, with a long stay in infamous and recently built prison camps assured. Quatro, the name of the most notorious prison camp, was where the most persistent allegations of the gross violation of human rights emerged, many with a great deal of justification. In the early 1990s, an ANC-appointed investigation, known as the Motsuenyane Commission, characterised Quatro as a 'dumping pit' in which 'manifest abuses of human rights' took place.[23]

When MK cadres were informed that they were about to join an MPLA offensive in Angola, it was the kindling needed to ignite already flickering tensions. Throughout 1983 and 1984, MK soldiers in camps throughout the ANC catchment area mutinied, demanding that a consultative conference be arranged to address their various grievances. The response was swift and uncompromising: despite offering only unarmed resistance, the mutineers (particularly the leaders) were arrested and held for months and years in camps like Quatro, some only being released at the same time as Nelson Mandela.[24] Many of the ANC leadership had become aware of the treatment at Quatro, but all the evidence suggests that little was done to rein in the abuses.[25] This, above all, has given the impression that the exile leadership of the ANC, hand-in-glove with its intelligence forces, tolerated the abuses, demonstrating an approach to intelligence that was markedly anti-democratic.

This was not the only important legacy bequeathed by the ANC's experience in exile. Indeed, another key development in ANC intelligence services in the late 1980s would cast a long shadow over South Africa's democracy and Jacob Zuma's ascent to power: Operation Vula and its closely associated programme, Operation Bible. Vula was arguably the most successful ANC intelligence operation, infiltrating extensive numbers of agents back into South Africa in heavy disguise.[26] The use of new technology – primitive modems and satellite phones – allowed communication out of South Africa in a way not previously seen: at one point, Nelson Mandela was able to communicate with Oliver Tambo in exile while Mandela was meeting with the NP's spooks in Pollsmoor.[27]

Vula was shrouded in secrecy. Indeed, almost the entire leadership of the ANC was unaware of the Operation. Elaborate cover stories were woven to explain the disappearance of operatives from ANC structures: Mac Maharaj, one of Vula's leading operatives, was said to be recuperating from a kidney operation in the Soviet Union, all the while undertaking daring trips under assumed identities.[28] Indeed, according to Maharaj, only Joe Slovo, Jacob Zuma and Oliver Tambo were made aware of the project, outside of its operatives. Operation Bible, the project run by the MJK Unit, led by the Shaik brothers, was similarly secretive, although it was largely integrated into Vula by the fact that Bible continuously fed intelligence to the Vula high command (and, at the top of the hierarchy, Jacob Zuma).[29] The result was that, by the time it was uncovered in July 1990, Vula operated as a virtually distinct intelligence network within the ANC, one that endorsed keeping the lines of trust short. As James Sanders has noted about the Vula experience:

> The operation's deeply problematic contribution to the struggle was that it had established, in addition to DIS and MK's Military Intelligence, a third ANC intelligence network ... Vula's most dominant legacy to the ANC and the new South Africa would be that it cemented a single message into the minds of ANC politicians: the importance of possessing a private intelligence network.[30]

This was the worrisome legacy bequeathed to the post-apartheid state: intelligence services on both sides that had previously engaged directly in anti-democratic practices and gross human rights violations, and which displayed dispiriting attitudes to non-partisanship.

In the post-apartheid period little seemed to change.

Zuma, Mbeki and intelligence: the preview

The ANC's failure to deal with this dispiriting legacy is nowhere more clearly illustrated than in the succession battle between Thabo Mbeki and Jacob Zuma. Factions within the intelligence services frequently came to the aid of one man or the other over a period of close to a decade. Often this was done with little consideration of the governing principles of the Constitution, which determined that no member of the security or intelligence forces 'may in the performance of their functions prejudice a political party interest that is legitimate in terms of the constitution or further, in a partisan manner, any interest of a political party.'[31]

It is often forgotten that the roots of the Zuma–Mbeki antipathy may very well have stemmed from one of the country's frequent intelligence imbroglios. In April 2001, Safety and Security Minister Steve Tshwete revealed that intelligence had been received indicating that there was a 'coup plot' to oust Mbeki. But this was no ordinary political coup. Tshwete indicated that Mbeki may have been put in 'physical danger'.[32] Remarkably, the three main plotters were identified as the *crème de la crème* of the ANC generation to which Mbeki belonged: Cyril Ramaphosa, Tokyo Sexwale and Mathews Phosa[33] (the latter two would later publicly line up against Mbeki in the run-up to the Polokwane Conference). Based on information from an Mpumalanga ANC Youth League official, James Nkambule, it was alleged that the three had been spreading gossip to the effect that Mbeki had a hand in the murder of his one-time rival Chris Hani, a disinformation campaign designed to stoke emotions on a sensitive topic.[34]

Almost no evidence has emerged to support the claims. The ANC's alliance partners were livid and rubbished the reports out of hand,[35] seeing Tshwete's move as no more than a blunt power game aimed at cementing Mbeki's hold on the party. The international media, meanwhile, wondered whether the announcement was an indication of the weakness of Mbeki's support within the ANC.[36] Nkambule, for his troubles, was declared a notorious liar (he would later be found dead in suspicious circumstances after alleging widespread corruption in the construction of World Cup stadiums in Mpumalanga). And Mbeki, at last, was forced to concede publicly that the allegations should not have been made public. Little damage, it seems, had been done to the ambitions of any of the alleged coup plotters, though the *Guardian* did wonder whether Tshwete's statement was an implicit threat of surveillance of any pretenders.

Not so for Jacob Zuma. According to the unparalleled biography of Thabo Mbeki by Mark Gevisser, Mbeki had gotten wind of the coup plot months before Tshwete's announcement. Due to a complicated set of circumstances, Mbeki allegedly came to believe that Zuma had been implicated in the coup plot by providing information to Mathews Phosa.[37] Mbeki confronted Zuma, forcing him to issue a bizarre and humiliating statement. Out of the blue, Zuma appeared on television to confirm that he had no designs on the presidency of the ANC, projecting a hagiographic portrait of Mbeki that would have been unthinkable seven years later at Polokwane:

> In recent months there have been rumours and unverified so called 'intelligence reports' circulating that I might stand for the position of ANC President during the next national conference of the African National Congress.
>
> I have felt it important to state publicly that I have no intention or desire to stand for the position of President. I believe our current President is certainly capable of leading both the ANC and the country and my confidence in him remains unwavering.
>
> He has grown up within the ANC, occupied leadership positions and has been a part of its leadership collective for many years.
>
> He has a profound understanding of the movement, has provided excellent leadership to South Africa during its most trying times, and continues to do so. He has my full and unqualified support as the President of both the ANC and the country.[38]

Emerging out of an intelligence operation of dubious provenance, this bombshell was as much a remnant of the ANC's exile past as it was a pointer to the future. For South Africa's two top politicians, it was the beginning of the end.

The hoax email saga

The next substantial step in what now became the Mbeki–Zuma power struggle came in 2003, when Schabir Shaik was charged with corruption relating to the Arms Deal, as described in Chapter 2. It was in this context that a deeply confusing mini-drama unfolded. In early September 2005, shortly after Shaik was found guilty, Saki Macozoma, a prominent businessman with ties to higher-ups in the ANC, made a startling phone call to the Minister of Intelligence, Ronnie Kasrils. According to Macozoma, he and his family had been 'harassed' by intelligence agents from the National Intelligence Agency over the course of two days in August 2005.[39] A few days later, perhaps concerned that his complaint was not sufficient, Macozoma instructed his lawyers to apply for an interdict against the NIA to prevent the surveillance.[40] Kasrils claimed that he had no knowledge of the surveillance operation, suggesting that it had been initiated and conducted by another senior member of the intelligence team. Determined to get to the bottom of the matter, he requested the matter be investigated by the Inspector-General for Intelligence.[41]

What the Inspector found was remarkable: Macozoma had indeed been monitored, but he was far from being alone. Indeed, as the *Sunday Independent* later reported, Macozoma was one of 13 individuals whose communications were monitored by the NIA, including Cyril Ramaphosa, ANC Chief Whip Mbulelo Goniwe, ANC spokesperson Smuts Ngonyama and the parliamentary offices of the DA.[42] The monitoring had taken place as an intelligence exercise, reportedly the brainchild of the Director-General of Intelligence, Billy Masetlha. 'Project Avani' was initiated without ministerial knowledge as a '360 degree horizon scan with no bias' whose main function was to 'gather, correlate, evaluate and analyse intelligence in order to identify any threat or potential threat posed by the presidential succession debate, foreign services interests there-in, the impending Jacob Zuma trial and poor service delivery impacts and dynamics to the security and stability of the Republic'.[43]

Avani was conceived in such broad terms (with an implicit eye on developments in the ANC) that it was almost inevitable that it would be drawn into the wider power-play of the succession. In the middle of August, according to the Inspector-General for Intelligence, the Project Avani team were made aware of a series of emails between senior members of the ANC, the Scorpions and the DA. The emails seemed to prove, once and for all, that there was a concerted conspiracy, led by a 'Xhosa faction', designed to keep Jacob Zuma out of office, and which also targeted Kgalema Motlanthe and Billy Masetlha himself.[44] The emails also seemed to prove that the corruption charges levied against Jacob Zuma were nothing more than a political connivance: one 'faction' that was said to be represented in the emails was a group of reactionary white functionaries (incidentally all senior members of the Scorpions investigating unit) who were attempting to foment division in the ANC and prevent Zuma's rise to power.[45]

It is here that things get mightily complicated. According to the Inspector-General for Intelligence, the emails were, in fact, a hoax.[46] Nothing of the sort had actually been sent between the members of the alleged conspiracy. Instead, paper versions of a series of fake emails were allegedly fabricated to give the impression of a conspiracy against Jacob Zuma[47] with manufactured evidence designed to give credence to cloak-and-dagger claims often made by Zuma supporters. By inference, they were meant to spur on the Avani Project towards greater monitoring of those considered to be unsupportive of Zuma's presidential push – an elaborate ruse to secretly gather real intelligence on Zuma's opponents, which is where the monitoring of Macozoma and others came in. If this was true, it suggested that Billy Masetlha had tried to subvert the aims of Project Avani to further the aims of a Zuma presidency. Manufacturing a conspiracy *was* the conspiracy, according to this version.

As a result of the investigation into Avani, Mbeki dismissed Masetlha, citing a 'breakdown in trust' between the two. Soon after, Masetlha was charged with fraud, along with two accomplices. One of these – Muzi Kunene – was alleged to have been an outside agent hired on contract by Masetlha and paid with Avani funds, despite NIA regulations prohibiting the employment of contractors to undertake interception work.[48] Khunene was later found to be of somewhat limited trustworthiness. In 2009 he was sentenced to life imprisonment after being found guilty of the murder of a Ballito estate agent from whom he was renting a property.[49] He is currently facing additional charges of attempted murder for allegedly shooting at his son, who planned to testify against his father in the Ballito estate agent trial.[50]

But the claims levelled by the Inspector-General for Intelligence – that Masetlha had actively overseen the composition of the hoax emails – were treated with suspicion in some quarters. Masetlha, for one, denied any involvement. According to his version, the emails had been handed to him by the ANC Secretary-General, Kgalema Motlanthe, whose own source was unknown.[51] To further complicate the tale, Masetlha claimed that there were, in fact, two sets of emails: the hoax emails and a set of genuine emails intercepted by Project Avani. The latter, he claimed, without divulging their content, were in an NIA office.[52]

Other investigations into the hoax email saga also cocked a snoot at the findings of the Inspector-General's report. The parliamentary committee overseeing intelligence argued that the report was technically flawed and should be treated with caution.[53] An internal ANC investigation into the report – instigated at the reported prompting of Kgalema Motlanthe – also dismissed the findings, clearing Masetlha of any wrongdoing.[54] However, when the findings of the internal ANC investigation were presented to the NEC, they were, in turn, rubbished. When the matter proceeded to court, the fraud case against Masetlha and his alleged co-conspirators was revealed to be full of holes. In particular, the state's own IT specialist confirmed that it was impossible to show conclusively that the emails had been generated on a laptop belonging to Muzi Kunene.[55] One laptop that was seized from Kunene did seem to contain keyword fragments that matched some of the hoax emails. But there was no solid evidence that the emails had been written on the laptop, and the fact that it was not secured with a password meant that the IT specialist could not rule out its having been tampered with prior to their investigation.[56]

When the dust settled, it thus seemed that Masetlha had finally been vindicated and the matter laid to rest. But, in reality, the hoax email

saga was only superficially resolved, leaving more questions than an-
swers. The fake emails were incontrovertibly composed by someone and
distributed widely. But who drafted them, and for what reason? Was it
an audacious triple bluff, seemingly setting up Masetlha in such a way
that he could eventually be cleared, confirming, in a back-handed way,
that there was a conspiracy against himself, Zuma and Motlanthe? If
Motlanthe did indeed distribute the fake emails, what was his source,
and why did he believe them to be real when even a cursory examination
would have confirmed their dubiousness? What had happened to the
original, genuine emails that Masetlha claimed to have seen, and did
the information they contain really justify the electronic surveillance of
13 targets under Project Avani? Why did Masetlha hire Muzi Kunene
to undertake email interception when this could have been conducted
by the NIA itself? Why, indeed, was he even working with a man whose
later conviction for a brutal and premeditated murder has cast suspicion
on his character? Who, in the end, had decided to initiate Project Avani?
The Inspector-General claimed it was started at Masetlha's own instiga-
tion, while Masetlha alleged he had been approached by Cabinet – but
if this was so, why was Ronnie Kasrils, a Cabinet Minister, unaware of
the Project?

All that is clear, in the end, is that some unknown person, of unknown provenance and for unknown reasons, decided to use the cover
of an intelligence operation to introduce the fake emails into circulation. As such, it served as warning of the ease with which the secrecy
and subterfuge involved in intelligence operations could be manipulated
and abused, with major political consequences. And it also illustrated
perfectly the burden of uncertainty placed on ordinary South African
citizens who knew that something dastardly had happened, but had no
solid evidence as to why and how.

The Browse Mole Report

On 7 May 2007, a top-secret report was faxed to the offices of Cosatu's
General Secretary, Zwelinzima Vavi, widely known to be supportive of

Jacob Zuma. Known as the Browse Mole Report, its contents were the essence of political combustibility. Over the course of 18 pages, the report outlined a series of allegations that sought to prove that 'Deputy President Jacob Zuma's presidential ambitions are fuelled and sustained by a conspiracy playing out both inside South Africa and on the African continental stage'.[57]

The report began by discussing the source of Zuma's funds, which it believed had been sourced largely via presidential circles in Africa. In particular, it alleged that Zuma had become close to senior figures in the Angolan administration after being introduced to them by Brett Kebble, who was considered 'Zuma's then major funder'.[58] As a result, Zuma had pursued a number of diamond deals in Angola; none of which, it is alleged, came to fruition. But, in 2006, the report continued, Zuma used his family connections with a South African judge to overturn the impound order on a jet owned by Angolan interests. The result: 'in exchange for the favour Zuma was given an oil concession in the north of Angola'.[59] Further, the report claimed to be in possession of intelligence that suggested that Zuma had been given access to other oil and diamond concessions as a result of a directive from Angolan President Eduardo dos Santos,[60] widely seen as hostile to Thabo Mbeki.

Another alleged continental benefactor was Libya's Muammar Gaddafi. According to an intelligence document received by the investigator who compiled Browse Mole, Zuma had travelled to Libya on at least three occasions and met senior Libyan figures after being introduced by the SACP's Blade Nzimande. The result was a reportedly substantial donation:

> In the course of these visits, according to the report, Zuma met with Musa Kusa, Muammar Khadafi's Chief of External Intelligence, and in one meeting a sum of $5m was handed over. The purpose of this donation was allegedly to promote the mobilisation of mass support at street level against the status quo in South Africa and in support of Zuma's presidential campaign.

The money was understood to be the first instalment of an

ongoing commitment, though it is unclear whether further moneys have yet been forthcoming.[61]

There were startling allegations that a coterie of supporters around Zuma had started to lay plans for some form of military intervention to ensure his ascension to the Presidency. This, the report claimed, would be undertaken by both South African conspirators and supporters on the African stage. It was alleged that a number of senior African officials had met in April 2006 at an 'unknown venue' as part of discussions around the Great Lakes conflict. According to a source within the body-guarding sector, plans were drawn up to provide paramilitary support for Zuma's 'revolution':

> Among those allegedly present at the meeting in question were the following, or their representatives:
> ❏ General Abdusalam Abubakar, the northern leader in Nigeria
> ❏ Muammar Khadafi
> ❏ The President of Côte d'Ivoire, Laurent Gbagbo
> ❏ Denis Sassou Nguesso, President of Congo Brazzaville
> ❏ Unnamed rebel leaders from the DRC
> ❏ Unnamed Angolan representatives
> Possibly military support for the Zuma cause was allegedly discussed in the context of a rolling ground-level revolution in pursuit of Zuma's presidential ambitions.[62]

This meeting, the Report claimed, was preceded by a meeting in South Africa at Shaft 17 at the Nasrec Conference Centre. The Nasrec meeting was allegedly attended by senior former MK leaders then serving in the SANDF, African diplomats and former SANDF chief Siphiwe Nyanda:

> Though detail around the meeting remains sketchy, the sources concur that a possible alignment of the military in support of Zuma was raised by Nyanda, as well as the possibility of a military coup, or use of the military to force Mbeki to stand

down. Such discussions were in the context of foreign military assistance.

According to the protocol source, mention was made in the course of the meeting of military or paramilitary formations being trained in northern Mozambique, to operate as part of a destabilisation strategy inside South African borders. Apparently ambassadors present at the meeting were to pledge military support in this regard.

The exact nature of these paramilitary or military formations remains unclear. It was specified, according to the source, that – prior to the acquittal of Jacob Zuma on rape charges – plans had been laid to blow up South African courts if a guilty verdict were returned. It is however possible that such formations could be connected to criminal actions, like cash-in-transit heists, as a means to both the destabilisation of the State and securing funding.[63]

The report concluded by recommending that a broader investigation be undertaken by both the Scorpions and the Reserve Bank into 'conspiracy to sedition' and money laundering, among other things.

There is little doubt, now, of the provenance of the Browse Mole Report. It has long been established that it was produced by a Scorpions 'special investigator', Ivor Powell, who had previously worked as an investigative journalist. In 2009, Powell broke a nearly two-year silence to confirm that he had begun his investigations that informed the Browse Mole Report in early 2006 at the insistence of the then head of the Scorpions, Leonard McCarthy. Moreover, Powell also admitted that he was the 'sole author' of the report, subject to 'two caveats': 'that McCarthy passed certain pieces of (unsourced) information to me during my inquiry and he instructed that certain passages, written by himself, be inserted into it'.[64]

It was immediately clear that the investigation that led to the Browse Mole Report was instituted with an eye on the succession debate; perhaps, it has been intimated, as a means to undermine Zuma's credibility at a key time, or as justification for mobilising additional state resources to sift through the detritus of his political campaign. What was less clear at the time, however, was how spectacularly the tactic would backfire.

Days after the report was leaked to Cosatu, the organisation, along with the SACP, wrote a number of letters to the DSO and other bodies requesting that its provenance be investigated.[65] Only days later, sections were being run in the media. Finally bowing to political pressure, Thabo Mbeki agreed to institute an investigation into the report, headed by the NIA's Arthur Fraser – a move that, as we will see later, may have had a major impact in clearing Jacob Zuma's path to power. The NIA's findings were, in turn, handed to Parliament's Joint Standing Committee on Intelligence, which fairly eviscerated the Browse Mole Report in its own release in 2007. Concurring with the findings of the NIA, the Joint Standing Committee found that:

❏ The Browse Mole Report is reflective of typical information peddling traits;
❏ The DSO has fallen prey to dubious activities of information peddlers. The context to this is that the DSO is involved in intelligence collection activities for which they do not have the required competency neither the experience. Further, that they believed in the substance of the information generated. The DSO made use of private intelligence companies;
❏ Law Enforcement Agencies have as yet not taken action against these peddlers, even though they are known to produce and disseminate defamatory and subversive documents;
❏ Indications are that information peddlers make use of 'facilitators' and or have access to some senior leaders of the ruling party;
❏ The probability exists that the leakage was timed, due to the non responsiveness of the law enforcement agencies. The determination is that these peddlers are driven by a need to create division within the ruling party; and,
❏ These peddlers have links to foreign government including Foreign Intelligence Services. This raises serious concerns

about the role played by these Foreign Intelligence Services in this matter.[66]

With these damning parliamentary findings, it was hard to dispute the idea that those hostile to Jacob Zuma were using state resources to undermine his campaign for the presidency; that there was indeed a political conspiracy. What had started as a search for a smoking gun to stop Zuma's campaign had turned into the biggest advertorial for his claims of innocence.

That the Browse Mole Report was undertaken by the Scorpions – despite their not having the mandate to conduct intelligence – also seemed to prove that the entirety of the organisation was inflected with partisan prejudice: the unfortunate and certainly incorrect inference being that Zuma's corruption charges, emanating from a Scorpions investigation, were fabricated in a similar manner. Just when the Scorpions were starting to face the loudest calls for their disbandment, despite their stellar performance in fighting organised crime, the report confirmed what many had long been saying: it was time to remove their sting. Such was the institutional cost of the Zuma–Mbeki confrontation, and the (mis-) use of intelligence functions.

The loss of the Scorpions was not the only burden placed on the public by the Browse Mole debacle. Certainty was also a victim, with many questions left unanswered. In particular, citizens were left to grapple with one key concern: how much of the report was a pure fabrication, and how much accurately described reality? According to the *Mail & Guardian*, the claims of military intervention were clearly bunk that 'blend[ed] fact with fiction'.[67] However, the reports that Zuma may have relied on the financial and political support of Angola appeared sounder. In particular, the *Mail & Guardian* noted that the source that was relied on for the Angolan information had been used in the past by both the National Intelligence Agency and the South African Secret Service, which was not exactly how an 'information peddler' would be treated.[68] Indeed, it was reportedly this source that had tipped off the South African government about the coup plot in Equatorial Guinea. Zuma insiders, too, confirmed that Angola had sought to provide political support to Zuma, but that the promised funding had never materialised.[69]

Another mystery also remains unresolved: just who had leaked the Browse Mole Report to Cosatu? Parliament's Joint Standing Committee on Defence found that it was Powell, himself, who had sent a fax of the document to the organisation.[70] Powell, however, has disputed this vociferously.[71] In addition, no convincing evidence has been provided to explain why he would leak a document that would be so clearly damning to himself and the Scorpions, the organisation he worked for. Perhaps this is just an academic matter: the real infraction was committed by those in the Scorpions who decided to initiate the investigation. But, at another level, it illustrated that, somewhere in the bowels of the security apparatus, somebody was watching Zuma's back.

The Zuma trial

Though Zuma may often have seemed to be on the back foot in these intelligence exchanges, he proved to have both means and inclination to retaliate. Indeed, on two separate occasions, both related to the corruption charges brought against Schabir Shaik and, later, Zuma himself, intelligence was used to try and prevent the trial being brought to court.

In August 2003, Bulelani Ngcuka, the National Director of Public Prosecutions, announced to the nation that the NPA was about to prosecute Schabir Shaik. The charges: that Shaik had engineered a corrupt relationship with Jacob Zuma, which included the solicitation of a bribe from the French arms maker Thomson-CSF on Zuma's behalf.[72] Zuma, meanwhile, was not to be prosecuted, despite there being an alleged 'prima facie case' against him.[73] While it was almost certainly a major misstep to fail to prosecute Zuma at this stage, and the ambiguity was a source of considerable angst for him and his supporters, Zuma's political career would be inextricably bound to the trial about to unfold.

Slightly over two weeks after Ngcuka's statement, *City Press* ran a now-famous article that drew extensively on documents written and compiled during the ANC's Operation Bible intelligence project, which had been staffed primarily by the Shaik family and supervised by Jacob Zuma.[74] The documents pointed to a bizarre allegation, namely, that

Bulelani Ngcuka had once served as an apartheid spy with the code-name RS452. It was all quite incontrovertible, according to Moe Shaik, Schabir Shaik's brother and a key mover and shaker behind Operation Bible: 'By late 1989, the unit in South Africa had come to the conclusion that there was a basis for suspecting Bulelani Ngcuka as being RS452.'[75]

It was immediately obvious that the Operation Bible documents had been leaked in order to sully Ngcuka's name following his 23 August announcement. A respected journalist, Jovial Rantao, commented: 'There can only be one reason for unleashing allegations as damaging as these. It is the desire by people – desperate people – to turn the focus away from themselves. It's a smokescreen ... Quite clearly, these are tough times and there are desperate people out there. They are not only desperate but it would seem they are afraid. The innocent are never afraid. They never get desperate.'[76] Moe Shaik would later confirm much of this point. 'I went public with the allegations about Ngcuka in order to defend the honour of the deputy president of this country,' he explained. 'I believe this ongoing personal investigation is because [Ngcuka] is aware that Zuma conducted an investigation into him in the late 1980s.'[77]

The publication of spy allegations would undoubtedly have touched a nerve with Thabo Mbeki, who had, at various times in exile, been falsely accused of being a counter-revolutionary agent.[78] In order to get to the bottom of the matter, Mbeki appointed a Commission of Inquiry led by Judge Joos Hefer. As matters proceeded, it was quickly apparent that the Hefer Commission was likely to be a farce. Only days after the public hearings began, the claims against Ngcuka were fatally undermined. In a front-page exposé, the former Eastern Cape human rights lawyer, Vanessa Brereton, admitted that she was agent RS452.[79] The codename had been given to her by her handlers in the apartheid security forces for an intelligence exercise – 'Operation Crocus' – designed to gather information on the activities of the 'white left'. For Brereton, who felt enormous guilt for her actions during apartheid, the linking of Ngcuka to her agent number was simply unconscionable: 'I was RS452,' she confirmed, 'and I have had enough of the lies and deceit.'[80]

The situation clearly needed rescuing, and sure enough, another set of complicated claims was presented against Ngcuka at the Hefer Commission.[81] These focused on the arrest of three comrades who had run an underground unit in Natal during apartheid. According to the new allegations, Ngcuka had informed on the members of the unit, leading to their incarceration. But even this allegation could not stand up for long. One leading member of the unit (Ntobeko Maqhubela), who testified before the Hefer Commission in October 2003, claimed that it was 'impossible' for Ngcuka to have sold the unit out to the security police[82] – he had not even been aware of the unit's existence before he was similarly arrested and placed in detention along with the unit's members. More to the point, Maqhubela confirmed that those who ran Operation Bible were well aware of this fact,[83] suggesting that the reworked claims against Ngcuka had been levelled without much care for the truth of the matter.

The findings were unsurprising. According to Judge Hefer, 'Mr Ngcuka probably never acted as an agent for the pre-1994 government security service ... the allegations of spying have not been established. The suspicion which a small number of distrustful individuals harboured against him 14 years ago was the unfortunate result of ill-founded references and groundless assumptions.'[84]

The Hefer Commission of Inquiry had quite clearly exonerated Ngcuka on this point. But it also had another impact: it sent a message, loud and clear, that the extensive intelligence archive on which Vula and Bible operatives sat could not be used to score political points in the post-apartheid era. Outing opponents as apartheid spies could have only limited political clout and would likely be followed by some sort of investigation that could only point to the rawness of primary intelligence data gathered in extreme circumstances. But this was not to suggest that Zuma's camp did not still have some very useful friends in key places in the intelligence community.

In April 2009, Mokotedi Mpshe, the Acting Head of the NPA, delivered a much-anticipated address to the nation. The will-he, won't-he of the case against Zuma seemed to have reached a point of no return. Mpshe began by announcing that he had reached a decision he characterised as the 'most difficult' of his life.[85] Based on a series of spy tapes that had been acquired by Zuma's legal team and presented to the NPA, Mpshe's team had come to the conclusion that the former head of the NPA, Bulelani Ngcuka, had conspired with the head of the Scorpions,

Leonard McCarthy, along with others, to manipulate the prosecution against Jacob Zuma for political ends. The result: 'an intolerable abuse has occurred which compels a discontinuation of the prosecution'.[86]

Mpshe quoted extensively from the tapes that had been presented to the NPA. References in the conversations to 'the big man' have led some to speculate that the conspirators were engaging with Thabo Mbeki, giving a Watergate-like air to the recordings. And the language was certainly expressive: shortly after Mbeki's defeat at Polokwane, one voice-mail message left by Leonard McCarthy was quoted as saying 'we are still wiping the blood from our faces, or egg, or egg and blood from our faces. Saw the man on Friday evening, we are planning a comeback strategy.'[87] The inference was, of course, that the charges of racketeering against Jacob Zuma were nothing more than a political conspiracy of the highest order.

How Zuma's legal team got hold of the spy tapes is something of a mystery. If they were recorded privately, they were almost certainly legally questionable. And if they were provided by a member of the security services prior to declassification, that, too, would have been a serious offence. 'If the South African Police Service and the National Prosecuting Authority (NPA) took seriously its job to uphold the law and act without fear, favour, or prejudice (in other words, if it adhered to the rule of law), it would be hard at work preparing for the prosecution of those responsible for breaking the law,' Professor Pierre de Vos, a respected Constitutional Law specialist, commented. 'One or more members of the intelligence service or the SAP obviously broke the law by leaking the tapes to the Zuma camp (or perhaps President Zuma, if he was shown to ever be in possession of the tapes) also broke the law by receiving those tapes. This is because private citizens (which both Hulley [Zuma's lawyer] and Zuma were at the time) are not allowed to possess such classified information.'[88]

What is known is that, when Mpshe's team were evaluating the spy tapes, they approached the National Intelligence Agency for confirmation. The NIA could confirm that the tapes were genuine, and for a deeply ironic reason: they had monitored the very same people who appeared in the Zuma spy tapes as part of an investigation into the Browse Mole affair.[89] Browse Mole, if it was intended as a means to smear Zuma, had thus backfired in two spectacular ways: it confirmed, at the time of its leaking, that there were elements in the Scorpions who were abusing their office to thwart Zuma's presidential ambitions; and it provided the means by which the tapes that secured Zuma's release from prosecution could be independently verified.

This has led some to suggest that, in fact, Zuma had secured the tapes from the very same source that had verified them: the NIA investigative team that was investigating the Browse Mole affair. According to a *Mail & Guardian* investigation, it was alleged by three independent sources that the tapes had been leaked to Jacob Zuma's legal team by Arthur Fraser, the deputy head of the NIA. Fraser, importantly, had headed the Browse Mole investigation, and had conducted legal surveillance of those mentioned in Mpshe's decision. One source claimed that Fraser felt the need to ingratiate himself with the new administration.[90] Fraser and his office have denied the allegation.

Another theory suggests a different source. According to papers filed by Faiek Davids in the Commission for Conciliation, Mediation and Arbitration, the former deputy of the Special Investigating Unit, who was mentioned in the spy tapes, Willie Hofmeyr, who had listened to the tapes on Mpshe's behalf, had claimed that the tapes had been leaked by police intelligence. As such, these recordings would have been made illegally and for deeply nefarious purposes. Davids further alleged that the recordings had been made by police intelligence functionaries (in an operation revealingly titled 'Destroy Lucifer') in order to illegally monitor the progress of a Scorpions investigation into police chief Jackie Selebi.[91]

It seems unlikely that the South African public will ever know the true source of the tapes that secured Zuma's release. Shortly after the charges were dropped, the Inspector-General for Intelligence, Zolile Ngcakani, conducted an investigation into how his legal team had acquired the tapes. Ngcakani had written the initial report into the hoax email saga, fingering Masetlha and his colleagues as the authors of the fake emails. His report into the spy tape issue was, in turn, handed over to Parliament's Joint Standing Committee on Intelligence in 2010.[92] However, the Standing Committee, much to the chagrin of opposition parties and commentators, refused to publish the report or allow any public access to its findings. ANC MP Cecil Burgess, who has also chaired the committee overseeing deliberations into the Secrecy Bill (see below), reportedly claimed that he saw no need for it to be released to the public. The DA, meanwhile, has indicated that it intends to file a Promotion of Access to Information request to access the document, as it clearly does not relate to any issue of national security.[93]

South Africans were left scratching their heads. How Zuma's legal team got hold of the spy tapes was not the only unanswered question; there was the veracity of the charges themselves, and also the wisdom of Mpshe's decision. The latter's credibility soon took a battering when it emerged that the most substantive part of his announcement – a detailed legal justification for the decision – had been extensively plagiarised from a judgment delivered by the Hong Kong judge Colin Seagroatt.[94] What was more, Seagroatt's judgment had been overturned on appeal – it was not even considered 'live' jurisprudence in the jurisdiction where the judgment was delivered.[95] When Seagroatt was interviewed about Mpshe's decision, he was bemused that Mpshe had even relied on his original reasoning: '[I find it] impossible to identify why he was relying on my judgment ... It is very strongly arguable that [Mpshe] should have let the trial process begin before a judge, leaving the aspect which seems to have dominated his proper role as a prosecutor (the old adage being a "prosecutor's job is to prosecute") to be determined by a judge.'[96]

There was also the issue of what the spy tapes actually illustrated. A close reading of the transcripts included in Mpshe's decision suggested that McCarthy and co had been discussing the timing of the charges to be brought against Zuma. Certainly, if this was the case, it was a highly questionable course of action. But it did not show in any way that the charges against Zuma had been manufactured from thin air, or that the entire prosecution (including the actions of all those involved in the case, such as the prosecutors and detectives who worked in the Scorpions) was undertaken for any other reason than to present objective evidence that could be tested before the courts.

Vitally, Mpshe's decision also flew in the face of a Supreme Court decision that had only recently been delivered. After Judge Chris Nicholson had decided to squash the charges against Jacob Zuma, finding, as an additional matter, that there was 'baleful' political interference in his trial, the matter had been referred to the Supreme Court of Appeal.[97] In a unanimous decision reached only three months before Mpshe's announcement, the five judges of the Supreme Court lashed Nicholson for making his findings on the matter of political interference even though the matter was not 'an issue that had to be determined' by Nicholson. The result was that Nicholson 'changed the rules of the game, took his eyes off the ball and red-carded not only players but also spectators'.[98]

Most importantly, the Supreme Court found that, even if there was a political motivation in bringing the charges, this was irrelevant: what mattered was whether or not there existed a reasonable case against Zuma, which was something he never denied:

> A prosecution is not wrongful merely because it is brought for an improper purpose. It will only be wrongful if, in addition, reasonable and probable grounds for prosecuting are absent, something not alleged by Mr. Zuma and which in any event can only be determined once criminal proceedings have been concluded. The motive behind the prosecution is irrelevant because ... the best motive does not cure an otherwise illegal arrest and the worst motive does not render an otherwise legal arrest illegal. The same applies to prosecutions.[99]

Remarkably, when Mpshe announced his decision, he admitted that the decision to drop the charges against Zuma had nothing to do with whether the case was reasonably constructed on the basis of evidence at the Scorpions' disposal:

> The representations submitted by legal representatives pertained to the following issues:
> ❏ The substantive merits
> ❏ The fair trial defences
> ❏ The practical implications and considerations of continued prosecution
> ❏ The policy aspects militating against prosecution.
>   I need to state upfront that we could not find anything with

regard to the first three grounds that militate against a continuation of the prosecution ...[100]

In other words, Zuma's representations could do nothing to prove that
there was not a reasonable case against him, that he would not receive a
fair trial, or that a trial would be unusually burdensome from a logistical
standpoint. Instead, Mpshe relied on the matter of political interference, which the Supreme Court had explicitly ruled out as a reason to
halt the prosecution taking place.

And what of the substantive charges that had been laid against Zuma?
As should be obvious to anyone with a passing interest in South African
politics, Zuma should be treated as innocent until proven guilty. But
this does not mean that it is necessarily wrong to believe that he had a
strong case to answer. This much was made clear when Schabir Shaik
was found guilty by Judge Hilary Squires in 2005. In reaching his judgment on whether Shaik and Zuma had a 'mutually beneficial symbiosis',
Squires found that the evidence presented by the prosecutors was 'overwhelming'.[101] Some choice findings included:

> ... in our view that Zuma did in fact intervene to try and assist
> Shaik's business interests. While it may be accepted that his
> intervention on behalf of Shaik to relieve the threatened ex-
> clusion of Nkobi interest in ADS and the munitions suite con-
> tract, was undertaken as Deputy President of the ANC and
> would not, in the absence of any alleged and known duty vest-
> ed in that office that was discharged or subverted for Shaik's
> benefit, constitute a contravention of Act 94 of 1992. But it
> clearly shows ... a readiness in both Shaik to turn to Zuma for
> his help, and Zuma's readiness to give it ...
>
> In our view no sane or rational businessman would conduct
> his business on such a basis without expecting some benefit
> from it that would make it worthwhile ...
>
> It would be flying in the face of commonsense and ordinary
> human nature to think that he did not realise the advantages
> to him of continuing to enjoy Zuma's goodwill to an even
> greater extent than before 1997; and even if nothing was ever

said between them to establish the mutually beneficial symbiosis that the evidence shows existed, the circumstances of the commencement and the sustained continuation thereafter of these payments, can only have generated a sense of obligation in the recipient.

If Zuma could not repay money, how else could he do so than by providing the help of his name and political office as and when it was asked, particularly in the field of government contracted work, which is what Shaik was hoping to benefit from. And Shaik must have foreseen and, by inference, did foresee that if he made these payments, Zuma would respond in that way. The conclusion that he realised this, even if only after he started the dependency of Zuma upon his contributions, seems to us to be irresistible.[102]

It is entirely unclear what Zuma's defence would be if these findings were ever to be contested in court; he has never, in any affidavit, provided any details as to how he would contest the facts presented in court and in the original indictments against him beyond alleging that the case against him was politically motivated. Some indication of what his defence might have been was given in his official ANC biography, released on 5 May 2009. In a paragraph that has since been removed from the ANC website, the biography claimed that:

Over the course of eight years, his [Zuma's] rights, privacy and dignity were repeatedly violations [sic]. The accusations arose out of his relationship with friends and comrade, Schabir Shaik, who was his financial adviser.

This relationship has been frequently misrepresented. The plight of returning exiles forced them to seek financial support from friends and relatives. In the case of Shaik, Zuma solicited a loan with an undertaking to repay, which Zuma had started to do. Despite the fact that Zuma had no involvement in the arms deal, and had no power to 'protect' companies involved in the deal, prosecutors tried to link the loan to the arms deal.[103]

Many of these defences had already been dealt with in the trial of Schabir Shaik and rejected out of hand in the light of evidence presented. Notably, the courts in question had rejected the claim that the payments from Shaik to Zuma were loans – mostly because Zuma was never in a financial position to feasibly make the repayments. But, most importantly, the 'loans' were issued without interest at the very time that other banks and lending institutions would be reluctant to lend to Zuma. 'Even if these could be regarded as loans despite all evidence to the contrary,' Judge Squires commented in his judgment, 'the basis on which they were made would, in our view, unarguably amount to a "benefit" within the meaning of the word in the Corruption Act.'[104]

South African citizens are thus thrown into an odd situation. On the one hand, the full details of the judgment against Schabir Shaik have been in the public domain for years. On the other, Zuma cannot be accused of any wrongdoing in this regard without defaming his character. It is a schizophrenic position, to say the least. South Africans will never know what Zuma's defence is, or indeed whether there is sufficient evidence to convict him of a raft of incredibly serious charges. It cannot but be considered darkly ironic that this situation of confusion, doubt and uncertainty was facilitated by the use and abuse of the intelligence services.

A broken record: intelligence and the Zuma presidency

When Zuma finally took power in 2009, many hoped that it would mark the end of the intelligence wars as the partisan demands of the Mbeki–Zuma contest faded into the past. In reality, the uses and abuses of intelligence have remained a persistent feature of the South African political environment; so much so, that one of the most democratically questionable pieces of legislation proposed since the end of apartheid may indeed emanate from the continuing predominance of intelligence's partisan politicking.

That intelligence, and private intelligence networks, would remain a feature of the post-Mbeki era was confirmed soon after Zuma took power as the head of state. Wielding a large broom, he swept away the most obviously pro-Mbeki functionaries from his Cabinet. To replace them, he did not turn exclusively to the assorted Alliance members who had backed him during the succession race. For many key functions (notably in the intelligence and security clusters), he turned to long-trusted comrades from the days of Operations Vula and Bible. According to an intriguing article by Zuma's biographer, Jeremy Gordin, luminaries of these operations who would feature prominently in the administration included Siphiwe Nyanda (Zuma's first Minister of Communications and Chief of the SANDF during the Arms Deal); Moe Shaik (a close confidant whom Zuma appointed head of the country's Secret Services); Nathi Mthethwa (Zuma's Minister of Police); Pravin Gordhan (Zuma's Finance Minister); Raymond Lala (one-time head of SAPS intelligence) and Solly Shoke (currently Chief of the SANDF).[105]

Of all the appointments, Moe Shaik's promotion to the position of foreign spy chief was the one that attracted the most criticism. The DA, for example, commented that Shaik's 'appointment has clearly been made to consolidate the Zuma faction's hold over the South African intelligence community'.[106] The Congress of the People, meanwhile, argued that 'Shaik has distinguished himself as being unprofessional [and] partisan.'[107] And while the ANC claimed he was appointed due to his vast experience of intelligence functions, it was hard not to recall the Hefer Commission debacle as evidence that Shaik was willing to use confidential intelligence for partisan and personal political ends. Such criticism was ramped up in January 2011, when the inflammatory site Wikileaks released confidential US embassy cables describing meetings between Shaik and US diplomats. In one 2008 meeting only two days before Judge Nicholson squashed the charges against Zuma, Shaik threatened to 'expose' the 'political skeletons' of anti-Zuma individuals if the charges were not dropped.[108] Hardly the words of a man who was ignorant of the political power of selective use and abuse of intelligence, or of one likely to accept the outcome of judicial processes.

Confirmation that intelligence was still a key political battleground during Zuma's presidency was received in early 2011. In March of that year, the head of Police Intelligence, Richard Mdluli, appeared in court.

He was charged with a number of offences, most notably that of murder. According to the state, Mdluli and two accomplices had plotted the murder of one Oupa Ramogibe in 1999, additionally engaging in a cover-up to prevent the matter reaching court.[109] It was alleged that Ramogibe had married Richard Mdluli's former lover, and that Mdluli had orchestrated the murder and cover-up.[110]

Mdluli loudly protested his innocence, and to prove it, declassified yet another inflammatory intelligence report that soon found its way to the media. The 'ground coverage intelligence report', allegedly funded to the tune of R200 000 by Police Intelligence,[111] emerged from a police investigation into alleged corruption involving police chief Bheki Cele. It outlined a sophisticated plot to remove Jacob Zuma from power and to discredit the name of Richard Mdluli himself. Once again, Tokyo Sexwale was alleged to be at the centre of the plot, leading what was named the Mvela Group (referring to Sexwale's company, Mvelaphanda) in an attempt to replace Zuma at the ANC's 53rd National Conference in 2012.[112] The Mvela Group allegedly included Bheki Cele, along with a number of other high-profile politicians.

Most in the ANC responded with incredulity to the 'ground coverage intelligence report'. Sexwale was the most vocal, hosting a media briefing to explicitly deny the existence of an anti-Zuma plot and to call for a full investigation into its compilation.[113] Some were less critical. In a bizarre move, Billy Masetlha, firmly in the Zuma camp following the hoax email saga, claimed that the report had some credence. 'There is no smoke without fire,' he explained to the *Mail & Guardian*. 'I know who they [the plotters] are talking to and how they want to do this. I am not going to keep quiet and watch people destroying the organization.'[114] Zuma himself was reported to have treated the report with scepticism,[115] although questions remained as to why he had sat on it for so long without informing other members of the NEC, since it had been sent to him months before the charges were laid against Mdluli.

In late 2011 and early 2012, the Mdluli story took a bizarre turn. All the charges against him, which included not only murder but also fraud and corruption related to the alleged abuse of witness protection funds, were suddenly dropped.[116] The official explanation was somewhat confusing: the NPA suddenly believed that the best way to pursue the charges was by means of an official inquest rather than a court case. The decision was further clouded by the suspension on charges of misconduct of Advocate Glynnis Breytenbach, a senior specialised commercial crime unit investigator. Rumours abounded that she had faced suspension for pursuing the Mdluli case, among others, with somewhat too much commitment,[117] rumours the NPA denied wholeheartedly.[118] Similar rumours alleged that Mdluli had the ear of Jacob Zuma, and was keen to assume Cele's old role at the apex of the police.

Once again, South African citizens are left scratching their heads, although perhaps the country's recent history of intelligence splurges has made some sceptical of the various claims and counter-claims. But what is certain is that the intelligence services, and the security cluster as a whole, are still engaged in the dirty business of compiling dossiers on political enemies, leading South Africa on yet another roller-coaster ride in the run-up to the 2012 elective conference. The *Mail & Guardian*, for example, commented that the report and its fallout had a 'depressingly familiar quality'.[119] *The Witness*, meanwhile, let loose some more light-hearted barbs: 'Conspiracies, the whispering of names, intelligence structures, an upcoming election of leaders ... sound familiar?'[120] And there is cause for suspicion that only more will follow: 'Bugged telephone conversations allegedly proving a political conspiracy against Zuma helped Zuma in his corruption case. Expect more of the same in the run-up to Mangaung.'[121]

The dreaded Secrecy Bill should perhaps be viewed through this prism. The proposed legislation, officially named the Protection of Information Bill, sets the legal limits for the distribution of classified information.[122] The draft Bill significantly broadens the power of relevant Ministers and government officials to classify documents at will. It stipulates incredibly harsh jail terms – a maximum of 25 years, in one instance – if someone publishes, distributes or merely holds possession of a classified document.[123] Despite repeated calls from civil society to radically modify the Bill, and to include a public interest clause, the ANC has remained steadfast in support of the legislation. Unless there is severe political pressure, it is difficult to see how the legislation could pass muster if challenged in the Constitutional Court – it so drastically undercuts the freedom of the press and constitutionally mandated provisions of access to information that any other finding by the Court would have to be viewed askance.

Much of the commentary about the Secrecy Bill has focused on its impact on the media and accountability, which is not surprising, considering that the draft Bill was submitted at the very same time that the ANC began the process that would have led to the creation of a much-feared Media Tribunal. But less attention has been paid to the fact that the Bill would drastically consolidate power in those hands already on the tiller of the state. It is the possession clause, above all, that gives rise to the suspicion that it is aimed at reining in potential rogue intelligence agents. It would be illegal, if the Bill were to pass, for rogue intelligence reports to do the rounds in the ANC's back rooms, finally emerging into the light of the media. It would also prevent leaks that might be embarrassing to any state incumbent, whether threatening to national security or not.

And yet it would not prevent intelligence from being gathered, coursing through the state to the executive, who would have the legal right to view it and, if necessary, declassify it ahead of a strategic leak. Intelligence would, under the Bill, be given legal cover to undertake the most severe abuses of power and partisan politicking it could conceive: but it would be only one faction – the one in control of the state – that could harness it for their own ends.

If information is power, then the Secrecy Bill strictly constrains who is able to wield it and to what end. In the contest over political ideas, the Secrecy Bill would thus make the political playing field uneven to the point of farce.

Chapter 6

The Last Bastions: Judiciary, Media and Civil Society

Paul Holden

Over the last 18 years, South Africa's democratic institutions, and especially those that exist in the orbit of the legislature and executive, have been buffeted by attempts to limit their independence. Chapter 9 institutions and Parliament in particular have, as we have seen in the previous two chapters, been brought to heel to ensure that their activities exercise only limited accountability over the executive and the ANC. Those institutions and sites that exist outside of executive and legislative purview have faced similar pressures, but have to date put up a far stronger resistance than the country's other more compromised institutions.

Outside of the political tent exist three key sites of independence and accountability: the judiciary, the independent media (largely print and online) and civil society organisations. Each has acted as a powerful and deeply necessary corrective against the more authoritarian proclivities of various public figures. But, as a result, they have incurred the wrath of the ANC. If one thing could unite the Mbeki and Zuma factions, it would likely be distaste for the media and meddlesome think-tanks and protest groups. Recently, such pressures have intensified, with each of these three sites facing their most severe challenges to date. How well they weather the storm – if they do at all, which is far from certain – will do much to determine the robustness of South Africa's democratic future.

The guardians of the Constitution

During apartheid, power was concentrated within the executive and Parliament in a way that militated against the establishment of an independent judiciary. South Africa was run in the Westminster style: Parliament was tasked with debating and enacting legislation, over which the judiciary had strictly limited powers of review.[1] The judiciary were merely asked to interpret the existing laws and could do little – seldom beyond making stray judicial observations – to ensure that they adhered to universal principles of human rights. The appointment of Chief Justices and other senior judges exclusively from within the ranks of senior counsel limited the type and world views of the judges who would interpret such legislation. In addition, it was made abundantly clear that career progression for judges would be based on political affiliation and an eager executive-mindedness. One such example was Chief Justice LC Steyn, whose 'meteoric' rise to the position of Chief Justice in the early 1980s was scathingly described by now-Judge Edwin Cameron; Steyn's seniority ensured that the apartheid state was often able to rely on a pliant judiciary to enforce its network of constrictive and racist laws.[2] The result of these factors, according to judicial commentator Hugh Corder, was a largely stolid and conservative judiciary that failed to question South Africa's fundamentally questionable laws:

> The overall picture [of judicial attitudes] which emerges is one of a group of men who saw their dominant roles as the protectors of a stability ... The judges expressed it in terms of a positivistic acceptance of legislative sovereignty, despite a patently racist political structure, and a desire to preserve the existing order of legal relations, notwithstanding its basis in manifest social inequalities.[3]

The post-1994 dispensation was to be fundamentally different – in a way that would ensure that no tyranny of a future authoritarian Parliament would be able to erode 'universally accepted'[4] human rights. Parliament would, in this system, be free to enact the laws it chose. The judiciary, and in particular the Constitutional Court, could, however, overturn these laws if they did not abide by the precepts of the Constitution and the Bill of Rights – arguably the most important document of the post-1994 consensus. In addition, the pre-eminence of the Constitution as *the* supreme law of the land meant that government action (as well as private action, such as discrimination) was subject to the overview of the Constitutional Court. If government acted unconstitutionally – as has been found on a number of occasions, as described later – the Constitutional Court was empowered to order it to desist in such activity as well as provide remedies to ensure such infractions did not occur again. The Court was also empowered to overturn the judgments of the lower courts (the Supreme Court of Appeal, High and magistrates' courts) in matters dealing with constitutional issues, a powerful means of ensuring that, in the immediate post-apartheid period, the rest of the judiciary (then still to be transformed) infused constitutional principles into their jurisprudence. Thus, while South Africa's governance structure was to be predicated on a separation of powers between the executive, judiciary and executive, the Constitutional Court was, in a sense, 'first among equals'.[5]

This does not mean that the Constitutional Court operates without oversight from the other arms of government. First, judges of the Constitutional Court are to be appointed by the President, who is required to apply his mind to the recommendations given by the Judicial Service Commission (JSC). The JSC is a 23-member council that undertakes the interviewing of potential judicial appointments (for the Constitutional Court and other courts) and makes recommendations to the President on the basis of these interviews.[6] The make-up of the JSC is purposefully heterogeneous, but, importantly, includes at least six members of the National Assembly and three other persons specifically appointed by the President.[7] This process of appointment means that judges who do ascend to the Constitutional Court have to be considered fit and proper, but, also, according to the perception of certain critics, at least largely adhere to the principles of the contemporaneous political environment. Second, judges can be removed from their positions by political processes – if the JSC finds that the judge 'suffers from incapacity, is grossly incompetent or is guilty of gross misconduct', and the National Assembly adopts a resolution that has the support of two-thirds of its members.[8]

In the immediate post-1994 period, the creation of the Constitutional Court did much to mitigate the worries of how a discredited judicial class could be relied upon to protect and guide democratic jurisprudence. By widening the net of judicial appointments to include academics and other suitable candidates (rather than just the limited paddling pool that marked the apartheid era), it was also possible to rapidly install new judges more obviously committed to the democratic order. Both moves granted the judiciary a legitimacy it may not so easily have expected, considering its apartheid legacy.[9] Indeed, the Constitutional Court was considered of sufficient legitimacy to act as the body to certify the final Constitution itself, suggesting it had considerable cachet amongst all members of the negotiating teams.

As is well known, the country's final Constitution was adopted in 1996, after much debate in the Constitutional Assembly. Prior to promulgation, however, it was sent for certification to the Constitutional Court, which assessed the draft according to 34 constitutional principles that the negotiating parties had agreed to and included in the Interim Constitution, 1993. Upon reviewing the draft, the Constitutional Court found certain instances where the draft did not abide by the principles, and ordered that the document be amended to do so.[10] The Court was thus not only birthed by the (interim) Constitution; the (final) Constitution was also midwifed by the Court itself.

The Constitution itself is remarkable for any number of reasons, not least because its anti-discrimination clauses ensure that previously persecuted minorities – gay and lesbian communities in particular – are finally afforded the dignity of liberty. But equally important is the fact that the Constitution sees South Africa as a dynamic society: it both enables and demands a fundamental reshaping of the socio-economic landscape. In a major insight, the esteemed legal expert and advocate Geoff Budlender noted that 'our Constitution differs from many others in a fundamental respect. Most Constitutions reflect the outcome of a change which has already taken place, and lay down the framework for the new society. A key theme of *our* Constitution is the change which is yet to come – the transformation which is yet to come.'[11] In one key judgment (*Soobramoney*, discussed below), the Court made this fact abundantly clear:

> We live in a society in which there are great disparities in wealth. Millions of people are living in deplorable conditions and in great poverty. There is a high level of unemployment, inadequate social security, and many do not have access to clean water or to adequate health services. These conditions already existed when the Constitution was adopted and a commitment to address them, and to transform our society into one in which there will be human dignity, freedom and equality, lies at the heart of our new constitutional order. For as long as these conditions continue to exist that aspiration will have a hollow ring.[12]

The transformation envisaged by the drafters of the Constitution is most clearly codified in the Bill of Rights, which 'applies to all law, and binds the legislature, the executive, the judiciary and all organs of state'.[13] In particular, three sections stipulate that every person in South Africa has the right to certain baseline economic necessities: section 26 states that 'everyone has the right to housing'; section 27 secures the 'right to have access to health care services, sufficient food and water, and social security assistance'; section 29 does the same for basic education. Sections 26 (health care) and 27 (housing) further stipulate that the state would have to take active steps to achieve these rights: 'The state must take reasonable legislative and other measures, within its available resources, to achieve the progressive realisation of each of these rights.'[14] It is in this way that the Constitution was most radical – for the first time ever in South Africa (and in contrast to the majority of Western democracies), citizens can take government institutions to court for failing to meet their basic socio-economic needs as stipulated in the Constitution. Socio-economic rights are, simply put, justiciable.

The inclusion of justiciable socio-economic rights in the Constitution broadens the purview of the Constitutional Court. It provides the mechanism by which the Constitutional Court is empowered, in appropriate cases, to assess government action according to constitutional principle. It is certainly a much more substantial role than merely ensuring that legislation passes constitutional muster, and almost inevitably has introduced an extra element of tension into the relationship between the judiciary and the executive. And seeing as the ANC has bridled at limitations on executive power and the easy path granted by handsome legislative majorities, some sort of conflict between the government and the Constitutional Court has been predictable.

Despite the noises now emanating regarding the powers of the Constitutional Court (dealt with below), this tension is arguably something to which the judiciary has often been alive – arguably leading to a more cautious jurisprudence than many social activists might desire. Three key cases illustrate the Constitutional Court's approach to litigating socio-economic rights. In the first, *Soobramoney v Minister of Health, KwaZulu-Natal*, the litigant (Soobramoney) attempted to get the Constitutional Court to order that he should be placed on life-saving dialysis by a state hospital to prolong his life, despite the fact that his general physical health (terminal illness) meant that such treatment was usually not given to people in his condition.[15] In the second, *Government of South Africa v Grootboom*, the Court was asked to assess whether the eviction of citizens was constitutional when the state could not provide adequate replacement housing.[16] In the third, *Minister of Health v The Treatment Action Campaign* (TAC), the Court was asked to review the failure of the state to provide pregnant mothers with access to antiretroviral drugs that could prevent mother-to-child HIV transmission as well as prolong the lives of those afflicted with the disease.[17] The results for the government were mixed. In the Soobramoney case, the Court found in favour of the state's policies, while in both the Grootboom and TAC cases, the Court determined the government's actions were unconstitutional.

To adjudicate the cases, the Constitutional Court had to decide on what basis it could determine the constitutionality of government action: it had to 'fill in' the content of the broad (and vague) clauses included in the Bill of Rights. One potential avenue would have been to adopt what is known as the 'minimum core' approach. The 'minimum core' principle has been most clearly articulated by the UN's Committee on Economic, Social and Cultural Rights, which is empowered to oversee the International Covenant on Economic Social and Cultural Rights.[18] In a major piece of clarification published in 1990, the Committee argued that it was incumbent on all states who were party to the Covenant to ensure that a basic minimum of socio-economic services were to be delivered to every citizen.

If the Court had adopted this position, the impact would have been profound: it would effectively have established itself as a potential governance monitor, prescribing that the government provided a basic level of socio-economic services to every person in the country. It would have hugely increased the Court's remit and would have encouraged the Court to establish a universal 'minimum core' of obligations that the government had to fulfil – what could be construed as a form of 'intense judicial activism' or, at the very least, an adoption of a policy-making function that is typically the preserve of government.[19] Some activists and legal experts were in favour of such an approach, as it would act as a mechanism that provided a baseline of delivery against which the state could be measured.[20] Without it, it was feared, enforcement of the Bill of Rights would lack 'teeth'.[21]

Instead of adopting the 'minimum core' approach, however, the Constitutional Court developed a different line of argument, referred to as 'reasonableness'.[22] As Murray Wesson has neatly summarised, the Court reasoned in *Grootboom* 'that a program implemented in order to realise a socio-economic right must be "comprehensive", "coherent", "balanced" and "flexible". More importantly, the Court insists that a "program that excludes a significant sector of society cannot be said to be reasonable."'[23] In the judgment on the *Grootboom* matter, for example, it was found that the state did have a reasonable and integrated national policy on the progressive provision of housing, but it had not instituted reasonable measures (in legislation or policy) that would provide temporary relief to those in immediate and dire need in the community: those, for example, who had, as in the case of the *Grootboom* litigants, been evicted from their land with no alternative accommodation provided.[24] As such, government policy, in this limited regard, was unreasonable and thus unconstitutional.

Reasonableness was also used as litmus test during the Treatment Action Campaign's much discussed Constitutional Court challenge. If a 'minimum core' approach had been taken, one would have expected that the Court would have stipulated that a minimum level of HIV care was due to all. Instead, the Court limited itself (in broad terms) to finding that, amongst other things, the low cost of providing ARVs and their proven efficacy meant that not providing the treatment was unreasonable. As the Court concluded:

> The [HIV treatment] program to be realised progressively within available resources must include reasonable measures of counselling and testing pregnant women for HIV, counselling HIV-positive pregnant women on the options open to them to reduce the risk of mother-to-child transmission of HIV, and making appropriate treatment available to them for such purposes.
>
> The policy for reducing the risk of mother-to-child transmission of HIV as formulated and implemented by the government fell short of compliance with the requirements ...[25]

The judgments in *Grootboom* and *TAC* were not only notable for the fact that they constituted some of the first ever jurisprudence regarding socio-economic constitutional rights; they were also notable for their keen awareness of the dangers of judicial over-reach. In *Grootboom*, for example, the adoption of reasonableness as a measure meant that the Court could countenance a multiplicity of policy approaches, as long as they met the standards of comprehensibility, flexibility, coherence and balance. The Court would not go so far as to stipulate which policies would lead to the most efficient progressive realisation of rights. Part of this was due to the fact that the Court felt it did not have sufficient research capacity or information to make such judgment calls. Another factor was that the Court was keen to recognise that, in a democracy, policy choices are more appropriately made through Parliament and democratic contestation. To quote, once more, from *Grootboom*:

It is not possible to determine the minimum threshold for the progressive realisation of the right of access to adequate housing without first identifying the needs and opportunities for the enjoyment of such a right. These will vary according to factors such as income, unemployment, availability of land and poverty. The differences between city and rural communities will also determine the needs and opportunities for the enjoyment of this right. Variations ultimately depend on the economic and social history and circumstances of a country. All this illustrates the complexity of the task of determining a minimum core obligation for the progressive realisation of the right of access to adequate housing without having the requisite information on the needs and the opportunities for the enjoyment of this right. The [Committee on Economic, Social and Cultural Rights] developed the concept of minimum core over many years of examining reports by reporting states. This Court does not have comparable information ...

A court considering reasonableness will not enquire whether other more desirable or favourable measures could have been adopted, or whether public money could have been better spent. The question would be whether the measures that have been adopted are reasonable. It is necessary to recognise that a wide range of possible measures could be adopted by the state to meet its obligations. Many of these would meet the requirement of reasonableness. Once it is shown that the measures do so, this requirement is met.[26]

The Court's reasoning in the *TAC* judgment was even more forthright in its judicial minimalism. The Court clearly indicated that the role of the Constitutional Court, properly understood, was one of relative restraint in adjudicating government policy. The reasons were both practical (the Court was insufficiently equipped to do so) and principled (the need to strike a balance between judicial, executive and legislative branches of government):

It should be borne in mind that in dealing with such matters the courts are not institutionally equipped to make the wide-ranging factual and political enquiries necessary for determining what the minimum-core standards are ... nor for deciding how public revenues should most effectively be spent. There are many pressing demands on the public purse ...

Courts are ill-suited to adjudicate upon issues where court orders could have multiple social and economic consequences for the community. The Constitution contemplates rather a restrained and focused role for the courts, namely, to require the state to take measures to meet its constitutional obligations and to subject the reasonableness of these measures to evaluation. Such determinations of reasonableness may in fact have budgetary implications, but are not in themselves directed at rearranging budgets. In this way the judicial, legislative and executive functions achieve appropriate constitutional balance.[27]

Whether or not the Court made the correct decision to adopt reasonableness from a legalistic point of view is still a matter of debate.[28] For Geoff Budlender, it is somewhat beside the point: 'the Court has made clear that the "minimum core" approach will not be used in future'.[29] Nevertheless, the adoption of reasonableness was a clear indication that the Court was sensitive – perhaps even over-sensitive – to the separation of powers envisaged in South Africa's democratic Constitution. It seems that, in the Court's mind, it was clear who ruled South Africa: Parliament and the executive, with the Court acting as a collaborative partner that would give the state broad leeway within the bounds of reasonableness to fulfil its mandate.

This has made more recent complaints against the judiciary less than credible. Starting in 2008, the courts have come under increasing vocal attack, largely from senior members of the Alliance. The heat was generated by the Arms Deal, in particular the friction caused by Jacob Zuma's push for power and the corruption charges that he faced for his alleged role in the Deal. As noted in the previous chapter, Zuma's legal approach to the charges involved challenging technicalities while simultaneously developing the narrative that the charges were a fabrication woven together in a political conspiracy to keep him from the presidency.

This is not to suggest that Zuma was entirely unsuccessful during his appearances in court; not only were charges of rape against him dismissed by the High Court, but he also succeeded in having search warrants against him declared unlawful (a decision to be overturned later by majority decisions in the Supreme Court and Constitutional Court) and in having his charges struck from the roll in 2006 after the prosecution's application for postponement was dismissed. Nevertheless, only a few months before his corruption charges were dropped in 2009, the Supreme Court of Appeal overturned one of Zuma's major victories in his quest to have his prosecution dismissed on the basis of the alleged conspiracy against him – the Nicholson judgment – and provided a framework by which the fairness of pursuing the corruption charges against Zuma could be assessed. This finding indicated that Zuma would struggle, on the basis of his legal strategy to date, to have the charges against him dismissed.

Writing in 2012, four years after the most intense noises were made about Zuma's charges and the perfidious judiciary, it is easy to forget just how violent the political discourse had become, and how fragile the institutions of democracy seemed in the face of the so-called 'Zunami' and the repeated characterisation of the judiciary as 'counter-revolutionary'. Examples of the attacks on the judiciary were legion, but none gave a clearer flavour of the tone of the time than a vituperative volley from Gwede Mantashe, newly appointed as Secretary-General of the ANC, in 2008. Reacting angrily to news that Constitutional Court judges had laid a complaint against Judge John Hlophe (see Chapter 2), Mantashe claimed that the Court was part of a larger attempt to thwart Zuma's ambitions:

> This is psychological preparation of society so that when the Constitutional Court judges pounce on our president we should be ready at that point in time ... Our revolution is in danger; we must declare to defend it to the very end ... You hit the head, you kill the snake. When there is an attack on him it is a concerted attack on the head of the ANC. Everybody

says it's an innocent attack on him. We will know that it is an attack on the ANC.[30]

Since Zuma's charges were dismissed, attacks such as this on the judiciary appear to have lessened, at least in frequency. Nevertheless, the judiciary has faced a constant drip of criticism emanating from senior ranks in the ANC. While earlier criticisms consisted of broad swipes and character assassinations, some of the more recent attacks have been more rigorously formulated. The major emergent critique appears to be the claim that the Constitutional Court (and the judiciary as a whole) has started to overstep its boundaries by overturning government policies. In July 2011 Zuma delivered a speech at an Access to Justice conference that clearly articulated this view:

> While acknowledging the strides we have made, it is our well-considered view that there is a need to distinguish the areas of responsibility between the judiciary and the elected branches of government, especially with regards to government policy formulation.
>
> The Executive, as elected officials, has the sole discretion to decide policies for Government …
>
> This means that once government has decided on the appropriate policies, the judiciary cannot, when striking down legislation or parts thereof on the basis of illegality, raise that as an opportunity to change the policies as determined by the Executive area of government.
>
> There is no doubt that the principle of separation of powers must reign supreme to enable the efficiency and integrity of the various arms of the State in executing their mandates.
>
> Encroachment of one arm on the terrain of another should be frowned upon by others, and there must be no bias in this regard.
>
> In as much as we seek to respect the powers and role conferred by our constitution on the legislature and the judiciary, we expect the same from these very important institutions of our democratic dispensation.

> The Executive must be allowed to conduct its administration and policy making work as freely as it possibly can.
>
> The powers conferred on the courts cannot be superior to the powers resulting from the political and consequently administrative mandate resulting from popular democratic elections.[31]

The weakness of these critiques is obvious. First, the Constitutional Court had already indicated that, by adopting the reasonableness approach, it was attempting to respect the balance of powers by giving as much leeway as possible for policy formation by appropriate democratic institutions within the bounds of the Constitution – hardly indicative of a desire to write government policy. Secondly, the claim that the powers of the judiciary should not be superior to those of the executive fundamentally misunderstands what a constitutional democracy entails. The Constitution is *the* pre-eminent law in the country, and every person and institution has to abide by that law equally. That is what is meant by constitutional supremacy. As the highest court empowered to decide constitutional matters, the Constitutional Court is empowered to seek to remedy any breach of these principles. If the Constitutional Court did not have that power, South Africa would not be a constitutional democracy. And, as any reasonably well-read student of history knows, the alternative – parliamentary supremacy and majoritarianism – provides no guarantee of ethical behaviour or just laws.

Regardless of the overwhelmingly negative response to Zuma's speech in the media and legal communities, the push towards a possible new arrangement of the constitutional deckchairs has continued apace. Only a few months after Zuma's much-discussed speech at the Access to Justice conference, Cabinet released a statement indicating that it was planning to conduct a study to 'review' the powers and jurisprudence of the Constitutional Court. The opinion of some that such a review was aimed at clipping the wings of the judiciary in retaliation against Zuma's less than spectacular legal successes appeared to gain further credence on 27 March 2012, when the Department of Justice and Constitutional Development released the terms of reference for the anticipated review. In a surprise move, the Department reported that the review would also now look at the functions, power and jurisprudence of the Supreme Court of Appeal.[32] The week previously, the Supreme Court of Appeal had ruled that the spy tapes upon which Zuma's counsel relied to have the charges dismissed would have to be made available to the applicant (the DA) and that the matter would have to be returned back to the High Court to decide if a review could take place. So much for the rather unambiguous statement in a Department of Justice discussion document released only weeks before Zuma's Supreme Court reversal: 'While it may be desirable to assess the impact of the decisions of the Supreme Court of Appeal and the High Courts in relation to the transformation of society, it is desirable to limit the focus on the Constitutional Court, which is at the apex of the transformation agenda in relation to our evolving constitutional jurisprudence.'[33]

In addition to complaints about judicial over-reach, senior figures in the ANC have wondered aloud whether the judiciary has not hindered broad socio-economic transformation. The argument has been made that the apparent willingness of the Constitutional Court to deliver judgments that overturn government decisions has encouraged conservative groups to pursue legal recourse with the alleged intention to block transformation. In August 2011, for example, Mantashe brought out the big guns in an interview with the editor of The Sowetan, in which he appeared to link judicial over-reach with apartheid sympathisers:

> The independence of judiciary and separation of powers must never be translated into hostility, where one of those arms becomes hostile to the other. My view is that there is a great deal of hostility that comes through from the judiciary towards the executive and Parliament, towards the positions taken by the latter two institutions. Unless this issue is addressed deliberately it's going to cause instability. It undermines the other arms of government and this could cause instability ...
>
> If the Constitutional Court positions itself to create a perception that it overturns anything passed by parliament, it is going to make nonsense of the democratically elected parliament. Look at the kind of people taking matters to the Constitutional Court. It is people like Paul Hofmann, Hugh

Glenister, AfriForum and many others. All these are people and institutions resisting transformation in society. They are beneficiaries of the past regime. They use the courts to overturn any progress made that is transformative in society.[34]

To claim that the judiciary is overtly hostile towards the executive must surely count as one of the more outrageous statements of recent times. The Constitutional Court, in particular, has exercised considerable restraint in giving the state leeway to determine legislative and policy approaches that can be tested against the reasonableness criteria. Indeed, the Court has, in many instances, actually been remarkably deferential to the discretion exercised by government when the adjudication of socio-economic rights has been necessary. If the Court has given the state considerable leeway to pursue a transformational agenda, but transformation has not been forthcoming, it can hardly be rationally considered the fault of the Court.

Mantashe's argument also contains an irony that not many have considered. If the Constitutional Court were to have pursued a more actively transformational agenda with regard to socio-economic rights, it would almost certainly have had to adopt a 'minimum core' approach. But a 'minimum core' approach would entail making direct decisions about budgetary allocations, policy interventions, legislation and other matters. An activist Court, in other words, would have been forced to adopt a far less restrained approach to judicial oversight than that which has been followed to date. One cannot demand that the judiciary pursue socio-economic transformation while simultaneously denying that the Court has the power to review action that happens outside of the realm of the judiciary. To demand that the Court abrogate its power of review while still pursuing transformation is to ask the impossible. As far as arguments go, Mantashe's is a stinker.

It is tempting to view these critiques as a possible backlash against a series of reverses the state (and members of the ANC) had suffered during various legal proceedings, rather than a sincere engagement with constitutional principle. It has been an unsightly spectacle. 'At the level of the President, you need a leader who speaks in a way that affirms the role of the Constitutional Court and respects the institution,' argues Sipho Pityana, the current chairperson of the Council for the Advancement of the Constitution. 'That doesn't mean he cannot engage with the decisions of the Constitutional Court and the executive should be at liberty to participate in those debates. But to express such unhappiness with those decisions that you start to run a process that you want to change the powers of that institution smacks of intolerance.'[35]

Perhaps the response of some senior ANC leaders has not been predicated entirely on the simple reversal of government decisions. A pertinent example is provided by the Glenister case, the outcome of which had the Constitutional Court finding that the South African Police Services Act, which created a new crime-fighting unit, 'the Hawks', did not allow for sufficient independence for the unit. Perhaps it was the tone that the judiciary struck in reaching such decisions that really rankled. Two judgments involving the state, in particular, are notable for the manner in which the courts found it necessary to remind the state how democracies functioned. Considering the cases the courts were deciding, they were arguably right in doing so.

The first judgment, delivered in December 2011, overturned the appointment of Menzi Simelane as National Director of Public Prosecutions (NDPP).[36] Simelane had been appointed to the position despite both the Public Service Commission and a parliamentary inquiry finding that his previous conduct, in particular during the Selebi affair, raised questions about his integrity.[37] In the course of the judgment – which ruled that the decision to appoint Simelane was invalid – the Supreme Court of Appeal went out of its way on two separate occasions to reiterate the importance of the principle of constitutional supremacy:

> The rule of law is a central and founding value. No-one is above the law and everyone is subject to the Constitution and the law. The legislative and executive arms of government are bound by legal prescripts. Accountability, responsiveness and openness are constitutional watchwords. It can rightly be said that the individuals that occupy positions in organs of state or who are part of constitutional institutions are transient but that constitutional mechanisms, institutions and values endure. To ensure a functional, accountable constitutional

democracy the drafters of our Constitution placed limits on the exercise of power. Institutions and office bearers must work within the law and must be accountable. Put simply, ours is a government of laws and not of men or women ...

One further aspect requires brief attention. It will be recalled that in para 115 above a paragraph from the heads of argument on behalf of the President was quoted, in which it was submitted that, because the President is the people's choice, the Constitution vests the power in him to appoint an NDPP and that the power is exercised based on the President's value judgment. It is implicit in that submission that a court cannot scrutinise the President's exercise of a value judgment. I have already dealt with the power of courts to ensure compliance with the Constitution. It is necessary to say something about whether in doing so the popular will is subverted. Dealing with critics who suggest that the power vested in the judiciary to set aside the laws made by a legislature mandated by the popular will, itself constitutes a subversion of democracy, former Chief Justice Mahomed, in an address in Cape Town on 21 July 1998 to the International Commission of Jurists on the independence of the judiciary, stated the following:

'That argument is, I think, based on a demonstrable fallacy. The legislature has no mandate to make a law which transgresses the powers vesting in it in terms of the Constitution. Its mandate is to make only those laws permitted by the Constitution and to defer to the judgment of the court, in any conflict generated by an enactment challenged on constitutional grounds. If it does make laws which transgress its constitutional mandate or if it refuses to defer to the judgment of the court on any challenge to such laws, it is in breach of its own mandate. The court has a constitutional right and duty to say so and it protects the very essence of a constitutional democracy when it does. A democratic legislature does not have the option to ignore, defy or subvert the court. It has only two constitutionally permissible alternatives, it must either accept its judgment or seek an appropriate constitutional amendment if this can be done without subverting the basic foundations of the Constitution itself.'

These statements are beyond criticism and apply equally when actions or decisions by the executive are set aside.[38]

A similar tone was struck in the March 2012 Supreme Court of Appeal finding that the DA had the necessary legal standing to use the courts to challenge the decision to drop the charges against Jacob Zuma in 2008. Early on in the judgment, the Court once again emphasised the importance of judicial review and the rule of law. In what some may see as a broadside against Zuma's more heated statements regarding the judiciary, the Court also emphasised that the rule of law was the best defence a democracy could have:

> Section 1(c) of the Constitution proclaims the supremacy of the Constitution and the concomitant supremacy of the rule of law. In fulfilling the constitutional duty of testing the exercise of public power against the Constitution, courts are protecting the very essence of a constitutional democracy. Put simply, it means that each of the arms of government and every citizen, institution or other recognised legal entity, are all bound by and equal before the law. Put differently, it means that none of us is above the law. It is a concept that we, as a nation, must cherish, nurture and protect. We must be intent on ensuring that it is ingrained in the national psyche. It is our best guarantee against tyranny, now and in the future.[39]

It has to reflect poorly on the democratic record of the government, and particularly on the presidency of Jacob Zuma, that two separate judgments have taken such clear steps to reiterate the role of the rule of law and judicial review in South African society. And it also clearly indicates that, if there is an attempt to review such powers, the judiciary will likely prove a formidable opponent. Unfortunately, as South Africa approaches yet another ANC elective conference at the end of 2012, the supremacy of the Constitution and judicial review cannot be taken for granted. A major and uncontested victory for Zuma, especially if that victory is followed by further reverses at the hands of the courts, could easily embolden certain senior ANC leaders to take the fight to the judiciary. And, if that happens, South Africa's democratic institutions could, finally, collapse under the weight of executive pressure.

Guardians of the (many) truth(s): media and civil society

The media and civil society have also had to labour under the burden of the ANC's efforts to control outcomes in its favour. Both have remained fiercely independent, refusing to bow to alternating demands and requests to be more forgiving of government action. Unfortunately, the independent print and online media remain only a small part of the media landscape, which is dominated by the public broadcaster, the South African Broadcasting Corporation (SABC).

Created during the apartheid era, the SABC was initially conceived as a public broadcaster and established along very similar lines to the British Broadcasting Corporation (BBC). Indeed, the original SABC charter was written in 1933 by John Reith, the first Director General of the BBC (he also wrote the public broadcasting charters for Canada, Australia, India and Kenya).[40] The original Reithian principles included a belief in the power of the public broadcaster to educate and improve, as well as a firm commitment to political neutrality and independence. Ironically, as Ruth Teer-Tomaselli observed, 'the translocation of the BBC ethos to South Africa in the 1930s suited the National Party's policy of apartheid after the 1950s, as neither Reith nor the NP recognised black Africans as part of the listening/viewing audience except on white terms.'[41] Considering apartheid's hegemonic project, it was unsurprising that, under the NP, the SABC shifted from being a public broadcaster that projected a multiplicity of views to being a state broadcaster, projecting only the state-sanctioned version, and filling the airwaves with virtually unceasing apartheid propaganda.[42]

Thus, in the post-1994 period, the general public's relationship with the media would largely be shaped by whether or not the SABC – whose media infrastructure and reach dwarfed those of any independent media outlets – would be reconstituted as a public rather than state broadcaster. In a country with persistently high rates of illiteracy, radio penetration has always been the biggest avenue for delivery of news and events. A 2007 study by Statistics South Africa found that 9.5 million households owned a radio – 76.5 per cent of the population.[43] By comparison, only 900 000 households (7.2 per cent of the population) had access to the internet and the alternative media sources this made available.[44]

By far the majority of radio listeners tune in to SABC stations, the biggest of which are African language stations. The two largest radio stations in South Africa are Ukhozi FM (broadcasting in Zulu) and Umhlobo Wenene (broadcasting in Xhosa), which attract 6.38 million and 4.76 million listeners respectively.[45] Television coverage, too, is dominated by the SABC. According to the SABC's own figures, its television network – of three free-to-air channels and one pay TV channel – attracts a daily viewership of 17 million adults: 74 per cent of the total adult viewership.[46] These figures far outstrip the reach of the largely independent print media, which has also faced reduced circulation figures in line with the rest of the international media. In the first two quarters of 2011, for example, the core circulation of daily tabloids and broadsheets was measured at just over 1.3 million – a drop of 300 000 from a recent peak of 1.6 million in 2007.[47]

The SABC was rapidly transformed, with a focus on demographic representativity quickly changing the population and character of its newsrooms and support staff – a move that any viewer with a memory of the dour and biased pre-1994 coverage has to celebrate. Yet, despite a high-minded editorial policy that 'strive[s] to disclose all the essential facts and … not suppress relevant, available facts, or distort by wrong or improper emphasis',[48] there have been frequent complaints that the SABC has shown a distasteful executive-mindedness in its reporting and coverage. The claims were hard to verify for the first decade of the SABC's existence – the vagaries of media interpretation often preclude a simplistic judgement about the political bias of media content. But, by the mid-2000s, hard evidence started to emerge that substantiated worries that political control was being exercised, either directly or indirectly, over the SABC's news coverage.

In June 2006, for example, Karima Brown and Pippa Green, both of whom had served in senior positions in the SABC, wrote articles that indicated that political pressure and self-censorship had led to a distortion of coverage. 'The organizational culture and ethos at Auckland Park newsroom [the head SABC newsroom] promotes self-censorship,' Brown wrote in a damning column in *Business Day*. 'Under the guise of transformation, the SABC has been all but hi-jacked by a clique of self-serving government lackeys who believe they alone know what the public should see and hear. These individuals are not just in news management. They are on the SABC board, in the newsrooms and they even include senior journalists.'[49] Green, meanwhile, worried that 'when top managers of the SABC are appointed more for their perceived political loyalties than professional experience, judgment is often blurred and many dance complicated two-steps to do what they *think* will please those in power.'[50]

Both Brown and Green were writing mainly about the activities of one Snuki Zikalala, a former ANC commissar in exile (where he received a doctorate in journalism from Bulgaria's Sofia University), who was appointed to the position of managing director of news and current affairs during Mbeki's presidency. On 20 June 2006, the *Sowetan* ran a story alleging that a number of experts – William Gumede, Aubrey Matshiqi, Karima Brown and Vukani Mde – had been blacklisted on Zikalala's orders.[51] All the experts banned were considered to be critical of Thabo Mbeki and his administration. The story broke the dam walls: soon, further examples of blacklisting and bias in the newsroom came to light. In one of the more damning allegations, it was claimed that coverage of the 2005 Zimbabwe elections had been subjected to gross manipulation, partially by banning both Moeletsi Mbeki and Elinor Sisulu from being interviewed on the country – a decision that Zikalala later confirmed under oath, claiming that they were out of touch with developments in the country.[52] Not coincidentally, both had already indicated their distaste for the Mugabe regime and were critical of Mbeki's 'quiet diplomacy' approach to Zimbabwe.

Nine days after the *Sowetan* story ran, a Commission of Enquiry was appointed by Dali Mpofu, SABC Group Chief Executive Officer, to assess the allegations. The resulting report was highly critical of both

Zikalala's actions and the lack of internationally benchmarked editorial standards. Perhaps as a result of this, the SABC went out of its way to keep the report secret:[53] it has still not been officially published, although a draft version was leaked to the *Mail & Guardian* and made available online. A full airing of the facts was only achieved when the Freedom of Expression Institute decided to take the broadcast regulator, Icasa, to court. In a judgment delivered in January 2011, the court ran through a number of incidents in which experts were banned or coverage actively manipulated, the most notable of which was the manhandling of the coverage of Zimbabwe's elections. Surveying the evidence, the judgment was damning about the conduct of the SABC and Zikalala in particular:

> The evidence reveals a number of incidents in which the SABC's News Management and Dr Zikalala in particular, manipulated its news and current affairs, that they dishonestly tried to cover up this manipulation when it was publicly revealed and that the SABC's Board subsequently failed to take any action when the manipulation and dishonest cover-up was exposed by its own Commission of Enquiry.[54]

The end of Zikalala's tenure at the SABC raised the hopes that such obvious manipulation would fade into the background. Unfortunately, persistent claims about executive interference in the operation of the SABC have continued to surface. The SABC has been in the near-permanent throes of a governance crisis, rocked by frequent resignations and allegations of political interference in the make-up of the board.[55] The most recent flare-up occurred in February 2012, when it was alleged that the board had attempted to 'parachute' Hlaudi Motsoeneng into the position of Chief Operation Officer, despite the fact that the SABC was interdicted from making an appointment to that position by the High Court as the previous hopeful, Mvuzo Mbebe, believed that he had been given the green light by the previous Communications Minister, Ivy Matsepe-Casaburri.[56] Motsoeneng had previously been fired by the SABC in 2007 after an internal investigation into various wrongdoings, including the falsification of his qualifications.[57] In the course of a year from his re-appointment to the SABC in 2011, he was promoted three times. 'What instruction, which we as the SABC do not know about, does the board have from Luthuli House?' an unnamed official queried.[58]

Admittedly, the governance crisis at the SABC (in terms of constant resignations and contested appointments) has been somewhat overshadowed by a related problem, namely endemic fraud and corruption. In September 2009, the Auditor-General published a report that pointed to widespread financial mismanagement. In certain cases, the sums were not insubstantial: a total of R174 million was awarded in seven separate tenders despite the tender hearings not meeting minimum requirements; a R326 million contract with a consultant was entered into by two senior SABC employees despite not having the authority to do so; and a two-year investigation between 2007 and 2009 had found R111 million in irregularities such as double payments, overpayments and needless repurchasing of show licences.[59] An astonishing 1 465 employees were found to have interests in outside companies, which made it difficult to countenance the absence of any central register of these interests or employee approvals.[60] And yet, despite the report and its recommendations being presented in 2009, the SABC was forced to admit to Parliament, during a hearing in March 2012, that 'there was little or no implementation of the recommendations at 30 November 2011'.[61]

Whether or not the viewing public intends to punish the SABC's perceived bias and corporate dysfunction by withholding their ears and eyes has been an open-ended question to which there has been no definitive answer. However, figures released in mid-March 2012 suggested that the SABC was beginning to lose a substantial number of viewers of its news programmes to the independent commercial station, e-TV. Between October 2011 and January 2012, the SABC was reported to have lost over a million viewers during the news timeslots across its three channels, while e-TV reported a 100 000 viewer increase.[62] For the National Union of Mineworkers, the figures could only be construed as the audience recoiling at political bias: 'The NUM is not surprised by these developments as the SABC particularly its television component has long ceased to be a public broadcaster and turned itself into a self-promotion propaganda instrument for certain factions. The National Union of Mineworkers congratulates e-TV, a private broadcaster which almost adequately fulfils the mandate of a public broadcaster for refusing to be drawn into narrow factionalist coverage.'[63]

Outside of the direct political control of the ruling party, the independent media have retained their fierce autonomy, despite frequent and robust criticisms being directed in their direction by senior ANC members. Indeed, if anything, the independent print media, and especially titles such as the *Mail & Guardian*, *City Press*, *Sunday Times* and *Beeld*, have become increasingly trenchant in the face of heavy-handed attacks and the deluge of corruption stories and allegations of government malfunction. Indeed, many media practitioners now view the role of the media as more than simply reporting the news or providing insight into government activities; the media, instead, should be actively involved in exposing abuses of power. Ray Hartley, the current editor of the *Sunday Times*, for example, believes the media should fill a multiplicity of roles:

I think that we do see the media as having an obligation beyond simply reporting. We have a constitution which tries to encourage the society to go somewhere, to build a democratic nation, to increase the empowerment of ordinary people. It is an activist constitution in that sense. And we would see ourselves in tune with that. But the primary mission remains to unflinchingly report the news. And, as a weekly newspaper, to break news and to expose abuses of power.[64]

For Nic Dawes, the editor of the *Mail & Guardian*, these roles – to inform, to act as a mechanism of accountability and as a forum for an exchange of ideas – are not merely identified by an arrogant media elite keen to extol their own virtues. Instead, the role of the media in assuring accountability is fundamental to South Africa's constitutional democracy:

The Constitutional scheme is very clear. South African democracy functions both by having a properly designed state with appropriate roles for the executive, judiciary and parliament, and by making space for a range of other mechanisms of engagement and accountability that overlap with the institutions of the state. This is one reason that the media is given a special place in the constitutional architecture first of all as a mechanism of accountability, and also, and no less importantly, as a forum for the exchange and testing of ideas and the development of the proper democratic public sphere.[65]

When it has come to exposing abuses of power, the print media has a remarkable record. Almost all of the major corruption scandals that have surfaced over the last 15 years have been investigated and broken by the print media. Its continued attention to the topics, and dedication to uncovering as much of each sordid story as possible, has often been solely responsible for South Africans gaining a modicum of insight into each situation. The examples of the Arms Deal, the police leasing scandal and the Jackie Selebi corruption story are clear statements of how the media has played a vital democratic role in forcing a modicum of accountability. In each of these, media attention has empowered those in the justice cluster to pursue the cases despite their political awkwardness. As a result, the Arms Deal is now subject to a Commission of Inquiry; the police leasing scandal is currently under investigation and prompted the suspension of the Chief of Police; and Jackie Selebi is currently serving a lengthy term after being found guilty of corruption.

But perhaps the best example of how the media has been able to force the state to fulfil its democratic functions has been the Oilgate saga (see Chapter 7). Suffice to say that that saga involved the ANC allegedly agreeing to supply political support to Saddam Hussein's beleaguered Iraq in return for favourable oil allocations. The allocations and their sale were overseen by the late Sandi Majali, who was alleged to have repaid the ANC for its political support by diverting some of the Oilgate funds into the ANC's books. The story was first broken by the *Mail & Guardian* in the face of severe pressure: Majali's company, Imvume, successfully sought a temporary interdict to prevent publication, only for the information later to be made available in Parliament by the Freedom Front. Over the course of the next few years, the newspaper was able to unravel the deal's sordid conduct, in the process fingering such luminaries as Kgalema Motlanthe.[66]

It seemed, for a while, that it might have been a pyrrhic endeavour. The allegations were forwarded for investigation to the Public Protector, who found that 'much of what has been published in the *Mail & Guardian* was factually incorrect, based on incomplete information and documentation and comprised unsubstantiated suggestions and unjustified speculation'.[67] Upset by the finding, the *Mail & Guardian* approached the High Court for relief. The Court found that the Public Protector's investigation was of dubious quality. In June 2011, the High Court's judgment was upheld by the Supreme Court of Appeal, which found that the Public Protector's 'investigation was so scant as not to have been an investigation, and there was no proper basis for any findings that were made'.[68] As a result, the Public Protector's report was set aside, meaning that the allegations would have to reinvestigated afresh, which the current incumbent, Thuli Madonsela, has indicated she will do. By investigating the Oilgate scandal and challenging the Public Protector, the *Mail & Guardian* not only served democracy by providing access to information that many within the ANC would rather not have seen published, but also made great strides in ensuring that the Public Protector properly performed its role as envisaged in the Constitution. It would be hard to imagine any future investigation by the Public Protector cutting corners so obviously or behaving in a manner apparently so biased towards the ruling party – a major victory for democratic governance and accountability.

For both Nic Dawes and Ray Hartley, it is precisely the success of the independent print media in fulfilling its role of exposing the abuse of power that has led to the rapid deterioration in the relationship between the media and the ANC. Asked about when he felt the relationship between the media and the ruling party started fraying, Hartley was adamant:

> I think it was when corruption at a very high level began to be exposed, particularly around Tony Yengeni who was then a rising star in the party. That's when we got a lot of people who would have cooperated being a little bit on edge. And then I think that the whole unfolding Mbeki versus Zuma saga, which actually has its roots way back during Bulelani Ngcuka's tenure, when the media started to expose and get

> involved in that, it was perceived as acting on the part of one faction and not the other, and the reverse. It became a very tense relationship from that point ... Zuma for his part perceived the media to be acting against him in concert with Ngcuka and Mbeki to damage his public profile. And I think he bears that grudge to this day.[69]

During Mbeki's tenure, attacks on the media were frequent and vicious, especially in his weekly 'ANC Today' column. 'Mbeki acted as a one-man media tribunal in his Friday letter,' Nic Dawes pithily notes. But, beyond these attacks, little attempt was made to directly bring the media within the ambit of government control. It was only in 2007, at the Polokwane Conference that elected Zuma as the new ANC president, that a resolution was passed supporting the creation of the so-called Media Appeals Tribunal. That resolution was fleshed out in more detail in a 2010 ANC discussion document, although even this remained vague:[70] all that was clear was that the ANC supported the creation of a body (possibly based in Parliament) that would have the power to review the content of the media and seek remedy if it found that a media report was biased or an individual's dignity was violated. Considering the ANC's parliamentary majority, the judgments that such a body would reach when confronted with issues of bias in the representation of the ANC would be somewhat predictable.

To support the moves towards a Media Appeals Tribunal, the ANC has claimed that the media is under-regulated in South Africa. The Press Ombudsman, in particular, which is empowered to adjudicate complaints about press coverage and make orders that provide a measure of restorative justice, has been portrayed as little more than a press patsy, as the Ombudsman is usually an ex-editor or academic – conveniently ignoring that, if the Ombudsman's decision is appealed, it is heard by a retired judge. As an attempt to undermine the Ombudsman's credibility, the claim appears to have been unsuccessful. In February 2012, for example, the Ombudsman reported that there had been a 70 per cent increase in complaints to the Ombudsman from 150 in 2009 to 255 in 2011: hardly indicative of a body to which the public refused to turn.[71] The Ombudsman also noted that the majority of the decisions it had reached had been in favour of the complainants and against the major media houses.[72] 'There are many times when I would much rather prefer to be in court than in front of the Press Ombudsman,' Ray Hartley noted. 'In many cases I feel I could have better defended a story legally than in front of the Ombudsman who has a looser, less legalistic approach.'[73]

Hartley's mention of legal defensibility raises another inconvenient fact: the press is already regulated in the form of defamation and privacy law, and is constrained, as are all private actors, by the dictates of criminal law. In addition, complaints can also be laid with both the Gender and Human Rights Commissions, and the Equality Court, which have the power to make determinations in relation to media articles. The media is also now subject to an additional level of scrutiny via the social media, which has proven incredibly robust in detecting errors and making them known. But perhaps the greatest regulator is credibility: if newspapers are considered to be overtly politically biased, unfair in coverage or consistently linked to incorrect information, the public is less likely to turn to those sources. 'The *New Age* newspaper [funded by members of the Gupta family, which is reportedly close to Zuma, and launched in 2010] has mobilised vast resources, but it still doesn't have great traction,' Hartley argues. 'It's not a bad paper at all, but there is a suspicion that it will not give you the unvarnished truth. There is a culture of scepticism and it's not surprising in a situation where the truth has been suppressed for so many decades.'[74]

The Media Appeals Tribunal appears, on the face of it, to be a solution where there is no problem. The inference that this leads to is that it has been conceived of primarily as a means to reassert a degree of control over a media that has not refrained from pointing out the problems in the ruling party. This suspicion has been compounded by another Zuma-era development: the Protection of State Information Bill (also known as the Secrecy Bill), as it stands in its current form. As we saw in the last chapter, the Secrecy Bill, whose passage is still being debated by the National Council of Provinces at the time of writing, imposes, for instance, severe prison sentences on any person found to be in possession of classified documents. In addition, the Bill lacks any public interest defence, meaning that classified documents cannot be published even if their publication would uncover corruption or other abuses of power. Nic Dawes believes that the Media Appeals Tribunal and the Secrecy Bill are part of a concerted effort to manage the output of the media and limit negative news reportage. Moreover, in his view, the fact that this is to be achieved via a Secrecy Bill is an indication that the ANC's intelligence and security heritage (also discussed in the previous chapter) may have convinced key members of the ANC that the best means to achieve such control is via a state security framework:

> It does at times feel as if the ANC tries to run the country as if it were an exiled liberation movement operating out of a flat in London. There is a pervasive feeling amongst those people that you subsist in a world of enemies and that you are to understand negative press coverage in terms of a conspiracy of some kind to bring down the movement and as the product of the machinations of the forces opposed to change. There is a belief that power changes hands by conspiracy and that if you see activity out there that you don't like, it is the function of a conspiracy. There is an intelligence focus and paranoiac attitude that developed out of the world of exile ...
>
> The Media Appeals Tribunal and the Secrecy Bill are efforts which have identified freedom of information as a particular risk to the hegemony of the ANC. There is an 'ANC of fear' – the Mbokodo ANC – that believes you deal with challenges by identifying the conspirators and nailing them. The reaction of the 'ANC of fear' is to seek mechanisms of enhanced control and the natural response is through a security apparatus style intervention. Amongst the Zuma crowd, it's the default setting.
>
> I think that that the Secrecy Bill did start as a process to reform unconstitutional legislation. But it got lost in the process, setting off for the city on the hill and falling into a ditch, haunted by spooks on the way. It became an attempt to gain control over leaks, over the activities of people who they believed were undermining the party, and they decanted all that into a national security framework.[75]

It is beyond argument that if the Media Appeals Tribunal were to be implemented and the Secrecy Bill passed, they would both have a chilling impact on the types of stories covered by the independent media. They would hamstring the ability of the media to uncover and publish stories of major national importance and would run the risk of bringing the media firmly into the sordid world of intelligence machinations and manipulations. Needless to say, much rides on how successful the media is in resisting these impulses.

But this is a fight that is not only being waged by the media. Indeed, civil society organisations have played a powerful role in ensuring that the topics remain part of the national debate. The best example of this is the Right2Know (R2K) campaign, which emerged out of concern about the impact of the Secrecy Bill. Operating from its base in Cape Town, the Right2Know campaign has united a large range of individuals and civil society organisations to protest the passing of the Bill. It has been able to source enough funds and manpower to ensure that most parliamentary hearings into the Bill were attended by an R2K representative, who could then provide feedback as to the various deliberations around the Bill. Partially as a result of the pressure brought to bear by the R2K movement in the form of protest marches, submissions and statements, numerous amendments to the Secrecy Bill were included in its current draft, improving what was a hangdog piece of legislation into something slightly less shoddy. Nevertheless, despite the attempts, it has failed to convince the relevant powers to include a public interest defence clause and has indicated that, if the Bill is passed in its current form, it will contemplate challenging the Bill in the Constitutional Court.

If it does so, it will be in good company. While civil society organisations are arguably no longer as influential in the corridors of power as they were in the early 1990s, when the groundswell of political engagement engendered by the UDF was still a force in contemporary politics, there are numerous examples of successful civil society campaigns directed at changing government policies. The most famous example has already been mentioned above, namely, the Treatment Action Campaign. Not only did the TAC raise awareness about the HIV/Aids pandemic (which it continues to do), it also successfully challenged the non-provision of ARVs to pregnant mothers in the Constitutional Court.

Another civil society movement that has achieved some remarkable successes is AfriForum, which emerged out of the trade union Solidarity. While AfriForum has been criticised for its perceived conservative proclivities, it has launched a number of successful legal applications. The most notable of these involved charging Julius Malema with hate speech for singing the struggle song, 'Kill the Boer [farmer]'. To many people's surprise, AfriForum were successful in this appeal, and Malema and others were ordered to refrain from singing the song in public in future.

These are not achievements to be sniffed at. But the observant reader will have noticed a feature that links these campaigns: they all, in the end, had to turn to the courts to ensure that illegal or unconstitutional government policies were overturned. The ANC's parliamentary majority, and its historic role as the country's liberator, has insulated it from the need to too rapidly respond to civil society campaigns. It appears that the party has often found it easier to cast the organisations as patsies of capital or Western governments (as the R2K was outrageously described in Parliament) than to respond to the demands of a robust civil society. The message is simple: a robust civil society that aims to change government policy simply has to have access to a system of judicial review, especially in the context of a one-party dominant state.

Yet even this is a simplification. The reality is that all three spheres of independence discussed in this chapter – the judiciary, the media and civil society – are interrelated and interdependent. Civil society needs a free media from which it can glean important information about the government and disseminate its own views. The media, meanwhile, requires a robust civil society to ensure that the public sphere features a multiplicity of voices, without which media coverage becomes remarkably bland and hegemonic in its own way. In the current climate, the active support of civil society for press freedom is additionally vital in acting as a corrective to the idea that the media is resisting the Media Appeals Tribunal and the Secrecy Bill purely out of self-interest. For the courts to have a transformational role in society, as envisaged in the Constitution, litigants must bring cases, which would hardly be possible in an environment where civil society fails to robustly engage in South Africa's political future. And both the media and civil society require that the rights guaranteed by the Constitution are protected, which would simply not be possible if the judiciary was stripped of its power to review government action (as appears to be contemplated by Gwede Mantashe, amongst others) and enforce the law without fear or favour.

Democratic institutions, especially in states that have only a short history of democratic contestation, are both fragile and mutually dependent. If one institution is attacked and undermined, all of the rest of the institutions of democracy are impoverished. The ANC has already shown its willingness to manhandle those institutions that fall under its direct political control – Parliament, Chapter 9 institutions, security agencies, just to mention three – doing damage that could take years to reverse (if it is reversed at all). If the attempts were to be successful in clipping the wings of either the judiciary or the media, in so doing fatally wounding civil society, the democratic future that was once promised in the halcyon days of transition will be nothing but that – an unfulfilled promise.

The Way In –
Money, Money, Money

Chapter 7

Ensuring Reproduction: The ANC and Its Models of Party Funding, 1994 to 2011[1]

Paul Holden

In the heady days after the fall of apartheid, the ANC basked in political goodwill at home and abroad. Its liberation credentials and the unquestionable charisma of its leading lights – the most notable being Mandela, although Tokyo Sexwale and Cyril Ramaphosa both swiftly became media darlings – masked the fact that the party itself was frequently in disarray. Its bureaucracy had to be created in double-quick time following exile, and often on the tightest of budgets. While the old political elite of apartheid could draw on nearly 50 years of state patronage, the ANC had to rely on a frayed party core that leant heavily on the abilities of individual leaders.

This was not to last long. One of the central narratives of the post-apartheid period is the transformation of the ANC from a liberation movement into a modern political party with its attendant bureaucracy and formalised funding structures. Central to this process was a project to make the ANC financially secure and self-sufficient. It was no smooth process, and at least two models were tried out before settling on its current vision – namely, business fronts benefiting from state contracts that pass profits back to the ANC's treasury.

In so doing, the ANC has fundamentally reshaped key elements of the power dynamic in the new South Africa, freeing itself from dependence on often unreliable donors while achieving an election kitty that dwarfs that of the opposition. Despite fears that the 'elite pact' struck in 1994 would render the ANC and its allies financially powerless, the ANC has successfully turned political power into economic power. And, as any canny commentator knows, economic power begets further political power.

Power on the cheap

The ANC had always struggled financially. Unlike the NP, which could leverage the apartheid state for its economic well-being, the ANC in exile relied exclusively on the kindness of strangers. By far the largest donors were the Soviet Union and Sweden, and much of the support provided was in kind rather than cash – tractors, clothes and basic supplies, and was barely enough to keep the ANC's comrades out of the direst poverty. By the mid-1980s, for example, the ANC in exile was receiving $24 million from the Soviet Union and $20 million in cash from Sweden's Nordic Africa Institute.[2]

By the early 1990s even this modest source had turned to a trickle. The Soviet Union was collapsing at a tremendous rate, cutting off key supplies and aid. Sweden continued to fund the organisation up until the 1994 elections, the Nordic Africa Institute being the largest funder. By 1993, the ANC was receiving an estimated R40 million from Sweden.[3] These donations helped it stay afloat, but only barely – many of its leading lights had to take up residence in flats offered by friends and sympathisers and ANC functionaries were paid minuscule salaries. When the ANC took power in April 1994, this source of party funding dried up entirely, as its Scandinavian donors believed that the ANC, newly installed in the Union Buildings, could now take care of itself.

The result was that, from 1994 until at least the mid-2000s, the ANC was constantly short of funds. In December 1994, it was reported to the ANC national conference in Bloemfontein that 'ANC structures are

having to operate in an environment where foreign funding has dwin-
dled to a trickle. The years of illegality have bred a dependence on external funding which the ANC is finding difficult to escape from. No
comprehensive plans have been developed – at national, provincial and
branch level – to make the ANC financially self-sufficient.'[4] At the 1997
Conference, this picture was clarified. In 1994, for example, the costs of
repatriation and contesting an expensive election meant that the ANC
was operating 'with an overdraft of billions of rand'.[5] Worryingly, 'there
were no fundraising structures or strategies in place'. As a result, between 1994 and 1997, the ANC flitted between just solvent to close to
bankruptcy. 'Wiping out the overdraft was not an insurmountable task.
In fact by April 1995 we were in the "black",' the 1997 report noted. 'But
by June we were already deep in the red again. This in and out of the red
was to characterize our period in office.'[6]

The ANC's finances did not look a great deal rosier a decade later.
In 2007, the ANC's Treasurer-General, Mendi Msimang, would report
that, at the time of the 2002 Stellenbosch Conference, the ANC 'was
going through the most difficult period in its financial life'. Indeed, for
14 months between January 2003 and April 2004 the ANC struggled
to pay salaries to its staff on time, which led to the resignation of 171
staff members.[7] As this indicates, the ANC struggled to cover its basic
monthly operating costs out of regular membership dues. In 2003, for
example, it had to pay salaries equal to R6 million a month (or R72 million a year).[8] In the same year, the ANC's total income was R107 million,
of which R55 million was earned via ad-hoc fundraising. Thus, without
this additional fundraising, the ANC would be unable to function at all.

Problems with funding were compounded by a sclerotic ANC bureaucracy that failed to maintain regular standards of accounting. In 2007,
for example, Mendi Msimang fretted about the organisation's ability to
establish working budgets:

> It is extremely worrying that after all these years, we still
> do not enjoy the response from almost all the sectors of our
> Movement to furnish us with the necessary information to
> enable us to construct monthly budgets. The implication
> for this was clearly demonstrated when we came out of the

Stellenbosch Conference. Due to the challenges of capacity coupled with Local Government Elections, we incurred a blistering overdraft because we were not working on the basis of budgets ... Comrades, we can no longer work without budgets because that will expose us again to financial mismanagement and debt. It is sufficient that we have lived through that painful experience.[9]

But by far the largest strain placed on the ANC's creaking finances was the need to fund expensive election campaigns. The 1994 election, for example, left it at least $20 million in debt.[10] During the 1999 election, it was estimated that all South Africa's political parties had spent a joint total of between R300 million and R500 million, only R66 million of which was raised from the public purse.[11] Exactly how much the ANC spent during the 1999 campaign was never confirmed, although an estimate of between R100 million and R150 million is considered reasonable. Of this, R33.5 million was raised from public funds, while another R4.3 million would have been raised from membership fees,[12] leaving a figure anywhere between R60 million and R110 million to be raised from outside sources. During the 2009 election, the ANC was reported to have a campaign kitty of R150 million, allegedly raised mostly from donations from the ruling parties of Libya, Angola, China, India and Equatorial Guinea.[13]

The ANC was thus often in a bizarre situation – unable to cover its monthly costs yet still able to raise considerable amounts for its local and national election campaigns. To do so, it relied on two main fundraising models, which brought their own disadvantages and controversies born from the organisation's financial vulnerabilities. By the mid- to late 2000s, these had been sidelined in favour of a third model – the party business. The result was that, by 2007, the ANC was newly flush with cash. 'To build a sound portfolio of investments has taken us a long time to put together, but it has been worthwhile,' Mendi Msimang told assembled ANC delegates at the Polokwane Conference in 2007. 'I am happy to announce that the market value of all our investments stand at no less than R1.75bilion. That is what the Movement owns.'[14]

Making money: the ANC's fundraising models
1994–2011

The first approach that the ANC used could be broadly described as the foreign charitable model, which drew heavily on the bankability of Mandela as the world's most famous freedom fighter. From the early 1990s, Mandela almost single-handedly raised external funds for the ANC. Unfortunately, many of the donations were of somewhat questionable provenance. Some of the more notable funders were President Suharto of Indonesia, running a brutal military-style dictatorship, King Fahd of Saudi Arabia, running a dictatorial monarchy ravaged by corruption and rent-seeking, and Sani Abacha, the former president of Nigeria, intimately linked to allegations of gross human rights violations.

A considerable amount of money flowed as a result of these links. During a speech in 1999, Mandela admitted that Suharto had donated $60 million to the ANC.[15] King Fahd of Saudi Arabia's $10 million was piddling by comparison, although the $50 million received from Sani Abacha ranked close to Suharto's generosity.[16] Abacha's $50 million donation, incidentally, was made in 1995 – the same year as a very public bust-up between Mandela and Abacha over the execution of Ken Saro-Wiwa, one of Nigeria's most respected human rights activists. Colonel Muammar Gaddafi was another funder – he donated $10 million to the ANC, according to London's *Telegraph*.[17] As Suharto was the most generous donor, he also received the highest plaudits. In 1997, he paid a visit as a special guest of the President, received a 21-gun salute and was awarded the Order of Good Hope, one of South Africa's highest honours.[18]

Trading diplomatic recognition for donations was a slippery slope and could potentially give off signals that South Africa's diplomatic largesse could be bought for the right amounts. Certainly, this was the impression given by South Africa's liaison with Taiwan in the early 1990s. From 1994 to 2000, Taiwan established a £100 million slush fund under the direction of President Lee Teng-Hui that was used to lobby and buy influence around the world, reaching as far as Republican senators in the US.[19] In June 1994, soon after attending Mandela's inauguration,

President Lee agreed to donate $10 million to defray the ANC's $20 million post-election debt,[20] which he hailed as an encouraging example of what could be achieved with the appropriate donations.

When Eugene Loh I-cheng, the Taiwanese ambassador to South Africa, was interviewed he recalled that the main contact point within Mandela's inner circle was none other than Treasurer-General Thomas Nkobi[21] (who, incidentally, received the money in small denominations).[22] Loh believed that the donations achieved their aim, namely, to ensure that South Africa only withdrew diplomatic recognition from Taiwan (which had historically close ties to the apartheid regime and whose friendship was considered damaging to a future alliance with China) two years later than it had initially planned.[23] Indeed, the Taiwanese–South African relationship was only disbanded on 1 January 1998, nearly four years after the ANC's election and a great deal longer than outside observers believed was probable.

If the ANC's foreign funding sources raised eyebrows, this wasn't a touch on the controversy of its second model: the 'comrades in arms' model. With this approach, the ANC would identify ANC comrades that would be deployed into business and given the support of the ANC to succeed; a distinct advantage in the world of politically loaded Black Economic Empowerment. With the ANC's support, these businessmen would often secure contracts from entities with close relationships to the state, or from the state itself. In turn, the ANC would receive generous donations from the businessmen as and when needed. That the ANC used this model consciously is not speculation, as evidenced by the speech of the ANC's Treasurer-General to the ANC's 1997 Conference. Addressing the ANC's fundraising concerns, Makhenkesi Stofile noted that

> ... there were a number of options. One was the National Party option, which formed companies and gave them contracts which produced a steady stream of income. We didn't think this was a good thing to do. We then considered joint ventures and also thought that they would not be viable and would be a source of conflict. We opted for the role of facilitators for black business in the country. There are black

businesses whom we have been able to turn to when we're in trouble.[24]

The often negative publicity generated by these relationships has ensured that they have remained far from secret. Perhaps the most notorious of these relationships was that established between the ANC, the businessman Sandi Majali, and the Iraq government of Saddam Hussein – a nexus known colloquially as the 'Oilgate' scandal.

Following the first Gulf War, in which Saddam Hussein's regional ambitions were thwarted by a united international response, there was a concerted effort to ensure that Iraq would struggle to cobble together the same powers it wielded when it fatefully decided to invade Kuwait in the wake of the decade-long Iran–Iraq war. Key to this process was the imposition of sanctions, designed, much like those levied against apartheid South Africa, to emasculate Iraq's leadership corps. Aware of the potentially grave human costs of sanctions amongst ordinary Iraqis, the UN established the Oil-For-Food programme, which was established in December 1996.[25]

The Oil-For-Food programme worked simply. According to the programme, the UN would oversee the sale of Iraqi oil to different bidders. The money raised from oil sales would be deposited into a UN-controlled escrow account, out of which food, medicines and other supplies could be bought and distributed to ordinary Iraqis. It was a truly massive programme: between the end of 1996 and the US invasion of Iraq in March 2003, roughly $64bn in oil was sold via the arrangement.[26] It was a figure equal to the GDP of many small to medium-size countries, and one which ensured that any number of schemes would be concocted by various agents and bodies around the world to wrangle their own slice.

The Oil-For-Food programme had two key weaknesses that ensured such manipulation could take place. The first was that the Iraqi government (via the Ministry of Oil and its related marketing arm, Somo) was able to decide to whom oil could be sold and how much oil each recipient would be entitled to lift. This allowed the Iraqi government to leverage this discretion to exert – and, most importantly, buy – political influence. Those who offered to bat for Iraq on the world stage would receive allocations, while those associated with countries or companies that were at odds with Hussein's regime would be 'punished' by being denied allocations. To quote from the Volcker Report, the excoriating independent investigation of the Oil-For-Food programme:

> As early as Phase II of the Programme, the Government of Iraq began directing oil allocations to particular countries and individuals. Iraqi officials took the position that it was within their discretion to sell oil to countries 'friendly to Iraq' and individuals perceived as being able to influence public opinion in favour of Iraq. The Government of Iraq also believed that it had the discretion to cease oil sales to companies based in countries perceived as less friendly to Iraq.
>
> Subsequent oil allocations fell into two categories, which appear in SOMO allocation tables beginning in Phase II. 'Regular' oil allocations were given to established oil companies, many of which regularly had purchased Iraqi oil prior to the imposition of sanctions and had proved to be reliable purchasers. 'Special' allocations were given to individuals, organizations, and political parties considered to be 'friends' of Iraq or perceived as holding political views supportive of Iraq.[27]

The second weak spot was that the Iraqi government was able to slap surcharges onto each sale, in violation of the terms of the programme. The surcharges were usually in the region of $0.05 per barrel – a figure that, over the course of the entire programme, netted the Iraqi government in excess of $220 million.[28] Central to this system was the fact that the surcharge payments would not be paid via the UN escrow account, but instead directly into the accounts of the Iraqi government itself, allowing it to skim considerable funds off the top despite the best efforts of the UN. In reality, the surcharge payments were nothing more than bribes, as they simply had to be paid by buying companies in order to get their desired contracts. These bribes would be directly responsible for funding the Iraqi government and its abusive state machinery.

According to the Volcker Report, South Africa's involvement in the Oil-For-Food scandal was one of the most clear-cut cases of abuse for political purposes uncovered by investigators. Indeed, it was a prime 'example in the Programme of exploitation of the symbiotic relationship between a country's closely aligned political and business figures and the Government of Iraq ... [T]he principals ... used their relationships with South African political leaders to obtain oil allocations under the programme.'[29]

For Iraq, a friendship with South Africa offered many advantages. In particular, it was keen to draw on the considerable international diplomatic cachet that South Africa's government carried in the years following the overthrow of apartheid. This diplomatic leverage was confirmed in 1997 when Thabo Mbeki, then deputy president, was appointed as the chairperson of both the Non-Aligned Movement (NAM) and the African Union. As head of NAM, South Africa was loud in its support of Iraq, especially in the lead-up to the Iraq War. In 2002, for example, South Africa decried international meddling in the work of international weapons inspectors examining Iraq's alleged stockpile of nuclear warheads and biological weapons, even going so far as to send its own weapons inspection team to bolster the UN-led efforts. Most importantly, South Africa, as head of NAM, was able to call a number of extraordinary meetings of the UN Security Council to make the case for the peaceful resolution of the weapons of mass destruction imbroglio.

When Iraq was finally invaded in March 2003, the ANC condemned the invasion in the strongest possible terms, and committed support for 'all efforts to end the unilateral aggression of the United States and other countries'.[30] There was, of course, much to protest about, not least the clearly fabricated and sexed-up evidence that Iraq was in possession of weapons of mass destruction. But whether the ANC and the South African government issued their protests purely out of a sense of moral obligation is muddied by the fact that, by then, it had already received a considerable amount of money from the Oil-For-Food programme.

The man at the centre of this arrangement was one Sandile Majali who, from at least 2000 onwards, was considered close to both Thabo Mbeki and, especially, Kgalema Motlanthe. In December 2000, Majali secured his first 'win' in his dealings with Iraq. He was introduced to Iraqi Deputy Prime Minister Tariq Aziz by an Iraqi-American businessman and attended a series of meetings in Baghdad to discuss a possible oil allocation to his company, Montega Trading. The result was that Montega, with no prior experience in logistics, oil or shipping, was granted a concession to lift two million barrels of oil,[31] Majali's inexperience having paled into insignificance next to the information that he had the official blessing of the ANC. Indeed, when Somo drew up the first order letter, it listed Montega as being under the control of 'Sandi Majali – Advisor to the President of South Africa'.[32]

Remarkably, even after this deal went sour – Iraq claimed Majali had failed to pay the requisite surcharges – Majali was able to secure further deals, this time through his newly formed company, Imvume Management. By March 2002, Imvume had secured an additional deal to lift a further two million barrels intended for the Strategic Fuel Fund, which manages South Africa's fuel reserves, with a further concession of another 6 million barrels for June 2002. To do so, Majali once again leaned heavily on his political connectivity. In September 2001, as joint head of both the South African Business Council for Economic Transformation and the South Africa-Iraq Association, he led a delegation of officials from the South African Department of Minerals and Energy and the Strategic Fuel Fund to Baghdad.[33] To confirm Majali's status as the ANC's selected representative, Kgalema Motlanthe smoothed the way for the trip with a letter to the South Africa-Iraq Friendship Association stating that Majali's position in the Friendship Association had been granted the ANC's 'full approval and blessing'. Remarkably, Motlanthe further claimed that Majali had been approved by the ANC 'as a designated person to lead the implementation processes arising out of our economic development programmes'.[34]

Majali, meanwhile, impressed upon Somo and the Iraq Oil Ministry that any deals with Imvume would be used to strengthen ties between the ANC and Iraq's Baathist Party. In September 2001, for instance, he wrote to Somo requesting an allocation of 12 million barrels of oil, noting that 'a joint effort between the ANC and the Arab Ba'ath Party will add a lot of value towards achieving common political objectives'.[35] He even went so far as to ask for a considerable discount, requesting that that a 12 million barrel allocation be granted 'with particular attention to the competitive pricing of this transaction for the benefit of both parties in order to build financial resources to support political programmes. I am convinced that you do appreciate that such financial resources are crucial for the long term sustainability of the political pro-grammes that [the ANC and Ba'ath] parties will be implementing and to run seminars, workshops in order to develop effective political devel-opment strategies.'[36]

There was no doubt in anyone's mind that Majali was being awarded his contracts purely on the basis of his political connections rather than his abilities as an oil shipper. Once allocations had been granted to his company, the barrels were lifted, shipped and sold by the international company Glencore. Imvume was then paid a commission on the sale, like all good political middlemen. Indeed, when Majali was questioned by UN investigators about his role in the Oil-For-Food programme, his lawyer sent a response that articulated his role beyond any doubt:

> Majali admits to a long standing close relationship with and membership of the ANC. Both Majali and the ANC had admitted that the ANC promoted the business activities of Imvume, with the authorities of the former Iraqi government. This was in the course of legitimate, above-board political support and the promotion of Imvume as an emerging Black Empowerment resources trading company, in the restructur-ing of the South African oil and fuels industry. It is ordinary, standard, everyday, commercial business practice for compa-nies to receive political support and be promoted, at a politi-cal level, in international trading activities. It is routine for high-level political delegations throughout the world to in-clude business delegations and to receive introductions, en-couragement and political support in business opportunities. This is precisely how Majali 'used his close ties' with the ANC in pursuing business opportunities in Iraq.[37]

Unfortunately, these arguments rubbed up against the fact that Majali was, at the same time, receiving contracts from the state and passing on considerable funds to the ANC. This was done relatively simply. In March 2002, as we saw above, Imvume was granted a concession to lift two million barrels of oil. This was done to satisfy a tender that Imvume had won from the South Africa Strategic Fuel Fund. To ensure that Majali got the concession, despite his failure to pay surcharges under the Montega deal, the Fuel Fund wrote to Iraqi officials to calm their fears, stating the Imvume was a 'strategic partner' in the restructuring of South Africa's oil market.[38]

Things took a strange turn soon after Imvume was granted the concession. Before the oil was even lifted out of Iraq, the Fuel Fund made an advance payment to Imvume for $2 million out of a contract of $10 million.[39] Almost immediately thereafter, Imvume allegedly transferred the bulk of the advance into the account of the ANC: four cheques totalling roughly R11 million that the ANC intended to use to pay for a portion of the 2004 election campaign.[40] But this meant that Imvume was without the necessary cash to pay Glencore, threatening to scupper the entire deal. To resolve this issue, PetroSA, the South African parastatal, agreed to pay Glencore directly to ensure that the deal went ahead and that the Mossel Bay refinery it was intended for would still receive its payload.[41] In effect, PetroSA had paid for the delivery twice over – once to Glencore and once to Imvume, more than doubling the cost to the state to R33m when it was initially priced at R15 million. In effect, by some fancy footwork, PetroSA had paid money to the ANC via Imvume.

But the 'Oilgate' saga had the downside of considerable negative press coverage. In addition, much as happened to Schabir Schaik, Majali would be faced with legal troubles linked to investigations by the UN or by local South African legal minds. When Majali was found dead in his room at the Quatermain Hotel in Sandton at the end of December 2010, for example, creditors representing PetroSA claimed that they intended to try and recover funds from the Oilgate transaction from his estate.

The result was that the 'comrades in arms' model was arguably both too controversial to pursue as a long-term strategy and, vitally, unreliable in ensuring a continuous flow of money to the ANC's election coffers. The result was that the ANC adopted its third, and current, model of party funding that offered considerably more reliability: the party business.

Addressing ANC delegates in 2007, Mendi Msimang explained the new approach and its huge success:

Notwithstanding the fact that our Movement continued to work ceaselessly with local business as well as with sympathetic organisations in different countries of the world, it became abundantly clear that for the ANC to survive in order to carry out its mandate to lead and provide a better life for all the citizens of the country, it had to strive hard to generate funding within the Republic of South Africa rather than depend on external funding ... It was important that we establish our own platform to be self-sufficient ...

To build a sound portfolio of investments has taken us a long time to put together, but it has been worthwhile. We have now managed and already used part of these investments to provide part of the resources for this Conference. I am happy to announce that the market value of all our investments stand at no less than R1.75bn. That is what the Movement owns.[42]

The best known case of the ANC effectively running a business front is that of Chancellor House, a story broken due to the stellar investigative work of the *Mail & Guardian* and the Institute for Security Studies during a joint project. Chancellor House – named after the building in which Nelson Mandela and Oliver Tambo ran their law firm – were formed in 2003 and based in the suburb of Rosebank in Johannesburg. While it is known that the notable ANC historian Bernard Magubane was its original founder, its shareholding and ultimate beneficiaries were initially kept purposefully opaque. According to share registers, Chancellor House and its subsidiaries are owned by the Chancellor House Trust. The Chancellor House Trust is, in turn, listed as a charitable institution, suggesting that all its earnings are diverted to 'charity'. However, the original trust deed indicates that the Chancellor House Trust retained considerable political connections. The main trustees, for example, were Popo Molefe, an ANC NEC member and former provincial premier, and Salukazi Dakile-Hlongwane, the CEO of BEE company Nozala Investments.[43]

While the ultimate ownership of Chancellor House was initially kept under wraps, it was nevertheless widely considered by senior ANC leaders as, effectively, the ANC's internal investment vehicle. Various senior figures in the ANC interviewed by the ISS and the *Mail & Guardian* confirmed this fact. One who agreed to be interviewed anonymously recalled that the ANC Treasurer-General Mendi Msimang had been pitching for contracts from the Department of Minerals and Energy as early as 2002: 'It said the money was for the ANC ... You can speak to any ANC leader. There is no question, Chancellor House is regarded as an ANC company. It is officially supposed to be an entity for ANC funding.'[44] In 2007, Kgalema Motlanthe admitted to the *Financial Mail* that Chancellor House was an 'ANC vehicle' devoted solely to raising funds for the party.[45] And, in 2010, in a report compiled by the Public Protector, it was readily accepted by investigators that the ANC had a direct and material interest in Chancellor House.[46]

Since its formation, Chancellor House had gained shares in a wide number of companies, mostly focusing on large-scale engineering, mining and energy projects – all of which frequently touched on state spending and state regulation. In 2004, for example, Chancellor House was part of a large BEE deal involving the massive engineering and industrial equipment firm, Bateman Engineering. Bateman Africa, the company's local subsidiary, was split so that BEE partners received a 51 per cent stake in the company – 10 per cent of which was granted to Chancellor House.[47] Bateman, meanwhile, is frequently involved in large mining and infrastructure projects, all of which could founder on the sharp-edged rocks of regulation overseen by the state. While it is unclear how much money Chancellor House could have made from this shareholding, it was reported that, in 2009 alone, Bateman Africa was due to earn a R20 million profit.[48]

What Chancellor House may have offered to its business partners has been made particularly clear in its involvement in the mining sector. According to the investigation conducted by the *Mail & Guardian* and the ISS into the fund, Chancellor House was able to take a stake in the Continental Consortium (the exact size of the share is unclear). Continental, in turn, owned 23 per cent of Wits Gold, a potentially controversial company.[49] Wits Gold was listed in April 2006 and allegedly operated as a BEE outsourcing company – in other words, a shell via which key mining houses could ensure that their mining ventures achieved BEE eligibility. With a 40 per cent empowerment index, Wits

Gold took control of the resources of a number of major players, including AngloGold Ashanti, Gold Fields and ARMGold-Harmony. Once these resources had been taken over, Wits Gold applied for new mining rights, freshly armed with new BEE credentials – mining rights that would be regulated by the state and the Department of Minerals and Energy. Vitally, the original sellers of the mining resources retained the right to purchase back 40 per cent of the original mines once Wits Gold had moved them to the 'bankable feasibility' stage.[50] This has only heightened the suspicion that Wits Gold's only value is provided by having the right demographics and political connections.

Chancellor House entered into another potentially fraught mining deal at roughly the same time. According to the deal, it became the strategic equity partner of the Russian minerals group, Renova, in a project that involved the mining of potentially massive manganese deposits in the Kalahari. Chancellor House owned roughly 25 per cent of the company that was given rights – once again, by the state – to mine the concession, by the name of United Manganese of Kalahari (in which Renova retained a 49 per cent stake).[51] Almost immediately after it was formed, United Manganese was valued at $20 million, suggesting that Chancellor House's share would be valued at $5 million. It is entirely possible that the ANC may earn considerably more than this – the project, once manganese extraction begins, is said to be worth roughly $1 billion.[52]

But by far the most controversial Chancellor House deal got off the ground in 2005, when the international engineering and industrial project giant Hitachi established a South African subsidiary. Hitachi Power Africa (of which Chancellor House held a 25 per cent stake)[53] was formed in order to take advantage of the massive recapitalisation to be undertaken by the national state-owned power utility, Eskom. It was a truly huge project – Eskom had pledged to construct at least three large coal-fired power stations to overcome the shortage of electricity that had led to widespread blackouts across the country. In 2008, it was announced that Hitachi Power Africa had been awarded two contracts to supply boilers for new power stations in Limpopo and Mpumalanga, at a total value of R38.5 billion.[54]

How much the ANC may make off these projects is unclear. In 2010, Hitachi Power Africa claimed that the ANC would only make

R50 million as a result of the boiler projects.[55] Other estimates, however, suggest that it could rake in as much as R1 billion profit.[56] Either way, the ANC is in the invidious position of attempting to manage the health of its bank balance while still serving the needs of the country. Indeed, while the economy as a whole reeled at the news in 2010 that Eskom intended to hike its rates by 25 per cent to pay for the recapitalisation, the ANC was in a conflicted position – it would benefit financially from the rate hike as this would pay for the contracts earned via Hitachi Power Africa, but would struggle to meet its stated socio-economic goals in the face of such extreme inflationary pressure.

The news that Hitachi's Eskom contracts had been awarded while Valli Moosa was the Chairperson of Eskom also raised eyebrows.[57] Moosa, a former Minister, retained close connections to the ANC, serving on the NEC. Vitally, he served on the ANC Finance Committee, and admitted to being involved in fundraising activities 'from time to time'.[58] According to an investigation by the South African Public Protector, it was established that Moosa had failed to recuse himself from discussions relating to the Hitachi Power Africa contract even though, as an ANC member, he was in a position of conflict of interest in overseeing the award of a contract to a company in which Chancellor House had holdings: 'Mr Moosa failed to manage his conflict of interest in compliance with the Conflict of Interest Policy of Eskom and therefore acted improperly,' the Report concluded.[59]

While the Report also found that no undue pressure had been brought to bear in the selection of Hitachi Power Africa, Chancellor House has become a conflict-of-interest time bomb. Public officials with ANC affiliations are often placed in a position that enables them to award or decline contracts to companies affiliated with their political home. And, being so closely connected with the ANC leadership, there is little to suggest that sufficient controls have been put in place to ensure that Chancellor House does not receive the 'inside track' on new and forthcoming government contracts. As a governance issue, Chancellor House reeks.

A foul smell continues to emanate from another version of the party business: the Progressive Business Forum (PBF), established in 2006.[60] The PBF's model is simple and disarmingly unethical. Businessmen are invited to join by paying a substantial fee. A tiered system of party friends, ranked in platinum, gold and silver, much as casinos reward high rollers, pay between R3 000 and R7 000 for the privilege. Companies are invited to join, too, paying between R12 500 and R60 000 directly to the ANC itself.[61] In return for their membership, PBF's friends are granted a series of benefits, including direct access to important government and ANC officials for mutually beneficial one-on-one meetings.[62]

When news broke of the PBF's existence in 2007, the ANC was quick to rise to its defence. One argument was that the PBF only granted members access to ANC members rather than government officials – ignoring, of course, that almost all senior ANC members also hold senior state positions. The other argument, articulated most recently by Jacob Zuma, was almost syndicalist in tone. A close relationship between business and the party, so the argument went, was reflective of a healthy, cooperative and communicative society, rather than an ethical minefield. Speaking to reporters in September 2010, Zuma waxed lyrical about the relationship between business and the ANC, in so doing articulating almost the exact opposite of what his Alliance partners must have been thinking. 'Politics and business go together,' Zuma claimed. 'Now, once business gets closer to a political party, you must know that things are going very well in the country. It means in South Africa, things are going very well. Business, the ruling party don't have a problem. They are together. Wonderful.'[63]

How much money has been raised by the PBF is unclear. Payments are repeated annually and, by 2007, it was reported that it had 2 000 members, although no information was provided as to what proportion of these members were high-paying businesses.[64] What is certain is that the funds raised are not insubstantial. In September 2010, during the PBF conference at which Jacob Zuma was quoted above, the PBF raised R500 000 from members in return for spaces in exhibition areas, breakfasts with ministers and seats at a NGC dinner; presumably over and above annual contributions.[65] Since businessmen are always keen to press the flesh with powerful political figures, organising a large number of conferences must be relatively straightforward, suggesting that the ANC has a useful spigot that can be turned on at will.

Of course, it is not just the ANC that needs to raise funds to operate; other parties, too, have to rely on the peripatetic goodwill of donors to survive. As a result, many have been reluctant to support any change to legislation around party funding that would lead to increased disclosure. The Democratic Alliance indicated in 2002 that it supported legislation that would require a disclosure of all donations in excess of R50 000. By 2005, it had made an about-face, and even went so far as to join the ANC in opposing litigation around party funding initiated by the Institute for a Democratic South Africa (Idasa). How much money it raises from donations is somewhat unclear. The only indicative figures come from 2004, when it was claimed that the DA raised about R21 million from private funders.[66]

In defending its secrecy, the DA has argued that donors may baulk at disclosure of their donations on the basis that ANC members in government may 'punish' DA supporters.[67] It is not an unreasonable argument, although it does little to erase concerns that the DA has, on this point at least, foregone its oft-stated commitment to transparency and accountability. Equally compelling has been the argument that, for long periods of time, the DA held no political power of note, controlling only the city of Cape Town (and then under the broader provincial leadership of the ANC). Donating to the DA purely for political influence would therefore be folly, suggesting that donations were made by individuals and businesses that identified with the DA's largely free market ideology. This, of course, is no longer the case: the DA now controls the Western Cape, one of three wealthiest provinces in South Africa (along with Gauteng and KwaZulu-Natal). The temptations of office and the power of patronage are now firmly DA concerns; how well these are managed, and how honestly the DA conducts itself in this arena, will be major contributors to how it is perceived by the broader population in its struggles to become a truly national power.

Chancellor House and power politics in the new South Africa

Chancellor House raises serious questions about political and corporate governance in South Africa and the frequently blurred line between the

ANC, the state and business. But it also deeply impacts on the power politics of South Africa.

At the simplest level, Chancellor House and the ANC's formalised approach to corporate funding (via bodies such as the Progressive Business Forum) suggests a growing political inequality in South Africa. Fundamentally, the democratic project, and any democratic system, draws its legitimacy from the idea that each individual has an equal say, expressed by means of the vote and facilitated by other political freedoms such as the right of association. Chancellor House and the Progressive Business Forum suggest that this is not the reality; in the latter case, a well-placed donation grants immediate access for the corporate community to the ANC's elite; in the former, companies that are willing to share their stakes with the ANC are arguably provided with an unfair advantage in the competition for state contracts. As corruption expert Susan Rose-Ackerman notes, 'the worry is favouritism. Groups that give funds to elected officials might expect returns whether it be from preference when seeking contracts and state tenders, or in terms of favourable policy outcomes. When the interests of such wealthy groups conflict with those of the general public, this undermines democratic values and outcomes.'[68]

A key example of this process is the status of the government's BEE programme. For many of those in the ANC and the Alliance as a whole, BEE is an eyesore, a game of backhanders that only enriches a tiny politically connected elite. Cosatu, for example, has pulled no punches in decrying the way in which BEE has merely transferred funds to a small coterie of fortunate souls. Regardless, the ANC, via Chancellor House, has a powerful financial stake in the maintenance of a deeply unpopular system. Indeed, Chancellor House's success relies almost entirely on BEE and (presumably) the political connectivity of its central operators. How likely is the ANC to revisit BEE when so much of its financial muscle derives from its continued prominence?

Generating a portfolio of close to R2 billion within only a few years of establishment is no mean feat. The rise and stellar success of Chancellor House has sped up the transformation of the ANC from a liberation movement into a fully fledged political party. On one level, the additional funds allow for the creation of a professional party bureaucracy no longer dependent on volunteerism and activism for its operation. More fundamentally, the formalisation of the ANC's funding has cemented a process whereby political power is now wielded with commensurate economic clout. The ANC of 2012 is hugely different from that of 1994 in many ways, but none more so than its ability to draw on the resources of the state in order to maintain power. Perhaps, when reviewing the outcome of the 1994 negotiations, this new reality should be borne in mind. Perhaps those who negotiated South Africa's democratic transition always knew that radical economic transformation was not necessary at the time. Political power begets economic power, especially when a flexible approach to the boundaries between business, the state and the party is added to the mix.

Chapter 8

Precarious Power: BEE and the Growth of South Africa's Black Middle Class

Paul Holden

The model lay delicately half-naked on the bonnet of a white Lamborghini, her pale body serving as platter for a display of freshly rolled sushi. All around, some of the leading lights of South Africa's newly empowered elite eyed the scene hungrily. Only a handful would have been thinking about the nutritional value of the cucumber maki. Bad taste aside, it was a triumphant occasion, celebrating the fortieth birthday of one Kenny Kunene, one of post-apartheid's most notable empowerment successes. The setting was Kunene's nightclub, which, since its formation, had become a must-go destination for the new elite and all their various hangers-on. High-powered politicians thronged in the gaudy lights, in particular Julius Malema, with whom Kunene had expressed a mutual understanding. The tab: considerably more money than most South Africans would see in decades, let alone in a single evening. When Kunene was attacked by Cosatu's Zwelinzima Vavi for his ostentatious show of wealth, his response was hubristic. In an open letter to Vavi in which he told him to 'go hang or go to hell,' he also happily took the time to 'correct [Vavi's] misapprehension that my party cost R700 000. It cost more.'[1]

Such confidence on the part of the party's host and revellers could easily fool the outside observer into believing that these were the new rulers of South Africa (if not quite the masters of the universe seen strutting on Wall Street), a wealthy black elite that drifted across political and business worlds, riding high on the knowledge that their political backup – the ANC – was likely to hold power for the foreseeable future. In some senses this is true – this particular black business elite has assumed remarkable importance within the upper echelons of the ANC. But such a simplistic reading ignores many of the subtleties of the situation, not least how precarious many of the fortunes of the new breed of black millionaires are – and how tenuous their position within the political firmament. Far from being the uncontested ruling elite of the New South Africa, the new black empowerment elite is only one amongst a jumble of forces contesting power, using the economic muscle and political connectivity that are their stock in trade. And its existence, until now, has been made possible only because of a unique alignment of political winds, which could change direction at any time: a situation that would no doubt please the ANC's alliance partners.

A short history of Black Economic Empowerment

That some form of economic restructuring would need to take place after the end of apartheid was clear to almost all observers during the dying years of that foetid regime. Within the ANC and the broader liberation movement, the reversal of South Africa's economic exclusivist structure was a given: the economy would have to be deracialised in one way or another. But the exact means to do so was unclear, and, while some sort of economic transformation was envisaged, the exact terms were slightly fuzzy.

The closest that the ANC came to fully articulating a post-apartheid plan was the ANC's most popular exile theory – the National Democratic Revolution. The NDR was, in one way, a means of reconciling the socialist and nationalist/Africanist poles in the alliance. The end-point, it was long claimed, was a non-racial socialism – rejected by many, privately, as a utopian vision, and certainly one that was to receive a knock following the fall of the Berlin Wall. But it was inconceivable that South Africa's racially segregated economy would be able to move directly into the socialist future. Instead, there would exist a first phase – the slow deracialisation of the economy through the creation of a black bourgeoisie. That no time frame was put on the period during which the black bourgeoisie would rule the roost allowed nationalists within the organisation to believe that a period of mutual enrichment could occur for quite some time into the future, while those on the left could console themselves in the knowledge that the 'true' path to liberation lay in socialism.

But, as this suggests, the idea of a forceful and acquisitive black bour-geoisie was one that was treated with some degree of distaste within the ANC in exile. A black middle class was not necessarily desirable: it was to be tolerated on the way to socialist utopia. Such distaste was, in many ways, cemented by the actions of the late apartheid government. From at least the early 1980s, white capital in South Africa had argued for a relaxation of the less productive elements of apartheid, in particular the job-reservation policies that forbade employing black South Africans as semi-skilled or skilled labour at much lower rates of pay than the artifi-cially protected white working class.[2] Indeed, it was this group – white capital, including both English and Afrikaner businesspeople – that was the first group to publicly make contact with the ANC in exile in 1984, sig-nalling, for many, the coming end of apartheid in its current formation.[3]

Buffeted by the ongoing civil war and upbraided by white capital for being a block on unfettered acquisition (and for unsuccessfully nego-tiating South Africa's pariah status and the economic sanctions that followed), the apartheid state initiated a process of reform. The most publicly obvious step – and the most widely reviled – was the creation of the Tricameral Parliament, which provided limited voting rights to coloured and Indian South Africans while completely excluding African aspirations. The idea behind this widely reviled policy was to try and widen the beneficiaries of apartheid, adding additional buffers to pro-tect the apartheid state – buffers that could be drawn from other South African minorities.

While Africans would be excluded from political representation, economic integration was envisaged as a key part of trying to create a new pro-apartheid alliance. From the early 1980s onwards, the apartheid state began loosening certain restrictions on black business in the townships, actively promoting the creation of a black middle class that would believe it owed its success to its erstwhile overlords.[4] That a newly emergent black middle class could become a political ally of the NP was not an entirely ludicrous idea. As part of its project of social engineering, the apartheid government had overseen the creation of ethnically exclusive homelands, also known as bantustans. Each bantustan was to be the official 'home' of the different ethnicities of black South Africans. Powers of governance – except over defence matters – were granted to bantustan rulers such as Lucas Mangope. Leveraging grants from central government, as well as from limited tax receipts from remitting migrant workers, bantustan leaders created a not insubstantial network of patronage tied to government employment, facilitating the emergence of a politically complacent black middle class. It was out of this milieu that one of the ANC's fiercest critics – Chief Mangosuthu Buthelezi and his Inkatha Freedom Party – emerged to complicate the transition from apartheid.

For the ANC in exile, and for the liberation movement more broadly, the cynical creation of a black middle class in the bantustans and townships only served to further sully the idea that a black middle class would necessarily be progressive (read: support the ANC). It was an idea not without foundation. As protest mushroomed in the homelands, the apartheid security apparatus often worked hand-in-glove with bantustan rulers and their patchwork patronage network of government employees and petty businesspeople to torture and kill activists.[5] The result was not only distaste amongst the liberation movement for ethnic chauvinism, but an equally wary eye cocked in the direction of black businessmen claiming progressive intentions.

Ambivalence towards the idea of a black bourgeoisie meant that, while some form of black economic empowerment was anticipated, the exact details remained unclear. The clearest statement as to what BEE might entail was included in the seminal RDP document. Even here, however, beyond a few broad statements regarding preferential procurement, no great plan was articulated:

The domination of business activities by white business and the exclusion of black people and women from the mainstream of economic activity are causes for great concern for the reconstruction and development process. A central objective of the RDP is to deracialise business ownership and control completely through focused policies of Black Economic Empowerment. These policies must aim to make it easier for black people to gain access to capital for business development. The democratic Government must ensure that no discrimination occurs in financial institutions. State and parastatal institutions will also provide capital for the attainment of BEE objectives. The democratic Government must also introduce tendering out procedures, which facilitate BEE. Special emphasis must also be placed on training, upgrading and real participation in ownership.[6]

In the absence of any clearly stated direction, the first steps towards a process of empowerment were taken by white business itself in a canny move that helped to both cement its democratic intentions and also provide an early model for how empowerment could function. Equally important was the fact that BEE provided the means and momentum via which South Africa's major conglomerates (of which only four held 83 per cent of all assets on the Johannesburg Stock Exchange[7]) could begin a process of unbundling in order to focus on core internationally competitive assets. Far from being an entirely altruistic move, many of the conglomerates were more than happy to sell off chunks of businesses they no longer wanted to handle.

The earliest such move was taken by Sanlam, which, as early as 1993, sold 10 per cent of its holdings in Metropolitan Life to a black empowerment consortium headed by Nthato Motlana.[8] Numerous deals followed shortly thereafter, a flood of transactions in which black empowerment groups were sold stakes in some of the largest companies in South Africa. By 1998, significant progress had already been made. In 1994, for example, only 0.5 per cent of the shares on the JSE had been owned by black investors. By 1998, by some estimates, this had reached 20 per cent[9] (other, more conservative estimates, put it in the region of 10 per cent).[10] At its highest point in 1995, BEE deals accounted for 38.7 per cent of the total value of all transactions on the JSE (although this had dropped to 10.8 per cent by 1999).[11]

The deals, however, quickly ran into trouble. The root cause was the fact that the emerging black elite had little or no access to ready-made capital resources. To undertake the deals, as a result, they had to raise significant funds in the form of loans. To do so, numerous special-purpose vehicles were created, almost all of which relied on high dividends and rapidly increasing share prices to remain feasible. If neither of these materialised, the special-purpose vehicles were left with highly leveraged assets whose earnings were not enough to cover interest payments on loans.[12] Following the Asian crisis in 1998, these fears were realised: the stock market dipped and interest rates rapidly increased on the back of fears of the massive outflow of speculative capital.

A number of newly empowered entities struggled in such choppy waters and the percentage of black ownership on the JSE dropped precipitously. To rub salt in the wounds, many of the multinationals, now flush with cash following international re-listings and the original BEE fire sale, were able to buy back the shares from black investors at a snip. In one instance, Anglo American sold its shares in Johannesburg Consolidated Investments (JCI) to empowerment groups at R54 a share. Following the Asian crisis, Anglo used the drop in asset prices to buy back two of JCI's major assets – profitable gold mines – at a much reduced price. The total profit for Anglo on the deal was R140 million. The 'only smile belonged to Anglo,' commented one media outlet. '[It] made a handsome profit on a sale it had originally declared would be a magnanimous gesture towards wealth-sharing.'[13] Remarkably, as Carmody has noted in an insightful study in 2002, those with pre-existing access to capital were able to take greater control of the JSE following the collapse of the first phase of empowerment: Afrikaner businessmen, for example, grew their shareholdings in the JSE from 24 per cent to 36 per cent between 1996 and 1999.[14]

The first phase of BEE, however, was not entirely devoid of state intervention. While the ANC had been reluctant to engage directly with the thorny issues of legislating the racial redistribution of ownership, it was quick to tackle the issue of employment. In 1998, legislation was passed to give effect to employment equity (also known as affirmative action). The legislation required that a certain number of employees in any company be drawn from historically disadvantaged communities.[15] It was this legislation, rather than the flashy yet unsustainable early BEE deals, that would have a lasting impact on the South African political economy. As we will see in greater detail below, employment equity – and the mass re-staffing of the state bureaucracy to bring it into line with equity requirements – almost single-handedly fostered the creation of a sizeable black middle class.

When the second phase of BEE began is difficult to pinpoint exactly, although it seems to have been in full swing by the middle of 1999. The key difference between the first and second phases of BEE was the role of the state: now, unlike during the five years of much flash but little substance that preceded it, the state would become directly involved in ensuring ownership transfers and management staffing. The most significant step in this regard was the appointment of the quasi-official BEE Commission in 1999.[16] Chaired by Cyril Ramaphosa, the Commission was tasked with evaluating past experiences of BEE and making suggestions as to state policy. The outcome – the official Commission Report in 2001 – called for the adoption of legislation and a mechanism that contemplated the monitoring and formalisation of 'industry charters'.[17] The charters stipulated industry-wide targets as to the levels of ownership to be transferred by agreed dates. In addition, the charters committed industry to ensuring that black staff were also appointed to positions of control – rather than just ownership – by providing guides as to the levels of black employees that would need to appear within the managerial and director corps, aided by a commitment to skills transfers.[18] By focusing on issues beyond just the transfer of ownership, it was hoped that empowerment could become more holistic or, to use the official phraseology, broad-based.[19] These issues were to be monitored by means of BEE scorecards, which allocated points to entities based on their adherence to BEE targets.[20] If a company failed to score decently on its BEE scorecard, it would be excluded from all state procurement (even at the third or fourth remove) – a not insignificant threat, as state spending equalled roughly 20 per cent of GDP.

The shift to an interventionist approach towards BEE was matched by a remarkable sea-change in the content of political discourse. The socialist endpoint of the NDR was quietly dropped, while key figures preached that social transformation and the eradication of poverty would be achieved by the creation of a black middle class, or, in the parlance of the time, a 'patriotic bourgeoisie'. In 1999, for example, Thabo Mbeki, in an address to the Black Management Forum, argued that the ANC and its partners should drop any sense of shame in the desire to create a black middle class:

> Ours is a capitalist society. It is therefore inevitable that, in part – and I repeat, in part – we must address this goal of deracialisation within the context of the property relations characteristic of a capitalist economy.
>
> As part of the realisation of the aim to eradicate racism in our country, we must strive to create and strengthen a black capitalist class.
>
> Because we come from among the black oppressed, many among us feel embarrassed to state this goal as nakedly as we should ...
>
> All this frightens and embarrasses all those of us who are black and might be part of the new rich. Accordingly, we walk as far and as fast as we can from the notion that the struggle against racism in our country must include the objective of creating a black bourgeoisie ...
>
> As part of our continuing struggle to wipe out the legacy of racism, we must work to ensure that there emerges a black bourgeoisie, whose presence within our economy and society will be part of the process of the deracialisation of the economy and society.[21]

Underpinning the idea of the creation of the black bourgeoisie was the notion that black capitalists, or black managers, or black employees, would, due to community bonds, avoid the pitfalls, prejudices and predations of apartheid capitalism. It was an idea that was picked up with gusto by many of the biggest names in the empowerment world. In 2005,

for example, Saki Macozoma – one of the 'Fab Four' who constituted
the wealthiest empowerment figures – gave a candid interview to *Time*
magazine. 'You need the same kind of person who was the bedrock of
the A.N.C. to be bedrock of a society that is based on a middle class,'
he explained. 'There is no way I would support a free-enterprise system
that tolerates poverty. But with five or six of us spread out through the
economy, that can make a difference in a very fundamental way.'[22] ANC
spokesman Smuts Ngonyama, never known for his subtlety, presented
the crasser side of the black bourgeois argument: 'I didn't join the struggle to be poor,' he explained in a huff in 2007.[23]

While BEE was intended to be broad-based, most of the deals following the BEE Commission Report – and most of the charters that
were introduced – focused on South Africa's larger sectors: minerals,
telecommunications and finance key amongst them. Other sectors were
slower to reform and adopt industry charters. Partially this was due to
market demand: minerals, finance and telecommunication offered quick
profits and considerable social cachet. Others, which would have required a longer period to produce sustainable profits, were ignored – in
particular, agriculture, which has retained many of its apartheid charac-
teristics despite government's reiterated commitment to land reform.[24]
There was also the reality that the state's reach was limited: it could
most effectively lobby for empowerment (and wield the necessary stick)
in industries over which the government had leverage via the issuing of
licenses, concessions and contracts.[25] Without such reach, or the induce-
ment of access to state procurement contracts, empowerment was slow
to show in the broader economy.

Nevertheless, the publication of industry charters (starting in 2000),
the publication of the BEE Commission Report in 2001, the passing into
law of the Broad-Based Black Economic Empowerment Act of 2003, as
well as the gazetting of 'codes of good practice' in late 2004 and 2005,[26]
provided regulatory focus and encouraged a boom in empowerment
deals. From 2003 to 2006, an average of 222 empowerment transactions
took place every year. At its peak, in 2004, 243 deals were concluded.
The value of the deals was not insignificant, reaching a total of R204.3
billion, nearly R70 billion more than all deals that had taken place in
the preceding nine years. And while the number of transactions slipped

in 2007 to 125, the total value of the transactions reached their highest ever level: R96 billion. Without the global recession, the scale of empowerment deals would undoubtedly have continued to grow, instead of stuttering, as it did, to a relatively meagre 58 deals worth R36.5 billion in 2009.[27]

These dry figures cannot however convey the popular conception of BEE, or the manner in which the seemingly daily deals dominated the political discourse in the country. At a symbolic level, the period from 2003 to 2008 was the one in which South Africa went BEE-mad, with paper millionaires created seemingly from nothing – or, at the very least, from the magic generated from the friction of financial engineering and political connectivity. Nowhere was this clearer than in the virtual obsession with the biggest BEE players, most notably Cyril Ramaphosa, Tokyo Sexwale, Patrice Motsepe and Saki Macozoma, or in the taste of some of the newly empowered for high-profile luxury fripperies such as Kunene's ill-conceived sushi party. For some, the new BEE elite was a travesty, the epitome of the betrayal of the struggle. But for a new and growing element within the ruling class, BEE millionaires were role models, the respected face of an aggressive African nationalism that revelled in the fruits of freedom. It has been this focus – this public focus on BEE and its personalities – that has created the impression that the BEE elite are the new rulers of South Africa: the new Randlords, as *Time* dubbed them in 2005.[28] But socio-political realities are seldom so simple.

Some features of the patriotic bourgeoisie

There are several features of the way in which the process of empowerment and accumulation has played out that need to be understood before we can 'insert' empowerment into the question that guides this volume – who rules South Africa?

The first is that while the raw figures around empowerment are impressive, they mask the fact that black ownership and control of the economy remain small and financially precarious. Certainly, there is little doubt that a considerable amount of value within the country has been brought under black control, with the total value of BEE deals reaching R535 billion in the years from 1995 to 2009.[29] To put this in perspective, the annual output at basic prices of the mining and quarrying sector has averaged around R180 billion per year from 2002 to 2010.

Even more impressive figures are generated when one calculates the percentage of all mergers and acquisition activity taken up by BEE. From 2003 to 2009, BEE deals have never fallen below 23 per cent of transactions (in 2007). At their peak in 2004, BEE deals made up 42.2 per cent of all ownership transactions. Between the years 2003 and 2009, BEE deals constituted, on average, 29 per cent of all ownership trans-actions.[30] Unsurprisingly, these transactions have occurred at the same time as a virtual explosion in the number of black directors serving on the boards of JSE-listed companies. From a figure of only 12 black di-rectors in 1992, the JSE now boasts a total of 770 black directors on the JSE, 526 of them men and 244 women. At the highest level of influ-ence, there are, as of October 2011, 157 black executive directors serving on the boards of JSE-listed companies.[31] The growth in black directors has been particularly strong over the last three years; between 2008 and 2010, the number of black directors on the JSE increased by 58 per cent from 487 to 770.[32]

And yet, while the figures above may seem impressive, they begin to take on a different sheen when compared to the financial might of the rest of capital (both white and foreign-owned) in South Africa. Simply put, at the level of ownership and directorial control, the levels of black involvement in the economy are still a mere fraction of the total. Thus, while BEE deals have been struck left, right and centre, black ownership still accounts for only 17 per cent of all shares on the Johannesburg Stock Exchange.[33] It should be noted that this is a figure given by the JSE, with which the Black Management Forum disagrees: they believe it is more in the region of 5 per cent. Importantly, of the JSE figure, only 8 per cent of this market share is owned directly by black inves-tors – the remaining 9 per cent is indirectly owned 'by black investors through mandated investments such as pension funds'.[34] The number and influence of black directors, too, needs to be put into perspective. While the growth in numbers has been spectacular (from 12 to 770), black directors (both male and female) constitute only 22 per cent of the 3 500 directors serving on the JSE. More importantly, only 20 per cent of all black directors on the JSE hold these positions as executive directors (those directors with major influence on board decisions).[35]

In addition, the total transaction value of BEE deals (which we noted to be valued at over R535 billion between 1995 and 2011), may also be misleading, partially as a result of the collapse of the first round of empowerment companies and partially due to the fact that empowerment partners are incentivised to sell shares quickly if share prices increase exponentially (allowing the creation of massive short-term profits). This, indeed, was the model by which Mzi Khumalo, a major BEE player, secured his fortune: after buying shares in companies that were willing to offer them on good terms (an effective discount) due to empowerment commitments, Khumalo rapidly on-sold his shares,[36] making both a personal fortune and a mockery of the concept of empowerment acting as a solid vehicle for the long-term and sustainable transfer of assets. While newer empowerment deals have now included clauses that prevent shares being sold by BEE partners within a decade, it is clear that overall black asset ownership has decreased as a consequence. Indeed, according to Anthony Butler, writing in 2010, the total value still tied up in BEE deals is around R250 billion – far less than the R535 billion in empowerment transactions between 1995 and 2009 would suggest. By comparison, the private sector is estimated to hold assets in the region of R6 trillion, suggesting that black ownership in the broader economy remains relatively trivial.[37]

More worrying for proponents of BEE is the concern that many of the deals struck in the heyday of empowerment – from 2003 to roughly 2008 – may have been structured in a way that could lead to another cataclysmic collapse of BEE investments. Writing in 2010, the noted commentator and co-founder of BusinessMap Foundation, Jenny Cargill, argued that it is 'reasonable to be pessimistic about BEE investments' surviving what could be a protracted global recession.[38] The reasons for this pessimism are remarkably similar to the underlying cause of the first BEE bubble bursting in the late 1990s. First, Cargill notes, the flood of BEE deals done during and after 2003 were concluded when the JSE was 'a bull market' – when the economic outlook was rosy and share prices extremely high. BEE firms could thus not expect an explosion in share prices and, more importantly, would be heavily stretched if the market entered a dip.[39]

This interacts directly with the second cause for concern: that virtually all BEE deals are financed by debt.[40] Paying off the interest on the debt is possible when dividends are good; but if the market enters into a slump – as it did with the fall of commodity prices in the late 2000s and during the international credit crunch – BEE firms are left with the bag, forced to pay escalating interest charges but unable to finance this with profits from business activity. A drop in the share price would cause even greater calamity: BEE investors would be left with a debt that is higher than the underlying assets – the shares. They would experience the bane of small property holders all around the world following the Credit Crunch: negative equity.[41]

Admittedly, the complete collapse of existing BEE deals is unlikely. One the one hand, it is politically inconceivable, since existing capital would more than likely be aware of the inevitability of major social fallout if property relations were to return to their apartheid levels. If Moeletsi Mbeki is to be believed, Black Economic Empowerment had long been envisaged as the means by which white capital would ingratiate itself into the new democratic dispensation.[42] BEE was part of a pact, the reverse side of which was an assurance that the state maintained market-friendly policies (most clearly represented by the adoption of the remarkably neo-liberal policies of GEAR in 1996). If this pact were to dissolve, white capital would have little means of ensuring continued 'buy-in' on the part of the black political elite, potentially leading this elite to adopt a more rigorously redistributive approach to property relations.

In addition, because many BEE enterprises folded in the late 1990s precisely because of the two structural problems noted above, empowerment deals have been increasingly nuanced. Most deals now try to strike a balance: BEE partners are forbidden to sell their shares for a stipulated period of time (to prevent the Khumalo means of capital accumulation), and, in return, the company being empowered underwrites the loans (and therefore carries the can if the BEE entity goes bust). This has the effect of providing a degree of security to the transactions, although it simultaneously means that BEE capital is constrained in the area in which capital always demands the maximum: the freedom of mobility.

What emerges from a deeper reading of the situation, then, is that the muscular image of BEE is somewhat misplaced. As a result of structural problems and the global economic crunch, BEE deals are in somewhat of a state. Take one of the poster children of BEE: Mvelaphanda. Established by the current Minister for Housing, Tokyo Sexwale, in the early 1990s, Mvelaphanda made its name by stitching together a whirlwind of BEE deals – mostly in resources – that saw it acquire assets in the billions. Following the collapse in mineral prices in 2008, Mvelaphanda was left with a massive debt burden, necessitating the sale of millions of shares in the mining company Gold Fields, the proceeds of which were then ploughed back into a refinancing drive.[43] Most recently, Mvelaphanda has proceeded to unbundle a large portion of its assets, trying to resolve its debt issues at the same time. Far from being the future diverse behemoth in the style of Anglo, it has had its wings clipped to the extent that one newspaper felt comfortable enough to call Mvelaphanda 'the most prominent BEE failure', 'twisting and turning ... to get off the hook of crippling debt'.[44] In this context, it is unsurprising that Sexwale's support for the nationalisation of mines[45] has raised eyebrows, with the left wing in particular postulating that his support for state intervention derives solely from his desire for a bail-out of his struggling mineral portfolio.[46]

It is not, of course, all doom and gloom. The past 17 years have also been marked by another development: a marked increase in the size of the black middle class. Putting exact figures to this is somewhat tricky and depends much on how 'middle class' is defined.[47] One method that seems intuitively sound is to calculate the number of individuals and households earning enough to live a middle-class lifestyle: that is, measured by a universal standard of affluence rather than simply by calculating the number of people who sit in the middle of income distribution in South Africa. By these calculations (specifically the number of people earning between R1 400 and R10 000 per capita per month), South Africa's middle class now numbers 9.9 million people, of whom 49.8 per cent are African.[48] This may not seem a massive leap, considering that the figure was roughly 29 per cent in 1994;[49] but this ignores the explosion in pure numbers of new middle-class South Africans. Between 1994 and 2000, for example, the size of the entire South African middle class increased from 3.5 million to 5 million,[50] and almost doubled – according to the affluence definition – to 9.9 million in 2011.[51]

Even these figures should be taken with a pinch of salt. For many middle-class South Africans, especially those who have had to overcome a generational asset deficit that stemmed from the systematic impoverishment of their elders, finances remain tight and a middle-class status still markedly dependent on monthly income. The ratio of household debt to earnings has, in the last two years, reached its highest ever level in South Africa's modern history: a total over 70 per cent.[52] The greatest growth in the ratio occurred from 2003 onwards, correlating neatly with the explosion of middle-class South Africans that took place at the same time. Forfeitures and asset seizures were not that far away: in 2008 alone, 10 per cent of South Africa's black middle class reported that they had had items repossessed in the previous year.[53]

The severity of debt problems experienced by South Africa's emergent middle class was made clear in a sadly under-read report published by the Public Service Commission in 2007. The report examined the indebtedness of public servants – a relevant area of investigation, considering that the transformation of the public sector has been one of the key drivers of black middle-class growth in South Africa. According to the report, over 20 per cent of all public servants had been served with garnishee orders.[54] Of this 20 per cent of public servants with garnishee orders, 86 per cent were African, 9 per cent coloured, 4 per cent white and 1 per cent Indian.[55] Garnishee orders, simply put, are instituted when a person has defaulted on credit repayments, leading to the intervention of a third party. This third party then secures an agreement on the part of the employer, in this case the state, to pay the debt directly out of the employee's salary, ensuring that the credit is settled. At an indicative level, a garnishee order says: this person is over-indebted. The impacts are, of course, potentially profound. As the report bluntly noted:

> During 2006/2007 there were 216 857 public servants who made garnishee related payments through PERSAL [the state's salary system]. This figure amounts to a staggering

20% of the total number of public servants employed within the Public Service. This means that a fifth of all public servants are over-indebted. This could have severe consequences if such public servants resort to unlawful practices to relieve their personal circumstances. Such actions could include fraud and corruption.[56]

The second key feature of the process of empowerment is one that has long dominated popular perception: that BEE has benefited a small class of individuals, most of whom are connected in some way to the upper echelons of the ANC. Certainly, the public face of BEE has the stamp of the political about it. Of the 'Fab Four' of Tokyo Sexwale, Cyril Ramaphosa, Saki Macozoma and Patrice Motsepe, only one – Motsepe – has not held a position on the ANC's NEC. Motsepe is still, nevertheless, politically connected: one of his sisters is married to Cyril Ramaphosa, another to government stalwart Jeff Radebe.[57] Both Ramaphosa and Sexwale have consistently been linked to runs for the position of President of the ANC. More recently, Sexwale has been seen to be manoeuvring to develop a power base separate from Jacob Zuma via his support of Julius Malema. The perception that BEE has benefited only a small group of cadres has only been made worse by the fact that there has been a tendency by empowerment companies to strike more than one empowerment deal at a time. In 2003, for example, it was reported that a full 72 per cent of all BEE deals had flowed to only six BEE heavyweights.[58]

Amidst the deluge of BEE deals from 2003 onwards, it was difficult not to gasp at the more incestuous deals that seemed to make a mockery of applying the term 'broad-based' to BEE. While there are many to choose from, one of the most notable was Absa's empowerment deal with Batho Bonke. In April 2004, Absa announced that it had agreed to sell 10 per cent of its shareholding to Batho Bonke, bringing the bank in line with the black ownership requirements stipulated in the financial services sectoral charter.[59] Batho Bonke was presented as the essence of broad-based empowerment, as it could claim to have a total of 1.1 million beneficiaries due to its trust-like shareholding.[60] In reality, the deal had been put together under the guiding hand of Tokyo Sexwale, who himself owned a not insignificant stake due to the fact that that a large portion of Batho Bonke was, in fact, owned by Mvelaphanda Holdings.[61] Indeed, according to William Gumede, one of the fiercest critics of the Mbeki regime, Batho Bonke was as much about empowerment as it was about Sexwale cultivating friends on the right places. Large swathes of shares had been liberally distributed (for free) to a whole range of powerful players in politics, the media and judiciary, as Gumede noted in 2007:

> Beneficiaries [in Batho Bonke] include Matthews Phosa (the former premier of Mpumalanga and also touted as a presidential candidate); Manne Dipico, the former premier of the Northern Cape; and the Western Cape ANC chairman, James Ngculu. He has also given shares to the spouses of key individuals on the ANC's national executive committee, including Nompumelelo Maduna, the wife of former justice minister Penuell Maduna, Thuthukile Skweyiya, the wife of welfare minister and ANC 'elder' or 'wise man' Zola Skweyiya, Thami Didiza, the husband of Thoko Didiza, the minister of public works, and Mbeki's wife, Zanele.
>
> Sexwale has also extended his patronage to those outside politics. He has given shares to the political editor of the SABC, Sophie Makoena, the Natal judge president Vuka Tshabalala, who oversaw Zuma's corruption case, Xolela Mangcu, a prominent analyst, King Goodwill Zwelethini, the head of the National Intelligence Agency, Manala Manzini, leading black empowerment business leader Danisa Baloyi, journalist turned businessman Thami Mazwai, and many of Mandela's children.[62]

Of course, the popular narrative has focused almost exclusively on the perfidy of political cadres using their political clout to amass personal fortunes. But this has ignored the other driving force of BEE's political bias: the fact that, for many white businesses, if they are forced to engage in the dilution of their ownership via BEE, they are likely to try and extract other value out of the process, more particularly, political goodwill. The use of preferential procurement – driving state business to black companies – only added further incentive to choose politically active partners who could ensure that the faucets of government spending flowed freely. As Ben Turok, one of the ANC's most respected thinkers and MPs, has noted:

> Favoured BEE partners are those with inside knowledge of the government and easy access to Ministers and top officials. The golf course is a favourite contact point. There is a great deal of socialising among top people in government and business where informal talk may prove a great asset. Americans call it 'schmoozing' and it brings in a great deal of business.[63]

The perception that transformation has benefited only a small handful of ANC comrades has only been reinforced by the use of cadre deployment in the civil service. Recall, as we noted above, that the rapid racial transformation of the civil service has been one of the major drivers of the growing black middle class. Cadre deployment, in simple terms, was the decision to place officials throughout the civil service – but mostly at the top – based on their political loyalty to the ANC rather than their ability or other criteria. At a local level, it has created the impression that employment by the state is based on loyalty to the ANC. Moreover, it has been hard to escape the impression that local government has become merely a string of political fiefdoms unconcerned with delivery and staffed by individuals who, due to their political connections, remain unaccountable to the broader electorate or more universal standards of merit and achievement. Certainly, this was one of the key worries of the SACP during the Mbeki period. In a widely circulated discussion document published in May 2006, the SACP fretted about the construction of an 'alliance between emerging black capital and ... state-related technical/managerial strata'[64] that was thwarting a left-wing agenda in the ANC. In this way, elite enrichment via BEE was joined at the hip with cadre deployment in the imagination of the left wing of the Alliance, even if the two groups – a black capitalist class and a black technocratic elite – may in fact have very different agendas and class positions.

That BEE has been perceived to benefit a narrow 'band' of ANC operatives has only exacerbated the first major feature of BEE that we noted above: that the power of the BEE elite remains precarious. On the one hand, BEE's elite focus has made it unpalatable to the broader Alliance, many of whom are horrified by the more gauche proclivities of their one-time comrades. It has created a political elite that is, in a sense, compromised by its own enrichment. On the other hand, the link between politics and empowerment has meant that members of the BEE elite are over-represented at the top levels of the ANC. This may explain why the popular perception of a muscular BEE elite on top of the world is so pervasive – it is hard not to develop that impression when the faces decorating the covers of financial magazines are the same as those dominating the dailies. It also means that the BEE elite, as the balance of power now stands, wields political clout that is out of proportion to its actual economic power. And, because of the financial difficulties of many BEE companies, they remain heavily reliant on the state, monitoring and cajoling existing capital to retain whatever economic gains they have. If the political winds were to change – if BEE were to be substantially reconfigured by a new left-wing alliance in the ANC, for example – the continued existence of this already narrow band of businessman would be far from assured. And there has been no evidence that BEE will, of itself, produce a black businessman who enters politics – that traffic has been entirely one-way – suggesting that it has not, as yet, grown economically powerful enough to articulate a class position outside of the political world of the ANC.

The third key feature of the process of empowerment is that it has occurred in the context of growing inequality. Since 1994, levels of inequality have increased in South Africa, despite post-apartheid promises. The most popular measure of inequality is the Gini co-efficient, which measures imbalances across the entire economy. According to the co-efficient, a country with a score of zero has absolute equality, while a country with a score of 1 would have absolute inequality (one person owning everything). South Africa's Gini has, distressingly, increased since 1995. In 1995, it was measured at 0.64. By 2005, it was measured at 0.69;[65] most recently, it was measured at 0.68, making South Africa one of the most unequal countries in the world.[66] The data is even more interesting when it is broken down by race, which shows that income inequality has increased across all racial groups (although it is most pronounced amongst the coloured population). In *every* racial group, to put it simply, the rich have gotten richer, and the poor have gotten poorer (or at least stagnated).[67]

Some of this inequality, it must be admitted, has been ameliorated by the creation of the South African welfare state, which disburses grants to disadvantaged people throughout the country. According to one study, when social grants are added into the income equation, South Africa's Gini co-efficient may be slightly lower than reported: 0.59.[68] This still suggests major inequality, however. The simple fact is that the South African experience remains schizophrenic and disjointed: a wealthy, now largely multiracial middle and upper class exists in a first-world bubble that is miles away from the penury of a bottom-half that has seen few gains from the post-apartheid period. This is not to suggest that empowerment and affirmative action are entirely responsible for this increased inequality between and within racial groups. Far more attention, I feel, should be paid to the over-arching liberalism of post-1994 economic policy: an economic policy that has been shown, time and again, to increase inequality throughout the world.

But this is beside the point. The fact that there has been the emergence of a well-heeled black middle class and an empowerment elite in the context of growing inequality has only compounded public perception that BEE has not only empowered a small group of well-connected businessman, but also actively contributed to the widening of income gaps in the economy. Empowerment, according to this perception, is part of a series of measures that have increased inequality, rather than a measure that might have reduced inequality. This much is clear from the widely held belief – held with some compelling justification – that empowerment was part of an elite pact to retain key features of the apartheid economic model in the face of a redistributive politics. Empowerment has become tied up, at least in the popular imagination, with all the other anti-poor policies that constituted the so-called '1996 class project': privatisation, GEAR, fiscal austerity and supply-side economics generally. The fact that many early empowerment deals were concluded on the back of privatisation efforts – such as Telkom's privatisation and the resultant empowerment deals struck with the Elephant and Lion consortiums – only confirmed this perception. Empowerment, as a result, does not sit outside these policies – it is considered part of their fabric. Attacking the '1996 class project', as happened so radically in the lead-up to Polokwane, thus also involves attacking the process of empowerment and an elite that may actively pursue anti-poor policies.

The fourth and last feature of empowerment is that its conduct since 1994 has widely discredited the idea that a black patriotic bourgeoisie would act more ethically than other capital formations in South Africa. At the simplest level, this perception has been cemented by the crasser statements of some of the newly empowered elite. Statements such as Mzi Khumalo's 'We are here to run a business. I'm not for any of this brotherhood stuff',[69] were frequently made, especially when the left wing of the alliance questioned elite enrichment. But no better example of the 'fall' of the idea of a patriotic bourgeoisie can be found than in Thabo Mbeki. In 1999, as we saw earlier, Mbeki aggressively supported the creation of a patriotic bourgeoisie during a speech to the Black Management Forum, urging the black middle class to drop any sense of embarrassment in the articulation of this goal. And yet, in 2006, at the very height of a wave of empowerment deals and only seven years after his speech to the BMF, Mbeki was castigating the black elite for losing sight of its political mission in pursuit of wealth and status. Running throughout Mbeki's critique was a painful awareness of just how bad the elite was making itself look in the eyes of ordinary South Africans:

> ... the capitalist market destroys relations of 'kinship, neigh-bourhood, profession, and creed', replacing these with the pursuit of personal wealth by citizens who, as he says, have become 'atomistic and individualistic'.
>
> Thus, everyday, and during every hour of our time beyond sleep, the demons embedded in our society, that stalk us at every minute, seem always to beckon each one of us towards a realisable dream and nightmare. With every passing second, they advise, with rhythmic and hypnotic regularity – get rich! get rich! get rich!
>
> And thus has it come about that many of us accept that our common natural instinct to escape from poverty is but the

other side of the same coin on whose reverse side are written the words – at all costs, get rich!

In these circumstances, personal wealth, and the public communication of the message that we are people of wealth, becomes, at the same time, the means by which we communicate the message that we are worthy citizens of our community, the very exemplars of what defines the product of a liberated South Africa.

This peculiar striving produces the particular result that manifestations of wealth, defined in specific ways, determine the individuality of each one of us who seeks to achieve happiness and self-fulfilment, given the liberty that the revolution of 1994 brought to all of us.

In these circumstances, the meaning of freedom has come to be defined not by the seemingly ethereal and therefore intangible gift of liberty, but by the designer labels on the clothes we wear, the cars we drive, the spaciousness of our houses and our yards, their geographic location, the company we keep, and what we do as part of that company.[70]

A large part of why and how the black elite has fallen from grace has been discussed above – its narrow focus, the fact that it exists in the context of growing inequality, the gaucheness of some of the conspicuous consumption. But this fall from grace has also been cemented by black empowerment's association, in some major public instances, with corruption and specifically anti-labour policies. This is not to suggest that black empowerment is by definition corrupt, or that its beneficiaries have uniformly acted in corrupt and unethical ways. That is a patently unfair claim. Rather, it is simply that *enough* of black empowerment's conduct has been corrupt and unethical to create this perception, especially amongst those who populate the left wing of the political spectrum.

Cases of corruption involving black empowerment are, unfortunately, too many to mention, but perhaps the clearest example of this process was the Arms Deal. As we have seen elsewhere, a good chunk of the corruption in the Arms Deal took place via the mechanism of black empowerment, where politically connected companies were made partners in companies that were to win lucrative contracts. Futuristic Business Solutions, staffed by relatives of Joe Modise, was the pre-eminent example, becoming the BEE partner of Thomson (which also featured Schabir Shaik's Nkobi Holdings as a shareholder).

But by far the most powerful illustration of all the problems of BEE is that of Aurora, which is explored in considerable detail in the chapter on corruption in this volume. Suffice to say that it took over the reins of two mines previously owned by another BEE company (Pamodzi Gold) that was struggling to make ends meet. Aurora featured a number of politically connected individuals on its board, most notably Khulubese Zuma, nephew to the president. Over two years, Aurora was alleged to have asset stripped the mines under its administration, destroying millions of rands worth of infrastructure. Moreover, despite Khulubese Zuma and his co-partners owning billions of rands in assets, workers on the two mines went for months without receiving payments, sending almost all of them directly into the poor house.

It is against this background that the broader nationalisation debate must be seen. As discussed elsewhere, a key fault line within the Alliance developed in 2010 and 2011 when the ANC Youth League began to loudly proclaim the need to nationalise South Africa's mineral wealth. The call was rejected by many members of society, none more ferociously than Cosatu and the SACP. The significance of this stance on the part of the left wing of the Alliance, and its key reasons for rejecting the nationalisation proposals, have tended to be overlooked. It cannot be ignored that nationalisation has been one of *the* central policy planks of the left wing of the liberation movement since at least the 1960s; an ideal that was loudly proclaimed after apartheid's fall in 1994. Indeed, the fact that the ANC rejected nationalisation has been seen, by the left wing at least, as one of its greatest post-apartheid failings, reflective of an organisation that sold out its membership to white and foreign capital in its drive to implement the 'Washington consensus'.

It should also be acknowledged that Cosatu and the SACP rejected the Youth League's calls for nationalisation for very particular reasons. They did not contest nationalisation because the ideology no longer formed part of their ideological firmament: nationalisation, as a concept, remained appealing. What they contested was the manner in which nationalisation was to be undertaken and the conduct of the political elite that would oversee it.[71] The inference is simple: those who had benefited from BEE since 1994, especially those with political connections, had conducted themselves in a manner that suggested that they simply could not be trusted to manage South Africa's mineral resources to the benefit of the majority. And the left wing would oppose nationalisation – one of its most cherished ideals – in order to prevent it.

Consequences and conclusions

A black economic elite, created by empowerment, remains over-represented on the top rungs of the ANC. Its economic power, while marginal in the broader political economy, remains a potent force in the ANC's various succession and factional imbroglios: campaigns need to be paid for, transport covered, posters printed, avenues opened and deals cemented with patronage. Yet it must be remembered that this is primarily political power, and it cannot be exercised outside of the rarefied air of the ANC's upper echelons.

This is equally true of South Africa's emerging black middle class, albeit with some caveats. It has long been predicted that South Africa's black middle class will provide a solid 'middle' to the ANC, articulating a law-and-order position that contests the outwardly redistributive policies of labour and the unemployed poor. Certainly, this was the impression that was generated with the creation of the Congress of the People in 2009 after Thabo Mbeki's recall as State President. Cope was a largely black (although not strictly so) middle-class party that felt far more affinity with the formalism of Mbeki than the 'populist' strains of Jacob Zuma and the 'alliance of the angry'. And yet Cope collapsed as quickly as it emerged, only partially as a result of its interminable power struggles. Key to Cope's collapse was the fact that it was made abundantly clear by the ANC and Cosatu that those who left the ANC would find their economic opportunities diminished. This much became obvious, in our view, when Icasa, the state-run communications agency, attempted a last-minute interdict to prevent the listing of Telkom shares

on the JSE, a listing that was set to earn Telkom's empowerment partners a significant sum of money. These empowerment partners included
some individuals – Smuts Ngonyama, Gloria Serobe, Wendy Luhabe
and Lyndall Shope-Mafola in particular – who were closely linked to
Cope and its higher reaches.[72] The message was simple: step out of line
and we will use the very same political levers that made you rich in order
to make you poor.

This is also the implicit agreement at the heart of the policy of cadre
deployment. Cadre deployment has been seen primarily as a means of
buying influence by creating networks of patronage that generate political support for certain individuals and factions. Underpinning this
is the acknowledgment that, if members of the bureaucracy change
political allegiance, their cushy contracts may face the chop. In this
sense, cadre deployment is a class-wide reality that has kept the black
professional bureaucratic class on a short leash. Cadre deployment
has not just prevented the creation of a professional bureaucracy, it
has also prevented the emergence of a middle-class grouping that can
articulate demands outside of the ANC and its upper reaches. Much
like the small elite that has benefited from BEE, the broader beneficiaries of the transformation of employment in state organs thus remain overwhelmingly reliant on political favour to cement and retain
their status. And yet, within the realm of politics, the fact that cadre
deployment has taken place at the same time as the virtual collapse
of local government and frustration with service delivery, has kept it
politically precarious, seen with a jaundiced eye by the left and pro-
democracy campaigners horrified by its impact on accountability and
good governance.

The four features of the BEE elite and empowerment more generally,
combined with the points raised above, thus suggest a complex picture.
As it stands, empowerment politicians remain over-represented at the
top levels of the ANC, with political power that exceeds their actual
economic clout. And yet this position is precarious, partially because
the elite are seen with such distrust by the left wing of the Alliance and
progressive civil society more broadly. The fact that the BEE elite remain
economically marginal within the broader economy also means that it
cannot exert a great deal of pressure outside of the Alliance and the

backrooms of the ANC, and it certainly cannot yet risk articulating an independent class position outside of the ANC. Perhaps time and the process of slow acquisition will change this. But for now, the message from the Alliance is clear: you are rich because we allow it, but our patience is not infinite.

New Centres of Power, New Contests

The One That Got Away: How Helen Zille Built a Political Fortress in Cape Town[1]

Martin Plaut

Since the end of apartheid the African National Congress has retained the support of the overwhelming majority of South Africans, allowing the party to dominate the country's political and economic life. It has used its position to 'deploy' its senior cadre throughout the upper echelons of the civil service, as well as the companies and non-governmental organisations controlled by the state. At its National Conference in 1997 the ANC adopted a 'Strategy and Tactics' policy[2] that resolved to 'transform the instruments of power' by 'adopting a cadre policy ensuring that it plays a leading role in all centres of power'. Such cadres would be controlled by the party leadership, which would 'exercise maximum discipline among its members, and ensure that, after ideas have been exchanged and decisions taken, all its structures and members pursue the same goal'.

The ANC 'blurs distinctions between party and state (and between legality and illegality)', as Roger Southall argues.[3] Yet one province has escaped its control. This is the Western Cape, which has been taken by the Democratic Alliance (DA). The party has used its hold on the province to show what it can do, and to attack the ANC's hold on the rest of the country.

The DA has its strengths, but also its weaknesses. Its ability to win might in the end lead to a real challenge to the ANC. This would answer the troubling question of whether or not South Africa is a real democracy, for democracy will only be consolidated once the governing party has shown that it is willing to have its hold on power ended at the ballot box. That is unlikely to happen in the immediate future, but until it does no one can be certain of the country's democratic credentials.

Blessings from on high

There is a well-established tradition in Africa for anti-colonial movements to present themselves as the natural parties of government once they assume office. While parties across the continent have portrayed themselves as the embodiment of their people's hopes and aspirations, once in government they have tended to treat all opposition as suspect, an act of treachery, undermining the happy unity of the nation.

The ANC is no exception. Thabo Mbeki, in particular, was fond of peppering his speeches with references to the role of the ANC as the 'vanguard movement' in South Africa, reinforcing the notion that the party was the natural expression of the people's will.[4]

Indeed, at times it has gone further, deploying religious imagery to bolster its rule by suggesting that the ANC is divinely sanctioned. In 2008, the mayor of Bushbuckridge, Milton Morema, told an ANC–SACP rally that 'the ANC will rule this country until Jesus Christ comes back home'.[5] The most elaborate and direct use of religious symbolism has come from President Zuma. During a rally at Mthatha on 5 February 2011, he was quoted as saying:

> When you vote for the ANC, you are also choosing to go to heaven. When you don't vote for the ANC you should know that you are choosing that man who carries a fork ... who cooks people.
>
> When you are carrying an ANC membership card, you are blessed. When you get up there, there are different cards used

but when you have an ANC card, you will be let through to go to heaven.

When [Jesus] fetches us we will [find those in the beyond] wearing black, green and gold. The holy ones belong to the ANC.[6]

Newspapers received sackfuls of letters criticising the President's 'blasphemy', while opposition parties condemned the statement. The ANC claimed it was meant only as a figure of speech, but the point had been made. Zuma is, after all, a wily old campaigner and knows full well the power of such imagery.

In general the South African public identifies strongly with the ANC government. Support for the party in elections has remained remarkably solid. In the 2009 general election the ANC won 65.90 per cent of the vote, taking 264 of the 400 seats in the National Assembly.[7] The remaining votes were scattered among 25 other parties. The only opposition party that even made a dent in the ruling party's dominance was the DA. With 16.66 per cent of the vote it took 67 seats – hardly a challenge to the ANC's hold on power.

Nonetheless, the result unsettled President Zuma's party, for the 2009 election saw the ANC lose control of a province for the first time. In the Western Cape, the DA won 51.46 per cent of the vote, pushing the ANC into second place with just 31.55 per cent support.[8] The DA's leader, Helen Zille, was jubilant.[9] 'The results are very good for South Africa,' she told the BBC. 'They are very good for democracy ... The Democratic Alliance has grown by more than 30% nationally and we have doubled our vote in the Western Cape, where we've won the province which is wonderful.'

The loss was a rude shock for the ANC, which wasted no time in going on the offensive. They attacked Zille for her choice of Cabinet, which was – apart from herself – entirely composed of men. The trade union movement declared that the Western Cape was to be run by a 'pale, male' executive.[10]

Helen Zille, never one to be caught on the back foot, responded in kind. She told *The Sowetan* newspaper that she would not take lessons on sexism from the ANC or its allies. She was quoted as saying that:

'Zuma is a self-confessed womaniser with deeply sexist views, who put all his wives at risk by having unprotected sex with an HIV-positive woman.'[11]

The remark, although true (since Jacob Zuma had admitted as much during his rape trial) touched the rawest ANC nerve. Zuma had just won the presidency and was in the first flush of popularity. The Youth League accused her of appointing only men so that she might 'sleep around' with her 'boyfriends and concubines'. Umkhonto we Sizwe's Military Veterans Association threatened to render the Western Cape 'ungovernable' by sending troops to the province if Helen Zille continued insulting the newly elected president.[12] Zille herself complained that her remarks had been taken out of context and that she was only responding to the sexual slurs made against her.

When she got to see President Zuma later that month, Zille used the opportunity to try to lay the matter to rest. 'During a conversation with President Zuma ... I asked him to regard the Western Cape as an opportunity, and not as a threat,' she said. 'I told him that we would always act in good faith and in the interests of all our people when we propose alternative approaches to solve some of our country's most pressing problems. I said that we need the space to implement them.'[13]

The incident was perhaps trivial in itself, but it highlighted something more profound. It indicated how novel the situation was for both parties. For the ANC the feeling that electoral support was ebbing away, no matter how slightly, was distinctly unsettling. For the DA, governing its own province offered an opportunity to show what it was really made of. For a party that had, in various incarnations, criticised governments from the sidelines for 50 years, this was an entirely new experience.

How the Democratic Alliance was built

The origins of the Democratic Alliance are to be found in the turmoil that beset South Africa following the Second World War, the same period that was so formative for the ANC, the Communist Party and their allies in the trade unions. In 1959, twelve MPs broke away from

the United Party over its refusal to oppose the apartheid legislation being brought in by the National Party government.[14] The rebels formed
the Progressive Party. They elected Dr Jan Steytler, the son of a Boer
War veteran, who had studied medicine at Guy's Hospital in London,
as their leader. It was a position he was to hold until his retirement in
December 1970.[15]

The Progressive Party opposed apartheid, calling for an entrenched
Constitution in which the powers of the provinces or federal states
would be protected. It also stood for an economy based on unfettered
capitalism.[16] The party received financial support from big business, and
Anglo American in particular, but it did not fare well at the polls. After
the general election of 1961 the party was virtually wiped out. Only
Helen Suzman was able to retain her seat.[17] The lone parliamentary
voice speaking up for South Africa's oppressed, Suzman became internationally famous for her outspoken criticism of NP policies. She was
an outstanding orator, holding her own as an English-speaking woman
of Jewish descent in a Parliament dominated by male Afrikaners.[18]

Suzman retained her seat for a further 13 years as the sole principled
opponent of racial discrimination in Parliament. She fought against detention without trial, pass laws, influx control, job reservation on the
grounds of colour, racially separated amenities, forced removals, capital
punishment, the banning of the Communist Party, and gender discrimination, especially against black women. It was often a lonely position to
be in, but it stood her and her successors in good stead.

In 1974, six more Progressive Party members won seats in
Parliament. Soon thereafter, fellow anti-apartheid activist Harry
Schwarz and others left the United Party to form the Reform Party, which
in turn merged with the Progressives to form the Progressive Reform
Party (PFP) in 1977.[19] In 1977 the party was further strengthened by
more defections from the United Party. Under the leadership of Colin
Eglin, and with the ANC still banned, it became the official opposition.

In 1988, Zach de Beer took over as party leader and through con-
tinuous negotiations, ultimately succeeded in successfully merging the
Independent Party, National Democratic Movement and Progressive
Federal Party to form the Democratic Party (DP) on 8 April 1989.[20]
The National Party called for an election in September that year. Under

the combined leadership of Zach de Beer, Denis Worrall and Wynand Malan, the DP won 36 seats in Parliament.

These were the dying days of white rule. The National Party itself had fractured, with groups of MPs leaving to form the Conservative Party. Then in February 1990 President FW de Klerk unbanned the ANC and other parties and the whole edifice of apartheid came tumbling down.[21] In 1994, South Africa held its first truly democratic election. The ANC won a resounding victory, leaving the DP with just 1.7 per cent of the national vote.[22]

The new era ended the goldfish-bowl of white-dominated politics. Even a new political party with an honourable record of opposing apartheid, like the DP, would have to reinvent itself. It was an unpromising beginning, yet gradually the party began to carve out a place for itself, taking a growing share of votes in national elections.[23]

Year	Votes	Percentage	Seats	Leader	Result
1994	338 426	1.73	7	Zach de Beer	ANC victory
1999	1 527 337	9.56	38	Tony Leon	ANC victory; DP becomes official opposition
2004	1 931 201	12.37	50	Tony Leon	ANC victory; DA retains official opposition status
2009	2 945 829	16.66	67	Helen Zille	ANC victory; DA retains official opposition status and wins Western Cape province
2011	6 393 889	23.94	Local elections	Helen Zille	ANC victory; DA retains official opposition status, retains Western Cape and wins support in black only wards

Under the leadership of Tony Leon, and with only a handful of MPs, the party attempted to find a new role, fighting for the legitimacy of the opposition, and for transparency and accountability in government. Gradually the strategy began to pay dividends. The 1995 municipal elections began to show a swing back to the DP. This was continued during the 1999 national elections, where the party won over 9.56 per cent of the national vote and returned 38 members to Parliament.[24] The DP had become the largest opposition party.

Tony Leon attacked the government of Thabo Mbeki for its centralisation of power and its installation of ANC loyalists and cadres in key positions in media, business, public and private sectors, as well as sport, culture and even the offices of the Public Protector. The DP argued that democracy in South Africa could only be strengthened and protected by building a strong opposition able to limit the one-party dominance of the ANC.[25]

Attacks on the government, while essential for an effective opposition, would not of themselves bring the DP to power. Leon knew that he could not wait for electoral unpopularity to gradually erode support for the ANC. A new strategy was called for. The National Party was in terminal decline. Tony Leon saw an opportunity to construct a wider alliance. For a party whose roots lay in fighting apartheid, making a bid for the MPs and supporters of the renamed New National Party was both risky and painful. Leon decided it was the only way his party could make progress, but it did move the party to the right. As one observer put it:[26]

> The DP (Democratic Party) transformed itself, under the leadership of Tony Leon, from a liberal, English-dominated voice for freedom to a more conservative party offering vocal, aggressive opposition to the ANC. This enabled it to win much of the Afrikaner vote from the NNP (New National Party).

In 2000, the Democratic Party reached an agreement with Dr Louis Luyt, of the Federal Alliance. Talks also commenced with the New National Party, and this led to the final change in party name, with the formation of the Democratic Alliance.[27] The deal drew fierce criticism from some party loyalists, including the doughty Helen Suzman, who told Leon in no uncertain terms that he had made a 'huge mistake' and would 'come to rue doing business with these people'.[28] It was, as Leon himself was later to describe it, a 'marriage made in hell'. Yet the strategy paid dividends. The New National Party brought with it large numbers of coloured supporters, many of whom feared they would lose those privileges they had enjoyed under apartheid, which had differentiated them from the rest of the black population. In December 2000 the newly named Democratic Alliance won a number of municipalities, including the jewel in the party's crown: the city of Cape Town.

The DA struggled with serious tensions over the personalities and allegiances of its new partners. A break finally came in October 2001, when Tony Leon suspended the controversial mayor of Cape Town, Peter Marais, from the party.[29] In response, Marthinus van Schalkwyk, the former New National Party leader, left the DA to form a new alignment with an even more unlikely partner – the ANC.[30]

In the 2004 general election, the DA began to build momentum, gaining 12.37 per cent of the vote and a total of 50 seats in the National Assembly.[31] In absolute terms the party expanded its support by over 400 000 votes, despite the fact that an estimated 114 000 fewer votes had been cast in the election. The DA was the fastest growing opposition party, increasing its support in eight out of nine provinces.

The 2004 elections established the foundations for the party's performance in the 2006 local government elections.[32] These saw the DA increase its national share of the vote to 16.3 per cent – a 4 per cent rise. It also increased its number of representatives in all six of the metropolitan councils, notably in the Cape Town area, where its share of the vote rose from 27.1 per cent in 2004 to 41.9 per cent. This put the DA ahead of the ANC.

On 15 March 2006, Helen Zille, until then a DA MP and the party's national spokesperson, was elected mayor of Cape Town. A former journalist who had broken the story of Steve Biko's death, Zille was a rare example of a white South African politician who learned Xhosa as an adult. The race to lead Cape Town was fiercely contended, but she won the position by forging a seven-party coalition. Zille became mayor with a slim three-vote majority, including one ANC councillor who secretly voted for her. It was a fragile hold on power in the city, but Zille gradually cemented her position. In August 2010, after difficult and protracted negotiations, the DA managed to persuade the Independent Democrats – a predominantly coloured-based Cape party – to join them.[33]

On 26 November 2006, Tony Leon announced that he would step down as his party's leader in 2007. Helen Zille was elected as his successor at the party's 2007 Congress.[34] The 2009 general election saw a further increase in DA support, with the party winning control of the Western Cape province. The party maintained its position as the largest opposition party and showed that it was gradually increasing its reach into ANC territory.[35]

At the same time the ANC remained the predominant force in South African politics. Indeed, the most striking fact about the country's post-apartheid politics has been the stability of the ANC's support. Since the first truly democratic national election in 1994 the ANC's backing has fallen by less than 1 per cent.

The rise of the DA can be explained, in part, by the decline in support for other opposition parties since 1994. The mainly Zulu Inkatha Freedom Party has lost votes, while the New National Party has merged with the ANC. Only the emergence of the Congress of the People (Cope) in 2008 has provided any alternative to the DA as the party of opposition. But the spectacular falling out between its leaders, Mosiuoa Lekota and Mbhazima Shilowa, has left the party in such difficulties that it is hard to see how it will recover.[36]

Year	Party	Votes	Percentage	Seats
1994	Inkatha Freedom Party	1 371 477	8.58	34
	New National Party	1 098 215	6.87	28
2009	Inkatha Freedom Party	804 260	4.55	18
	Congress of the People	1 311 027	7.42	30

In a 2008 report, opinion polling and strategic research company MarkData put forward a detailed report which analysed the results of a political opinion survey on party support patterns and inter-party co-operation.[37] While the report is now somewhat dated, its findings remain interesting.

Although the DA is frequently perceived to be a 'white' party, the report found the party's political vote was significantly multiracial. Though its white support accounted for 54 per cent of its total vote, its African support stood at 21 per cent, its coloured voters made up 17 per cent, and its Asian voters 8 per cent.[38]

In addition, the report found that the DA's growth prospects would be somewhat limited by the considerable hostility to it among African voters: while 14 per cent admired Helen Zille, 65 per cent disliked her. But this hostility was not based on race, since African voters had almost the exact response to leaders of other political parties – the United Democratic Movement's Bantu Holomisa (Xhosa), the Independent Democrats' Patricia de Lille (coloured) and the Inkatha Freedom Party's Mangosutho Buthelezi (Zulu). Rather, it was argued that the hostility was due to 'liberation solidarity', which, according to the report's author, Laurence Schlemmer, explains 'the tendency among ANC activists and spokespeople to vilify and stereotype any leader outside the ANC Alliance. While the vilifications are usually no more than very loose rhetoric, like all stereotypes their effects are remarkably persistent.'[39]

The May 2011 local elections may have been something of a turning point. Helen Zille's campaign attempted to move voters away from these racial stereotypes. Her key phrase, repeated throughout the election campaign, was 'making the issues the issue'.[40] She relentlessly highlighted her party's record in government, while refusing to become involved in the racial attacks of the ANC in general and Julius Malema in particular. Malema, in typical fashion, described Zille as a 'madam' and suggested that her attempts to dance at party rallies were 'like a monkey dancing for votes'.[41] When the election was over, Malema refused a debate with the DA's spokeswoman, Lindiwe Mazibuko, describing her as a 'tea girl'. 'I was never asked to debate Lindiwe ... She's a nobody, she's a tea girl of the madam. I'm not debating with the service of the madam,' he declared.[42]

In the event, the local elections saw the DA's vote increase by 7.7 per cent, while the ANC's share of the vote decreased by 2.7 per cent. Had the ANC not routed the Inkatha Freedom Party in KwaZulu-Natal, its losses would have been much more dramatic. As it was, the DA strengthened its support in 78 per cent of the municipalities it contested in 2006, growing by 17.8 per cent in the Western Cape, the region it already dominated.

Political commentator Steven Friedman said the ANC should be concerned, not by the opposition, but by the decline in its own support, because it showed that voters were no longer comfortable with the ruling party.[43] 'This is the second election where the ANC vote has gone down. It declined in eight of the nine provinces. This should worry the ANC,' he said.

In reality, the May 2011 elections produced two clear results. Firstly, they showed that the DA could win seats in wards in which there were only black voters. The party could claim that it had captured 6 per cent of the black vote – not huge, but a breakthrough nonetheless.[44] This was, at least in part, because it had chosen a number of high-profile black candidates in key seats and gone out of its way to give them prominence during the campaign. At the same time, its appeal in the townships was limited. Although it won 133 wards from the ANC, only about nine were could be considered '100 per cent black' – including two in the Transkei, one in East London, two in Vereeniging and one in the Tswaing municipality in North West.[45] Even in its heartland, the Western Cape, it was trounced in the townships, where the ANC took some wards with more than 95 per cent of the vote. 'We have to look at our current leadership there who, despite numerous resources available to them, have failed to make significant electoral gains for the party,' said a DA official, speaking on condition of anonymity.[46] The party had established more than 24 branches along the 'N2 Constituency', which encompasses most of the city's black townships, holding several events there and putting up ward candidates. This produced just 6 154 votes for the DA in all of Cape Town's townships.

Secondly, the election reduced the South African political scene to a two-horse race (some commentators suggest that this process has been under way for some time.)[47] Between them, the ANC and the DA took 89 per cent of the vote in 2000, 86 per cent in 2006 and 91 per cent in 2011. The DA is now the ANC's only real competitor, with its nearest rival, Inkatha, reduced to just 3.8 per cent of the vote.

The Democratic Alliance's vision: dream or nightmare?

The issue facing Helen Zille as she attempts to transform the DA from a party of opposition into a party of government is how to escape its image as a party of the white elite. It is an attack on the party that is the constant drumbeat of the ANC and its allies. This critique by Zwelinzima Vavi is typical:[48]

> ... we only have to look at the Western Cape, to see the nightmare we can expect if the Democratic Alliance were to gain any ground next year ... The DA will always be the party of the rich and privileged, with no time for the interests of the majority.

The difficulty for the DA is that it cannot escape its past (any more than the ANC can), or its association with the liberal, well-heeled white constituency that maintained it through the apartheid years. Nor can it deny that many of its current supporters are white and a fair number are rich. What it can address is the political policies it offers the South African electorate and – probably more importantly – the policies it pursues once it is in office in the towns and cities that it controls.

So, what does the DA offer in theory and how does it behave towards its more vulnerable citizens in practice?

The party's basic philosophy is spelt out in its vision statement, entitled Our Vision:[49]

> Our dream for South Africa is of an open opportunity society in which every person is free, secure and equal, where everyone has the opportunity to improve the quality of his life and pursue her dreams, and in which every language and culture has equal respect and recognition.

This vision is then given substance in three simple objectives:
1. Individual freedom under the rule of law – an open society;
2. Opportunity with responsibility – an opportunity society; and
3. Full equality for all.

It is worth comparing these statements with the aims and objectives of the ANC.[50] These are the following:

> The ANC's key objective is the creation of a united, non-racial, non-sexist and democratic society. This means the liberation of Africans in particular and black people in general from political and economic bondage. It means uplifting the quality of life of all South Africans, especially the poor. The struggle to achieve this objective is called the National Democratic Revolution.

This is then elaborated as encompassing the Freedom Charter of 1955, which is described as the party's 'basic document'.

The statements are diametrically opposed. The DA offers freedom and opportunity regardless of race or creed. The ANC's vision is focused on the African majority and on the needs of the poor. Without attempting to provide a textural analysis comparing the policies of each party line by line, the trend is clear. The ANC is a party of the centre-left, offering welfare benefits to those in need. Indeed, following the 2011 budget an economist, Mike Schussler, described South Africa as the 'biggest welfare state in the world'.[51] The government was unapologetic, with the Social Development Minister, Edna Molewa, observing: 'It is difficult for the government to close its eyes and look at people when they are suffering and do not have anything to eat.'

The government estimated that following the 2011 budget just under a third of all the country's citizens would be recipients of some form of social welfare payments.[52] The National Treasury projection indicated that by 2011/12 there would be 16 million social grant beneficiaries. This is an increase of 2 million people in just a year. Whether this is the right direction for South Africa to take is a matter of debate, but the DA takes a very different view. Presenting what it described as an 'alternative' budget, the party said:[53]

> At its current acceleration rate, the social security net is becoming increasingly unaffordable and crowding out other priorities. The DA believes that a caring society must demonstrate its support for its vulnerable members, including

the aged, the disabled, the young and the unemployed. The problem with the social security net is not that it is generous, but rather that it supports too many recipients.

The social security system places a safety net below vulnerable members of society who cannot enter the formal economy. The aim of any kind of social spending must always be to empower as many citizens as possible to help themselves over the long run. Within the ANC's model of the Developmental State, social security creates a system of hand-outs. This is turn breeds dependency on the state and a culture of patronage, and it is destroying potential for using the social security system for more long term benefit.

The implications are clear; fewer benefit recipients and an end to a system of patronage and hand-outs. This is the classic formula proposed internationally by parties of the centre-right. The question for the DA is whether this vision can be sold to the electorate. In a country in which more than a quarter of its citizens are out of work and poverty is endemic, telling people to get on with their lives and enjoy the benefits of an 'opportunity society' is not an easy platform from which to win votes.

In reality, the DA is not opposed to welfare grants and state assistance, as long as these are kept within what it considers reasonable limits. Rather, it is the perception that the party does not provide for the black majority, whom the ANC regards as its bedrock of support that is important. Poor black people could easily believe that their precarious financial position could be made even more difficult if the DA were to take over the reins of power. This might appear to be an almost insuperable obstacle, but in one region it does not apply: the Western Cape.

From theory to practice – the case of the Western Cape

The DA has managed to transform the Western Cape into something of an electoral fortress. It has done so at least partly because this is one of the few provinces in which the demographics are tilted in its favour.

It is the province furthest away from the centres of traditional black population groups like the Eastern Cape and KwaZulu-Natal. During the years of apartheid it was designated a 'coloured preference area', which slowed the rate at which black people arrived in the province. As a result, the coloured and white communities were a majority of the population at the time of the 2001 census, at 54 per cent and 18 per cent, respectively.[54] Since then the black population of the Western Cape has grown rapidly, so that their share of the population increased from 20.9 per cent in 1996 to 30.1 per cent in 2007.[55] Yet despite an influx of black people into the province they remain in a minority. The only other province in which this is the case is the Northern Cape, where black people made up 39.8 per cent of the population in 2007.[56]

The coloured population, with around half the entire vote, is critical to every party's prospects in the Cape. The politics of the coloured people has a long and complex history, but it is – in the end – a history of marginalisation. Coloureds have seen themselves, as the academic Mohamed Adhikari put it, as caught between the white and the African populations. The author quotes the sociologist, Zimitri Erasmus, as saying: 'For me, growing up coloured meant knowing that I was *not only* not white, but *less than* white: *not only* not black but *better than* black (as we referred to African People).'[57]

The question for the coloured people has always been which side of this racial divide to support – and, at least for the moment, this decision has gone decisively in favour of the DA. A breakdown of the 2009 election concluded that the party 'made huge gains and increased its share of the vote in coloured majority communities, making significant inroads in some ANC constituencies in these areas'.[58] The party's merger with the Independent Democrats, which has drawn most of its support from the coloured population, has strengthened this relationship.

For the DA, the question is really whether it can break the racial glass ceiling and begin winning support from the black population. Failure to achieve this would condemn the party to permanent opposition, since black people make up 79 per cent of the total population. The prospects are not promising. A careful analysis of the 2009 election in the Western Cape points to the various population groups voting almost exclusively along racial lines.[59] Despite working hard to try to win over sections of the black population who live in the townships surrounding Cape Town, the DA failed to achieve the breakthrough they were hoping for.[60]

> The DA received little reward for its effort to reach out into black areas: its poll share reached 1% only in 7 of the 81 voting districts of Khayelitsha, 4 of the 20 districts in Philippi and in 15 of the 48 districts of Langa, Nyanga and Guguletu, and was below 2% almost everywhere.

Even those rare mixed suburbs of Mowbray, Observatory and Woodstock showed much the same pattern of racially defined voting. This analysis is supported by another study which confirms that in some wards in townships like Gugulethu and Langa, the DA received as little as 1 per cent of the vote.[61] In summary:[62]

> ... [though] the DA was able to record an outstanding performance in the Western Cape provincial poll, and was indeed able to draw voters away from the ANC in both urban and rural areas, it did not meet its key objective of capturing significant numbers of African supporters, who remained extremely loyal to the ANC.

So is the outlook for the DA entirely bleak? Is it doomed to remain trapped within the Western Cape, an irritant to the ANC, but little more? The same author – Anthony Lemon – suggests not. He points out, probably correctly, that the electoral support of the parties will depend on the performance of the government, the alignment of the political parties and, critical for Helen Zille, the ability of her party to act as a viable alternative to the ANC's administration. Here the message for the party is considerably more positive. The DA has a record of service in the towns and rural areas that it administers that are the envy of the rest of the country.

In its 2009 assessment, the international credit rating agency, Global Credit Ratings, awarded the city of Cape Town's Metropolitan

Municipality one of its highest long-term debt ratings: AA- (double A minus). This was because of the city's 'sustained operating growth over the review period, supported by the city's stable increase in development, which in turn, has lead to a steady increase in the municipality's cash generation and, as such, has supported year on year growth of 16 per cent in cash & cash investments over a four year period'.[63]

In October of 2009, another agency, Empowerdex, found that 'Cape Town is clearly the best city in the country for service delivery', and that 'at 89.5% Cape Town delivers the best service, followed by Johannesburg at 88.5%'[64] The agency considered the provision of a wide range of services like housing, water, sanitation, electricity and waste removal. It combines household access to service with an improvement index over 6 years. The Western Cape was also alone in receiving a clean bill of health from the Auditor General, who found it was the only province in which there was no unauthorised expenditure in 2010/11.[65]

The most comprehensive indication of DA's ability to deliver services in the Western Cape came from the government itself. The Basic Services report, published in October 2010, showed the province as the best service provider in almost every category.[66]

Province	Access to water (%)	Water backlogs (%)	Access to sanitation (%)	Sanitation backlogs (%)	Access to electricity (%)	Electricity backlogs (%)	Refuse removal (%)	Refuse back-logs (%)
Eastern Cape	84.1	15.9	67.9	32.1	58.9	41.1	37.0	63.0
Free State	98.6	1.4	66.6	33.4	75.0	24.8	74.4	25.6
Gauteng	96.8	3.2	87.4	12.6	76.7	23.3	84.8	15.2
KwaZulu-Natal	81.7	18.3	75.4	34.6	65.7	34.3	50.4	49.6
Limpopo	80.0	20.0	47.2	52.8	73.1	26.9	17.6	82.4
Mpumalanga	87.9	12.1	60.2	39.8	82.1	17.9	39.6	60.4
North West	89.4	10.6	65.0	35.0	72.5	27.5	52.6	47.4
Northern Cape	92.5	7.5	77.1	22.9	78.3	21.7	71.4	28.6
Western Cape	97.6	2.4	93.6	6.4	86.1	13.9	90.3	9.7

Welcoming the report's findings, Cape Town mayor Dan Plato said the city was 'very proud' of its number one ranking but warned there was 'much room for improvement'.[67] A government spokesman would only respond, somewhat sourly, that the report contained no surprises.[68]

The ANC has reacted nervously to the DA electoral and administrative success. Gwede Mantashe admitted the ANC has major problems with its local councillors, and can learn something from the opposition.[69] This sentiment was echoed by others inside the ANC, with an anonymous party stalwart bemoaning the quality of ANC local politicians: 'It's not as if the ANC has a truckload of decent councillors that it can just pick from and install.'[70]

A major problem for the ANC has been the divisions within its own party structures in the Western Cape. These pitted the 'Africanists' – who argued that the growing black population would soon swamp the coloured and white electorate – against the non-racial elements in the ANC, who believed the party should appeal to the whole electorate. These issues have been admitted, but solutions to the problem appear to be elusive. Speaking at a local government seminar, the premier of KwaZulu-Natal, Zweli Mkhize, said: 'Ineffectiveness is caused by instability within the ANC. The causes are our own ill-discipline and inability to manage our own structures. That issue is what we need to cure.'[71] Mkhize went on to accept that 'a lot of work done by Helen Zille is fulfilling what the ANC manifesto is saying should be done'.

President Zuma has accepted that his party's operation in the province has been a shambles. The ANC in the Western Cape has been 'fighting itself', he said, giving other parties the opportunity to win elections as ANC supporters stood back because of the internal party battles.[72] He has also admitted that the ANC is failing to mount a creditable challenge to the DA, while support for the party in the province has declined and new membership is growing 'very slowly'.[73]

A story of toilets and evictions

The statistics on service delivery are clear. At a macro level, the DA's

administration in the Cape Town area is ahead of comparable adminis-
trations around the country. But this is not the end of the story. Critics
have singled out two issues in particular as examples of the party's un-
caring attitude towards the poor. Zwelinzima Vavi referred to them in
the speech quoted earlier in this chapter when he said: 'The mass eviction of poor communities and the open toilets saga are just the two best
known episodes in the DA administration's war against the working
class and the poor.'[74]

This 'war' is being fought out in two of the poorest communities in
the Cape Town area: the informal settlement of Makhaza on the edge of
Khayelitsha, and Hangberg, on the outskirts of Hout Bay. Neither confrontation was simple: the brevity of this account does neither justice.

At Makhaza, Helen Zille says she reached an agreement with local
residents in late 2007, while she was mayor of Cape Town, to build
toilets for each of the 1 316 households in the area.[75] These were in
addition to the communal toilets already provided, and in return the
residents agreed to enclose the toilets to give themselves privacy. With
the toilets in place almost all the residents (96 per cent) enclosed them,
but 55 did not. The ANC Youth League complained to the South Africa
Human Rights Commission that this was a violation of the citizens of
Makhaza's rights, since they were having to use the toilets with blankets
around themselves in full view of the public.[76]

What happened next is a matter of controversy. The city says it began enclosing the toilets with galvanised iron structures on 19 March
2010, only to be met by local people demanding concrete enclosures.[77]
The galvanised iron enclosures around 26 toilets were removed, apparently by members of the ANC Youth League, who joined the protests.
The mayor of Cape Town, Dan Plato, told the *Cape Times* that he had
recently met the Youth League and community leaders, and they had
agreed to tell residents that open toilets would be enclosed. He said the
corrugated metal sheets used to enclose them were not inferior to the
material people had used to build the homes they were living in and that
if people wanted to destroy the new structures he would 'walk away'.[78]

The crisis was clearly escalating. The Youth League's regional secretary issued an open threat to the Cape Town administration. 'We are
going to destroy everything and make the city ungovernable,' said the

regional secretary, Loyiso Nkohle. 'We are calling on all youth to do this [vandalise the city], especially those living in informal settlements.'[79] In a letter to the Minister of Human Settlements, the Youth League explained: 'Our complaint is based on the reality that African people residing in Makhaza, Khayelitsha, are forced to shit in full view of the public.'[80]

The city responded by removing the offending unenclosed toilets, with the mayor calling on the residents to protest against what he called ANC Youth League 'hooligans'. 'We are willing to go back and reinstall the toilets as soon as the community reaches an agreement with the Youth League,' Dan Plato said.[81] The ANC condemned the city's decision, while the Youth League referred the matter to the Human Rights Commission.

On 4 June 2010 the Human Rights Commission found that the DA had failed to respect the dignity of the residents who had been provided with toilets without enclosures.[82] While the Commission commended the city for providing toilets to every household, it found that Cape Town:

> … was constitutionally obliged to come to the aid of those who, due to poverty and their particular disadvantaged socio-economic status, could not afford to enclose their toilets. The Commission notes that such action violated the right to dignity of the community members. Consultation processes appear to have been inadequate. The aforementioned considerations in this instance are of particular significance in light of an Apartheid past in which the least amount was spent on basic services for those classified 'African'.

The DA promised to study the ruling and has attempted to reinstate the toilets on several occasions, but with little success.

The matter was taken to court and when Judge Nathan Erasmus delivered his verdict on 29 April 2011, close to the May election, it must have made very unpleasant reading for the party. The judge, who had gone to inspect the area himself, was scathing. He said the way local people had enclosed the toilets was 'unsatisfactory to dignity and privacy'.[83] Justice Erasmus was also critical of the city of Cape Town's consultation with the community, which had been given only four days to consider the options before it. No minutes had been taken of the meeting in 2007 with the community, which had been attended by just 60 people, said to represent approximately 6 000 residents. He also found that the communal toilets provided in the area – many in a filthy state – did not provide an alternative the community could rely on. At the conclusion of a judgement that took three hours to deliver, Judge Erasmus found that the constitutional right to dignity of the residents had been violated.

Julius Malema was triumphant.[84] 'Spread the message,' he told supporters outside the court. 'We are here today to bring down Helen Zille. Convince everybody here to vote for the ANC.' Helen Zille, no doubt through gritted teeth, told journalists that she accepted the ruling, saying the toilets would be enclosed. 'We have tried to do this on several previous occasions and each time enclosures were destroyed by the ANC Youth League,' she said. 'We will, however, try again.'

The demolition of shacks at Hangberg in Hout Bay followed a similar pattern. On 21 September 2010, a squad of the Cape Town land invasion unit demolished 23 unoccupied homes that had been built in a firebreak on the side of the mountain.[85] 'The structures are built on the slopes of the Sentinel, a world heritage site,' said an unnamed city spokesman. 'People just started building illegally here and the area is not safe for them as it is a firebreak.' Attempts to achieve a negotiated settlement to the issue had failed, after some of the residents attacked Zille, forcing her to leave the area under cover of her security guards. The demolition squad arrived at 6.30 in the morning and were met by protests. Stones were thrown and 15 police officers were injured; 62 people were arrested.

The trade union movement, which has no love for Helen Zille or her administration, weighed in. The local Cosatu representative, Tony Ehrenreich, condemned the violence, calling it an attack by the Western Cape government on the people of Hout Bay.[86] 'The attack on the poor community of Hout Bay is nothing new … this high-handed action we are seeing now from government is typical of DA,' he said. He went on to describe the incident as a 'war against the poor' by the party, which had promised to protect the interests of the rich white community of Hout Bay.

President Zuma entered the fray, promising a commission of enquiry into what he described as 'extreme brutal force' by the police, which had resulted in three people losing their eyes.[87] Protests continued for several days and the Human Rights Commission decided to investigate the incident. This drew a sharp response from Helen Zille, who attacked the Commission as the 'political hit squad of the ANC'.[88] The Commission responded by describing the allegation as untruthful, wild and unsubstantiated.[89]

Should the DA be concerned by two incidents that are – on the scale of things – relatively minor? After all, service delivery protests have become almost routine in the rest of the country, while ANC local authorities have frequently used contractors, known as the Red Ants, to forcibly remove squatters. Nor was the DA the only party to fail to enclose toilets. In April 2011 it was revealed that in the small Free State town of Moqhaka the ANC had built 1 600 toilets as far back as 2003, which had never been enclosed. The ANC at first denied knowing about Moqhaka, but finally conceded the truth. The Human Rights Commission, coming under pressure to reveal the findings of an investigation into the issue before the local elections, finally put out a report saying that the residents had had their rights and dignity violated.[90] President Zuma was left to lament that: 'Of all the stories pertaining to service delivery that I came across during campaigning, the open toilets saga broke my heart.'[91]

The impressions of black voters in the Cape Town metropolitan area are what counts, since this is the electorate the DA is seeking to win. Here the anecdotal evidence is that both the toilets and the removals mattered. Lwazi Mabizela, a Khayelitsha resident, was quoted as saying he was not sure who to vote for in the 2011 local elections because he does not trust any party.[92] 'When the ANC was in charge of Cape Town we thought our lives would change, but nothing changed, we continued to suffer,' Mr Mabizela said. 'We thought the DA would improve the basics like access to housing but we are still waiting ... nothing has changed for us, so it just means my vote is useless.' Gugulethu resident Mzwandile Khojane said whoever wins in Cape Town will be under 'serious' pressure to deliver 'because communities are tired of waiting'.

Some analysts support these assertions, saying that the basic services provided in the townships have not been as effective as the Cape Town administration would suggest. Gavin Silber and Angy Peter of the Social Justice Coalition attacked the administration in Cape Town for making assertions that simply did not stand up to scrutiny:[93]

> In March, the city issued a statement in which it claimed that 'there is access to toilets in townships'. Last year's city annual report noted that '100 percent of households have access to basic water and sanitation'. This is patently untrue, as anyone who has ventured into Khayelitsha will know, and indeed, according to the city's own data, which shows that just over 45 000 households don't have access to basic sanitation. Recent research by Water Dialogues has shown that the true figure is probably closer to 100 000 households.

Justin Sylvester, from the Idasa think-tank, partially supports this case, arguing that the delivery of services by the city to the central business district has been clear, but it has not been felt in the townships.[94] 'This is the challenge the Democratic Alliance faces,' he says. At the same time he argued that the problem of the toilets and removals might have been overplayed. 'It is quite clear that the DA has generally done better than the ANC, especially administratively. They have not had any major scandals, in contrast with the ANC when it governed the city. The Hangberg and the Makhaza issues were highly politicised but in the broader context I do not think they will hurt the DA's chances in the polls.' The outcome of the May election bore this out. At the same time there is probably merit in the observation of the political analyst, Daniel Silke. 'It is not a surprise that most black voters remain suspicious of the DA even if it has positive intentions ... perhaps the DA needs to look at all this from a public relations point of view to market (itself) in black communities.'

This problem has been both exacerbated and ameliorated in recent months. Helen Zille has managed to become entangled in acerbic debates. The first was over the treatment of HIV/Aids, when she suggested that men who have multiple sexual partners and refuse to use condoms be charged with attempted murder. Then she was criticised for launching a competition with cash prizes for people who visited testing centres and were tested for the HIV virus. To this she responded by pointing out that as a result of the prizes a record number of people now know their HIV status.[95] Zille also became involved in a heated exchange with the musician Simphiwe Dana over whether Cape Town is a racist city. Zille attacked her opponent directly: 'You're a highly respected black professional. Don't try to be a professional black. It demeans you,' she said in a Twitter exchange.[96]

Where to from here?

Neither debate will have enhanced Helen Zille's reputation in the eyes of some black people. These perceptions might be strengthened by Zille's recent battles over her tweets suggesting that students are arriving in the Western Cape as 'refugees', because the quality of education in the Eastern Cape is so low.[97] While she has never been afraid to court controversy, she has not allowed matters to rest there. Zille has had a long-standing campaign to increase the number of black Africans in senior positions in the DA. This has not been easy, given the party's incorporation of some sections of the former National Party. Recently, she has managed to get two key DA positions filled by Africans, in a move which could pay dividends in the years to come. In both cases it has meant removing senior, loyal white party officials. Mmusi Maimane has become the party spokesman, and Lindiwe Mazibuko has become the party's parliamentary leader.

These measures will go some way towards blunting attacks on the DA as a white-dominated elitist party. It is a tactic the ANC has deployed time and again, and it is not just hotheads like Julius Malema that have played the race card. The Deputy General Secretary of the Communist Party, Jeremy Cronin, used much the same tactics. 'The party is run by two stooges and a white madam,' he told a May Day rally in De Aar.[98] 'The boss lady. We all know who she is.' Can the DA find an answer to this kind of slur?

The local elections of 2011 were an important test for the party. It has made major strides since its disastrous showing in the 1994 election and is today the major opposition party in the country, attempting to hold the ANC to account. It has promoted black voices in Parliament and on councils up and down the country. The party now has the support of 5 per cent of the black population – not a huge number, but a beginning.[99] In women like Lindiwe Mazibuko, it has found a confident speaker who is not afraid to challenge the ANC. The party has a clear vision of how it would like to change South Africa, and a record of administration in the Western Cape of which it can on the whole be proud. Yet still the doubt remains: can the party break through to the black majority, who have until now proved so loyal to the party they supported for all these years – the ANC?

Perhaps the most perceptive remark has been from the editor of *Business Day*, Peter Bruce: 'the next test for the DA will be the national elections in 2014. Service delivery can't be central to its messaging then. Neither can the 'opportunity society' it currently uses. It's too complicated. What it needs is a core economic message people can relate to.'[100]

Chapter 10

Crime, Corruption and Connections[1]

Martin Plaut

An autumn day dawned grey and cloudy across Cape Town. Newspaper vendors selling copies of the morning paper at the traffic lights were warmly dressed against the unseasonable cold. The *Cape Times* of Thursday, 31 March 2011, had STATE CORRUPTION BOMBSHELL plastered across its front page. The story merited the treatment.

Willie Hofmeyr, head of the Special Investigation Unit probe into government corruption, had told 'visibly shocked' members of Parliament the previous day that 16 government departments and public entities were being investigated for fraud, corruption and maladministration. There were, he said, serious irregularities in the construction of 33 police stations and in the tenders for 10 000 homes for the poor, while the state broadcaster, the SABC, was being investigated for awarding R2.4 billion in contracts to firms in which its management had a stake. 'I think we should all accept that corruption is a serious problem in our country,' Hofmeyr said, 'but I am hopeful that we will make good progress over the next few years.'

On the same day, the *Times* led with a different but equally dramatic headline: 'Crime intelligence boss arrested'. This was the story about how the chief of police intelligence, Richard Mdluli, was wanted for a murder committed 12 years earlier. While the case apparently concerned a dispute over a woman, the papers went on to suggest links to other cases: the murder of a Cape Town gangland leader, Cyril Beeka, and the arrest of a Czech fugitive, Radovan Krejcir.[2]

Just one day's papers contained all the elements that have so scarred South African life in recent years: government corruption, national and international gangland bosses, links between senior police officers and the underworld, and unsolved murders. Yet there was little unusual about Thursday, 31 March. Readers inured by the frequency of such reports probably turned to the back pages for rugby, cricket, soccer – anything for a little light relief.

This chapter will look at how corruption and organised crime inter- act and feed on each other; how the law enforcement agencies are fight- ing back, but how they have been undermined by politicians, and how serious the threat is that South Africa could become a 'predatory state' in the grip of criminal syndicates.

The historic context of crime and corruption

South Africa has never experienced a 'golden age' of clean, just and effective government. It should not be forgotten that dispossession, ava- rice and conflict are the bedrock upon which it was built. The nation was founded on conquest and imperial ambition, black as well as white, and its legacy lives on to this day. This violent inception was given added momentum by the discovery of vast wealth – diamonds, gold and then a host of other minerals – in the latter half of the nineteenth century. From the first, these resources were exploited with rapacious greed, leading to two of the most brutal colonial conflicts Britain ever fought: the Boer Wars. Definitions of legality and illegality depended on whose law and whose order were being imposed.

Rapid industrial development and urbanisation after the Second World War created an environment in which urban criminality flour- ished. In the townships on the outskirts of the cities, young boys formed gangs that were mainly involved in petty crime. During the 1950s, the Msomi gang operated from Alexandra, outside Johannesburg.[3] They were responsible for an organised reign of terror involving numerous armed robberies, murders, protection rackets and the fleecing of ordinary residents. Their local rivals were the Spoilers, a 250-strong gang known for their violence. Among the Spoilers members was Joe Modise, of later Arms Deal fame.[4]

There is some evidence that in this period the ANC Youth League made informal use of criminal gangs during political protests. Although the Youth League members were much more political and respectable than the gangs, they were not averse to using these young thugs to enforce bus boycotts. They could be trusted to 'board a tram and beat up those who were on the tram and in that way help to make the tram boycotts more effective'.[5] Gang members were used to enforce political boycott campaigns and stayaways, although they were not formally organised as party 'storm troopers'.

Don Mattera, a former gang member, maintained that during the 1960s ex-gangsters joined the ANC when it launched the armed struggle.[6] Although they represented a tiny fraction of the youths who became members of the ANC, Mattera says that they influenced the movement to become more militant and more violent: 'The violent arena was not new to the gangster,' Mattera is quoted as saying. 'He could kill now for a more worthwhile cause.'[7]

Joe Modise, like many of his peers, went into exile after the ANC was banned. He rose rapidly in the organisation, undergoing military and political training in the Soviet Union and Czechoslovakia. Having become a member of the ANC high command, he established bases in Tanzania, Angola and Uganda, and supervised training programmes for thousands of young blacks fleeing South Africa. But according to the author, RW Johnson, Modise ran Umkhonto we Sizwe with a mixture of ruthlessness and avarice.[8] Johnson quotes an ANC member, Sibusiso Madlala, who accused Modise of presiding over torture in the movement's camps in Angola, running stolen car rackets from Zambia and encouraging bank robberies.[9] How much of this was done for the ANC and how much for Modise's own benefit is unclear. What is evident is that Modise liked the good life, and there was no explanation of how this was paid for. 'When I met him in Lusaka,' another exile told Johnson, 'all he seemed to care about was building his house. He was obsessed about his lawn.' Modise was accused by an internal ANC commission of sending his troops into South Africa to do his shopping at great risk to themselves.[10] He is said to have shared a house in Lusaka with a cocaine dealer. 'It was generally assumed that Joe was using his contacts to make money out of the drug trade too,' says Johnson; 'he would, after all, stop at nothing and in any case other high-ranking ANC folk were known to be involved in the drug trade too.'[11]

Difficult as it is to assess the accuracy of these allegations, it is not the first time they have been made. Stephen Ellis and Tsepho Sechaba wrote about much the same issue in 1992, without naming Modise directly.[12]

> Rumours abounded that a clique within the leadership was involved in smuggling into and out of South Africa, using army [MK] personnel to take drugs into the Republic and bring out stolen cars, which were then sold in Mozambique or elsewhere for personal profit. Some senior ANC figures were said to have grown rich on rackets of this type, and to be investing their money in Zimbabwe especially.

The routes used to smuggle arms and fighters into the country for the liberation movements were to remain intact, also serving the more dubious interests of personal enrichment.

While this was taking place abroad, crime, rather than politics, was the focus of the South African gangs in the 1960s. The port of Durban became a haven for organised criminal groups.[13] The smuggling of marijuana, or 'dagga' as it is known locally, was important for gangs in the area. The international demand for 'Durban Poison' – the name given to the top-quality marijuana from the Transkei – was such that its export became a highly lucrative business.[14] By the early 1970s, the gangs had developed into regular narcotics syndicates. In exchange for exporting compacted dagga to Europe and Australia, they also obtained LSD and other drugs – initially from France and Britain – which were then smuggled into the country.

In Cape Town, street gangs also grew rapidly after the Second World War. Upon returning from active duty, unemployed soldiers of the Cape Coloured Corps came to live in neighbourhoods such as District Six, close to the city centre. Together with the local '*skollies*', they formed gangs such as the 'Goofies' and the 'Red Cats'.[15] The massive relocation and the forced removals of coloured people from areas like District Six in the 1960s to townships on the Cape Flats tore families and communities apart, while social structures, including clubs and some religious groups, collapsed, leaving crime to flourish.

The gangs in the Western Cape engaged in rackets like housebreaking, motorcar robbery and drug dealing.[16] The acquisition and distribution of Mandrax developed into a major activity. Asians ran the Mandrax syndicates during the 1970s, obtaining supplies from India and Pakistan, but refrained from handling the drugs themselves.[17]

There is evidence that during the 1980s and early 1990s the apartheid government may have augmented the supplies of drugs, including Mandrax, LSD, and Ecstasy. 'Project Coast', the notorious chemical and biological warfare programme run by Dr Wouter Basson, produced these drugs on an industrial scale at factories run at the headquarters of SADF Special Forces near Pretoria.[18] Dr Basson argued during his trial that its aim had been to 'infiltrate the drugs and arms routes used by the ANC's armed wing, Umkhonto we Sizwe'.[19] Exactly how much reached the wider public is not clear, but a UN report into the project concluded that it was possible the drugs had been produced to undermine black communities by increasing addiction.[20]

During the 1980s, the world saw a brisk growth of organised crime and transnational criminal activity. Intricate criminal networks extended their operations to a 'global village'.[21] Increasingly operating across international borders, criminal activities grew at a pace that surpassed the law enforcement agencies' ability to hamper them. Political changes created a new space for criminals. The demise of the Soviet Union prompted the rise of organised crime in Russia and Central Europe. The end of the Cold War and the development of more liberal regimes ushered in a new age of open borders, easy migration and debilitated state infrastructure. This period saw organised crime transformed from a domestic to an international issue, and from a law and order concern to a threat to national and international security.[22]

As the apartheid era drew to a close and the white elite began to see the writing on the wall, venality increased dramatically. Hardly an area of South African life remained untouched. The scale of the corruption was revealed in a seminal report drawn up by Hennie van Vuuren, of the Institute for Security Studies.[23] In it he began to dismantle the image that the apartheid government was somehow repressive but clean, or, as he put it: '"brutal" in the way in which it wielded power, yet "honest" in the way it managed its finances at the same time'.[24] The study revealed the quite extraordinary extent to which corruption and sleaze became part of the South African body politic, particularly after the gradual isolation of the country began to take hold in the 1960s and 1970s. Van Vuuren reveals how slush funds and secret payments were designed to break the growing strength of the anti-apartheid movement and the gradual progress of black liberation across southern Africa. The full extent of what took place will certainly never be revealed, since the failing National Party regime engaged in an orgy of destruction to hide the evidence of its political crimes as well as the rampant scale of corruption. So great was this purging of the vaults that even the furnaces of the steel company, Iscor, were employed to burn the mountain of paperwork.[25]

An opportunity to conduct a thorough investigation was missed when the Truth and Reconciliation Commission decided that corruption was not part of its brief.[26] But it did commission an important study by the Auditor-General into the scale of the secret funds that were used by the South African state to pay for its most critical functions without revealing them to Parliament or the public. By far the largest sums were spent on defence, but they included everything from Information Services to Foreign Affairs. The sums spent in this way between 1978 and 1994 were valued at R339.19 billion.[27] From funds to get around the 1977 oil embargo to money to buy influence in Hollywood, South Africa bribed its way across the globe. Closer to home, vast sums disappeared into the black homelands, while even wildlife had its price: 100 000 Angolan elephant and countless rhino were poached by the occupying army in northern Namibia and Angola, turning large areas into what were described as 'green lifeless desert'.[28]

The report spells out in detail the myriad scams that were used to divert covert as well as overt funds from their alleged use to private accounts. Large sums found their way into personal bank accounts in places like Switzerland. Funds earmarked for defence projects flowed into the pockets of senior defence force personnel. Even the Minister of Finance and then President, Dr Nico Diederichs, was implicated in feathering his own nest.[28] The editor of the *Sunday Times*, Ken Owen, concluded that the scale of the corruption in the apartheid government forced it to the negotiating table, resulting in 'the bankruptcy of a nation that had been looted until it could no longer honour its debts'.[30] This may have been something of an exaggeration, but he was not alone in this view. Speaking at a conference on Public Sector Ethics in 1989, Judge Victor Hiemstra declared that:

> There is a strange atmosphere in the land, as if people have no faith in the future and consequently want, as soon as possible, to make as much money as possible. By the time they are discovered, so they reason, the whole affair would have collapsed anyway ... an atmosphere of let us eat, drink and be merry for tomorrow we die.[31]

It was in this frenzied climate that the transfer of authority took place in 1994. The world had an image of a brave guerrilla movement, fighting against one of the most hated regimes in the world, and on the whole this was not misleading. With Nelson Mandela inaugurated as South Africa's first black president, there was little criticism of the new administration. However, the corrupt relationships of the state were still in place and would unavoidably reach their tentacles into the new administration. As the first post-apartheid Speaker of Parliament, Frene Ginwala, put it: 'In South Africa we inherited an intrinsically corrupt system of governance ... To survive, it created a legal framework that was based on and facilitated corruption.'[32]

Death shocks the nation

Since 1994, the reputation of the ANC government has been radically altered. This may have begun with the Arms Deal, which is reported to have provided large kickbacks to many senior government officials. But it was the death of a businessman, Brett Kebble, perhaps more than any other event, that shattered the image of a clean, well-functioning administration. What his killing did was to reveal the apparent nexus between money and politics; the relationship between some of the highest offices in the land and the criminal networks that lurk beneath the surface.

Sam Sole, the *Mail & Guardian's* veteran investigative journalist, who did so much to uncover the events surrounding Kebble's death, captured the essence of this story.

> Kebble's murder lifted a corner on what appeared to be a very extensive organised crime network – with tentacles in the police, in customs and revenue, into Joburg's bouncer gangs and the drug-distribution turf they controlled, into smuggling networks that reached back into apartheid-era covert operations, into seemingly respectable business empires with multimillion-rand cash turnovers.[33]

In the early hours of 28 September 2005, the South African Press Association published the first detailed description of the murder.

> The bloodied body of mining magnate Brett Kebble was still lying in his luxury German car, on a bridge over a Johannesburg highway, some four hours after he died in a hail of bullets at 9 p.m. on Tuesday … Kebble's silver grey Mercedes was parked with its front wheels on the pavement with the driver's door open while forensic experts pored over the scene.

A multi-millionaire who had built his fortune in gold mining, Kebble was a generous benefactor of the ANC and a well-respected sponsor of the arts. Even a country inured to violence was stunned by the killing. There was an outpouring of grief and much generous praise for Kebble. His funeral would have done justice to a senior politician. It was held in Saint George's Cathedral in Cape Town, the seat of the Anglican Archbishop of Southern Africa. The coffin, draped in the South African flag, was carried into the cathedral past a uniformed honour guard of ANC marshals. The great and the good packed into the cathedral.

Among them were leading members of the ANC, including the business tycoons Tokyo Sexwale and Saki Macozoma. President Thabo Mbeki sent one of his most trusted associates, the Minister in the Presidency, Essop Pahad, to deliver the main tribute. Pahad didn't stint in his praise for the man he had known: 'Today we salute the memory of a remarkable person who was larger than life and who shouldered controversy with a natural sense of fortitude and even puckish charm.'[34]

But Pahad – Mbeki's 'hard man' since his early student days in Britain – then went on to strike a strangely discordant note.[35] Attacking the media for what he described as 'unfortunate' and 'obsessive' reporting of the case, the Minister warned those present to keep what they knew of the man to themselves. 'What Brett said to any one of us in private should remain private,' he declared. As the days went by, a different picture of the dead man began to emerge.

A well-connected man

Brett Kebble was an extraordinary entrepreneur even by the standards of a country that has seen more than its share of swashbuckling adventurers. He was cast in the mould of the Randlords, the entrepreneurs who dominated the gold and diamond trade – and politics – for much of the early twentieth century. His unauthorised biographer, Barry Sergeant, described the businessman in colourful terms: 'When he was not in fitful sleep, Brett Kebble lived his life like a combine harvester running on an oversized tank of jet fuel. No matter the problem, project or person in his path, the Kebble juggernaut rolled on, chewed it up and spat it out, propelling countless shards of junk skywards, eventually to rain down fretfully on the scorched earth he left behind.'[36]

Kebble studied law at the University of Cape Town, graduating in 1986. He abandoned a legal career and turned to the world of mining in 1991, teaming up with his father, Roger, a successful mining engineer, to mount a hostile takeover of Rand Leases Gold Mining. Then he won a controlling interest in Randgold and Exploration in 1994.[37] Kebble knew little about the industry, but he was a wizard with companies. In a short time he worked a minor miracle, talking up the value of the company's subsidiary, Randgold Resources, from $5 million to $310 million by 1996. He did this despite doing no more than buying what Sergeant described as a 'wreck of a gold mine in Mali' that had tens of millions of dollars of debt.[38]

His next target was Johannesburg Consolidated Investments, or JCI, one of South Africa's oldest mining houses. In 1996 the Anglo American Corporation decided to sell off JCI, on condition that it went to black investors. The company was split up and Kebble moved in for the kill. He was not black, nor did he have the R2 billion asking price, but neither condition appears to have been an obstacle. Cutting his ties with Randgold, Kebble joined JCI as the head of its gold division. Using the company as his base, he then outmanoeuvred his black partners and began a series of financial transactions of mind-numbing complexity.

Companies were spawned, assets were bought, sold and subdivided, and a vast financial pyramid was constructed. At the heart of the process was his ability to issue shares. His main vehicle was Consolidated African Mines. In just one year, 1997-98, Kebble increased the number of shares in the company thirty-fold.[39] As Sergeant puts it: 'During Kebble's stellar rise from nowhere man to billionaire, zero to people's hero in less than two years, he had mastered the art of issuing paper.'[40] In his thirties, Kebble had become one of South Africa's most powerful mining magnates. He bought the choicest of properties in Johannesburg and Cape Town. He owned a fleet of limousines and Italian sports cars. Kebble flew around the country in a pair of private jets, the more opulent of which was a Gulfstream mark II, worth $16 million.[41]

Kebble also became an enthusiastic supporter of the ANC after it took power. He was a man who knew the value of cultivating friends in the right places. Unlike other white businessmen who remained aloof, he joined the ANC and supported the party's plans to widen ownership of the country's wealth through BEE deals. Kebble helped initiate many such transactions, making instant millionaires of some of his new black associates, most of whom remained his loyal supporters, even though some of the deals later collapsed.

The mining tycoon was also happy to fund the party when it found itself in difficulties. When the ANC in the Western Cape ran out of funds in January 2003, a reported R250 000 was donated to it by Kebble and empowerment groups associated with JCI.[42] 'I am a patriot and an ardent supporter of our new democracy,' he declared when the news leaked out. Kebble was particularly generous with the ANC Youth League, lavishing gifts on its senior members. As *Noseweek* put it:

> Kebble has spent a small fortune on keeping these youngsters in his camp. He's given them credit cards and the use of his mansions in [the posh Cape Town suburbs of] Bishopscourt and Kirstenbosch to hold wild parties involving plenty of booze and beautiful young women frolicking naked in swimming pools with important business and political contacts.[43]

Andile Nkuhlu, a member of the Youth League's National Executive, was among the group of people expecting Kebble for dinner on the night he died. When it came to Kebble's funeral Nkuhlu had some of the kindest words for his old friend. In a world where youth and inexperience are shunned, Kebble's 'outstretched hand' became 'the ultimate bridge to experience and maturity,' he told the congregation. 'In a country where what is black is still suspect, marginal and less credible, having Brett on your side made a world of difference.'[44]

Kebble had been an important source of funds for the ANC's Youth League. It was reported that the League's financial arm, Lembede Investments, had been started with R5 million from Kebble.[45] By 2008, this holding had grown to an empire worth R97 million, with a stake in a string of companies.[46] Individual members of the ANC Youth League had become very rich indeed. Kebble's circle of friends went right to the top: according to Sergeant, he was one of Jacob Zuma's 'staunchest and most public supporters'.[47]

After his death, the *Sunday Times* published a series of claims based on a list found on Kebble's desk.[48] Headed 'Loan Account', the list itemised money paid to the ANC and leading members of the ruling party. A total of R95 million is reported to have been paid out, with the ANC itself receiving R18 million. Further details of these donations gradually filtered out as the Kebble family attempted to retrieve some of the largesse that Brett had spread around his cronies. In court hearings, it emerged that sums donated between 2002 and 2005 included:[49]

❏ R2.4 million for the ANC in the Western Cape;

- ❏ R750 000 for the ANC in the Eastern Cape;
- ❏ R6 million for the ANC Youth League;
- ❏ R14 million given to Lunga Ncwana, a prominent member of the Youth League;
- ❏ R860 000 given to Songezo Mjongile, a member of the League's National Executive Committee.

The ANC resisted the family's demand for the return of the money, claiming that these had been political donations, which it was entitled to accept. Nor was it alone. It transpired that the DA had also been in receipt of R500 000 from Kebble. There was one difference: the DA accepted that the money had to be returned. South Africa's largest ever corporate swindler was clearly a man who understood the need to buy influence.

Murder or suicide?

There were many fulsome tributes to Brett Kebble at his funeral, but not everyone joined in what the *Sunday Times* described as a 'cacophony of eulogies'.[50] Instead the paper published a stinging editorial, calling him 'the Great Corrupter, a dirty businessman who had little respect for the law or codes of good practice. He corrupted politicians and created a parasitical network of politically connected beneficiaries who affectionately called him *"umlungu wethu"* (our white man).'

On the face of it this was a remarkably ungenerous assessment of a man who had just received what came close to a state funeral. Yet it soon became evident that Brett Kebble's detractors were right. He was a truly malevolent influence; a swindler who had bought his way into the highest echelons of power and ruthlessly used his contacts to bolster his failing enterprises. For Kebble's empire was a house of cards – an artifice that could no longer be sustained. Indeed, news of the magnate's financial difficulties was beginning to leak out even before he died.

In late 2004 *Noseweek* began publishing a series of articles alleging that despite a vast array of assets, Kebble had paid little, if any, tax.[51] Indeed, he had failed to submit income tax returns for more than a decade. This had finally caught the attention of the Revenue Service's Special

Investigations Unit, which opened an investigation into Kebble's tax affairs in January 2002. When this was first revealed, the tax authorities attempted to silence the magazine, as did Kebble. Undeterred, *Noseweek* proceeded with its revelations, pointing out that the tax investigation had been halted after representations from Kebble's legal team; two key investigators had resigned and still no tax returns had been filed.

By early 2005 JCI's debts stood at a staggering R2.9 billion.[52] Kebble sold houses and other assets to try to stay afloat, but with a habit of flying by private jet and keeping a host of associates and hangers-on in pocket, he was reported to be personally getting through R5 million a month. It was estimated that the magnate stole sums in the order of R900 million from three companies.[53] By the time of his death, the *Mail & Guardian* was describing the collapse of the Kebble financial empire as 'our Enron ... the largest corporate fraud in South African History.'[54] There was a warrant out for his arrest.[55]

Kebble was married with four children and it was revealed that in the weeks before he was killed he took out life insurance policies in his own name, worth R30 million.[56] Speculation grew that perhaps the magnate had arranged his own death, in an attempt to provide for his family, since suicide would have invalidated the insurance and left them penniless.

The darker side of Kebble's death was gradually uncovered. Glenn Agliotti, a convicted drugs trafficker, was charged with arranging the killing, in concert with others. Like any business tycoon, Kebble left detailed arrangements of his affairs to his employees – and his own death was no exception. According to testimony in his murder trial, the operation was allegedly planned and masterminded by the man in charge of his security, Clinton Nassif. An investigation found the three men who actually carried out the killing. They were Mikey Schultz, Nigel McGurk and Faizal Smith, and all turned state witness in return for immunity from prosecution. When Agliotti was brought to court for the murder the trial judge, Judge Kgomo, gave a memorable description of the killing. He said it was 'like a scene from a Mafia film – tragic, emotionless and comical – only that it was real and serious.'[57]

The killers' first really serious work for Kebble came after an accountant, Stephen Mildenhall, began digging up dirt on JCI. In 2005 he started asking why the company had failed to comply with stock exchange regulations, and tried to have Kebble prevented from running the company. Kebble, who was not used to having his authority challenged, was furious. He ordered Schultz, Smith and McGurk to have Mildenhall injured, but not killed.[58] The three set off for Cape Town, where Mildenhall lived, and he was shot in both shoulders.

With this task successfully completed, the hit-men were the natural candidates for Kebble's next mission – organising his own death. This was arranged via Clinton Nassif, who told them that the fee for the job would be R2 million.[59] The money was to be paid via Agliotti. It was decided that Kebble would drive to a dark and secluded street where he was to be shot. In the event the operation was badly botched and turned into a tragic farce, with the killing re-arranged on three separate occasions. It was finally on 27 September 2005 that Mikey Schultz drew up alongside Kebble's car and pointed the firearm at his willing victim's head. The gun jammed and then jammed again. It was only on the third attempt, with Kebble apparently looking pleadingly at his assassin, that the gun finally fired. 'I could see the disappointment in his face, he gave me a look like to say "get this over with, you're putting me through hell",' Schultz told the court. He leaned out of the window and this time aimed for Kebble's body. 'I pulled the trigger, this time the gun fired. I kept firing.' Kebble died on the spot.

This story, extraordinary as it already was, still had many twists and turns to come. As journalists dug through the rubble of Kebble's life, his connections to the highest echelons of South African society began to be unearthed. In the end, Agliotti was cleared of the murder, with the judge arguing that the prosecution had 'violated the accused's right to a fair trial'.[60] But in his judgment Judge Frans Kgomo made this remark about the Kebble murder, which sums up the entire saga:

> This case is about hidden and/or sinister agendas perpetrated by shoddy characters as well as ostensibly crooked and/or greedy business persons. It is about corrupt civil servants as well as prominent politicians or politically connected people wining and dining with devils incarnates [sic] under cover of darkness.[61]

Police and politicians

Glen Agliotti not only had excellent connections with the criminal underworld; like any Mafia godfather, he had cultivated his links with the police at the highest level. Agliotti had managed to befriend South Africa's Police Commissioner, Jackie Selebi. In words that would come back to haunt him, the Commissioner admitted in an interview that Agliotti was 'my friend, finish and *klaar*'.[62] The use of the word '*klaar*', the Afrikaans for finished, underlined just how definitive the statement was.

It was a careful courtship. Agliotti approached Selebi – a past president of the ANC Youth League, friend of Thabo Mbeki, and an NEC member – in the early 1990s when Selebi was in charge of organising the return of ANC veterans to South Africa. Agliotti came up with a scheme to import second-hand clothes from Japan, which would be sold to assist the returning former ANC cadres.[63] The scheme failed, but gradually Agliotti drew Selebi into his circle. It was to prove to be his most propitious and lucrative initiative. In October 1999, after being sworn in as the country's president, Thabo Mbeki asked Selebi to take on the post of National Commissioner of Police.

Despite his misgivings, Selebi thrived in the post. In 2004 he was honoured by the international police organisation, Interpol. Jackie Selebi became the first African to hold the presidency of Interpol, with the organisation's secretary-general welcoming his election as a 'historic moment'.[64] He was at the pinnacle of his power, but his links to his 'old friend' were to be his downfall.

Selebi's appointment as Commissioner of Police was a godsend for Agliotti. In the years to come the drugs trafficker was to wind Selebi ever more tightly into his grasp, until he was in a position to sell access to Selebi like a commodity. From the Kebbles alone, Agliotti received $1 million for providing access to Selebi, establishing a special company through which to handle the payments.[65] Selebi became a regular visitor at Brett Kebble's home in Johannesburg.[66]

In return for his favours, Jackie Selebi received sums of money from the drugs trafficker. For this he was convicted of corruption in July 2010.[67] During his trial it was alleged that he had received R12 million from Brett Kebble in order to make Kebble's tax problems 'disappear'.[68] The court heard how Agliotti took Selebi on shopping trips to luxury stores in Johannesburg and bought gifts for him in London, paying for suits, shirts, ties and shoes. In return, Selebi did favours for Agliotti, including allowing him to see a report British Customs and Excise had sent to their South African counterparts. The report was part of an investigation called 'Operation Chaser', outlining a plan to transport a shipment of cocaine from Venezuela via Angola and then to conceal it in furniture to be sent by container to Britain.[69] The court heard that Agliotti was working on behalf of an international drugs cartel.[70]

On the night of Kebble's death, Agliotti talked to the Commissioner of Police on at least one occasion. It is not clear exactly what the two men said to each other, but we do have Selebi's version of events.[71] 'At some point Glenn [Agliotti] phoned me to ask if I had heard [about the murder],' he recalled. 'I said, "Glenn, when you get to the place please call me, and confirm that this is what has happened."' Jackie Selebi, as Commissioner of Police, appeared to be relying on a convicted drug trafficker for information about a crime, despite having his own officers present at the scene of the killing.

Unanswered questions

The Kebble affair was emblematic of the state South Africa is in. It linked the raw power of money with the greed and naïveté of those who came to rule the country after the ANC took power in 1994. It showed how one corrupt businessman could weave a chain of connections that led to the most senior politicians in the country, while contaminating the man who headed the police.

It would, of course, be wrong to tar all South African business with the Kebble brush. Most of the country's enterprises are entirely above board. Indeed some former South African companies – including Old Mutual, Anglo American and SABMiller – are now highly successful global corporations. These multinationals, as well as most locally based businesses, are careful about their procedures and corporate governance. At the same time they are not unaffected by crime.[72] A study by PricewaterhouseCoopers in 2007 suggested that South Africa was more seriously affected by economic crime than most countries. This included asset misappropriation, money laundering, bribery and fraud.[73]Many questions remain unanswered. Why, for example, did President Thabo Mbeki stand so staunchly behind Jackie Selebi, long after there was sufficient evidence to indicate that his most senior policeman was seriously bent? Bulelani Ngcuka's successor as Director of Public Prosecutions, Vusi Pikoli, had briefed Mbeki for 18 months about Selebi's corruption, yet it was only in January 2008 that Selebi was finally suspended from his job.[74] Why did the insurance companies pay Kebble's family the policies he had taken out, despite being warned that his death looked like suicide?[75]

What is extraordinary about this story is that despite years of investigations the death of Brett Kebble is still as mysterious as ever. Mandy Wiener, a reporter for Talk Radio 702, followed every twist and turn of the case. She attended the court hearings assiduously, ate lunch with Jackie Selebi and wrote a lengthy book after having interviewed almost everyone involved. Yet she remains without a firm conclusion.[76] 'At the end of it all, I am left with a hollowness, an uneasy sense of not knowing. Someone must be lying. Perhaps everyone is.'

The events surrounding the killing showed the legal system at its best, since it obtained the conviction of the country's most senior policeman. But it also revealed the system's weaknesses, since it failed to find a convincing explanation for Kebble's murder. Even now, after court cases, a Commission of Inquiry, innumerable articles and reports and two lengthy books, the facts about the Kebble killing are still shrouded in mystery. As the forensic scientist, David Klatzow, observed: 'Brett Kebble died just as he lived – in a cloud of smoke and mirrors.'[77]

The scale of corruption

An indication of just how pervasive corruption has become can be found in the annual surveys conducted by Transparency International, which measures the perceived level of corruption in 180 countries.[78] In 1995 – the earliest survey available – South Africa ranked 24th, just below Japan and above Portugal. By 2011 it had fallen 40 places and was ranked 64th in the world. This trend is reflected in the views of ordinary citizens across the country's major cities, with 83 per cent feeling that corruption has become a way of life while 85 per cent believe that there is corruption at senior levels of government.[79]

Noseweek used an editorial to portray the current situation:[80]

> South Africa is drowning in a sea of corruption. It's every-where: hospitals, police, schools, traffic officers, every state department, with Home Affairs, CIPC [Companies and Intellectual Property Commission MP], Public Works and Mineral Resources and Energy among the most visible.
>
> It's never been as bad as this.
>
> Corruption, it seems, is driven less by poverty, more by greed, a sense – or culture – of entitlement, and opportunity. The trend is set by those on top of the social and economic pile, rather than driven from the bottom by need.
>
> In South Africa, those at the top – the powerful because of their wealth, their positions of political power – not only in-spire corruption by example; they actively condone it – if only because they are themselves so compromised.

It is hard to argue with this conclusion. As the death of Brett Kebble indicated, the tentacles of crime penetrated the highest echelons of government. Nor was he a lone example. In May 2011, Sheryl Cwele, the wife of the Minister of State Security, Siyabonga Cwele, was found guilty of drugs smuggling with a Nigerian, Frank Nabolisa.[81, 82] She had helped organise the smuggling of cocaine from Turkey and Brazil us-ing two South African women as 'mules'. Both the accused were sen-tenced to 12 years in jail. Significant as the crime was, some questioned how much her husband and President Zuma knew about the case, and when they knew it. The Sunday Independent suggested that both men were briefed on her activities well before her arrest.[83] The paper reported that a group of intelligence chiefs, led by a former National Intelligence Co-ordinating Committee co-ordinator, Silumko Sokupa, had briefed President Kgalema Motlanthe (before he handed the presidency over to Jacob Zuma in early 2009). A freedom of information group, the Right2Know campaign, called on President Zuma to explain what he knew about the case when he re-appointed Siyabonga Cwele to the Cabinet as Minister of State Security in May 2009.[84, 85]

A family affair

There is mounting evidence that the blurring of the distinction between public office and personal interest extends to the highest levels of government. Many senior ANC officials, politicians and ministers now see holding such offices as no bar to holding outside interests. In August 2011, it was reported that about three-quarters of the Cabinet's 35 members had financial interests outside their main occupations.[86] So did 59 per cent of the country's 400 members of Parliament.

The families of some of the 'politically well-connected' have also done remarkably well since the end of apartheid. President Jacob Zuma himself has been criticised for allowing his family to become so overtly involved in business. The President's wives, children and other persons closely associated with him are reported to have developed more than 220 businesses between them, many established since Zuma became President.[87] The Zuma family's interests have a regional reach, with links to the President of Mozambique's own substantial business empire.[88] Other members of the family are reported to have links with the Democratic Republic of Congo.[89] The Democratic Alliance's leader in Parliament, Athol Trollip, called for an investigation into the Zuma family holdings,[90] accusing his family members of benefiting from 'mega tenders' without proper procurement procedures or having the necessary experience to deliver the projects, arguing that this was hampering service delivery. Replying to Athol Trollip, Zuma said:

> There are no current plans to extend this to all family members apart from the obvious question and it is laughable to suggest whether a member of the executive could be adequately informed about all such family members or whether such family members could be placed under a legal obligation to explain their affairs.[91]

All the Zuma family's enterprises may be entirely legitimate, but to what extent did they exploit the President's name in gaining business? There is also growing unease about the Zuma family's connections to the Guptas – a wealthy Indian family headed by three brothers, Atul, Ajay and Rajesh, who have been in business in South Africa since 1993. President Zuma is reported to be a regular visitor to the Gupta home.

The Zuma–Gupta connection was highlighted when mining rights were acquired by a company in which both families have a stake – Imperial Crown Trading. Imperial, a shell company with no track record in mining, managed to obtain the rights to an iron ore mine from Kumba Iron Ore, a subsidiary of Anglo American.[92] In May 2009, both Kumba and Imperial Crown applied for the rights to the mine, but the award went to Imperial. Kumba alleged that Imperial copied its documentation and then submitted this paperwork as its own.[93]

If the arrangement had gone ahead it would have made the President's son, Duduzane Zuma, a very wealthy man, although both he and the Guptas complain that they have never made a cent from their government connections and that the Zuma name has closed doors rather than opening them.[94] However, in December 2011, a court ruled against Imperial Crown. The decision was seen as a major boost to confidence in South Africa's system of justice.

This pattern of corporate greed linked to political influence is exemplified by the case of the Aurora Empowerment group of mines. The chairman of Aurora is the President's nephew, Khulubuse Zuma. The managing director is Zondwa Gadaffi Mandela, grandson of Nelson Mandela, while another board member, Michael Hulley, is President Zuma's personal legal adviser.

In October 2009, despite having no previous experience in the mining industry, Aurora was awarded control of two mines formerly owned by the Pamodzi Gold group by a high court-appointed liquidator. Aurora outbid experienced mining firms with an offer of R605 million for the assets. Since then the company has been at the centre of major controversy, with critics claiming that Aurora has committed multiple legal and regulatory infringements.

When Aurora took over the gold mines it promised steady jobs, decent housing and education bursaries for the children of its workers. 'All these things, all these beautiful promises – that worried me,' reflected Frans Baleni, NUM Secretary-General.[95] 'They started to seriously default on the payment of salaries in December 2009, and in the following year, 2010, for the first three months, they were not paying workers' salaries at all.'

Many of the 5 200 mine workers employed at the two mines have since been living on donations and food parcels provided by the unions. In mid-2011, in the run-up to local elections in May, the ANC began delivering food parcels, but many miners were scornful of the largesse, accusing the party of blatant electioneering. It was revealed that Khulubuse Zuma had made a private donation of R1 million to the ANC for its May election campaign, despite failing to pay the wages the company owed its workers.

The union demanded that the money be handed to the destitute miners, but the ANC refused. One of the mineworkers at Orkney, Primrose Javu, was furious.[96] 'Khulubuse Zuma gave one million rands to the ANC. For what reason? He gave it to them just to shut [them] up. They must shut their mouths. They mustn't say anything about these conditions,' she said.

The ANC has, in the past, been quick to condemn other firms that mistreated their workforce, but not Aurora. NUM's Frans Baleni says there is a clear reason for this: 'Because of the names which are associated with this saga, we have got a barrier. The ANC has been very silent on this – not a single word, not a single statement.'

Since taking over operations in 2009, Aurora failed to secure the financing to buy the mines outright as it had planned. This is despite Khulubuse Zuma boasting on radio in July 2007 that the company had 'deep pockets', promising profits of '5 to 10 billion dollars' in the first 10 years of business.[97] Aurora made repeated public statements that a finance deal was 'imminent' and the problems would soon be resolved, but the money never materialised. It was suggested that a Chinese state-owned company, Shandong Mining & Exploration, was to invest $100 million in the two gold mines, but this fell through.[98] Finally, in May 2011, the company was given just three days to vacate the premises.[99] 'We are very disappointed that it took so long to remove Aurora. We know they stripped assets and had a very negative impact on the mines.

We can only hope that they're gone for good,' said Lesiba Seshoka, NUM spokesman. Commenting on the behaviour of Aurora's directors, Cosatu head Zwelinzima Vavi described the company as encapsulating 'capitalism at its worst and greed at its best'.[100]

While ordinary miners lost their jobs, the directors of Aurora appear to be doing rather well. Khulubuse Zuma, a man who in the mid-1990s owned nothing more than a taxi business, has thrived. The South African media has highlighted the differences between his lifestyle and that of the miners he employed. He was photographed arriving at a celebrity wedding in a new Mercedes-Benz SL 363 AMG Gullwing, with a starting price of $183 000,[101] apparently one of 19 cars at his disposal. The paper showed the photograph to Simon Khanjane, one of the miners whom Aurora had not paid. 'It is not right,' he commented. 'They have no decency. It is shameful.'

Khulubuse Zuma denies exploiting his political connections. 'I cannot change the fact that I came from a political family,' he says. 'But just as they chose politics I chose to be an entrepreneur like my father.'[102] He denies using family connections to win deals. 'I can provide you with paperwork related to the deals to show that [President Zuma] was not involved. Companies that use political connections are bound to fail,' he says.

Aurora is currently being wound up, with administrators attempting to recover what they can of the mining assets. While this was under way, Michael Hulley was promoted from personal to official legal adviser of President Zuma.[103] The liquidator is reportedly looking for up to R1.7 billion from the Aurora management – the replacement value of the assets allegedly stripped from the mines.[104]

Local government

While most attention focuses on the major allegations of wrongdoing at the national level, it is at the local level that some of the most serious evidence of corruption and crime is to be found. Hardly a day passes without yet another allegation of misappropriation of funds by local politicians, and there have been numerous investigations detailing the failures of municipalities. One report into the provision of key utilities, including water and electricity, for two of the country's most important cities, Johannesburg and Cape Town, came to this searing conclusion.[105]

> Local government remains a sphere in which there is strong contestation over powers, roles and responsibilities. In some cases, officials in the administration have found common cause with politicians in creating a 'spoils system', where corruption, fraud and nepotism have developed as accepted ways of working. In other cases, officials have used their powers of maladministration to subvert legitimate council decisions and obstruct the efficient operation of the council. Between these two extremes lurk every conceivable combination in the troubled interface between the political and the administrative.

What is extraordinary about this state of affairs is that the government not only knows, but acknowledges that this is the case. As Kgalema Motlanthe admitted in 2007: 'The rot is across the board ... almost every project is conceived because it offers certain people a chance to make money.'[106]

Dissatisfaction with the provision of services is high and rising. A survey of 21 municipalities in Mpumalanga, Limpopo, KwaZulu-Natal and North West provinces showed that just 11 per cent of people believed they were getting good quality services.[107] The citizens of these municipalities were clear about what they thought of the behaviour of their officials and councillors – a majority (66 per cent) saw them as corrupt and nepotistic.[108] The study concluded that residents are very aware of just how badly these problems affect their quality of life. 'They are aware of poor communication, lack of transparency, increased corruption and nepotism in their local government and the fact that these factors have a negative impact on the ability to deliver high quality services.'[109]

There have been remarkably few systematic academic reviews of this phenomenon in recent years, despite its prominence in South African public life. A study by Professor Doreen Atkinson concluded that municipal malpractice had become 'extensive'.[110] She set out just how these corrupt practices work:

> There are numerous ways in which municipalities lend them-selves to personal enrichment. Typical problems are the abuse of mayoral funds, unauthorised transfers of municipal money to outsiders, favouritism in procurement processes, the pay-ment of bribes to secure services, the abuse of travel allowances, fictitious tenders, involvement of councillors with companies which then win tenders, non-payment of municipal services by councillors, using municipal facilities for party-political or personal purposes, and irregular performance bonuses.

Across the country, anger at corruption, nepotism and the accompany-ing lack of service delivery has led to riots. Confrontations between the poor and the authorities are on the rise.[111] These clashes are increasingly violent and growing in size. Researchers concluded that: 'The data sug-gests protest activity is likely to increase if communities believe govern-ment officials are neglecting the service delivery promises made during election campaigns.'[112]

International crime syndicates

The end of apartheid brought with it an increase in foreign trade and tourism, together with a relaxation of border controls and a more open environment. Welcome as these were, they also proved a boon to inter-national criminal networks. South Africa's geographical position also assisted this process, since the country was ideally placed to become a hub for the global marijuana trade. It also became a transit hub for other drugs that it did not produce itself. Heroin-producing countries like Afghanistan, Pakistan, and Thailand lie to the east of South Africa, while the cocaine-producing countries of Columbia, Peru and Bolivia lie to the west. Furthermore, South Africa's colonial past gives it connec-tions to the United Kingdom and the Netherlands, two lucrative drug markets and gateways to the rest of Europe. On a regional scale, South Africa acts as a base for many criminal organisations operating in nearby Zimbabwe, Swaziland, Mozambique and Zambia, amongst others. The country's advanced economy and infrastructure, together with its concentration of world-class financial services, are an added attraction to criminal organisations.

The easing of political tensions under Nelson Mandela saw a gradual decline in the township conflicts that had taken up so much police time and energy, but it was also a period of intense uncertainty for the security services. Few in the services knew whether they had a future. The newly elected government concentrated on consolidating its political authority, on transforming state structures and formulating new policies, rather than on the effective running of the state structures it had inherited.[113] As far as the police were concerned, the immediate focus was on transforming and legitimising the service rather than enhancing its effectiveness. The difficult process of amalgamating 11 existing police forces into one new South African Police Service had to be undergone.[114] It is suggested that the political transition:

> ... has been accompanied by an upsurge of indigenous criminal organisations and the influx of groups from outside the country as well as an increase in the problems of drug abuse and drug trafficking and associated violence. Part of the reason is that transitions are characterised by one or more of the following features: the collapse and re-establishment of state structures, major shifts in the principles underlying economic management, a redefinition of the principles and values on which a society operates e.g. who is eligible for participation in political affairs and a re-orientation of relationships with the outside world usually involving an opening of the economy and the society.[115]

Crime, and particularly organised crime, flourished as controls were relaxed in the post-apartheid period. East Asian, Nigerian and East European groups bought into local criminal operations and expanded them or contracted subsidiary organisations to conduct their work for them.[116] The most extensive report on organised crime in southern Africa – a three-year study by the Institute for Security Studies – concluded in 2011 that:

> While some organised criminal groups have been around for much longer than 1994 (such as the Chinese triads), syndicates of many nationalities operate in South Africa including nationals of Russia, Italy, Portugal, China, Lebanon, Pakistan, Nigeria, Morocco and India.[117]

The gangs were involved in a vast range of activities, from the transport and sale of narcotics to prostitution and people smuggling. They dealt in body parts, illicit cigarettes, stolen cars and rhino horn.[118]

These syndicates used South Africa's generally excellent transport infrastructure to move their goods into and out of the country. They bribed staff of the national carrier, South African Airways, and corrupted ground staff at airports, particularly Johannesburg's main airport, OR Tambo International. The risk for these staff members was high, but the rewards enormous, with $30 000 offered for transporting $5 million worth of drugs.[119] With only a limited chance of their activities being uncovered, the ports have become a magnet for criminal activities. For example, Cape Town harbour handles 60 000-70 000 containers a month, yet the police are able to search only two a day – around 40 a month.[120]

As we have seen, South Africa has plenty of home-grown gangs, including some now dominated by former military personnel from Mozambique and Zimbabwe, who are responsible for highly organised attacks on money vending machines, or ATMs. But it is the international syndicates that control many aspects of the criminal underworld. Nigerian crime syndicates dominate the illicit cocaine trade in South Africa.[121] They established themselves in Johannesburg during the 1980s and have since established a countrywide network. The cocaine is brought in from South America using Nigerian expatriates, but also using Nigerian contacts in Austria, the Netherlands, the United Kingdom, Japan and Switzerland.[122] Organised criminal activities involving Russians came to the attention of the police in 1995.[123] In November 1998, the then South African Minister for Safety and Security, Sydney

Mufamadi, visited Moscow, providing the Russian authorities with a list of 23 names of persons suspected of criminal activities.[124] He told the media that Russian criminals in South Africa were involved in arms smuggling, fraud, car theft and drug trafficking. Russian gangs have also used the many small and unguarded airstrips across South Africa to offload and load goods.[125] Viktor Bout, the infamous Russian arms dealer now convicted by a New York court, used southern Africa as a base for his operations during the late 1980s and early 1990s, running Soviet guns to groups fighting in Angola, Liberia, Mozambique, the Democratic Republic of Congo and Sierra Leone. In 2010 he was arrested in Thailand in an American sting operation and finally sentenced to 25 years in jail by a New York judge in April 2012.[126]

Chinese triads are involved in criminal activities ranging from the smuggling of abalone, illicit trading in rhino horns and ivory as well as the importation and distribution of drugs, money laundering, the illegal trafficking of Chinese immigrants and the trading of contraband goods such as pirated DVDs.[127] During 1992 and 1993 police investigations were able to confirm that Chinese criminals active in South Africa were linked to at least three different Chinese triad organisations based in Hong Kong and Taiwan.[128] The increasingly lucrative rhino horn trade has encouraged Far Eastern networks to become involved in southern Africa in general and South Africa in particular. There are extraordinary profits to be made, with horns being sold locally for R65 000 a kilo ($8 500) to be resold on the black market for sums as high as R390 000 a kilo.[129] South Africa's rhino are being killed at a rate of over 400 a year. What takes place amounts to something close to a low-level civil war, with poachers using aircraft and helicopters and high-velocity rifles.[130] In a well-publicised recent case, Chumlong Lemtongthai, a Thai citizen, was accused of being behind a rhino poaching syndicate.[131] The group allegedly hired Thai prostitutes to pose as hunters, using legitimate permits to kill rhinos across the country.[132] The role of the Italian Mafia is perhaps the best-known example of an international syndicate operating in South Africa. Vito Palazzolo (who uses the name Robert von Palace Kolbatschenko) has lived in South Africa since the late 1980s.[133] In March 2009, an Italian court confirmed a 2006 nine-year sentence for association with the Sicilian Mafia[134] – an allegation he denies, claiming to have been the victim of mistaken identity. An investigating judge said Palazzolo was a Mafia banker, managing the investment portfolio of Salvatore 'Toto' Riina, the jailed head of the Corleone clan.[135]

Palazzolo first came to the attention of the authorities in both Italy and the United States while they were investigating money-laundering activities in the 'Pizza Connection' cocaine and heroin trafficking ring between Sicily and New York, which used pizzerias as a front to launder drugs worth an estimated $1.6 billion.[136] US law enforcement agencies officially estimate that Palazzolo helped launder more than $1.5 million in drug money through Switzerland. He was sentenced to three years in jail by a Swiss court, but in December 1986, while on a 36-hour parole from a prison, he absconded to South Africa on a false passport.[137]

Palazzolo travelled to the Eastern Cape, where a National Party member of Parliament had organised Ciskei residence for him. Palazzolo acquired Ciskei citizenship and it was now that he acquired his new name, Kolbatschenko.[138] The former Ciskei ambassador, Douw Steyn, told the Harms Commission, which investigated the so-called Palazzolo affair, that Ciskei law had been specifically amended to accommodate him, on condition that he donated money to the homeland.[139] Palazzolo was granted a South African residence permit in December 1987. By 1988, Swiss police had traced him to South Africa and informed their South African counterparts. The police raided Palazzolo's farm and arrested him. During the raid they found 10 guns and diamonds worth approximately R500 000, along with documents indicating that he had invested more than R25 million in businesses in South Africa and Namibia.[140] The South African government declared Palazzolo an undesirable person and returned him to Switzerland to complete his jail sentence.

In 1992, Palazzolo was back, once again reported to be living in the Ciskei, in a house belonging to the then military ruler, Oupa Gqozo, but he soon moved back to South Africa. President FW de Klerk approved a new South African residence permit for him in March 1993, despite the existence of an Italian arrest warrant. During his time in South Africa, Palazzolo forged many contacts with both the National Party and the ANC. He established businesses in southern Africa ranging from bottled water to diamonds. In 1996 President Nelson Mandela established a Special Presidential Investigation Task Unit to look into the Palazzolo case,[141] but the investigation ran into the sand, collapsing in allegations of corruption. In July 2006, the High Court in Palermo convicted Palazzolo, in absentia, of complicity in the Mafia and sentenced him to nine years in jail.[142] This conviction was confirmed by the Supreme Court in Rome. In January 2007, the Italian government requested his extradition.[143] It was the sixth request from Italian authorities since 1992. In June 2010, the High Court of South Africa blocked the extradition, as South Africa does not recognise the crime of Mafia association as conceived in Italy, but finally, in March 2012, Palazzolo's luck ran out. On a visit to his son, living in the Thai resort of Phuket, he was arrested by police on an Interpol arrest warrant.[144] It was only when he was finally going through emigration to leave the country, and not surrounded by the bodyguards who had accompanied him throughout his visit, that the Thai police moved, taking him into custody. Extradition proceedings could be lengthy, but Palazzolo is finally behind bars.

This outline of the penetration of criminal syndicates in South Africa is by no means exhaustive. The country is, of course, not alone in having to fight their activities. It could be argued that very few countries have escaped the attentions of organised crime. What is so toxic is that it comes at a time when corruption is so rampant and the mechanisms to fight crime have been so weakened by political interference.

Causes and consequences

This chapter has traced the links of South Africa's political class to crime and corruption over the course of more than 100 years. However, the ANC's policy of 'deployment' and the practices this has produced have given fresh impetus to the phenomenon.

Deployment is a system that places ANC members in positions of authority across the state as well as sectors of the economy. The ANC says that the practice dates back to 1998, when a deployment committee was established, chaired by Jacob Zuma.[145] Some 'deployed' party members perform their functions diligently and effectively, but for many the lure of easy money is just too great. They become 'tenderpreneurs', who use their positions of authority to procure state tenders for themselves, their families and their wider client base. This practice has become deeply entrenched. In the Eastern Cape, one of the worst affected provinces, it was reported by the Auditor-General that three-quarters of all government contracts were awarded to companies owned by state officials and their families.[146] In 2009-10 the province was unable to account for no less than R5 billion of government expenditure – the result of 'irregular, unauthorised, fruitless and wasteful expenditure'.

Professor Doreen Atkinson is one of the few academics to have engaged in a systematic analysis of the problem. She argues that the 'deployment' system allows party loyalists to be placed in key functions because of their relationship with the party, without consideration of their suitability. She quotes an ANC municipal mayor to show just how this leads to the personal accumulation of wealth: 'Pay your allegiance to the leadership of your patronage and you will easily become a mayor … or a municipal manager … Leaders will reward [comrades] by so-called deployment.'[147] The process has allowed positions to be sold to the highest bidder, with the winner gaining access to the resources of the state.

From here it is a short step to awarding contracts to companies owned or controlled by 'deployed' officials or their wider circle of friends and family. Unsurprisingly, Atkinson's research indicates that the quality of the goods and services bought for the community are of little relevance to 'community leaders' who have paid for their positions. This is the origin of the 'tenderpreneurs' so hated by the left in the Alliance. The practice has also been widely criticised by other political parties as well as civil society groups. The allegation is that deployment is directly tied to the entrenchment of corruption.

The ANC itself accepts that governance at a local level has eroded the party's standing as well as undermining its ability to provide for local communities. There was a lengthy and self-critical debate during the ANC's 2010 National General Council, questioning just how badly the efficiency of municipalities had been reduced by maladministration and corruption.[148] At the same time, the ANC robustly rejects criticism of the deployment process itself. 'Deploying cadres is not a flawed conceptual system,' Gwede Mantashe explained.[149] It is not a 'sin to give black people operational exposure' as part of correcting imbalances created by the apartheid regime. 'It helps to address the situation we inherited in 1994. We are not ashamed about that,' he said. While this is a powerful argument, it fails to deal with the unintended consequences that it produces. It ignores the reality of the situation and the endemic corruption that it has fostered. There is no doubting the centrality of the issue, with both the opposition and the ANC's allies continuously raising the issue, as the unions and the SACP warned in a joint statement:[150]

> The single biggest threat facing our revolution today is the danger of corruption and tenderpreneurs, who are encircling our movement like vultures to try and take over this glorious movement of Chris Hani, Elijah Barayi, John Gomomo, Oliver Tambo, Moses Kotane, Nelson Mandela, Dora Tamana, Violet Seboni, Ray Alexander, Mzala Nxumalo and many others, not to serve our people, but to enrich themselves at the direct expense of the overwhelming majority of our people.

In this way, the Alliance tries to present the corruption and 'tenderpreneurs' as an aberration – something that is not inherently part of the Movement. This explains the invocation of a long string of revolutionary heroes.

The unions and the communists wish to suggest that the scourge can be eradicated by yet more vigorous 'campaigns'. It is a position that rings increasingly hollow, especially as the state appears to be at a loss as to how to tackle the menace. It may well be that there are structural reasons for this. As has already been clear from the preceding chapters, the new forces within South Africa – and particularly the new BEE elite – are dependent in large part on the openings provided for 'tenderpreneurs' like themselves. Their success is frequently not based on a level playing field; rather, many of their business empires have been built on the state's largesse and the ANC's influence. The new elite has risen precisely because the ANC has been able to transform government into the 'market place for tenders and business opportunities for a few and well connected elites' that the leader of the union movement, Zwelinzima Vavi, so despises.[151]

Just one example illustrates the scale of the problem. In September 2011 an embarrassed Public Works Minister, Gwen Mahlangu-Nkabinde, had to explain that the Special Investigating Unit, better known as the Hawks, had uncovered more than 40 cases of tender irregularities involving at least R3 billion in her department.[152] Ms Mahlangu-Nkabinde was left to explain that she had been badly let down. 'Frankly, I have been lied to and deceived by people who, instead of serving the people of South Africa, were intent on lining their own pockets,' she complained. The minister did not remain very long at her post, being fired by President Zuma in October 2011.

Can the state fight back?

After it took power in 1994, the ANC set about tackling the problem of organised crime, bringing in a range of laws.[153] It also created new organisations. In addition to the normal agencies of the state, like the police, the country could boast two highly effective organisations under the National Prosecuting Authority: the Directorate of Special Operations or DSO (better known as the Scorpions) and the Asset Forfeiture Unit, which seized the proceeds of crime.

By April 2005, the government had a clear idea of the scale of the task before it when it attended the 11th United Nations Congress on Crime prevention and criminal justice.[154]

> The South African Government has determined that 341 organised crime groups are known to be operating in South Africa. Most of these criminal groups specialize in drug-related crime, motor vehicle theft, hijacking of motor vehicles (and trucks), fraud, corruption and the trafficking in non-ferrous metals, precious metals and stones. In view of the Government's effective strategies to address organised crime, 167 of these crime groups have been detected to date, while 174 are still under investigation. These strategies have led to the arrest of 467 leaders and 1 229 syndicate members.

The Scorpions had a strong case to make, informing the UN that they had undertaken no fewer than 234 investigations during 2004, with a 90 per cent conviction rate. Drugs worth $758.6 million had been seized.[155] As an elite unit made up of top investigators and prosecutors, they differed from the police in that they made use of a troika of activities including intelligence gathering, criminal investigation and prosecution, all within one team. The combination of skills and expertise led by qualified and experienced prosecutors meant that they were able to conduct investigations that were solid and stood up in court. Their successes included a conviction rate of 82-94 per cent. The number of people arrested by the unit rose from 66 in 2002 to 617 in 2006.[156] The Scorpions also formed close relations with international agencies such as the American FBI, the UK's Serious and Organised Crime Agency and the Economic and Financial Crimes Commission in Nigeria.

Despite their successes, the Scorpions had ruffled feathers by pursuing cases against a number of senior ANC members, in particular the investigations they began into the corruption allegations against the newly elected ANC president, Jacob Zuma. In 2008, when Zuma had been ANC leader for just a few hours, the party decided to disband the unit. This decision went ahead despite the findings of Judge Sisi Khampepe, who had been asked to investigate the role of the Scorpions and make recommendations as to whether they should be incorporated into the police. Khampepe spelt out just why the Scorpions had been created in the first place.[157]

> The history of the establishment of the DSO stems from the need to curb rampant organised crime which was threatening the political and economic integrity of the country. Some corrupt elements in the police force which existed at the time, necessitated the creation of a de novo entity, designed with the specific intent to pursue the elusive elements of organised crime.

She concluded that although the unit had some shortcomings and difficulties in its relationship with other intelligence and security organisations, the Scorpions should continue to exist: 'it is my considered finding that the DSO still has a place in the government's law enforcement plan'.[158] This recommendation was adopted by Cabinet and approved by President Mbeki.[159] There was also strong public support for the Scorpions.

Despite this, the ANC decided to go ahead with plans to establish a new unit, this time under the control of the police. The DA accused the ANC of wanting to kill off the Scorpions precisely because so many of its own members were being held to account.[160]

> The government's decision to disband the Directorate of Special Operations (DSO), in line with the ANC's resolution at Polokwane is a transparent attempt to destroy the most effective corruption-busting force in the country. The only conclusion to draw is that the ANC wants to get rid of the DSO to protect prominent members of the ruling party. Besides the seven convicted criminals on the ANC's National Executive Committee (NEC), six NEC members are currently the subjects of ongoing criminal investigations. At least two of these are under investigation by the DSO.

A new organisation, the Directorate for Priority Crime Investigations, also known as the Hawks, was duly launched in 2009. Among other objectives, it was to target organised crime, economic crime, corruption, and other serious crimes as determined by the National Commissioner of Police. However, the new body failed to live up to the achievements of its predecessor in the fight against organised crime. The number of new investigations fell by 85 per cent, while the value of contraband seized plummeted by a staggering 99.1 per cent.[161]

Then, in March 2011, the government received a major reversal. The Constitutional Court ruled that the replacement of the Scorpions by the Hawks was unconstitutional.[162] In a majority ruling, the Court found that the Hawks were at risk of being insufficiently independent of political influence and interference. The Court was particularly concerned that the Hawks would be directly answerable to politicians, through a Cabinet committee. They concluded that:[163]

> ... the power given to senior political executives to determine
> policy guidelines, and to oversee the functioning of the DPCI
> [the Hawks], goes far further than ultimate oversight. It lays
> the ground for an almost inevitable intrusion into the core
> function of the new entity by senior politicians, when that in-
> trusion is itself inimical to independence.

The court order gave the government 18 months to remedy the defect.
Stunned by the ruling, the government said it would study the findings.

Public confidence in the police has been badly undermined in recent
years. There has been a constant flow of stories linking the force with
the criminals they are meant to be fighting. In order to assess the scale
of the problem, the South African Institute of Race Relations decided to
conduct a survey. The results were alarming:[164]

> The Institute consulted journalists, media reports, and infor-
> mation from the Independent Complaints Directorate (ICD).
> Within a week, a list of over 100 separate incidents alleging
> and/or confirming the police's involvement in serious crimes
> was drawn up. The Institute's researchers stopped looking
> for more incidents after compiling this list of the initial 100.
> The 100 incidents do not include reports of petty crimes, poor
> service delivery, or the soliciting of small bribes by officials.
> Without exception, the 100 incidents identified in this report
> are related to very serious and often violent and pre-medi-
> tated criminal behaviour. These included ATM bombings,
> armed robberies, house robberies, rapes, murders, and serious
> assaults.

At least as worrying was the report's assessment that very few police
officers were ever held to account for what they had done. A similar
trend can be seen in the field of money laundering.[165] In the five years
from April 2003 to March 2008, 64 cases were before the courts, but
there were only 16 convictions. There were no successful convictions at
all for the years 2003-04 and 2006. The prosecution of civil servants has
moved in a similar direction, with a rising number given final warnings,

rather then being dismissed, once they are found guilty of financial misconduct.[166]

Recently, however, a different and more hopeful trend has emerged. President Zuma has begun to focus much more directly on the problem, setting tough goals for the sections of government charged with combating criminality. At a meeting between the President and the Minister of Justice on 5 November 2010, key targets were agreed.[167] These included one to: 'successfully investigate, seize/restrain the assets and prosecute 100 people who have accumulated assets through illicit means of at least R5 million.' There were also clear goals for this to be achieved, with 100 prosecutions to be initiated by 2012 and at least 100 convictions by 2014. To obtain this number of convictions for corruption in the next three years will be challenging.

Nor are these the only targets. The aim is to get South Africa back up the Transparency International league table, from number 64 to number 40, within the next three years. A number of changes have been implemented, including the formation of an anti-corruption taskforce in July 2010, and more recently there have been moves to bring the key crime-fighting units – including the Hawks, the Asset Forfeiture Unit, the Special Investigating Unit and the prosecutors – under one roof, tantamount to re-creating the competencies that once existed within the Scorpions and made them such an effective organisation. This sense of urgency is badly needed. Speaking off the record, one senior official warned that action had to be taken, 'otherwise we are heading towards becoming a banana republic'.[168]

These targets have been followed by action from the President himself. In October 2011, after sitting for months on a report into irregularities in government from the Public Protector, Thuli Madonsela, President Zuma acted. He sacked two ministers and suspended the Police Commissioner, General Bheki Cele, pending an enquiry into his conduct.[169] The Public Protector had accused the Minister of Public Works, Gwen Mahlangu-Nkabinde, and General Cele of irregularities in the leases of police offices that had allegedly cost the state R 1.7 billion. The Public Protector's report into the Minister of Co-operative Governance and Traditional Affairs, Sicelo Shiceka, alleged that he had told the presidency that a trip to Switzerland to visit his jailed girlfriend was an official study tour relating to the 2010 Soccer World Cup.[170] President Zuma's somewhat belated, but nonetheless decisive action, was greeted with a huge collective sigh of relief.

In 2010 an international report into corruption commented dryly: 'South Africa has experienced a number of high profile corruption scandals within public sector agencies, provinces and, more recently, serious allegations that have been linked to the highest levels of government.'[171]

This is clearly true. As we have seen, former President Mbeki chaired the committee that oversaw the Arms Deal. Although he himself was not implicated in the corrupt practices that accompanied the deal, senior officials in his administration certainly were. President Zuma is also indirectly tarnished by the Arms Deal, which saw his financial adviser jailed for having a corrupt relationship with Zuma. It was only the way the prosecution handled the case that prevented the President from facing charges of corruption himself. It remains to be seen what the new enquiry announced by President Zuma into this whole question will uncover.

Organised crime is now a serious force, with tentacles reaching into the highest offices in the land. Just how far they have penetrated other institutions of the country is less clear, but remains a serious concern. At the same time, some of the new ANC-aligned elite have grown exceedingly rich in deals that are, at best, of questionable ethics.

The trade unions have warned repeatedly that South Africa is in danger of becoming what they term a 'predatory state'.[172] Some areas of the country are clearly well on the way to earning this title. Five departments of government in Limpopo province and three in the Free State have been placed under administration after running up vast debts in conditions of endemic maladministration.[173] Is it any surprise that poverty in the Eastern Cape has officially been described as a 'national disaster',[174] when the province has a reputation for being among the most corrupt?

The ANC has attempted to put regulations in place to halt this trend. Following a year-long study of the issue, the NEC issued a ruling in February 1999 that no one could stand for public office if they had a 'criminal record of a non-political nature'.[175] This seems to have had only limited effect. Worse still, the ANC has continued to embrace those of its senior members who have been convicted of crimes. So when the former chief whip was released from jail in January 2007 after serving just four months of his four-year sentence for taking a bribe in relation to the Arms Deal, he was met by a convoy of luxury black limousines carrying local dignitaries, including the ANC provincial secretary.[176] Similarly, disgraced UDF leader Reverend Allan Boesak was welcomed by senior party leaders when he was released from jail in May 2001, after serving one year of a three-year sentence for misappropriating Danish church aid meant to fight apartheid.[177]

Having said this, it is important to recognise that South Africa continues to have at its disposal a range of weapons to fight crime. The judiciary has remained largely untainted by accusations of corruption, even if it has, at times, appeared to be swayed by political pressure. Sections of the police have been corrupted,[178] but there are still important institutions of law enforcement and individuals within organisations who are effective and mobilised to tackle organised crime. There is also a wide range of highly effective non-governmental organisations that hold government to account. So does the media, which is vociferous in its exposure of malpractice.

Perhaps the real question is how long these pillars of society can resist the rising tide of sleaze and crime, including the organised crime of international syndicates. To this there is as yet no definitive answer, but the trend is clear. As a senior South African intelligence source put it: 'Are senior ANC members captured by organised crime and know they are captured? To varying degrees, yes. The moral fabric of some ANC individuals have been shaken by sophisticated capture.'[179] While expressing optimism that the issue was being tackled robustly, he concluded sadly: 'Avarice is becoming a characteristic of the nation.'

The evidence points to two conclusions. Firstly, that South Africa is now affected by corruption at all levels of society. Attempts are being made to combat it, but so far they have failed to stem the tide. The institutions of the state are resisting, but they have major weaknesses and deficiencies. Secondly, that organised crime is a serious threat. Again, there have been efforts to halt it, but these are compromised by the scale of corruption. The three-year-long investigation into organised crime in southern Africa by the Institute for Security Studies was damning in its conclusion: 'This research has thus far found that corruption not only facilitates organised crime but is indeed an integral part of it. It plays a role in virtually every type of organised criminal activity surveyed.'[180] This does not imply that the country is in the grip of criminal networks, as some Latin American or West African states are, but the warning signs are there. Unless they are heeded the direction of travel is clear and the outcome would be disastrous for the country and the region.

Chapter 11

Sharing the Beloved Country: Land Reform Since 1994

Martin Plaut

There are few issues more difficult or more pressing for South Africa than land. More difficult because it involves competing historic and contemporary claims; more pressing because attempts to resolve the land question have so far failed.

At face value, this is a simple question of right and wrong. The black African population were dispossessed of the land of their forefathers. This was not in the dim and distant past. In 1913 the Land Act was passed, which forbade Africans from owning, or even renting, land outside of designated reserves that made up 13 per cent of the country. It was only the latest episode in a long history of dispossession, but it made an indelible mark. Who can forget Sol Plaatje's famous lament, with which he opens his political tract, *Native Life in South Africa*? 'Awaking on Friday morning, June 20, 1913, the South African Native found himself, not actually a slave, but a pariah in the land of his birth.'[1]

Dispossession continued throughout the intervening years and was intensified under apartheid. The path-breaking Surplus People Project of the 1980s found that in the 23 years up to 1983, a total of 3.5 million people had been forcibly removed from 'white' areas.[2] By the time

Nelson Mandela became president of the country, whites were estimated to own 87 per cent of all South Africa.

The government has gone a long way to redressing the wrongs brought about by the 1913 Land Act. A Restitution of Land Rights Act was passed in 1994 and since then the Commission on the Restitution of Land Rights has been processing and investigating restitution claims. They did this either by restoring land or by making payments described as 'equitable redress'. Since it came into being, the Commission has approved 76 023 of the 79 696 claims filed with it.[3] It has made payments of R22.9 billion. Just 3 673 claims are still being investigated. This task is coming to an end, even though the process has slowed to a crawl. Just 33 land claims were settled in the year 2009-10, with a 'huge budget deficit' blamed for the lack of progress.[4]

This process of restitution does not, however, deal with the land taken by colonial conquest prior to 1913. To deal with this, the ANC government set a target for the entire land reform programme (restitution, tenure reform, and redistribution) to transfer 30 per cent of white-owned land within five years.[5] When it became clear that this could not be achieved, the target date was extended to 2014.

If blacks viewed history through the lens of conquest and dispossession, the white farming community saw matters in a very different light. Many regarded themselves as descendents of tough pioneers who tamed the unforgiving soil down the years, using their skills and capital to bring forward a rich, but costly, harvest. White farmers acquired title to the land legally, and some farms have been in families for generations. As citizens of South Africa, they believe they have an equally legitimate right to live on the land of their forefathers. Would removing their land now not simply replicate the dispossession of their black fellow citizens down the years?

There are also those who question the assertion that the white minority owns the vast majority of the land. It is suggested that the often-quoted statistic that 87 per cent is in white hands is misleading, for it includes all state-owned land, which was considered to be white under apartheid. This meant that the country's giant game reserves were 'white'.[6] So too was land reserved for the military. It also included vast tracts of semi-desert, which are of limited agricultural use. Just 13 per cent of all South African land is suitable for growing crops.[7]

Others go still further, to suggest that the racial division of land, although still severely skewed towards whites, is today less inequitable than previously thought. Frans Cronje, of the South African Institute of Race Relations, points out that blacks, coloureds and Indians have been buying into the agricultural sector and this has changed the balance of land holdings.[8]

> Africans probably now own close to 20% if one adds in an estimated 2-million hectares purchased on the open market and 6-million transferred by the state through various land reform and restitution processes. The state owns possibly 25% of the country. That slice was previously part of the white 87%. It should now be subtracted from the white share and added to the black share, which pushes the latter up to about 45%. Add in coloured and Indian ownership, which some people estimate at a high 10%, and the total black slice rises to about 55%.

There is some evidence to support Cronje's suggestion that 'previously disadvantaged' communities have been going out and simply buying the land they want. They have done this with and without government help. A study of land purchases in KwaZulu-Natal between 1997 and 2003 found that most land transfers from whites involved either pure market mechanisms (cash purchases or mortgages) or a mixture of grants and mortgages.[9]

Farmland acquired by disadvantaged owners in KwaZulu-Natal, 1997–2003 (constant 2000 prices)

	Restitution and redistribution	Government grant and mortgage	Private mortgage or cash	Bequests
Number of transactions	189	20	579	481
Total area (ha)	95 597	5 905	82 296	19 502
Mean area (ha)	487–515	295	114–192	41
Price per hectare (R)	734–1 198	2 809	1 398–3 651	N/A

Source: MC Lyne and MAG Darroch, *Land redistribution in South Africa: Past performance and future policy*, BASIS CRSP Research Paper, Department of Agricultural and Applied Economics, University of Wisconsin-Madison, 2003.

These private or semi-private means of land redistribution have to be added to the overall totals, if an accurate picture is to be arrived at. When Pieter Mulder, leader of the right-wing Freedom Front Plus and Deputy Minister of Agriculture, attempted to use some of these facts to challenge the ANC's demand for radical land reform, he received short shrift from President Zuma.[10] The President warned him that the land question was not to be trifled with. 'It is extremely sensitive and to the majority of people in this country, it is a matter of life and death.'[11]

In reality South Africa has a bifurcated rural economy. On the one hand, there are the large, well-capitalised, modern farms run by the commercial sector, and on the other there is a vast, often impoverished subsistence sector, much of it in the former black homelands. Commercial farms support 40 000 farmers, while 1.3 million farmers work the subsistence sector.[12]

Most, but not all of the commercial farms are run by whites. Exactly how many commercial farms now belong to black, coloured and Indian farmers is something of a mystery. The agricultural census does not collect the statistics of farmers by race – rather surprising in a country still obsessed with racial classification. The main agricultural union, AgriSA, says it has no idea how many commercial farmers are black. The union representing black farmers, the National African Farmers' Union, has gone into decline. An alternative union, the African Farmers Association of South Africa, was founded in February 2011. Mike Mlengana, the first president of AFASA, says his organisation has 32 000 members, with the majority producing mainly for subsistence.[13] He estimates that 5 000 black farmers could be classified as commercial – selling their produce on the market. As we have seen in the case of KwaZulu-Natal, these farmers have supplemented their land holdings by going into the open market to buy up land, as farms and finance become available. Some academics are sceptical about these claims. Professor Ben Cousins suggests that many are not engaged in agriculture at all, but rather in other forms of business,[14] including small-scale enterprises such as a transport company, trading store or a butchery.

However accurate the conclusions about land holding and race may be, they are unlikely to assuage demands for land reform, which are now at the centre of a fierce debate. The ANC Youth League has made the seizure of white-owned land a key element of its political programme.[15] The political report to the Youth League's annual conference in June 2011 rejected the government's previous attempts to deal with this question by buying up white-owned land:

> The ANC has, for the past 17 years, tried to transfer land through the willing buyer-willing seller principle and approach and we all know that it has also failed dismally. We refuse to continue living like we are in a colony. The only solution available to us now is expropriation without compensation; because we carry an obligation to do so, and can do so without violence and war through the political power which we are given by the people of South Africa.

The Youth League quoted a statement made by Oliver Tambo in 1985 in which the ANC president said[16]: 'The dispossession of our people of the land that is theirs remains one of the most burning national grievances.' He described the loss of the land as a 'gross injustice' and a 'historic crime'. Tambo concluded that: 'The land question must be resolved, if needs be, the hard way.' The Youth League promised they would not let Tambo down.

Those representing commercial, mainly white farmers, like the former Transvaal Agricultural Union, now known as TAU SA, reacted strongly against Youth League' remarks.[17] Ben Marais, president of TAU SA, said that his organisation noted what he described as the explicit threats concerning nationalisation and ownership of land. But, he said: 'That does not mean that we as farmers will relinquish our land which we have preserved and tilled over many years, without any compensation. Private ownership is internationally recognised and protected, and farmers we will defend such rights. We will not accept accusations that we have stolen land. Based on recorded history, international historians have substantiated the view that farmers have acquired their land legitimately, and we stand by that.'

Of course the Youth League's programme is not the policy of the ANC. Yet the party itself is preparing for its next Congress in 2012 and the issue of land is certain to be on the agenda. How President Jacob

Zuma approaches this issue could be an important factor in deciding whether he wins a second term in office. These are not peripheral questions, but central to the debate over the future direction of South African politics. They also highlight one simple question: are all the country's citizens, irrespective of race, equal before the law? Should farmers, some of whose families have been in the country for hundreds of years, be seen as genuine South Africans or merely as white settlers?

The problem has been underlined by the perception that the government is indifferent to the problems facing the mainly white commercial farming community. Many farmers complain that they are often treated with outright hostility by government agencies and officials who have little understanding of or background in agriculture. They suggest that their contribution to the economy and food security is not appreciated. Worse still, some white farmers believe there is little concern for their safety and security. There are reports that more than 3 000 whites have been murdered on their farms since 1994.[18] A government enquiry into the problem accepted that crime on farms was a real issue that needed to be addressed, but put the figure somewhat lower:[19]

> The farming community has been plagued by farm attacks for many years. It seems that farm attacks have been increasing, and according to available statistics there were 6 122 between 1991 and 2001, resulting in 1 254 persons being killed.

In 2001 the majority (61 per cent) of farm attacks were on whites. The government report suggested that it was up to farmers to take out additional security and improve their relations with their workers. There have also been instances of the brutal treatment of farm labourers by their employers. In one particularly notorious example, a farmer was convicted of feeding a troublesome employee to a lion.[20] The case caused a national outcry, particularly after the farmer was freed after just three years in jail, on the grounds that there was no evidence that the labourer was alive when he was thrown into the lion enclosure.[21]

At the same time, it is important not to lose sight of one key fact: despite its difficulties, agriculture is a success story. As a recent report pointed out: 'Currently, South Africa is not only self-sufficient in virtu-ally all major agricultural products, but in a normal year is also a net food exporter, making it one of six countries in the world able to export food on a regular basis.'[22]

The same report quotes the main commercial farming union to de-scribe the two sectors of agriculture:[23]

> According to AGRI-SA over 100 million hectares are used for commercial farming purposes, farmed by close to 40 000 commercial farmers. The average size of a commercial farm is about 2 500 hectares. The 1.3 million small-scale farmers occupy over 14 million hectares and their average farm size is just over 11 hectares. Their main production consists of maize for porridge and for staple food consumption, sorghum or wheat for bread or beer, and vegetables such as potatoes, pumpkin, sweet potato and dry beans.

Another author puts the issue even more strikingly. Sam Moyo suggests that just 20 000 white commercial farmers produce 80 per cent of all agricultural output.[24] A further 40 000 (including, by his estimate, 2 000 black commercial farmers) produce 15 per cent, while 500 000 families living in the former homelands produce just 5 per cent of the total. The question for South Africans is how to maintain the country's success as a major agricultural producer while satisfying demands for land equity and addressing rural poverty.

Rural communities

The land issue is not just a symbolic question of restitution. It involves vast numbers of people, many of whom are among the poorest in the country. Getting agreed figures for exactly how many people are in-volved is not easy. The data is unreliable and most authors resort to estimates or partial surveys. Even defining a rural area raises difficulties. But Nancy Andrew and Peter Jacobs estimate that between 40 and 45

per cent of the South African population is rural.[25] They go on to con-
clude that:

> Following liberalization and deregulation of agricultural mar-
> kets, the 60 000 white farmers (less than one-half a percent
> of the population) controlling more than 80% of farmland
> in 1994 have decreased in number to some 45 000, although
> some still own multiple properties. Slightly less than one-third
> of the black rural population, or several million, live in the
> 'white' agricultural areas, meaning they are demographically
> predominantly black.

These rural communities are, of course, far from uniform. Some are
thinly scattered across the semi-desert areas of the Northern Cape while
others are concentrated in regions like rural KwaZulu-Natal. But a trend
is clearly discernable – the fall in formal rural employment. Between
1985 and 1995 agricultural employment fell by a third, from 1.3 million
to about 920 000.[26] The latest statistics indicate a gradual continuation
of this trend.[27] In 2009 there were 849 782 farm labourers, of whom
459 901 were full time and the rest seasonal.

Employment in commercial agriculture

1985	1993	2002	2007	2008	2009
1 300 000	1 093 265	940 820	770 933	814 524	849 782

Sources: P Jacobs, *Agricultural market reforms and the rural poor in South Africa*, PLAAS Poverty Workshop
2009; Statistics SA, *Agricultural surveys 2008 and 2009* (preliminary), 23 June 2011, p 4.

This decline has not always been voluntary. Agricultural workers and
their families continue to be evicted from farms to this day, despite government legislation designed to protect them. A lengthy study of evictions concluded that 940 000 people were evicted from farms in the 10
years following the end of apartheid (1994–2004).[28] These figures have
been questioned, since they do not tally with the census data, which
suggests a rise in the number of black Africans on commercial farms.[29]
Moreover, they would indicate a rate of eviction that is higher that those

that took place at the height of apartheid, which seems unlikely. Having said this, there is no doubt that many people have been forced out of the farms on which they have lived and worked, sometimes for generations.

Many of those who were evicted ended up in poverty, with 60 per cent of these households living below the official poverty line of R322 per person per month. The balance of evictees were only marginally better off.[30] Of these, two-thirds moved to the cities, frequently living off government social welfare grants. Not all of this process of urbanisation was the result of forced evictions: the study indicated that around 200 000 a year left agriculture of their own volition.

Why are commercial farmers using smaller numbers of employees, many of whom are then evicted? The researchers quoted in the earlier study came to the conclusion that the evictions were mainly the result of commercial pressures, including drought, increasing international competition and mechanisation. But uncertainty about future government policy was also a major issue. The ANC has attempted to improve the lot of the rural workforce, but its intervention appears to have had serious unintended consequences. The legal changes included providing farm workers with minimum wages and guarantees of security of tenure.[31] The Labour Tenants Act of 1996, for example, ensured that workers not only could not be evicted from the houses they lived in on the farms, but could also pass their homes on to their children.[32]

Farmers have reacted to these Acts by cutting back on labour, wherever possible. Temporary labourers have increasingly replaced full-time permanent farm workers. These had always been used to undertake seasonal tasks, but there has been a rapid rise in the use of temporary workers provided by labour brokers to get around the new legislation. A study of the Western Cape found that 60 per cent of farmers had reduced their permanent workforce, and around half were thinking of reducing the number of permanent jobs still further.[33] The farmers questioned said they felt 'under attack' from the government, with the new laws cited as a major reason for their alienation. The ANC has continued to introduce more legislation year on year, increasing the burden on the farmers.[34] As one grumbled: 'I run a business – unfortunately, I am not a charity.' Many farmers decided to put relations with their workers on a more formal basis. As a result, handouts of food, payments for hospital visits and time off for illness ceased or were reduced. The new laws marked the end of the paternalism that had been found in many parts of agriculture.

These findings are supported by the government's own report:

> Close to a million people were uprooted from commercial farms between 1994 and 2003, destroying jobs and undermining household food security. The dissolution of agricultural (control) boards, withdrawal of subsidies and rapid change in the tariff regime resulted in the kind of shock that the sector could not adapt to quickly enough. The impact of uncertainties deriving from the land restitution process, and the poor regulation of land use management, are still being felt. This has been compounded by low levels of production on most of the resettled and distributed land. All this raises critical questions about effectiveness of the state, including the phasing in and sequencing of policy.[35]

These are critical questions, as the government points out. But what are the solutions? Before considering this, it is important to acknowledge that many rural communities do not fall into the commercial sector.

Around 2.5 million black South Africans (Africans and coloureds) are involved in small-scale agriculture.[36] The majority (61 per cent) are women, and most live in what were once classified as the 'black homelands'. In 1997, the former homelands accommodated 31.4 per cent of the total population – some 12.7 million people.[37] Very few – just 3 per cent – saw farming as their main source of income, although it is an important source of food. They grew crops and reared livestock mainly to provide additional food for their families. Some surplus food was sold by the side of the road, often by women and children, but the majority of black, coloured and Indian farmers do not fall into the commercial sector, however defined. They are small-scale or 'emerging' producers who work the land mainly to help put food on their own tables.

Many rural communities are desperately poor. This is confirmed by official studies. One report that took a comprehensive look at the Eastern Cape declared starkly that: 'More than a decade into our successful democracy, the Eastern Cape Province remains trapped in structural poverty that shows in all aspects of its demographic, health and socioeconomic profile … Poverty in the Eastern Cape Province is a national disaster.'[38] The ability to provide support to these communities is undermined by the poor state of local government, which is frequently at its least effective in rural areas. The worst-performing municipalities are almost all found in rural areas, which were formerly 'black homelands'.[39]

The government's elusive targets and unsuccessful reforms

On assuming office in 1994, the ANC set about attempting to tackle the land question by redistributing 30 per cent of the land. But the government was criticised for a lack of clarity. Commercial farmers complained that what began as 30 per cent of land, changed to 30 per cent of agricultural land and then 30 per cent of commercial agricultural land.[40]

The target, however defined, has certainly not been achieved. By 2009, sixteen years after these goals were set, just 6.7 per cent of land was in black hands.[41] As the years went by and the target slipped, new ones were established. The current aim is to transfer a total of 24.6 million hectares by 2014.[42] Very substantial sums have been devoted to achieving this, with the government allocating around R4 billion to the programme.[43] Yet inefficiencies in the Department of Land Affairs, which is reported to have more than 1 000 vacant posts, has resulted in as much as R1 billion being unspent and returned to the Treasury.[44]

The real tragedy is that even this overestimates what has really been achieved. There is considerable evidence that much of the land that has been transferred now lies idle or abandoned.

In 2007 the SABC reported that 70 commercial farms in Limpopo that the government had bought for rural communities had collapsed.

The farms, which cost the government more than R100 million, were rendered unproductive, according to the province's agriculture MEC, Dikeledi Magadzi.[45] Ms Magadzi said: 'We can't leave the state assets, the state money being under-utilised. When we are saying we need to halve poverty we need to create jobs, to me that is unacceptable ... What is of essence is that the national assets and the national money cannot lie fallow like we see.' The failure to produce vibrant, productive farms was put down to factors such as infighting and lack of good financial management.

In early 2009 the *Sunday Times* published a lengthy exposé entitled: 'Farms collapse as land reform fails'.[46] 'South Africa's food security is threatened by its chaotic rural land reform programme,' reported Bongani Mthethwa. 'Thousands of once-productive farms, mainly in KwaZulu-Natal, Limpopo, Mpumalanga and the Eastern Cape, lie abandoned and are causing serious shortages of staple foods. The country now imports more food than it exports and local production of grain, fruit and vegetables can no longer keep pace with the growing population.'

The journalist described a two-week visit to farms around the country, during which he discovered:

- Twenty top crop and dairy farms in the Eastern Cape, bought for R11.6 million and returned to a Kokstad community, are now informal settlements;
- A once-thriving potato farm in the KwaZulu-Natal Midlands is now a makeshift soccer field;
- Ten thousand people given back 8 000 ha of prime fruit and macadamia farms in Limpopo are crippled by R5 million debt;
- A former multimillion-rand tea estate in Magoebaskloof in Limpopo has become an overgrown forest;
- More than five tons of a macadamia nut crop on a reclaimed Limpopo farm was so poor that it was dumped into the Levubu river; and
- A R22 million irrigation system built by the government to supply water to new farmers in KwaZulu-Natal lies unused.

The article went on to quote Ann Bernstein, executive director of the Centre for Development and Enterprise, who said that their research had shown that the economic viability of many rural regions was under serious threat. Some beneficiaries had no interest in farming but just wanted a secure place to stay, she said. 'The issue is that at least 50% of land reform projects have failed, and that means for many of the people involved their circumstances have not improved – and for some, have even got worse. And all this is happening in the midst of a rise in food prices,' Bernstein commented.

The acting chief land claims commissioner, Andrew Mphela, was quoted as saying that it was too early to measure performance or to talk of failure. He said that contrary to 'popular rhetoric and biased reporting from certain quarters', projects did not collapse but instead experienced 'challenges'.

While some of the claims in the article appear exaggerated, the idea that these problems are simply 'challenges' to be overcome is difficult to sustain.[47] In 2010 the government officially accepted that its strategy was not achieving the desired results. The Minister of Rural Development and Land Reform, Gugile Nkwinti, acknowledged publicly that up to 90 per cent of all land transfers have failed to result in viable farms.[48] 'We cannot afford to go on like this,' he said. Mr Nkwinti went on to warn that if land is not used by those to whom it has been given, it will be re-allocated to farmers who can run the farms productively. He declared that it was a case of 'use it or lose it'.

> Use it or lose it will work now, with the recapitalisation and development where the strategic partnerships will form with farmers, whether active or retired. Because our view is that give them a chance, establish a clear system of managing these farms, provide necessary support and those who do not want to work the land, take them out. There is not going to be any compromise on that part. The only thing we thought we should strengthen is the support now that does not refer to those people who got land through restitution but those who got land through Land Redistribution. If they don't use that land, we will take it. Just think about it we always talk about

people not using the land, a lot of money. We have not talked about the revenue which the State has lost because 5.9 million hectares' farms which were active and acquiring revenue for the State were handed over to people and more than 90% of those are not functional, they are not productive and therefore the State loses revenue. So we cannot afford to go on like that, we then say agricultural sector production as a proportion of gross domestic product (GDP) is going down. Part of the reason is that a lot of land has been given to people that are not using it, no country can afford that.

What is apparent from this frank admission is not just that the policy has failed, despite having had vast sums spent on it, but that a new way forward is required if the issues are to be resolved.

Why so many reforms have failed

The record is grim indeed. Not only has it deprived South Africa of valuable farms, the poorly designed reforms have ended the hopes and dreams of thousands of families, many of them among the poorest in the country. The explanation for this is not hard to come by. Potential farmers were provided with grants from the government with which to get their enterprises on their feet. Since 2001 this has involved a grant under the Land Redistribution for Agricultural Development programme (LRAD). This provided beneficiaries with a grant of between R20 000 and R100 000, with the recipients making a contribution of their own, starting at R5 000.[49]

Often pooling their grants, a group would then purchase a farm from a white farmer. But rather than marking the beginning of a successful enterprise, this has all too frequently been the high point of the exercise. For a start, it involved a group purchase of a farm, which required establishing a strong system of collective decision making. It meant that the group, who were sometimes unemployed people from informal settlements who had been living on the edge of town, had to begin farming when they had little if any experience of agriculture. It has also meant that dozens of families were attempting to make a living from land that had once made a reasonable return for just one family. Without many skills, capital or expensive equipment, this was a recipe for failure. A study by the Human Sciences Research Council in 2003 provided heart-breaking examples from across the country of how and why the schemes have failed.[50]

Edward Lahiff, who has written extensively on the subject, provides an eloquent insight into the obstacles these schemes face.[51] He points out that these new farmers get little, if any, support once they receive their land. 'Recent studies show that land reform beneficiaries experience numerous problems accessing services such as credit, training, extension advice, transport and ploughing services, veterinary services, and access to input and produce markets.'

Worse still, according to Lahiff, the new farmers are required to abide by preconceived plans drawn up by the government, which have little to do with their real needs. Effectively dumped on a once-productive farm, black prospective farmers have little chance of making a go of it. Visiting areas of KwaZulu-Natal, one is struck by the number of farms that now stand idle, with weeds growing rampant where there were once tall rows of maize. Stalls for cattle stand empty, while a few chickens peck the earth outside shacks and unemployed young men hang around, hoping for something to turn up.

The government tries again

Despite this dispiriting record, the government has attempted to press ahead with the reform process. In August 2011, after months of mulling over how to proceed, Gugile Nkwinti released a long-awaited Green Paper. The Minister rather wearily conceded that achieving a fair distribution of land without destroying the agricultural sector was no easy task. 'There are no silver bullets to the resolution of the post-colonial land questions anywhere in the world,' he explained, appealing for time to resolve the issue.[52] 'In our country we wanted to solve it yesterday – it's not possible, such an emotive issue. So we think it's going to take a bit of time and it will require patience.'

The Green Paper envisages a new system of land holding:[53] 'A single land tenure framework has been fashioned out, integrating the current multiple forms of land ownership – communal, state, public and private – into a single 4-tier tenure system.' The Minister said the Paper aimed to break from the past without significantly disrupting agricultural production and food security, and to avoid redistributions that did not generate livelihoods, employment and incomes. The Paper proposes four categories of land ownership: state land which would be made available for leasing, private ownership which would be subject to certain limitations, regulated land ownership by foreigners, and communal land where certain usage rights would apply.

Two key institutions would be established: a Land Management Commission to scrutinise and validate land holdings and a Land Valuer-General to adjudicate on the appropriate value of land. The plan came in for immediate criticism, but two objections stand out: the decision that the state would hold land for black farmers leasehold, and the suggestion that the state would value the land, rather than allowing a market for farms.

Explaining the leasehold issue, Minister Nkwinti complained that many farms transferred from whites to blacks were soon back in white hands. He estimated that 30 per cent of redistributed farms ended up in this circuit.[54] 'The government bought land and handed it over to aspirant farmers who then sold it again, in many instances back to the original owner,' said the Minister. In the future the government would hold the land and lease it to black farmers.

This option was deeply unsatisfactory, complained Mike Mlengana, of the African Farmers Association of South Africa.[55] 'Farmers will be seriously affected, this creates a situation where the government is the grandfather. When you lease land and cap the amount of land farmers can own, at what point do farmers become productive?' he asked. Nick Vink, a professor of agricultural economics at the University of Stellenbosch, found it strange that the government was saying that if you were wealthy and had the means, you could acquire private property, yet black emerging farmers would have no such property rights. 'What they are saying to black farmers is that they won't get title deeds as they will be held by the government. Black farmers were discriminated against in the past and are still discriminated against today. Nothing has changed.'

On the question of the Land Valuer-General determining the value of farms, the minister said that the open market produced distortions in land values.[56] 'The willing-buyer willing-seller model on its own, it's a problem, because it distorts the market,' said Nkwinti, pointing to prices of land being pushed up. 'There will always be a willing-buyer willing-seller model working, except we want to make sure that some of the vagaries would be dealt with.' This did little to mollify the government's critics, including the conservative South African Institute of Race Relations, which warned that the establishment of the Valuer-General was an attempt to 'oust the jurisdiction of the courts'.[57] The Democratic Alliance also attacked this issue. Describing land expropriation as a 'last resort', the party insisted that a fair price had to be paid by the government to the farmer and that the Department had to have the expertise to value the land correctly. The party concluded: 'The Constitution makes it explicitly clear that the burden of carrying the cost of land reform resides with the state and not the individual land owner; as such, individuals should not be forced to accept less than market-related compensation.'[58]

The irreverent, but always perceptive, Senior Political Reporter, Eyewitness News of Talk Radio 702, Stephen Grootes, put it rather differently:[59]

> The ANC reckons one of the big problems is that some land owners are exploiting the process of land reform and willing buyer-willing seller principle. They know there's a claim on their land, they find a couple of valuators to push up the price, government has to fork out and they go away happy. Pocketing the latest benefits of the fact their grand-parents paid just a few glittering beads for hundreds, even thousands of hectares. Even Agri-SA, not a great fan of the ANC, will admit publicly that this has happened many times. Hence a 'land valuer-general' to step in and sort it all out.

It remains to be seen just how the government's plans will proceed, but clearly there is a need to make progress. The danger, as most commentators agree, is a land-grab on the Zimbabwean model, which would dislocate the entire farming sector. As Gilingwe Mayende, head of research at Walter Sisulu University's Centre for Rural Development, put it, progress had to be made because 'failure to do so postpones the inevitable'.[60] Mayende called for the Constitution to be amended to remove the requirement for compensation for land, as it was 'a gross historical injustice and an unfair burden on the state. A trajectory that will land us in a situation similar to Zimbabwe must be avoided at all costs,' he said.

Looming from the north – the example of Zimbabwe

Almost everyone in the South African land debate refers, at some point or other, to the situation in Zimbabwe. It would be hard to forget images of white commercial farmers being driven from their homesteads by mobs of Zanu-PF party supporters, wielding torches and machetes. Or the attacks by so-called war-veterans on farm owners and their workers. Black Zimbabweans were forced to the edge of starvation by the programme of land reform. The country, once described as the breadbasket of southern Africa, was transformed into a bankrupt supplicant, surviving on foreign aid.

These images were once an accurate reflection of events, but times change and events move on. Today these memories may hinder rational debate. Zimbabwe's brutal programme of land redistribution appears to have been less damaging to the long-term prospects of agriculture than was once feared. The evidence is that the sector is recovering in a way that some might find surprising. As the World Bank's lead economist for Zimbabwe, Praveen Kumar, commented in May 2011, 'The revival of agriculture goes against commonly held wisdom.'[61]

At the time of Independence in 1980, land distribution was as follows:[62]

Sector	Million hectares	Percentage
Large-scale commercial	15.5	39.1
Small-scale commercial	1.4	3.5
Communal	16.4	41.4
National parks and urban areas	6.0	15.2
State land	0.3	0.8
All	39.6	100

The large-scale commercial farms were owned almost exclusively by whites, who constituted less than 1 per cent of the country's population. President Robert Mugabe initiated a land reform programme following Independence to increase the access of black Zimbabweans to land. The first phase covered the period 1980-1998, during which 3.5 million hectares of large-scale commercial farmland were acquired and 71 000 indigenous families were resettled. The second phase was initiated in 1998, but only 0.17 million hectares were acquired and 4 697 families were resettled.[63] This went fairly smoothly. It was the third phase, the 'Fast Track' resettlement programme, using laws enacted for the purpose, with compulsory acquisition and forced resettlement, that caused the real disruption. It was this phase that produced the scenes recalled above.

It is perhaps worth briefly recalling the events that led up to this change in policy. It involved a series of interlocking crises for President Mugabe that began in 1997, when payments to the War Veterans ran out, after it was discovered that corruption and theft had emptied the War Victims fund.[64] The Veterans attacked the Zanu-PF party headquarters and heckled Mugabe at a televised event. By the late 1990s, support for the Mugabe government was waning. Britain's Labour government decided to withhold funds for the redistribution programme after it became clear that choice farms were being dished out to the president's cronies. Zimbabwe's role in the war in the Democratic Republic of Congo also played a part in reducing support from the international community.

Then, in February 2000, the opposition Movement for Democratic Change (MDC), together with civil society groups, managed to defeat a referendum on changes to the constitution. These would have censored the press, granted the president sweeping emergency powers and allowed the seizure of farms without compensation. It was Zanu-PF's first defeat since Independence, and Mugabe saw the writing on the wall. Believing that he might be forced from office at the next general election, he unleashed the 'Fast Track' programme of land reform. Bryan Simms of the Institute for Democracy in South Africa sums up the reasons for the programme:

> In fact, when we look at the pattern of land invasions and land redistribution during this period, we can draw the conclusion the fast track land reform was used to systematically purge commercial farms in areas where the MDC received support from both farmers and farmworkers. The redistribution of the land was designed to placate key constituencies and individuals as a way to shore up support for Zanu PF.

The results were brutal in the extreme. Probably the worst affected were the farm workers, hundreds of thousands of whom lost their jobs and their homes in farm seizures. The attacks were the work of the government. A journalist, Basildon Peta of the *Independent,* described what took place: 'It was common knowledge that this was not spontaneous land invasions. The army led the invasions in [military] vehicles. They were used by the police and army to shift goods, loot farms. I saw them with my own eyes.'[65]

These policies, together with a severe drought, saw a massive fall in farm production. By 2002 the United Nations was issuing stark warnings:[66] 'Zimbabwe is facing a serious food crisis, even at harvest time, and unless international food assistance is provided urgently and adequately, there will be a serious famine and loss of life in the coming months.' Unusually for the UN, it did not mince its words about the role of the government's Fast Track land redistribution programme. 'These activities and processes have disrupted farming activities and contributed to the fall in maize and wheat production,' the report concluded.

In July 2002 the normally reserved Famine Early Warning System issued a report headed 'Zimbabwe is under threat of famine'.[67] Later that year, its report carried a map showing most of the country in bright scarlet – indicating the huge numbers in desperate need of food.[68] It laid the blame for turning the drought into a crisis firmly at the government's door. 'The Government's controversial land reform program has undermined commercial farming and crop production for both domestic consumption and foreign exchange earnings and rendered many rural households homeless and without access to livelihoods.' Zimbabwe, which had exported an average of 250 000 tons of maize a year during the 1990s, was reduced to relying on the rest of the world for its food needs.[69]

By December 2002, 49 per cent of the population were described in the jargon as 'extremely food insecure'. Their only realistic hope they had of getting through to the next harvest was to rely on food from the UN's World Food Programme.[70] Most – including 489 000 former workers on the white commercial farms – lived in rural areas. All had lost their jobs as Mugabe loyalists attacked rural communities. By the mid-1990s most white commercial farms had been seized. Today it is estimated that there are just 200-300 white farmers left working in the country. Instead, there is a black farming community consisting of smallholders and commercial farmers. Some 160 300 black smallholder farmers were allocated 7 million hectares. A further 28 000 black commercial farmers received 2 million hectares.[71] This is the farming sector today.

This raises the question of what has happened to the country's agricultural production. The answer is that in some sectors it has shown a remarkable recovery, while in others it still lags well below the levels of output achieved by the white commercial farmers. The maize crop is critical, since it is the country's staple food. Production in 2010 was more than double the disastrous harvest of 2002, which had led to near-famine conditions, and nearly three times the harvest of 2008.

Zimbabwe – Maize area, yield and production, 2000–2010

Year	2000	2001	2002	2003	2004	2005	2006	2007	2008	2009	2010
Area (000 ha)	1 374	1 240	1 328	1 352	1 494	1 730	1 712	1 446	1 722	1 507	1 803
Yield (t/ha)	1.18	1.23	0.46	0.78	1.13	0.53	0.87	0.66	0.27	0.82	0.74
Production (000 t)	1 620	1 526	605	1 059	1 686	915	1 485	953	471	1 243	1 328

Source: 1999–2007 CSO, 2008–2010 AGRITEX, quoted in Special Report, FAO/WFP: Crop and Food Security Assessment Mission to Zimbabwe, 9 August 2010.

What does this indicate? Firstly, farmers feel secure enough to invest in planting maize. One of the main reasons for the increased harvest was a sharp rise in the area under cultivation, which increased by 20 per cent. At the same time, this meant that areas of less suitable land were planted and the yield declined. Secondly, measures taken by the unity government of Zanu-PF and the MDC have removed restrictions on the sale of grain and now designate the Grain Marketing Board as the buyer of last resort. These measures, together with greater macro-economic stability in the country, have supported the agricultural sector.

Thirdly, despite these improvements, the country is still not able to provide enough food for its own people. Total commercial imports were forecast at 317 000 tonnes of cereals, including nearly 200 000 tonnes of maize, to satisfy domestic requirements.[72] A third of all rural households go hungry and require food aid during the lean months prior to harvest (January and February).

Zimbabwe's maize harvest has recovered, even if it is not back to the days before whites lost their farms. It is worth noting that maize production was declining even before the Fast Track programme came into operation. Government controls, exercised through the Grain Marketing Board, had discouraged farmers, leading to a move to non-controlled crops such as tobacco and cotton.[73] These have fallen substantially since 2000, with the tobacco harvest declining from 202 000 tonnes to 93 000 tonnes in 2009/10. Cotton has followed a similar path, down from 333 000 tonnes to just 172 000 tonnes.

Eddie Cross, economic spokesman for the Movement for Democratic Change, currently part of the unity government, but still very much

an oppositional force, believes the outlook for 2011 is somewhat better. 'In 2011 we expect tobacco to reach about 150 000 tonnes and cotton 250 000 tonnes – most of the crop is in and these numbers look
realistic.'[74]

This is hardly a triumph, but it is not as gloomy a picture as is sometimes portrayed. Eddie Cross questions the figures on maize production,
pointing out that the FAO/WFP figures are drawn from the government's Grain Marketing Board statistics. He believes these are highly
misleading, and that most maize currently being used in Zimbabwe is
imported because it can be bought on the open market at prices cheaper
than those offered to Zimbabwe's farmers. This, he suggests, is because
countries like Zambia and Malawi use genetically modified seeds, which
are banned in Zimbabwe. Using GM seed and more efficient systems of
production means that maize can be landed in Zimbabwe at $240-250 a
tonne. Domestic producers are offered $284 a tonne, which is translated
into around $350 once additional costs including transportation and
storage are included. As a result, he says, about three-quarters of the
tonnage registered by the Grain Marketing Board is imported:[75]

> I estimate that even today some 70% of the maize consumed
> is imported either as grain or more frequently as meal. Last
> year and this year 250 000 tonnes of maize has been purchased
> by the GMB funded by the State and has gone into a strategic
> reserve. This stock is 30 per cent more expensive than imports
> and will be difficult to sell.

Others take a different view. Professor Sam Moyo, Director of the
Southern Africa Regional Institute for Policy Studies, estimates that
crop yields have risen to around two-thirds of the output in 2000, while
independent economist John Robertson puts the figure at around half.[76]
This would suggest that Zimbabwe's agriculture has recovered, but the
recovery is fragile. In essence, a glass that is as half empty as it is full –
depending on your point of view.

But this obscures some of the costs associated with the exercise. For
a start, valuable export earnings have been lost as grain harvests have
failed to reach pre-land invasion peaks. The taxes which the commercial

farmers used to pay have also vanished. Few peasant farmers pay any taxes, leaving a hole in government revenues.

None of the 'new farmers' have any security of tenure. Most has no more than offer letters from the government. A minority have been given 99-year tenure. A promised land audit has failed to materialise and no one has title deeds to their property. All land is finally the property of the state. Banks, which used to be major sources of finance, cannot lend since the farms cannot be seized and sold on, should the borrowers fail to repay the money they owe. As a result, the new farmers don't have the money they need for investments. Their status is also so insecure that they remain dependent on President Mugabe's Zanu-PF for the land that they till. A system of patronage has been established that has created a network of dependency, with farmers knowing that if they vote the 'wrong' way they could lose their farms. This is not a theoretical possibility – it has already happened.

Finally, there is the plight of the approximately 300 000 farm workers and their families who used to earn a living on the commercial farms. While wages were not high, they frequently received additional income in the form of school fees, medical care and other payments in kind. Today these have all but vanished. According to the General Agricultural Plantation Workers Union of Zimbabwe, the workers are in a terrible condition. Many are trapped on the subdivided farms, eking out a living by picking up casual labour wherever they can. Some have become small traders. In interviews they spoke of the hardship they were still suffering, years after the commercial farms were broken up.[77]

What are the alternatives?

Zimbabwe's land redistribution was accomplished at a terrible cost, both in terms of lives lost and livelihoods ruined. As indicated above, it was driven by political expediency rather than ideals of equity. As South Africans consider what measures to take to deal with their own land question, it would be more constructive to debate the issues on the basis of the evidence, rather than the myths about Zimbabwe's farming experience. The country's agriculture has been severely damaged by the redistribution, but it has not collapsed.

A range of alternative futures for agriculture exist, which include the following:

- ❏ leave the situation broadly as it is, with slow but steady re-distribution of land gradually resulting in 30 per cent of agriculture in black hands;
- ❏ copy Zimbabwe's Fast Track model of redistribution;
- ❏ assist redistribution through an equity share scheme, contract farming and other systems to assist black or 'emerging' farmers;
- ❏ break up farms to produce a smaller-scale farming sector.

The first is the current policy of the government. The Fast Track model, with its nationalisation of the land, is the ANC Youth League's plan, as discussed above. The other proposals each have their proponents.

The Democratic Alliance backs the government's farm equity scheme programme, which enables owners wanting to sell their farms to do so through a scheme in which farm workers buy a percentage of the prop-erty. The government's Rural Development Department uses funds al-located for land reform. Since their inception in 1996 the government has invested R500 million in farm equity schemes.[78] But after criticism that some workers were not aware that they were part-owners of the farms, and that few farms paid dividends to their new shareholders, a moratorium was imposed on the scheme in June 2009. This was lifted in early 2011.

The Democratic Alliance's leader, Helen Zille, speaking at a National Farm Workers Summit held in 30 July 2010, spoke out strongly in favour of the scheme, while calling for it to be based on equal shares for both parties.[79] 'There is also evidence from government research that 50-50 equity share schemes are the most productive land reform model by far,' she said. Ms Zille then gave a list of farms on which this system of shared ownership and control had worked:

Talk to farmers involved in successful schemes like Jannie Bosman of Lelienfontein in Wellington and Bernhardt du Toit of Langrivier in Koue Bokkeveld. Better yet, speak to the workers on their farms who are benefiting from becoming part owners of the farms they work on. On Lelienfontein, farm workers have been issued share certificates for their 50% shares, are given counselling on how to invest their dividends, and trustees receive financial and management training. In 2019, these farm workers will be in a position to take full ownership of Mr Bosman's farms – 430ha of some of the Cape's finest vineyards. This is an opportunity that would have been unimaginable to a previous generation of farm workers.

While acknowledging that the model had its problems and detractors, she concluded that the scheme held many benefits: 'The fact is that when equity share schemes work, they are productive, sustainable and offer real empowerment.' Her endorsement was welcomed by the government, with Minister Nkwinti saying that he liked her proposal for a 50-50 division of shares.[80]

This process, mixing the existing pattern of ownership with partnerships with new black farmers, would appear to hold out some prospects for success. So too would suggestions that the major food retailers might help by extending 'contract farming' to the emerging sector. This would mean that supermarkets would have to do deals with many more small-scale farmers in their localities, rather than buying their stock exclusively from a handful of large farms. This clearly would be costly, but it would help the evolution of a more diverse and equitable farming sector.[81]

The final alternative to these programmes is the suggestion that landholdings in South Africa are far too large and that they should be broken up to allow the emergence (or re-emergence) of a peasant sector. This approach suggests that the concentration of land in the hands of large capitalists is the major barrier to real reform. Edward Lahiff is a proponent of this view:[82]

The failure to subdivide is arguably the single greatest contributor to the failure and general underperformance of land reform projects, as it not only foists inappropriate sizes of farms on people (and absorbs too much of their grants in the process) but also forces them to work in groups, whether they want to do so or not ... What is clearly missing at present is any small-farmer path to development, which could allow the millions of households residing in the communal areas and on commercial farms to expand their own production and accumulate wealth and resources in an incremental manner. This would undoubtedly require radical restructuring of existing farm units, in order to create 'family-sized' farms, more realistic farm planning, appropriate support from a much reformed state agricultural service and a much greater role for beneficiaries in the design and implementation of their own projects.

At present there seems little government appetite for going very far down this road. The ANC's Green Paper gives no indication that it wishes to embark on this kind of reform. It would appear that the most likely future would be a continuation of past policies, with some additional measures injected from the Green Paper.

In the end, the land question is just too difficult a problem to tackle with any simple set of measures, without disrupting the agricultural sector. As Theo de Jager, the deputy president of AgriSA, complained to the London *Independent* newspaper, 'The basic problem is that the government has never treated land reform and agriculture as two sides of the same coin.'[83] It is clearly vital for the country to continue to provide plentiful supplies of cheap food while at the same time dealing with the problem of past injustice.

What the chapter indicates is not just the complexities and sensitivities surrounding land, but the almost insuperable problems of reform. The pattern of land holding in South Africa has the injustices of past centuries embedded within it. To the immense frustration of the ANC, this issue has highlighted only too clearly the limitations of the party's powers in government and its inability to tackle an issue that it has been determined to confront for generations. The party certainly rules, but has so far been incapable of answering the Freedom Charter's call for all land to be 're-divided amongst those who work it to banish famine and land hunger'.

Chapter 12

Rumbles and Rifts: Service Delivery Protests

Paul Holden

In the late 2000s, South Africa exploded in a series of often violent protests. Nearly always, the location was the old 'location' – townships that featured a smattering of formal housing, shacks and over 50 per cent unemployment. The civic action was quickly described as 'service delivery' protests. These protests were about the failure of the state to deliver housing, electricity, sanitation and other services to areas of the country that had not changed substantially since the end of apartheid. Nearly always, the target of the uprising was local government: councillors and ward committee members who many believed had misused their position in a manner that prevented service delivery, or ensured that what services were delivered were distributed unfairly.

The protests were, in a sense, against local government. As such, they have not yet presented a major threat to the ANC's national hegemony, even if its representatives at a local level have not bathed the party in glory. But, if certain conditions remain unmet, it is entirely possible that the locally focused sparks of unrest may catch fire nationally, leading to the formation of a new national civil society movement that could unite the one group that is often left outside the formal and informal forums of power: an urban underclass of the unemployed, under-employed or simply unemployable who continue to chafe against South Africa's pathologically unequal society.

Scale and geographical spread of service delivery protests

The images that emerged from the service delivery protests were eerily familiar: they looked much like those in the dying days of apartheid. Poor black South Africans were toyi-toying and marching to express their grievances. The protests sometimes spiralled into running battles with the police, with flaming barricades erected, or infrequently escalated into arson attacks on the houses of local councillors as well as amenities such as libraries and community halls. The resonance with the past was amplified by the fact that the areas in which the protests happened did not look much different than they had under apartheid – a reflection of the staggered and uneven nature of post-apartheid delivery.

In many ways, the service delivery protests looked as if they were intent on making townships ungovernable, much as they had been in the years of protest that eventually led to apartheid's demise. Disturbingly familiar, too, was the response of the police, which was disastrously heavy-handed, leading to multiple injuries.[1] In the case of Andries Tatane, a 33-year-old protestor in Ficksburg, police action led to death. Tatane was fatally beaten by a number of police officers without provocation in April 2011.[2] Thus, despite the targets being much different in 2009 than they were in 1989, and the police staffed by a whole host of new recruits, the 'repertoire'[3] of protest and state response was largely unchanged.

It is this feature of the protests that has often caught the public eye, splashed across newspapers and making for compelling, if not great television. But because the focus is largely on those that escalate into violence (and police brutality), the sheer scale of protests, many of which are not violent at all, has often slipped under the radar. Data from the local government monitor, *Municipal IQ*, which has tracked the number of service delivery protests since 2004, confirms the scale. In 2004, only 10 protests were tracked, rising to 34 in 2005 but falling to only 2 in 2006. In 2007 and 2008, 32 and 27 protests were noted respectively. From 2009, however, the protests exploded: in 2009, 105 protests were recorded, rising to a high of 111 in 2010.[4] 2011 was a marginally more peaceful year: by November 2011, 81 protests had been recorded.[5]

The scale is simply remarkable: between 2008 and November 2011, South Africa witnessed an average of 8.5 significant protests a month.

It should be noted that these figures are not necessarily definitive. Research by the local government research group, Local Democracy, Peace and Human Security (LDPHS), has suggested, based on a slightly broader definition of community protest, that an even larger number of protests have taken place, although both sets of data show that protests escalated enormously from 2009 onwards. In 2007 and 2008, the LDPHS reports that the country experienced 8.73 and 9.83 protests per month respectively (a total of 105 for 2007 and 117 and 2008, much higher than the 32 and 27 suggested by *Municipal IQ*). In 2009, the monthly average was 17.75 (213 in total), falling to 11.08 (132 in total) per month in 2010 (partially due to a hiatus during the 2010 World Cup) and 8.80 per month in the first five months of 2011.[6]

Service delivery protests have not just increased since 2009; they have also grown proportionally more violent. Whether this is due to heavy-handed policing or greater frustration is uncertain, although the pattern of increasing violence is clear. In 2007, approximately 41 per cent of all protests were violent, dropping to 38 per cent in 2008. In 2009, however, 44 per cent of the protests were violent. In the last quarter of 2009 the percentage rose to 52 per cent, prefiguring the increasingly violent nature of protests in 2010, when 55 per cent of all protests involved violence. Within the first five months of 2011 – the latest data available from LDPHS – the proportion had risen yet again to 59 per cent, with a high of 61 per cent in the first quarter.[7] If a service delivery protest does take place now, it is more likely to be violent than not.

And yet even these worrying statistics may not capture the full scale and extent of service delivery protests in South Africa, especially in the light of another key source of data. This data, drawn from the Incident Registration System (IRIS) maintained by the South African Police Service, suggests that the number of protests have actually numbered in their thousands. IRIS data tracked the number of 'gatherings' taking place in South Africa numbering over 15 people (but with no upper limit). Many of the recorded reasons for the gatherings were, as Natasha Vally of the Centre for Sociological Research has noted, protest or 'unrest'-related. The raw stats suggest that 8 004 (622 of which were violent) gatherings took place in 2004/2005, growing to 10 763 in 2005/2006 (954 unrest related), before dropping to 9 446 (743 unrest related) in 2006/2007 and 7 003 in 2007/2008 (699 unrest related).[8] In 2008/2009, the figures dropped to 6 943 but showed an increase in unrest-related protests to 718.[9]

It could be argued that these figures, due to their unvariegated nature, cannot paint an adequate picture of how many of these gatherings were related to local service delivery. But this argument was undermined during a reply by the Minister of Police to a parliamentary question in 2010. Responding to a question as to how many gatherings took place in 2008 and 2009, the Minister noted that 'the most common reason for conducting crowd management (peaceful) gatherings was labour related demands for increases in salary/wages, and crowd management (unrest) was related to service delivery issues.'[10] The vast majority of gatherings listed above as unrest-related can, as a result, be considered service delivery protests. Thus, according to the SAPS' own records, the number of service delivery protests in 2008/2009 was actually over six times the numbers reported by *Municipal IQ* and LDPHS. And lest one think the majority of these were only small gatherings of malcontents, the same reply confirmed that the average size of the 'unrest' gatherings in 2008/2009 was 4 000.[11] Based on these figures, an estimated 2 872 000 people took part in service delivery protests that elicited police response in 2008/2009 alone; equal to roughly 5 per cent of the total population of the country.

The sheer scale of the protests would suggest, to the casual observer, that they are a truly national phenomenon. This is only partially true. While every province has reported service delivery protests, their geographical spread has been markedly uneven. By far the majority of protests have occurred in the two wealthiest provinces of the country, lending an intriguingly counter-intuitive aspect to the protests. In 2011 it was reported that 26 per cent of all protests took place in Gauteng, followed by 23 per cent in the Western Cape: just under half of all service delivery protests in 2011 took place in the two richest provinces in the country.[12] The three poorest provinces, meanwhile, only contributed a small fraction to the overall protests: protests in Mpumalanga constituted only 6 per cent of all national protests, followed by the Northern Cape with 3 per cent and Limpopo – by far the most destitute and arguably least well-run province in the country[13] – accounting for only 1 per cent.[14] Importantly, a good deal of the protests were not only located in the richest provinces, but also the richest metros – roughly 10 per cent of all protests took place within the boundaries of the City of Johannesburg (which notably excludes the old East Rand, Ekurhuleni), for example.[15]

Causes and claims

The outbreak of protest across South Africa – some of it contaminated with xenophobic violence – has led to a great deal of confusion as to the causes of the protest, partially because the raw statistics around service delivery (provision of housing, water and electricity primarily) since 1994 have been deeply impressive. Between 1994 and 2010, for example, the state built and distributed just under 2.4 million houses for the formerly homeless.[16] By 2010, 13 per cent of the country was said to be living in informal housing (shacks and other temporary accommodation), a substantial reduction since 1994.[17] Electricity connections have boomed. In 1993, a measly 36 per cent of the population had access to grid electricity.[18] As a result of a huge national push, 82 per cent of all households in the country were connected to mains supplies by 2010.[19] Just under 90 per cent of the country has access to piped water, a previously inconceivable number. And sanitation, a major health issue, has also improved nationally, with a relatively small 6.1 per cent of the country without access to toilets or bucket toilets in 2010, down from 12.6 per cent as recently as 2002.[20] On top of this, the rollout of a welfare safety net has provided (admittedly limited) relief from the country's high unemployment; as of 2010, 28.4 per cent of the country was accessing one of a number of social security grants.[21]

But dealing with the raw statistics at a national level hides many features. One of these is the fact that, as Doreen Atkinson has pointed out, while the statistics on the *provision* of services have been remarkable, this says nothing of either the quality or maintenance of the services.[22] One can see this clearly with regard to the consistent unhappiness with the quality of newly connected water supplies. In the Eastern Cape, for example, 28.5 per cent of the population worry that the water that is being piped to them is unsafe to drink. Satisfaction levels have also dropped: 63.6 per cent of the country are satisfied with water services as of 2010, down from 76.3 per cent in 2005.[23] Quality of housing delivered is now of as much concern as the previous non-supply; only a few short years after RDP houses had been built throughout the country, hundreds of thousands of units are reported to be suffering from major structural flaws such as cracking walls, leaking roofs and poor sanitation connections. One example, if somewhat extreme, is illustrative: in 2011 it was reported by the National Home Builders Registration Council CEO Sipho Mashinini that 80 per cent of all RDP houses examined during a sweep by the eThekwini (Durban) municipality needed to be demolished and rebuilt.[24]

That the service delivery protests took place in the wealthiest provinces in the country has also raised the possibility that the protestors were responding, not to absolute levels of unacceptable deprivation, but relative deprivation; that is, levels of deprivation that may not be as bad as in places like Limpopo with its disastrous levels of poverty and unemployment, but which seem far worse when compared within cities and municipalities with a high average income and level of infrastructure. Many analysts have drawn on the theorist Robert Gurr and his model of relative deprivation. Gurr, writing in 1970, wrote that relative deprivation can be 'defined as actors' perception of discrepancy between their value expectations and their value capabilities. Value expectations are the goods and conditions of life to which people believe they are rightfully entitled. Value capabilities are the goods and conditions of life they think they are capable of getting and keeping.'[25] A number of analysts have suggested that living in wealthy areas increases the expectation of service delivery, which then exceeds the levels of delivery by a large margin.[26] The expectation–reality gap creates the impetus towards protest and violence. This produces the counter-intuitive conclusion that the regions most afflicted with protest are those that have performed best – the wealth and delivery successes have encouraged a rapid influx of migrants into these rich metros over the last decade, thus outstripping the pace of service delivery.

Reliance on Gurr and relative deprivation might be somewhat misplaced: the relative deprivation theory has been shown, repeatedly, to be too simplistic to capture the nuances of political violence throughout the world.[27] More important, it seems, is the wide divergence in the regional delivery of services in the context of rapid urbanisation. Over the last century, South Africa has been witness to rapid urbanisation, a fact that scared apartheid ideologues enough to develop their harsh laws around right of access to urban settlement, typified by the pass law. Since the 1980s, when the hated influx control laws were either scrapped or imperfectly monitored, urban populations have exploded, made all too plainly visible in the mushrooming of shanty and shack settlements at the edges of the country's most wealthy cities. The process has continued unabated since 1994, as rural migrants move to seek whatever economic opportunities may present themselves in the city.

The result has been that, in certain provinces, despite a high absolute supply of services, the percentage of people without access to services has increased. Unsurprisingly, the provinces with the highest percentage of service delivery protests (Gauteng and Western Cape) have witnessed an increase in the percentage of people living in informal settlements, despite high absolute service delivery numbers. In 2002, for example, 14.5 per cent of households in the Western Cape lived in informal dwellings, while 19.1 per cent did so in Gauteng. By 2010, these figures had deteriorated. In the Western Cape, 17 per cent lived in informal dwelling (an increase of 2.5 per cent), while in Gauteng the number had reached 21.5 per cent (an increase of 2.4 per cent).[28] The third highest reported incidents of service delivery protests was in the province of North West, where the figures are even more clear-cut: from 12.2 per cent in informal dwellings in 2002, the figure increased to 18.8 per cent in 2010, with a high in 2008 of 23.7 per cent, exactly as the wave of protests kicked off in earnest. Unsurprisingly, the provinces with the lowest percentage of reported service delivery protests, despite being the poorest, were those whose statistics showed the reverse trend; Limpopo's percentage of households living in informal dwellings fell from 5.1 per cent in 2002 to 3.8 per cent in 2010, while Mpumalanga's dropped from 13.9 per cent to 9.9 per cent.[29]

What relative deprivation theory tends to ignore is that, in very concrete terms, the areas in which protests happen are, at any level, simply extremely deprived. This, according to a seminal paper by the Centre for the Study of Violence and Reconciliation (CSVR), suggests that there is no need to rely on relative deprivation, especially as micro-studies of afflicted municipalities have shown that the data simply does not conform to relative deprivation schematics. In other words, the scale of deprivation is enough to explain the protest,[30] as is the fact that, due to urbanisation and migration, certain areas have experienced a proportional decrease in the amount of services available to the average citizen over the last decade and a half.

Statistics provided by CSVR regarding sites of protest investigated by their researchers indicate the severity of economic hardship in affected areas, as well as the simply unacceptable levels of non-delivery of services: these afflicted areas generally suffered greater deprivation than was the national average. In ward 95 of the Slovoview informal settlement, for example, 57 per cent of households had no adequate access to water (versus the national average of 16 per cent); 61 per cent had no access to sanitation (the national average being 15 per cent); 67 per cent of households had no access to electricity (24 per cent national average); and, finally, 48 per cent of the households did not have a single employed member (against the national average of 35 per cent).[31]

That immediate suffering was a key cause of the protests is also clear from data about the time of year when protests took place. Numbers of protests peaked during winter months, reflecting how immediate hardships such as a lack of electricity and decent housing contribute to the urgency of protest. In some years, the number of protests in winter months almost doubled those taking place in the summer months. In 2008, for example, the yearly average was 9.83 protests per month, made up of a winter average of 10.67 versus only 5.67 per month in the summer months. Similarly, in 2009, the average number of protests taking place in winter months sky-rocketed to 28.67 against a much smaller 10.33 per month in summer. The only year that this trend reversed was in 2010, which was most likely due to the broader reduction in protests during the (winter) football World Cup.[32]

Explaining why these areas are so deprived, then, is key to understanding the reasons behind the protests. Here, many explanations can be brought to bear, not least the fact that, since the end of apartheid, South Africa has faced enormous challenges. Transforming an economy and a society so pathologically deformed by apartheid is a grand task, and the pace of delivery on that promise is necessarily constrained by resources. Nobody is denying these constraints. But there is also little doubt that the situation for those protesting citizens could be better than it is currently, even if one cannot expect all South Africans to be seamlessly integrated overnight into the modern formal economy. What has prevented this is the distressingly widespread dysfunction of local government in South Africa.

The figures around local government performance and mismanagement are shocking. Municipalities and local government structures have become notorious for failing to abide by basic standards of financial management. In 2009, the Auditor-General released its most recent report into audits of local government, finding that an astonishing 67 per cent of municipalities had failed to address major concerns in their previous year's financial statements. Despite a massive government campaign – Operation Clean Audit – 30 per cent of all municipalities received disclaimed or adverse audit opinions: a polite way of saying that they simply could not account for how and why they had spent money. Commenting on the poor quality of financial reporting, the Auditor-General fretted that:

> ... the high incidence of material errors and omissions in financial statements submitted for audit, which management corrected during the audit and thereby avoided their financial statements being qualified points to a lack of accounting discipline. The continued, extensive reliance by municipalities on consultants to assist with the preparation of financial statements and even with the correction of such errors during the audit, raises concerns about the sustainability of audit outcomes for many municipalities.[33]

In other words, the Auditor-General worried that many municipalities simply would not be able to submit adequate statements in future without major changes being made.

Financial malfunction on this scale arises from a crippling lack of skilled capacity within local government. This is only partially because of a generalised societal skill shortage. Equally important is the fact that, in the process of transforming local government, huge numbers of white ex-civil servants were retrenched in accordance with employment equity and affirmative action policies. In so doing, decades of institutional memory and bureaucratic competency – admittedly somewhat sullied by its history – were lost to local government. New appointees were given the unenviable task of delivering on incredibly tough mandates despite a lack of previous experience or, in many cases, the lack of appropriate skill-sets.[34] In 2004, a survey by the Municipal Demarcation Board found that, in certain provinces, up to half of all managers had less than five years of municipal experience and service.[35] When the South African Institute of Civic Engineers scanned local councils, they found that 74 out of 231 local councils had no civil engineers, technologists or technicians.[36] How these councils could hope to maintain installed infrastructure and continue to deliver services is a mystery.

Rapid and sometimes questionable transformation decisions are only one part of the problem; indeed, maybe only a small part. Arguably more important has been the use of cadre deployment in the public service, which we have discussed in limited depth in the chapters on black empowerment and crime and corruption. In many ways, South Africa's local government has become an extended patronage network, rewarding political supporters and preventing alternative political bases from developing. This is not to suggest that all political appointees were not up to the task of local government, with a high number of skilled, intelligent and capable people amongst these ranks. Instead, what cadre deployment has done is change the yardstick by which people's performances are judged. By emphasising the political suitability of appointees (and doling out jobs on the basis of political affinity), the importance of merit and accountability has vanished as a criterion for judging performance. If a public servant is appointed to fulfil a factional agenda, it is unlikely that they will be removed if they don't do their job. Similarly, even if a person is doing a sterling job in local government, if they fall foul of regional and local political actors, they could find themselves sacked. Not exactly a formula for sterling success.

Organisational confusion, a lack of financial management and the death of meritocracy in local government has provided fertile ground for corruption on a grand scale, as we have seen elsewhere in this volume. One of the most persistent complaints during service delivery protests has been that government functions have been undermined by municipal tenders being farmed out to friends and family members of those serving in local government. There is also a widespread suspicion that low-cost housing allocation is shot through with fraud, bribery and mismanagement.[37]

The ethical environment within the public service generally gives little reassurance when these concerns are raised. In 2003, for example, the Public Service Commission (PSC) conducted a series of workshops with public servants around reporting incidents of corruption, fraud and other criminal activity within the public service. The results were disheartening: 'when participants were asked to give practical examples of white-collar crime in the public service they readily gave examples of fraud and corruption occurring in the workplace. When asked, however, whether they would "blow the whistle" on such criminal acts, barring one or two employees who had done so in the past to their detriment, nobody was prepared.'[38] Overwhelmingly, respondents during the PSC investigation believed that they would suffer harassment and unfair dismissal if they reported criminal activities.

Concerns over corruption and a lack of accountability mechanisms has eroded trust in the ability and willingness of local government to deliver on its service delivery mandate. This perception has only been exacerbated by the striking manner in which newly appointed local councillors have used the resources of the state to project an image of wealth and conspicuous consumption. Salaries have been increased with remarkable speed, often reducing the availability of funds for the delivery of key services. Two examples provided by Doreen Atkinson give a flavour: in Phumelela Municipality, only 2.9 per cent of its budget had been allocated to capital expenditure; in the Mafube Municipality, 3.6 per cent of the budget was allocated to capital expenditure, a full 44 per cent less than the 47.6 per cent of its budget that it spent on salaries.[39] The result has been, as the CSVR points out, the creation of a local government political elite that has grown increasingly distant from its constituency.[40]

Distance and a lack of communication are both symptoms of local government dysfunction; they are one of the primary causes of the eruption of service delivery protests and, most importantly, their escalation into mass action outside the bounds of formal engagement. Numerous studies have pointed out that a persistent lack of response on the part of local councillors to demands, concerns and petitions has led to a spiral of increasingly frustrated and angry protests. In the face of repeated experiences of high-handedness and a lack of responsiveness, disruption and violence become the only means of effectively communicating unhappiness with service delivery and economic hardship. The fact that violence has, in the end, produced some political results has confirmed to many that, in the repertoire of protest, violence is the most effective tool. In Kungcatsha, the site of a major protest, one participant summed up the logic: 'Violence is the only language that our government understands. Look, we have been submitting memos, but nothing was done. We became violent and our problems were immediately resolved. It is clear that violence is a solution to all problems.'[41]

The example of one 'typical' service delivery protest taking place in Voortrekker in Mpumalanga illustrates how this particular concatenation of government and party-wide dysfunctions came together to precipitate violence. Protests kicked off in Voortrekker in 2009 (after Jacob Zuma's election to the presidency of the ANC). The impetus was the mismanagement of a community sports day, for which R150 000 in prizes had been allocated. In April 2009, it became clear that the prizes were not to be forthcoming. In response, a group of residents and local ANC leaders (not in government) formed a Concerned Group to protest the situation. The Concerned Group called for a mass protest in the local stadium, urging community members to attend and join the forum. After the stadium meet, the Concerned Group arranged a march on the municipal offices to present a memorandum of grievances that included issues around service delivery and corruption.

Perhaps alerted to the combustibility of the situation, the provincial premier visited the province a week later, promising to attend to the matter. However, when the townsfolk arranged a mass meeting that following week, the Premier failed to attend. Despite there being a number of provincial Cabinet members in attendance, the no-show was a snub.

That evening, after chasing the provincial delegation out of town in their 4x4s under a hail of stones, the community acted by erecting barricades and indicating that they were to travel to Johannesburg to present their grievances to the ANC head office. When the police attempted to interdict the protest, matters turned violent and, over the course of the next day, amenities were burnt in anger. Only when the local town council was placed under administration by the Premier's office did the protests abate.[42]

Corruption and mismanagement caused the frustration; a lacklustre response on the part of local councillors and provincial government caused the anger; and police heavy-handedness provoked the violence. And violence, in the end, was what brought about decisive political action. If the slow build-up of frustration and anger had, at some point, been mitigated by some form of responsiveness, or if the frustration had been prevented from occurring in the first place, violence would not have occurred. Instead, violence was confirmed as the only means by which to effect meaningful change – a message that would not have been lost on other protestors around the country.

Local hiccups or threat to ANC hegemony?

A national outburst of protest over socio-economic and governance failure could easily suggest that the ANC's authority throughout the country has been massively dented. In reality, the picture is far more mixed. Despite the scale of the protests, the ANC has faced little by way of comeback at the polls. During the 2009 national elections, the party won a remarkable 65.9 per cent of the vote, just shy of the two-thirds majority that would grant it the ability to change constitutional provisions. In the 2011 local elections, too, the ANC scored big, winning 62 per cent of the total votes, despite the fact that, for the previous two years, service delivery protests had reached a historic peak. Local dissatisfaction has not translated into electoral punishment.

This would suggest that, on the whole, service delivery protestors have retained faith in the ANC and its core mandate of a developmental state. The protests were not a revolution to change the nature of the state; the aim was the more efficient and equitable implementation of this mandate. That revolution has not appeared so far suggests that the blame has been put squarely on the malfeasance of local councillors. A systemic linkage between the failure of local government and the broader governance model of the ANC does not seem to have been made. However, this is only one way of interpreting the paradox of bitter local grievance and the ANC's national electoral success. Equally compelling is the fact that many communities may have felt that stepping out of the ANC's fold would not chasten the movement; instead, that the communities risked being punished for their electoral treason, compounding an already unsatisfactory situation. Such are the calculations in a realm of governance and community engagement after it has been sullied by the simplistic equations of patronage.

The local nature of the protests also insulates the ANC from a national challenge. In no instance has a national movement emerged out of the protests, despite the universality of the grievances presented by protestors throughout the country. The protests have thus deeply impacted on local politics while having a mitigated impact on the broader national picture. Why this would be the case is unclear. Perhaps it is because the explicit link between non-delivery and the ANC's style of governance has not yet become a widely accepted belief, forcing the focus of attention purely onto local actors. Perhaps it is because many of those protesting lack the means to organise on a regional or national basis. Perhaps the symbolic strength of the ANC, the party of freedom, is so strong that it can survive the depredations of its local agents. Or perhaps the pain of recognising that the ANC is a crippled and corrupted organisation is simply too much for the poorest of the poor to bear. It is one thing being poor. It is another being poor and betrayed.

And yet there are indications that the protests may yet congeal into a new national movement that contests the ANC's hegemony, even if it is from within the organisation. One often overlooked fact about the protests is that they were highly organised and frequently led by those members of the community who were most engaged in local political developments, rather than being spontaneous outpourings of rage. One fascinating study published in 2011 by Ndodana Nleya, a researcher and

PhD candidate at the University of the Western Cape, found that active involvement in community meetings and local politics was a greater predictor of involvement in protest than attitudes and assumptions around service delivery issues in Khayelitsha.[43] The success of service delivery protests, measured both in terms of pure numbers of attendees as well as in the immediate political gains experienced by communities able to evict unpopular local councillors – illustrates a great deal of political *nous* on the part of the organisers. If, or perhaps when, this canniness is turned towards national objectives, the impact could be profound.

Equally important is the proportion of young protestors. This can partly be explained by resource mobilisation theory – that young protestors are also the most likely to be under- or unemployed, with time on their hands. Nevertheless, the service delivery protests have given notice that there is a new generation of activists in play, many of whom have lived their entire lives under ANC government. A child born in 1994 will be 18 in 2012, and, for many, freedom has yet to produce a life of dignity and decency. Without a drastic improvement in circumstances, this generation can confidently be predicted to be angry and active for a long time yet.

Then there is the simple matter of timing. During the first outbreak of protest, the failure of local government could be absorbed under the rubric of the contestation between Zuma and Mbeki factions within the ANC. Service delivery failures and local government dysfunction could be easily cast as the result of Mbeki's centralising tendencies, his imputed class and ethnic allegiances or his taste for technocratic solutions that were alienated and insulated from the rigours of local political contestation. Zuma was cast as the counterpoint: a man of the people, in touch with the realities of day-to-day struggle, emotionally available and sympathetic to the plight of the poor. It was powerful stuff. But it will seem considerably less powerful if his government cannot deliver on the services it promised upon election. Perhaps, then, service delivery failures will be seen, not as a function of greedy councillors and an unsympathetic leadership, but as a consequence of the ANC's approach to governance, development and democracy. Who *should* rule South Africa, rather than who currently does, would then be a question on everyone's lips.

So Who Does Rule South Africa?

Martin Plaut and Paul Holden

The history of South Africa during the lives of the most of its people has been the history of two political parties – the National Party, which brought about apartheid, and the ANC, which abolished it. Few can still recall living under any other party, and there has been only one change of government in living memory. South Africa remains what it has been since 1948: a one-party state, with democratic trimmings. None of the country's leaders has had to worry about being voted out of office by an electorate still dominated by concerns about race. Internal party machinations have been far more troubling to South African prime ministers and presidents than any criticism from the opposition.

On the face of it, the answer to the question of who rules South Africa is self-evident: it is the ANC. The ANC does not rule alone, however, and does not rule untrammelled. Nor is there a single monolithic ANC. As we have shown throughout the book, the ANC wields this power within a broader Alliance. It is a remarkably durable structure that has melded the various political strains – from communist to ultra-capitalist – into some sort of workable whole. Given the Alliance's sometimes schizophrenic components, it is unsurprising that the last decade of South African politics has been dominated by increasingly vicious battles for power between different factions. With so much at stake, these internal battles have undermined the democratic checks on government. As the over-used but ever so apt phrase has it, 'when the elephants fight, it is the grass that gets trampled'.

The ANC is no longer the movement it was during the fight against apartheid. The party has taken a long journey over the last 100 years. It changed from being an African nationalist and largely Christian organisation (with a distinct middle-class or at least petit-bourgeois bias) when it was founded in 1912 to become, in the 1950s, a multiracial, leftist party intertwined with the Communist Party and the unions. Today it is returning to its roots. It is not the organisation it was a century ago (like all parties it bears the scars of its history), but it is once more essentially an African nationalist organisation. It may sometimes use Third-Worldist, anti-Western rhetoric, and look to the Chinese for inspiration on how to run the party, but it has become an increasingly conservative force, representing an aspiring black middle class. The ANC has, over 100 years, moved through a radical arc and returned to its roots.

The movement that was born out of a black elite, led by tribal chiefs and religious leaders, is increasingly under the sway of a similar stratum, only this time they are the new moguls of Black Economic Empowerment. In 1943 Nelson Mandela described the party's leadership as 'a tired, unmilitant, privileged African elite more concerned with protecting their own rights than those of the masses'.[1] Is this a label that can be applied to the party once more?

This rightward trajectory leaves its partners in the SACP and the unions with a dilemma: should they tie themselves to this party, or move away? The ANC is by far the most influential force in South Africa, but it would be severely damaged if it lost its left-wing allies. They provide it with the legitimacy it requires to assert that it is acting on behalf of the vast majority of the population. For the left, the question is whether they are prepared to continue playing this role, despite losing effective influence over government policy. As we have seen, time and again, at key junctures the policies of the unions and the communists have been ignored. In economic policy, in particular, the left has little real sway. Orthodox tax and spending policies have been applied, with predictable results. The country remains solvent and on a path towards steady if unspectacular growth, but the scourge of mass unemployment remains unresolved.

If the left have had little say in ruling South Africa, who does? Simply, the most powerful political (but not necessarily economic) players are those BEE moguls and senior security advisers who have coalesced around the presidency of Jacob Zuma. Many have relationships with the President that go back a long way, while others have been elevated through Zuma's control of the ANC deployment committee after 1998, which allowed him to place friends and allies in key positions of influence. The President's grip on power in the ANC has been strengthened in early 2012, in part by taking disciplinary action against the one man who was willing to put his neck out to challenge his hegemony: Julius Malema. Those who predicted that Zuma would only serve a short and fractious five-year term as leader of the ANC were only partly right. It has certainly been fractious, but Zuma has proved to be far more durable than his critics expected.

To claim that Zuma retains this power alone, or with the help of a handful of cadres, is self-evidently absurd. In reality, Zuma appears to have relied on a trump card: a supportive and pliant intelligence and security sector. He has skilfully used current security officers and his old friends from his days in exile as head of the ANC's Intelligence Department. It was the security services that helped Zuma escape charges of corruption and racketeering in connection with the Arms Deal. It has made him a formidable opponent and given him unrivalled access to the one of the key currencies of political power: intelligence and information on his rivals. To maintain his control on information flows Zuma has, along with a number of intelligence figures, pushed hard for adoption of the Protection of State Information Bill (also known as the Secrecy Bill). As we saw in Chapter 6, the Secrecy Bill is not just a threat to media freedom. It is also a means of severely curtailing how information is distributed throughout the intelligence services and within the ANC itself. It gives Zuma's circle of friends and advisers a major advantage in a party that has become obsessed with conspiracy. As Nic Dawes, editor of the *Mail & Guardian*, has noted, the ANC has become 'the party of anxiety, of lies and spies, of permanent war'.[2]

Equally important has been the support of South Africa's 'new Randlords', the Black Economic Empowerment elite. While they are not monolithically aligned with Zuma, the President arguably has enough support from this group to benefit from it substantially. They have backed him in public debates and funded his needs. During his push for power against Thabo Mbeki, support from this group kept Zuma solvent and fighting – it costs a lot of money to campaign for power when excluded from the ANC's internal resources. In return, elements of this elite have benefited handsomely.

As we showed in detail in the chapter on BEE, this group's power is far from absolute. Clearly, it is a power wielded with disproportionate influence, but it is a power that is not reflected in the broader economy. The BEE elite has struggled to overcome major structural problems with the way in which BEE policies have been implemented. Many are now weighed down with debt and some BEE enterprises have reported major financial difficulties. In addition, its ownership of the broader economy remains small: white and foreign capital still rule the roost in the economic sphere. This explains why BEE capital is so keen to cosy up to political players: its power remains precarious, and is still heavily dependent on state support through legislation, enforcement and contracts.

This precariousness is only accentuated by the distaste with which the BEE elite is increasingly treated by the left in the Alliance and the broader public. Partially this is a result of the fact that a number of BEE deals – by no means all, but certainly many – have been linked to corruption and other corporate abuses. The left believes BEE moguls support nationalisation as a means of ending their financial difficulties. The same moguls would then undoubtedly have a hand on the tiller should mines be nationalised. Equally important is the fact that BEE has become associated with the post-apartheid compromises known as the 1996 'Class Project'. Simply put, the Class Project involved white business ending the ANC's anti-capitalist critique by making millionaires of its senior leadership. As the economist Hein Marais has written:

> BEE has served two primary functions. It has provided a vehicle for elite enrichment and the brisk engineering of a black bourgeoisie that rides side-saddle behind incumbent corporate capital ... And it has created a powerful political lobby inside and around the ANC against radical change.[3]

The result has been that white business remains a powerful, but frequently silent, player on the South African stage. It prefers to operate behind the scenes, allowing others to clash in public, but when the chips are down it is capable of flexing its muscles. Brett Kebble, who literally bought popularity and support from the ANC Youth League through his extraordinary largesse, who bribed his way into the heart of the police force and made links with politicians at the highest levels, is an extreme example of this trend.

Corruption has become endemic, from the lowest levels to the very top of government. This underlies certain attempts to neuter key areas of democratic accountability, in particular Parliament and the criminal justice system. As we explored in Chapter 1, Parliament's role in holding the executive and other arms of government to account has been curtailed. As a result of the party list system, MPs rely on powerful party leaders for their standing instead of being answerable to their constituents for their performance. This has been used to crack the whip, pulling Parliament into line when it strays into uncomfortable territory. The test case for this neutering of Parliament was the Arms Deal. Attempts by Andrew Feinstein and others on key parliamentary committees to investigate the scandal were ruthlessly crushed by the ANC. In so doing they set the limits of parliamentary scrutiny, which have been rigidly adhered to. The Arms Deal was the first of the country's major post-apartheid political scandals and sadly provided the template for many more. Political strings were pulled to ensure that most of its participants never faced justice. The as yet unsatisfactory resolution of Judge Hlophe's alleged attempt to influence the Constitutional Court is an ongoing stain on the reputation of the judiciary, the executive and Parliament.

As Chapter 10 (crime and corruption) indicates, crime and corruption have become endemic in local and national government. There is hardly a department which has not had senior officials convicted of corruption or named in a corruption enquiry. Billions of rands have gone astray, with some areas of local government (like Limpopo province) now so incapable of functioning that they have had to be taken over by national government. This process has been exacerbated by the ANC's policy of deploying party cadres to run key sectors of government and the economy. Some do their jobs diligently and are a credit to their party.

Others succumb to the lures of easy wealth available through the tendering system to line their own pockets. Organised criminal networks have grown in influence, threatening to bring sections of government within their grasp. The union movement is right in warning that South Africa is in danger of being ruled by a 'predatory state' that feeds on its people rather than serving them.

So far, the major opposition to these trends – elite enrichment, corruption and government dysfunction – has come from outside the ANC. These are the media, civil society, the unions and the judiciary. As we show in detail in Chapter 6, the ANC has an increasingly unhappy relationship with these alternative sites of power and influence. The media, which was so supportive of the ANC under Mandela, became increasingly disillusioned with Mbeki's centralising tendencies and his obtuse beliefs around HIV and Aids. Zuma, for many a bogeyman whose election heralded a new wave of corruption and abuse of power, has few supporters in the press. Outside of the SABC, which the state controls, the ANC is now faced with a media that consistently exposes its abuses. This not only threatens the ANC's control of key resources, it challenges the party's self-image as a bastion of the nation, 'uplifting the quality of life of all South Africans, especially the poor', as it's literature proclaims. Unsurprisingly, this threat has led the ANC to propose new legislation that would hamper media freedom, in the form of the Secrecy Bill and the much-fretted-about Media Appeals Tribunal.

Civil society has, since 1994, acted as a useful brake on the ruling party's hegemony. The post-apartheid slump that overcame so many groups associated with the United Democratic Front is now a dim memory. In Chapter 6, for example, we highlighted the role of the committed activists who formed the Treatment Action Campaign in forcing the distribution of life-saving antiretrovirals. More recently, bodies that have been formed in its mould, Right2Know and the Social Justice Coalition, have led campaigns against the Secrecy Bill and raised the concerns of impoverished communities. If the Secrecy Bill were to pass its final hurdles, it would be surprising if these groups and their associates did not launch a Constitutional Court challenge.

This highlights another feature of civil society's success: in the last instance, it could always turn to the courts to seek redress. This is how the TAC eventually forced the state to provide anti-retrovirals and how the opposition Democratic Alliance has tackled the handling of the criminal justice system under Zuma. The courts have consistently acted as the arbiter of last resort for those seeking to curtail the worst excesses of untrammelled political power. As a result the judiciary (in particular the Constitutional Court) now finds itself in the firing line from President Zuma and his clique. In a series of arguments that betray a fundamental lack of appreciation for the constitutional dispensation, Zuma has indicated that the ANC is looking at 'reviewing' the powers of the Constitutional Court. This explains the frontal attack on the constitutional order by Ngoako Ramatlhodi, a deputy minister and member of the ANC executive.[4] He suggested that the ANC had been outmanoeuvred during the negotiations to end apartheid, and as a consequence had been shackled by a Constitution that made real change difficult to implement.

> Apartheid forces sought to and succeeded in retaining white domination under a black government. This they achieved by emptying the legislature and executive of real political power. On the other hand, the liberation movement was overwhelmed by a desire to create a society bereft of any form of discrimination and, as a result, made fatal concessions. We thus have a Constitution that reflects the great compromise, a compromise tilted heavily in favour of forces against change.

That this is patently untrue is proved by the cases dealt with in Chapter 6, in which the Constitutional Court has acted as the *primary* agent for transforming South Africa along humanist and equitable lines. But attacking the constitutional order and the power of judges is still a powerful strategy, clearly illustrated during Zuma's run-ins with the courts when supporters loudly dismissed judges' rulings as 'counter-revolutionary'. This discursive foray may yet turn into an outright confrontation that will shape South Africa's political future in a most profound manner.

These trends are not just the whimsical concerns of commentators; they have had a material impact on the lives of ordinary South Africans.

Corruption has undermined the delivery of services and stripped government (local and national) of the resources it needs to tackle poverty. Many, employed as well as unemployed, find it increasingly difficult to make ends meet. Inequality has increased since the ANC took power and if it were not for the growing role of welfare payments, this inequality would be even greater. Many families, particularly in the rural areas, only survive on the pensions elderly relatives bring into the home. Poverty in the Eastern Cape, for example, has been officially labelled a 'national disaster'.

The government has attempted to react by launching initiative after initiative. Among them have been attempts to redistribute land. The skewed distribution of land – both under colonialism and during apartheid – has been much commented on. But attempts to redress the balance have gone awry. As the government now admits, 90 per cent of redistribution programmes have ended in failure. Suggestions by the Youth League that Zimbabwe should serve as an alternative model for agriculture fail to take into account the devastating impact this has had on output and employment in the farming sector. South African schemes to address these problems have so far undermined agriculture and displaced farm workers, while failing to address the historic injustices of land distribution.

Despite this, the country's poor have so far broadly stuck by the ANC, but this could change. Certainly there is a rising tide of anger in the townships. People have taken to the streets in vast numbers, mainly protesting against poor local service delivery, but also touching on broader themes of national importance – governance and corruption in particular. By our calculations, the demonstrations have involved more than 2 million people every year in the late 2000s. This is a rough estimate, but if it is remotely accurate it is a truly remarkable figure, highlighting the extent and depth of discontent. Currently, the protests have been localised and have, as a result, only really scared local and provincial government officials. It is not beyond the bounds of possibility that a movement could develop national organisational momentum. If that does happen, South Africa will have a new entrant into the politics of power: an organised underclass that, while sympathetic to the left in the ANC, may also chafe at the wage protectionism afforded by the unions, while being equally critical of the ANC's more brazen BEE nationalists.

The question: 'Who rules South Africa?' can only be answered today if one takes account of all of these forces, not forgetting to factor in the fluidity of South African politics and power more generally. The new BEE moguls represent the most powerful force in society, but they do not go unchallenged. Crime and corruption have strengthened the hold of the new elite, but have also exposed them to scrutiny and legal sanction. White business still has a major say in society, but has to play its cards carefully. Organised labour flexes its muscles, and threatens to withdraw it's support from the ANC, but fears it would be left in the wilderness. The poor clamour for their voices to be heard, but have, so far, had little hold over the mighty. Yet none of this remains written in stone. A new social movement, another grand corruption scandal, a popular groundswell in support of the constitutional order, or greater electoral success on the part of the Democratic Alliance; these are only some of the things that could dramatically influence the balance of power.

Perhaps this gives a clue to why South Africans should be optimistic about their future, for unlike much of the rest of Africa, the country has a powerful, well-developed civil society. It has newspapers that were founded more than 150 years ago. It has a union movement whose roots can be traced back further than the ANC itself, and a legal system that has largely proved itself to be a dignified corrective to non-delivery and the less salubrious authoritarian streaks of those in power. It has the finest universities in Africa, producing graduates who are equal to any in the world. And, after centuries of colonialism and decades of apartheid, South African citizens have developed a seemingly inexhaustible but vital resource: the will to fight for their rights, to question authority and to shape their own destinies.

South Africa remains a complex and contradictory society. It is a 'glass half full, glass half empty' story that cannot easily be encapsulated. There is much that is positive, including the many black businessmen and women who have built new enterprises from scratch and owe nothing to the largesse of the state. There are selfless civil servants who go about their daily business with nothing but the good of their community at heart. The success of the 2010 World Cup showed South Africa in its best light and revealed what it could, if all things went well, eventually become: an efficient, functional and fraternal country that exceeds expectations and serves as a beacon of success and good governance in a continent where such examples are sorely lacking.

Predicting what South Africa will look like in 10, 20 or 30 years is, as a result, very difficult indeed – so much is in flux and so many areas of power have yet to be developed. But some existing fault lines could develop in ways that would fundamentally change the nature of post-apartheid South Africa.

The first is perhaps the simplest: whether the centre will hold in the ANC. The left wing of the party has little to show for its years as a member of the ruling Alliance. The acquisitive strain of the party's right-wing nationalists and their association with corruption alienates not only the media and commentators but also their erstwhile comrades in the party. The crassness with which this wealth has been pursued and displayed can only stick in the craw of union members and the SACP rank and file. It is unwise, however, to suggest that this is an alliance that will be easily dismembered. It has proven remarkably durable over many difficult decades. Yet Cosatu's bluster has taken on a sharper tone in recent years, most notably when it floated the idea of leaving the Alliance for the first time ever in a public document in 2010. Putting this possibility down on paper made the prospect conceivable, rather than a remote suggestion muttered about in dark corridors. If Cosatu does not see some of its demands met in the near future and matters proceed as they are, a split becomes increasingly likely.

The second is whether the supremacy of the Constitution is challenged and the judiciary is assailed. There are those in the ANC who strain against the idea of judicial oversight over executive functions. Whether a radical initiative to reshape the formal political settlement enshrined in the 1996 Constitution would be successful is unclear, but it appears highly likely that some attempt will be made to, at the very least, clip the wings of what this faction regards as an overly independent judicial system. One law – the Secrecy Bill – could be the spark that ignites this confrontation. As we have suggested, the Bill in the form in which it was passed by Parliament appears unconstitutional. If this is the case, then the Constitutional Court, if left to its own devices, cannot fail to send the law back to its parliamentary drafters.

The Secrecy Bill has obvious flaws and has been rejected by important sectors of society. Despite this, it has been pushed relentlessly by Zuma and his core constituency in the intelligence community. It deals with confidential information and intelligence, and this has allowed its supporters to cloak themselves in a cape of spurious patriotism. If the law is overturned by the Constitutional Court it could trigger a showdown with Parliament and a constitutional crisis.

The third development is the electoral growth of the Democratic Alliance. As a party, the DA has made remarkable strides in consistently increasing its support. That it now runs the Western Cape – and seems to do so with a degree of goodwill and a lack of major controversy – gives it the ability to put itself in the shop window. If it learns from some of its disastrous previous campaigns – the 'Fight Back' slogan being virtually designed to alienate the majority of the population – and is able to successfully position itself as a multiracial party, the DA has the potential to make serious inroads into the ANC's electoral dominance. Its new strategy of promoting black Africans into senior positions – like the party's national spokesman, Mmusi Maimane, or its leader in Parliament, Lindiwe Mazibuko – is designed to do this. It is far from winning a general election, but the ANC now looks somewhat nervously over its shoulder at the Democratic Alliance. If it were to win over 35 per cent of Parliament (not an entirely unlikely event in the next decade) it could serve as a major obstacle to the ANC's parliamentary hegemony. Perhaps, then, Parliament could be re-enlivened, re-awakened from its moribund stupor and once more serve as the nation's real debating chamber.

The fourth issue is demography. During the 2009 elections, South Africans who were born on or after Mandela's release were able to vote for the first time. In 2014, it will be the chance of those who have lived their entire lives under an ANC government. It is a blindingly obvious point, but as time progresses, the lived experiences of the electorate change. Perhaps a new generation will be less willing to overlook the ANC's current infractions in the light of its historic role as the country's liberator. Certainly, it is difficult to imagine a new generation of young black South Africans who will not baulk at the prospect of their lives being little better than those of their parents. To an extent, we are already seeing this: service delivery protests have attracted a considerable following amongst the young (employed and unemployed) who are, importantly, engaged in local politics. How the energies of youth will be channelled is unclear. Will they go the way of the ANC Youth League, all brash populism with a forgiving take on the indiscretions of their leaders? Or will they develop into a civil movement that lauds the constitutional order and rigorous democratic battles? Such long-term developments are impossible to predict, but will have major implications for the future.

Finally, there is that most dangerous of political moments, which South Africans have yet to face. It is when a liberation movement finally confronts its own eclipse. The ANC has found it difficult enough to accept that it is, in reality, just another political party. It reacted with shock and anger when it lost the Western Cape. How will it respond when it finally has to confront electoral defeat? As we have seen, some in the ANC believe they will rule until the second coming of Christ, but all liberation movements gradually lose their sheen. The Indian Congress Party of Gandhi and Nehru held on to office for 30 years. African parties have also held on tenaciously, but even Kenyatta's KANU and Kaunda's UNIP finally conceded defeat.

Other precedents are not so positive. Facing the rejection of the electorate in the late 1990s, Robert Mugabe panicked. Combining populist land seizures with brutal repression, he hung on to power, but at a terrible cost to the country. What will the BEE moguls and the security operatives clustered around a future President whisper into his or her ear as the moment approaches? Will the ANC's proud democratic tradition prevail and the party accept the will of the people? Or will the President finally be persuaded to re-open the dusty manuals of the party's Soviet or East German tutors to find an alternative way forward? In the post-apartheid period the ANC has repeatedly claimed it is under attack both at home and abroad from unnamed shadowy enemies. It would be all too easy to conjure up these demons and wraiths.

Anyone can be a democrat in victory; the true test of democratic credentials comes with defeat.

Notes

Introduction

1 http://www.timeslive.co.za/local/article924877.ece/ANC-a-complete-mess – Wikileaks.

Chapter 1 The Uneasy Alliance

1 Technically, the Alliance – sometimes known as the Tripartite Alliance – consists of four members. The fourth, the South African National Civic Organisation (Sanco), is the rump of the United Democratic Front (UDF), the umbrella body founded in 1983 to bring 400 organisations together to fight apartheid. But after the ANC was unbanned the UDF was wound down, and Sanco is a pale reflection of it.

2 Quoted in H Mathisen and E Tjønneland, *Does Parliament matter in new democracies? The case of South Africa, 1994–2000*, Chr. Michelsen Institute Development Studies and Human Rights, working paper 1, 2001, p 1.

3 http://mg.co.za/article/2011-06-21-motshekga-whips-parliamentary-truants.

4 SACP Central Committee discussion document, 'Class, national and gender struggle in South Africa: the historical relationship between the ANC and the SACP', *Bua Komanisi*, vol 5, issue no 1, May 2006. http://www.sacp.org.za/main.php?include=docs/docs/2006/central.html#2.

5 *Ibid*.

6 'Report on the Tripartite Alliance Summit', 1 September 1997. http://www.anc.org.za/show.php?id=2454&t=Tripartite%20Alliance.

7 Z Vavi, address to the SACTWU National Congress, Cape Town, 23 September 2010. http://www.sactwu.org.za/component/docman/cat_view/59-speeches.

8 D Sikwebu, 'Foundation of the Alliance', *South African Labour Bulletin*, vol 26, no 1, February 2002.

9 http://www.polity.org.za/print-version/anc-zuma-address-by-the-president-at-the-100th-anniversary-of-the-anc-mangaung-08012012-2012-01-08.

10 J and R Simons, *Class and colour in South Africa*, IDAF, July 1983, p 44.

11 A Drew, *Discordant comrades*. Aldershot: Ashgate, 2000, pp 61–2.

12 J Baskin, *Striking back: A history of Cosatu*. London: Verso, 1991, pp 6–7.

13 Drew, *Discordant comrades*, pp 70–1.

14 http://www.polity.org.za/article/anc-gumede-international-congress-against-imperi
alism-10021927-2007-11-02.

15 J Zuma, Address to Progressive Business Forum in Polokwane ahead of the ANC's
99th anniversary celebrations, SAPA, 8 January 2011.

16 B Hirson, 'Bukharin, Bunting and the "Native Republic" slogan', *Searchlight South
Africa*, vol 1, no 3, July 1989, pp 51–66.

17 Drew, *Discordant comrades*, pp 94–111.

18 Baskin, *Striking back*, p 11.

19 Drew, *Discordant comrades*, p 254.

20 B Lapping, *Apartheid – a history*. London: Grafton Books, 1986, p 83.

21 T Lodge, *Mandela: A critical life*. Oxford: Oxford University Press, 2006, pp 36–7.

22 DJ Smith, *Young Mandela*. London: Weidenfeld & Nicholson, 2010, p 66.

23 Lodge, *Mandela*, p 38.

24 M Nyagumbo, *With the people*. London: Allison and Busby, 1980, p 72. Maurice
Nyagumbo, a Zimbabwean politician, became so enthralled by ballroom dancing
that he recalls how relieved he was when the CPSA was banned in 1950, as party
meetings ate into his practice time (p 80).

25 Smith, *Young Mandela*.

26 Stephen Ellis, 'Genesis of the ANC's armed struggle in South Africa, 1948–1961',
Journal of Southern African Studies (forthcoming).

27 Lapping, *Apartheid*, p 96.

28 V Shubin, *ANC – a view from Moscow*. Johannesburg: Jacana Media, 2008, p 5.

29 *Ibid*.

30 Quoted in E Sisulu, *Walter and Albertina Sisulu: in our lifetime*. London: Abacus,
2003, p 100.

31 '… those belonging to the other oppressed groups and those few white
revolutionaries who show themselves ready to make common cause with our
aspirations, must be fully integrated on the basis of individual equality'. First
National Consultative Conference: Report on the Strategy and Tactics of
the African National Congress, 26 April 1969. http://www.anc.org.za/show.
php?id=149.

32 T Lodge, *Black politics in South Africa since 1945*. London: Longman, 1983, p 69.

33 D Welsh, *The rise and fall of apartheid*. Johannesburg: Jonathan Ball, 2009, p 112.

34 Lodge, *Black politics in South Africa since 1945*, p 75.

35 Baskin, *Striking back*, p 13.

36 Quoted in *ibid*.

37 B Turok (ed), *The historical roots of the ANC*. Johannesburg: Jacana, 2010, p 76.

38 Turok, interview with author, 30 March 2011.

39 B Turok, *Nothing but the truth: Behind the ANC's struggle politics*. Johannesburg:
Jonathan Ball, 2003, p 82.

40 Turok, interview.

41 S Friedman, *Building tomorrow today, African workers in trade unions, 1970–1984*.

Johannesburg: Ravan Press, 1987, p 30.

42 *Ibid*, p 31.

43 *Ibid*.

44 Baskin, *Striking back,* pp 13–16.

45 Lodge, Mandela, pp 82–3.

46 Turok, interview with author, 30 March 2011.

47 This interview was accessed on 22 October 2011 at: http://www.youtube.com/watch?v=fPofm50MHW8.

48 R Suttner *The ANC underground in South Africa*: Jacana Media, 2008, p 18.

49 Ellis, 'Genesis of the ANC's armed struggle'.

50 H Barrell, *MK: The ANC's armed struggle.* London: Penguin, 1990, p 6.

51 *Ibid*, p 5.

52 Ellis, 'Genesis of the ANC's armed struggle'.

53 Suttner, *The ANC underground in South Africa*, p 34.

54 The South African Democracy Education Trust, *The road to democracy in South Africa*, vol 1, p 577, Interview with Joe Matthews. Matthews was a member of the Communist Party and was on the delegation to the Chinese Communist Party that met Chairman Mao.

55 Baskin, *Striking back,* pp 17–18.

56 Quoted in Martin Plaut, 'Changing perspectives on South African Trade Unions', *Review of African Political Economy*, no 30, September 1984, p 117.

57 *Workers Unity*, no 31, June 1982.

58 Friedman, *Building tomorrow today*, p 184.

59 J and R Simons, *Class and colour in South Africa.* London: IDAF, 1983, p 50.

60 E Webster, 'The Alliance under stress', in *Democratization*, vol 8, no 1, Spring 2001, Special Issue: *Opposition and Democracy in South Africa*, ed. R Southall, p 257.

61 R Southall, *Imperialism or solidarity: International labour and South African trade unions.* Cape Town: UCT Press, 1995, p 222.

62 N Kitson, *Where Sixpence lives.* London: Hogarth Press, 1987, p 214. At the time, the ANC in London argued that the only person who would be named in campaigns was Nelson Mandela, and that campaigning for anyone else would dilute this.

63 Author's interview with Mike Murphy, 25 August 2010.

64 A Butler, *Cyril Ramaphosa.* London: James Currey, 2007, p 224.

65 Baskin, *Striking back,* p 29.

66 M Plaut, 'The workers' struggle: A South African text revisited', *Review of African Political Economy*, no 96, 2003, p 308.

67 Friedman, *Building tomorrow today*, p 434.

68 *African Communist*, no 93, second quarter 1983.

69 Baskin, *Striking back*, p 53.

70 Jay Naidoo, *Fighting for Justice.* Johannesburg: Picador Africa, 2010, p 100.

71 Martin Plaut, 'The political significance of COSATU', *Transformation* 2, 1986, pp 66 ff.

72 Naidoo, *Fighting for Justice*, 2010, p 104.

73 *Ibid.*

74 V Shubin, *ANC: A view from Moscow*, second revised edition. Johannesburg: Jacana Media, 2008, p 142, for names of Central Committee members.

75 Published in the *South African Labour Bulletin*, vol 11, no 5, 1986.

76 Webster, 'Alliance under stress', p 259.

77 *Ibid*, p 100.

78 Author's interview, 31 March 2011.

79 Webster, 'Alliance under stress', p 260.

80 http://africanhistory.about.com/od/apartheid/a/AfrikaansMediumDecree.htm.

81 J Seekings, *The UDF: A history of the United Democratic Front in South Africa, 1983–1991*. London: James Currey, 2000, p 30.

82 *Ibid*, p 46.

83 Naidoo, *Fighting for Justice,* p 88.

84 H Barrell, *South African Review Two*. Johannesburg: Raven Press, 1984, p 14.

85 *Ibid*, p 90.

86 *Ibid.*

87 Seekings, *UDF*, p 231.

88 Norman Levy, 'The final prize: my life in the anti-apartheid struggle', *South African History Online*, 2011, p 414. According to Levy, a Treason Trialist and trade unionist, the final details of the relationship between Cosatu and Sactu were only hammered out in March 2000, with the veteran communist and trade unionist, Ray Alexander, declaring ecstatically that the 'SACP and Cosatu have found each other'.

Chapter 2 From De Klerk to Zuma: The Long, Hard Road of Post-Apartheid Politics

1 Welsh, *Rise and fall of apartheid*, p 344.

2 https://www.givengain.com/cgi-bin/giga.cgi?cmd=cause_dir_news_item&cause_id=2137&news_id=73749&cat_id=1595.

3 P Waldmeir, *Anatomy of a miracle*. London: Viking, 1997, p 133.

4 *Ibid*, p 35.

5 This view was shared by Joe Slovo, who said in 1986 that the ruling elite knew that they 'could not hold on for very much longer'. Interview with *Marxism Today* quoted in J Sanders, *Apartheid's friends: The rise and fall of South Africa's secret service*. London: John Murray, 2006, p 292.

6 The Reunion, BBC Radio 4, 18 September 2009. http://www.bbc.co.uk/programmes/boomjk5l. Dr Barnard explained: 'The crucial point is that the National Intelligence Service, from the very early eighties, believed there's only one way to find a solution to our country's future and that was to find a political settlement. And the only way to find a political settlement is to talk to the right people on the other side. And who is the right man on the other side? The right

man on the other side was Mr Nelson Mandela …We were certainly taking the lead in convincing PW Botha and his government that the only way to find a lasting settlement would be to find a negotiated settlement with the ANC.'

7   Waldmeir, *Anatomy of a miracle,* pp 185–7.

8   De Wet Potgieter, *Total Onslaught: Apartheid's dirty tricks exposed.* Cape Town: Zebra Press, 2007, pp 245 ff.

9   'The events in the Soviet Union and Eastern Europe […] weaken the capability of organisations which were previously supported strongly from those quarters.' FW de Klerk, Opening of second session of 9th parliament of Republic of South Africa, 2 February 1990. http://www.givengain.com/cgi-bin/giga. cgi?cmd=cause_dir_news_item&cause_id=2137&news_id=73749&cat_id=1595.

10 Quoted in T Lodge, *Mandela, a critical life.* Oxford: Oxford University Press, 2006, p 171.

11 Dr R Williams, 'The Impact of "Umkhonto We Sizwe" on the creation of the South African National Defence Force', *Journal of Security Sector Management,* vol 2, no 1, March 2007, p 17.

12 *Ibid,* p 18.

13 L Mashike, 'Age of despair: the unintegrated forces of South Africa', *African Affairs,* no 107, 2008.

14 SAPA, 28 July 2004. In October 2003, a year earlier, the Inkatha leader, Mangosuthu Buthelezi, explained that the weapons that had found their way to Inkatha had been destined for the Angolan rebel leader, Jonas Savimbi, but had been diverted to his movement in the dying days of the apartheid government.

15 Sanders, *Apartheid's friends,* p 342.

16 D O'Meara, *Volkskapitalisme: class, capital and ideology in the development of Afrikaner Nationalism, 1934–1948.* Cambridge: Cambridge University Press, 1983, pp 96 ff.

17 *Ibid,* p 182.

18 *Ibid,* p 250.

19 H van Vuuren, *Apartheid grand corruption.* Pretoria: Institute for Security Studies, May 2006, p 23.

20 *Ibid,* footnote 3, pp 265–6.

21 Moeletsi Mbeki, *Architects of poverty.* Johannesburg: Picador Africa, 2009, p 66.

22 *Ibid,* p 67.

23 *Time,* 29 February 1988.

24 *Sunday Times* (Johannesburg), 'Khumalo's running out of options', 21 March 2010. Interestingly, Khumalo's troubles began when no sooner had he won the bidding for JCI than the gold price started to crumble and, along with it, JCI's share price. Along came a major corporate crook, Brett Kebble, who ousted Khumalo with a fat severance deal but whose arrival scuppered any immediate hopes by Anglo of establishing its black-empowerment credentials.

25 Patrick Bond, *Elite Transition.* London: Pluto Press, 2000, pp 43 ff.

26 These findings were released by the Institute for Security Studies (ISS), which launched the 'Who owns what database', part of the institute's corruption and

governance programme. *Business Report*, 5 August 2011.

27 In 1995, the Gini coefficient (measuring inequality) stood at 0.64. By 2008 it had risen, indicating an increasing shift in wealth away from the poor, so that the index stood at 0.68. This won for South Africa the unenviable title of most unequal society in the world 'The battle against the predatory elite', Cosatu Central Executive Committee document, 8 September 2010.

28 Stephen Gelb, 'An overview of the South African economy', chapter 14, *The State of the Nation, 2004–2005*. Pretoria: HSRC, p 369.

29 Seekings, *UDF*, p 277.

30 *Ibid*, p 266.

31 See P Trewehla, *Inside Quatro: Uncovering the exile history of the ANC and Swapo*. Johannesburg: Jacana Media, 2009; and S Ellis and T Sechaba, *Comrades against apartheid: The ANC and the South African Communist Party in exile*. London: James Currey, 1992.

32 Seekings, *UDF*, p 321. This tradition continues to this day, with Cosatu far more open to democratic debate and discussion than the ANC.

33 From a sign hung in the headquarters of President Clinton's successful presidential campaign in 1992.

34 A Hirsch, *Season of hope*. Pietermaritzburg: University of KwaZulu-Natal Press, 2005. Chapter 2, 'From Kliptown to the RDP: The evolution of the ANC's economic policy', explains how this took place.

35 *Ibid*.

36 *Ibid*.

37 *Making democracy work: A framework for macroeconomic policy in South Africa*. A report of the Macro-economic Research Group of the Members of the Democratic Movement of South Africa. Cape Town: Centre for Development Studies, 1993. For a fuller discussion of these issues see JA van Wyk, *Cadres, Capitalists and Coalitions: The ANC, Business and Development in South Africa*, University of South Africa, Developmental Leadership Programme, Research Paper 01.

38 Naidoo, *Fighting for Justice*, p 215.

39 T Lodge, *The RDP: delivery and performance* in *politics in South Africa: from Mandela to Mbeki*. Cape Town: David Philip, 2003.

40 Naidoo, *Fighting for Justice*, p 227.

41 *Ibid*, p 251.

42 Thabo Mbeki, 'From resistance to reconstruction: tasks of the ANC in the new epoch of the democratic transformation – unmandated reflections', in Dale McKinley, 'Democracy, power and patronage: Debate and opposition within the ANC and the Tripartite Alliance since 1994', in R Southall (ed), *Opposition in South Africa's new democracy*, Seminar Papers, 28–30 June 2000, Kariega Game Reserve, Eastern Cape, p 68.

43 M Gevisser, *Thabo Mbeki: The dream deferred*. Johannesburg: Jonathan Ball, 2007, pp 663 ff.

44 *Ibid*, p 665.

45 *Ibid*, p 671.

46 Quoted in McKinley, 'Democracy, power and patronage', p 73.

47 Statement of the President of the African National Congress, Thabo Mbeki, at the 10th Congress of the SACP: 2 July 1998. http://www.sacp.org.za/main. php?include=10thcongress/thabospeech.html.

48 G Hannah, K O'Brien, A Rathmell, *Intelligence and security legislation for security sector reform*, June 2005, prepared for the United Kingdom's Security Sector Development Advisory Team, p 24.

49 B Gilder, 'To spy or not to spy?', p 47. 'And we had to do this in the face of specific obstacles that were incessantly thrown in our path: disgruntled apartheid-era intelligence officers who made it as difficult as possible for us to work; a burgeoning private security and intelligence industry that did its best to usurp us and spy on us; information peddlers who planted juicy but false information on us to divert us from the real issues; renegade officers who leaked (often false) information to the media; foreign intelligence services that sought energetically to infiltrate us and influence us to see the world as they saw it; and a public (and some in other arms of government) who saw intelligence in a post-apartheid and cold-war world either as an anachronism, or as an old-style repressive organ of state, the enemy of the people and of democracy.'

50 Gevisser, *Thabo Mbeki*, p 649.

51 W Gumede, *Thabo Mbeki and the Battle for the Soul of the ANC*, Zed Books, London, 2005, p. 379.

52 L Hutton, *Looking beneath the cloak: An analysis of intelligence governance in South Africa*. Pretoria: Institute for Security Studies, paper 154, November 2007, p 17.

53 *Noseweek*, Issue 37, November 2001.

54 For Mac Maharaj's view of Operation Vula see P O'Malley, *Shades of difference: Mac Maharaj and the struggle for South Africa*. London: Viking, 2007.

55 Thales is known in South Africa as Thompson. See Chapter 4 on the Arms Deal for details.

56 P Holden, *The Arms Deal in your pocket*. Johannesburg: Jonathan Ball, 2008, pp 180 ff.

57 RW Johnson, *South Africa's brave new world*. London: Allen Lane, 2009, p. 517. Johnson puts this decision down to the fact that Zuma is a Zulu and 'behaved as a Zulu man must', standing his ground and fighting.

58 Holden, *Arms Deal in your pocket*, p 118.

59 J Gordin, *Zuma, a biography*. Johannesburg: Jonathan Ball, 2008, p 90.

60 In October 2009, Zuma appointed Moe Shaik director general of the South African Secret Service.

61 Supreme Court of Appeal, Schabir Shaik and 4 Others v The State, Media Statement, 6 November 2006, http://www.justice.gov.za/sca/judgments/ sca_2006/2006_248.htm.

62 Constitutional Court of South Africa, Case CCT 86/06, [2008] ZACC 7, paragraph 80.

63 RW Johnson, *South Africa's brave new world,* p536.

64 RW Johnson, *South Africa's brave new world,* p 547.

65 *Ibid,* p 548.

66 SAPA, 9 May 2006.

67 *Special Report of the Joint Standing Committee on Intelligence (JSCI) on the Special 'Browse Mole' Consolidated Report document leaked to the public and investigated by Government Investigative Task Team, tabled in terms of section 6 (2) of Intelligence Services Oversight Act, Act 40 of 1994.* http://www.pmg.org.za/bill/20080226-brows-mole-report.

68 Gordin, *Zuma,* pp 210 ff.

69 *Ibid,* p 239.

70 *The Mercury,* 27 August 2008.

71 SAPA, 5 January 2008.

72 M Plaut, 'Threat to justice', *World Today,* Royal Institute International Affairs, October 2008.

73 *Business Day,* 3 September 2009.

74 *Times,* 24 April 2011. http://www.iol.co.za/news/politics/zille-wins-hlophe-battle-1.481159.

75 Freedom Under Law, Press release, 2 April 2012. http://www.freedomunderlaw.org/.

76 Confidential US dispatch, 25 July 2008 (Wikileaks).

77 Judgment in the High Court of South Africa, Natal Provincial Division, Case Number 8652\08, paragraph 170.

78 *Ibid,* paragraph 210.

79 Secret dispatch by US ambassador Eric Bost, based on a briefing from members of the Mbeki policy unit, 5 December 2008 (Wikileaks).

80 Statement by the acting National Director of Public Prosecutions, 6 April 2009. http://www.politicsweb.co.za/politicsweb/view/politicsweb/en/page71619?oid=124273&sn=Detail.

81 *Ibid.*

82 http://www.mg.co.za/article/2009-04-09-the-spy-who-saved-zuma.

83 http://www.mg.co.za/article/2009-05-01-browsed-and-beaten.

84 *Mail & Guardian,* 1 May 2009. http://www.mg.co.za/article/2009-05-01-a-closer-look.

Chapter 3 Political Hyenas and the Predatory State

1 *African Communist,* 1st quarter 2011, issue no 183, p 19.

2 His exact title is important. One of the objections to Manuel from the left is that he has titled himself Planning Minister, something they insist he is not. See Cosatu's submission to Parliament, 16 October 2009. http://www.cosatu.org.za/show.php?include=docs/subs/2009/submission1016.html&ID=2518&cat=Policy.

3 'Many months before the ANCYL president began publicly to campaign on this ticket, forces closely linked to the ANC had quietly begun to lobby for government

to nationalise the platinum sector. It was for this reason that, in December, and in response to the ANCYL, the SACP, while supporting the principle of nationalisation, warned that in the current conjuncture it could simply be a ploy to bail-out indebted BEE interests, diverting billions of rands of public funds to serve the interests of a narrow black (and white) capitalist stratum.' *African Communist*, issue 181, September 2010, p 74.

4 *Ibid*, p 75.

5 http://www.sacp.org.za/main.php?include=pubs/umsebenzi/2006/no57.html.

6 Political Report of the Central Committee to the Special National Congress, 10 December 2009, pp 13–14. www.sacp.org.za/docs/conf/2009/politicalreport.pdf.

7 Statement of the Cosatu Central Executive Committee, 23–25 August 2010.

8 Author's interview.

9 http://www.info.gov.za/speeches/2009/09090414151003.htm.

10 Beeld, 24 September 2009.

11 Cosatu 10th National Congress – Declaration, 21-24 September 2009. http://www.cosatu.org.za/show.php?include=docs/declarations/2009/declo925.html&ID=2440&cat=COSATU%20Today.

12 *Mail & Guardian*, 9 October 2009.

13 *Mail & Guardian*, 10 October 2009.

14 Statement of the Young Communist League of SA on Billy Masetlha, 11 October 2009.

15 Numsa statement on comments by Billy Masetlha, 9 October 2009. http://www.politicsweb.co.za/politicsweb/view/politicsweb/en/page71654?oid=146241&sn=Detail.

16 Address by the African National Congress President, at the second annual Raymond Mhlaba Memorial lecture, Port Elizabeth 12 October 2009. http://www.polity.org.za/article/anc-zuma-adress-by-african-national-congress-president-at-the-second-annual-raymond-mhlaba-memorial-lectures-port-elizabeth-12102009-2009-10-12.

17 http://www.anc.org.za/show.php?doc=ancdocs/pr/2009/pr1013a.html.

18 ANC National Executive Committee bulletin, January 2010. http://www.politicsweb.co.za/politicsweb/view/politicsweb/en/page71654?oid=158069&sn=Detail.

19 Blade Nzimande, Together, let's defeat capitalist greed and corruption! Together, build socialism now! Political Report of the Central Committee to the Special National Congress, 10 December 2009. http://www.sacp.org.za/main.php?include=docs/conf/2009/conf1210b.html.

20 http://www.timeslive.co.za/sundaytimes/article264348.ece/Malemas-war-on-Mantashe.

21 Confidential despatch by Ambassador Donald Gips, 30 December 2009 (Wikileaks).

22 Cronin is the Deputy General Secretary of the SA Communist Party and Deputy Minister of Transport.

23 http://www.sacp.org.za/main.php?include=pubs/umsebenzi/2009/vol8–20.html.

24 http://www.mg.co.za/printformat/single/
    2009-11-21-malema-cronin-scrap-over-mine-nationalisation.

25 Political report of the Central Committee to the Special National Congress,
    December 2009. www.sacp.org.za/docs/conf/2009/politicalreport.pdf.

26 Gwede Mantashe, Opening address by SACP Chairperson, Cde Gwede Mantashe,
    to the SACP Special National Congress, 10 December 2009. http://www.sacp.org.
    za/main.php?include=docs/sp/2009/sp1210a.html.

27 *City Press*, 10 December 2009.

28 *Ibid.*

29 http://www.mg.co.za/article/2009-12-11-young-communists-flay-drama-queen-
    malema.

30 *The Star*, 12 December 2009. http://www.iol.co.za/news/politics/
    anc-on-red-alert-1.467545.

31 http://www.mg.co.za/article/2009-12-14-ancyl-in-a-froth-over-malema-booing.

32 *Ibid.*

33 'The President of the ANC [Jacob Zuma] in summarising indicated that mistakes
    have been made on both sides,' the parties said in a joint statement following
    a bilateral meeting aimed at resolving differences caused by the incident. Both
    parties agreed that there would be 'no further personalised public attacks on
    each other'. The Communist Party – in the context of the discussions – 're-
    affirmed its regret' that the booing took place at its special congress in December.
    ANC secretary-general Gwede Mantashe said parties conceded that: 'Too many
    statements were issued against each other on both sides and that was a mistake.'
    SAPA, 11 March 2010.

34 *Times* (Johannesburg), 17 January 2010.

35 Cosatu CEC political discussion paper, September 2010. http://www.cosatu.org.za/
    list.php?type=Discussion.

36 *Ibid.* 'A key reason behind this paralysis, as we have said above, is that the
    predatory elite has subjected the leadership to so much beating, and blackmail
    tactics. It was hardly a year into their term when the predatory elite started making
    statements that some in particular the Secretary General and now increasingly the
    President will be replaced.'

37 *Daily Dispatch*, 22 August 2010.

38 *Mail & Guardian*, 28 August 2010. http://www.mg.co.za/
    article/2010-08-28-malema-warns-anc-leadership.

39 National General Council, 2010: Political report of the President of the ANC Jacob
    Zuma. http://www.anc.org.za/5921.

40 *Business Day*, 29 September 2010. http://www.businessday.co.za/articles/Content.
    aspx?id=122232.

41 Department of Labour, Annual Report, 2010.

42 *Ibid,* table 1.1.

43 Webster, 'The Alliance under stress', pp 261–2.

44 *Consolidating working class power for quality jobs – towards 2015: Programme
    arising from the COSATU 8th National Congress,* 9 October 2003. http://www.

cosatu.org.za/show.php?include=docs/policy/2003/2015plan.html.

45 Gumede, *Thabo Mbeki and the battle for the soul of the ANC*, p 340.

46 Cosatu CEC political discussion paper, September 2010, 'The Alliance at a crossroads – the battle against a predatory elite and political paralysis'. www.cosatu.org.za/docs/discussion/2010/dis0903.pdf.

47 *Ibid*, scenario 4, p 30.

48 D Pillay, 'Cosatu workers political attitudes in South Africa', in S Buhlungu (ed), *Trade unions and democracy*. Pretoria: HSRC, 2006, p 178.

49 SACP Central Committee discussion document, 'Class, national and gender struggle in South Africa: The historical relationship between the ANC and the SACP', *Bua Komanisi*, vol 5, no 1, May 2006. http://www.sacp.org.za/main. php?include=docs/docs/2006/central.html#2.

50 *Ibid*.

51 'Speech delivered in the Civil Society Conference – by the Cosatu President – Sidumo Dlamini, 28 October 2010'. http://www.cosatu.org.za/show.php?ID=4171. Dlamini concluded that corruption had to be fought, issuing this ringing declaration: 'Our struggle was not about converting our organisations into weapons to pave a way for better and juicy tenders! Our struggle was not about creating better chances for friends and closer circles to secure huge business deals!'

52 'Keynote address to the Civil Society Conference by Zwelinzima Vavi, General Secretary of Cosatu, 27 October 2010, Boksburg'. http://www.cosatu.org.za/show. php?ID=4170.

53 http://www.politicsweb.co.za/politicsweb/view/politicsweb/en/page71654?oid=2089 32&sn=Detail&pid=71616.

54 Cosatu's response to ANC statement, 2 November 2010. http://www.cosatu.org.za/ show.php?ID=4195.

55 The results are dealt with in more detail in Chapter 9.

56 SAPA, 24 May 2011.

57 SAPA, 27 May 2011.

58 http://www.timeslive.co.za/local/article1079140.ece/Cosatu-saves-the-day.

59 SAPA 19 September 2011.

60 *The Star*, 21 September 2011. http://www.iol.co.za/the-star/ anc-imploding-1.1141768.

61 ANC 52 National Conference, December 2007. http://www.anc.org.za/show. php?id=2539.

62 *Ibid*, para 59.

63 *Ibid*, para 63.

64 *Ibid*, para 236.

65 A Harber, *Diepsloot*. Johannesburg: Jonathan Ball, 2011.

66 *Ibid*, p 90.

67 *Ibid*, p 88.

68 *Ibid*, p 92.

69 *Ibid*, p 88.

70 *Ibid*, p 89.

71 'Zuma plot: Conspiracy stuck on repeat'. http://mg.co.za/
   article/2011-04-15-conspiracy-stuck-on-repeat.

72 'Tokyo tsunami, 2.0'. http://www.thedailymaverick.co.za/
   article/2011-04-11-analysis-tokyo-tsunami-20.

73 Also convicted by the party were his closest associates, including ANCYL
   deputy president Ronald Lamola, treasurer general Pule Mabe, secretary general
   Sindiso Magaqa and deputy secretary general Kenetswe Mosenogi. ANC *Public*
   announcement of the ANC National Disciplinary Committee hearings of
   Comrades Julius Malema, Ronald Lamola, Pule Mabe, Sindiso Magaqa Kenetswe
   Mosenogi and Floyd Shivambu, 10 November 2011, Chief Albert Luthuli House,
   Johannesburg. http://www.anc.org.za/show.php?id=9133.

74 Malema appears to have only limited support, even among young South Africans,
   with a poll indicating that 70 per cent believe his suspension was justified. SAPA,
   11 November 2011.

75 http://www.youtube.com/watch?v=pIiRsFYsRcg.

76 SE presents findings on black ownership on the JSE, 2 September, 2010. http://
   www.jse.co.za/about-us/media/press-releases/full-story/10-09-02/JSE_Presents_
   Findings_on_Black_Ownership_on_the_JSE.aspx.

77 http://www.politicsweb.co.za/politicsweb/view/politicsweb/en/page71654?oid=2383
   69&sn=Detail&pid=71616.

78 Martin Plaut, 'The workers' struggle', p 308.

79 Hein Marais, *South Africa pushed to the limit*. London: Zed Press, 2011, p 455.

80 'The alliance, Cosatu and the Constitution', *Daily Maverick*,
   13 December 2011. http://dailymaverick.co.za/
   article/2011-12-13-the-alliance-cosatu-and-the-constitution.

81 http://www.timeslive.co.za/opinion/commentary/2011/12/11/
   the-big-read-rock-of-south-africa.

Chapter 4   The Arms Deal and the Erosion of Parliamentary Power

1 This chapter draws on research that was conducted during the writing of
   P Holden and H van Vuuren, *The devil in the detail: How the Arms Deal changed*
   everything. Johannesburg: Jonathan Ball, 2011. The research was funded by the
   Institute for Security Studies, Cape Town.

2 See L Nathan, *The changing of the guard: Armed forces and defence policy in a*
   democratic South Africa, Johannesburg: HSRC Publishers, 1994, p 45.

3 RC Simpson-Anderson, 'The changing role of the South African Navy', *South*
   African Defence Review, no 10, 1993.

4 'Navy fires first salvo in push to keep afloat', *Sunday Times*, 8 May 1994.

5 See H Macmillan, '"The Hani Memorandum" – Introduced and annotated', in
   Transformation, no 69, 2009; S Ellis, 'Mbokodo: Security in the ANC camps,
   1961–1990', in *African Affairs,* vol 93, no 371, 1994.

6 *Ibid,* and *Report of the Motsuenyane Commission on the Treatment of ANC*

Prisoners, 23 August 1993, South African History Archives, AL2516 (ANC Commission of Enquiry Collection).

7 'Navy fires first salvo in push to keep afloat', *Sunday Times*, 8 May 1994.

8 J Modise, Speech in debate on vote no 7 – Defence (Appropriations Bill), 10 August in *Debates of the National Assembly (Hansard)*, Government Printers, 1994, col 1160–70.

9 'Guns vs. butter?', *Weekend Argus*, 26 February 1995.

10 See *Sowetan*, 21 April 1995; and 'A greater priority than new ships', *Cape Times*, 28 March 1995.

11 'Bengu pledge on national loan scheme', *Business Day*, 23 February 1995; and 'Students march to seek funding for education', *The Argus*, 23 February 1995.

12 J Slovo, Speech in debate on vote no 7 – Defence (Appropriations Bill), 4 August in *Debates of the National Assembly (Hansard)*, Government Printer, 1994, col 803–806.

13 M Sisulu, Speech in debate on vote no 7 – Defence (Appropriations Bill), 3 August in *Debates of the National Assembly (Hansard)*, Government Printer, 1994, col 745–746.

14 *South African Defence Review*, 1998, chapter 8, para 14- 39. Available for download from www.dod.mil.ac.za.

15 *Ibid.*

16 'Why Mbeki went for the Arms Deal', *Sunday Independent*, 10 August 2008.

17 According to information accessed via the Companies and Intellectual Property Rights Database.

18 *Ibid.*

19 'Modise linked to used MiG dealer', *Mail & Guardian*, 15 January 2001.

20 'Modise's greasy brotherhood', *Mail & Guardian*, 27 May 2002.

21 'Modise was bought', *Noseweek*, December 2003, issue 52; 'Three foresightful architects', *Citizen*, 16 December 2003; and 'The musketeers who bought the jets', *Mail & Guardian*, 2 February 2007.

22 'Arms and empowerment: cadres cash in', *Financial Mail*, 4 May 2001.

23 'German firm in R1.2m lobby agreement', *Mail & Guardian*, 12 April 2001.

24 'A deal that just won't go away', *TradersAfrica*, issue 7, July-October 2001.

25 H Squires, Judgment in the High Court of South Africa (Durban and Coastal Local Division) in the Matter Between The State and Schabir Shaik *et al.*, Case no. CC27/04, 31 March 2005. Available for download from www.saflii.org.za.

26 *Ibid.*

27 L Engelbrecht, 'South Africa's multi-billion arms programme revisited (part one)', The Arms Deal Virtual Press Office, 15 October 2001. http://www.armsdeal-vpo.co.za/articles03/revisited_one.html.

28 'BAe and the arms deal: Part 1', *Moneyweb*, 14 August 2007. www.moneyweb.co.za.

29 *Ibid.*

30 *Ibid.*

31 *Ibid.*

32 The Joint Investigating Report notes that in a workshop prior to the three-tier system being decided on, it was reported that 'the 2-tier system was not acceptable to the Minister of Defence'. See: *Strategic Defence Packages: Joint Report*, 2001, chapter 4, paragraph 4.3.1.4. www.info.gov.za.

33 'BAe and the arms deal: Part 1', *Moneyweb*, 14 August 2007. www.moneyweb. co.za.

34 *Strategic Defence Packages: Joint Report*, 2001, chapter 4, paragraph 4.3.6.3. Available at: www.info.gov.za.

35 P Holden and H van Vuuren, *The devil in the detail: How the Arms Deal changed everything*. Johannesburg: Jonathan Ball, 2011. See in particular Chapter 4.

36 *Strategic Defence Packages: Joint Report*, 2001, chapter 4, paragraph 4.5.1.10. Available at: www.info.gov.za.

37 *Ibid.*

38 'Pierre Steyn speaks out about the arms deal', *Mail & Guardian*, 2 February 2007.

39 'Strategic Defence Packages: Draft Report of the Auditor-General', chapter 7 – Selection of Prime Contractors: Submarines, undated, R Young/ C2I2 Personal Archive (PAIA Requests). Used with kind permission of Richard Young.

40 *Ibid.*

41 *Ibid.*

42 'MK boss was bought', *Noseweek* no 52, December 2003. See also P Kirk, 'Three foresightful architects', *Citizen*, 16 December 2003; and E Groenink and S Sole, 'The musketeers who bought the jets', *Mail & Guardian*, 2 February 2007.

43 'BAE denies it paid for Modise's cars', SAPA, 7 March 2003.

44 South African Government Information Service, 'National Industrial Participation (NIP) Defence Summary: Project Description', September 1999. http://www.info. gov.za/issues/procurement/background/nip.htm.

45 'Soldiering ahead in business', *Saturday Star*, 6 November 1999.

46 Feinstein, *After the Party*, pp 177–8.

47 G Murphy, British Serious Fraud Office, Affidavit submitted as Annexure JDP-SW12 in the High Court of South Africa (Transvaal Provincial Division) in the matter of *Ex Parte* the National Director of Public Prosecutions (applicant) re: an application for issue of search warrants in terms of Section 29(5) and 29(6) of the National Prosecuting Authority Act, No. 32 of 1998, as amended (2008).

48 *Ibid.*

49 'Treasury designates Mugabe regime cronies', statement issued by US Treasury, 25 November 2008. www.politicsweb.co.za.

50 www.johnbredenkamp.co.za.

51 G Murphy, British Serious Fraud Office, Affidavit submitted as Annexure JDP-SW12 in the High Court of South Africa (Transvaal Provincial Division) in the matter of *Ex Parte* the National Director of Public Prosecutions (applicant) re: an application for issue of search warrants in terms of Section 29(5) and 29(6) of the National Prosecuting Authority Act, no 32 of 1998, as amended (2008).

52 'Saab admits secret arms-deal payments', *Mail & Guardian*, 17 June 2011 and www.saab.com.

53 S Brümmer and S Sole, 'The house the arms deal bought', *Mail & Guardian*, 3 December 2010.

54 *Ibid.*
55 *Ibid.*
56 'The corvettes, the R130m "expenses" and Thabo Mbeki', *Sunday Times*, 16 July 2006.
57 *Ibid.*
58 'Excellent connections', *Der Spiegel*, 3 July 2006.
59 'On German kickbacks and the corvette contract', Politicsweb, 7 April 2008. Available at: www.politicsweb.co.za.
60 'Mbeki, Chippy and the Greek lobbyist', *Mail & Guardian*, 9 February 2007.
61 *Ibid.*
62 Feinstein, *After the Party*, p 226.
63 *Ibid.*
64 *Ibid.*
65 H Squires, Judgment in the High Court of South Africa (Durban and Coastal Local Division) in the Matter Between The State and Schabir Shaik *et al.*, Case no. CC27/04, 31 March 2005. Available for download from www.saflii.org.za.
66 *Ibid.*
67 *Ibid.*
68 In the High Court of South Africa (Durban Coastal and Local Division) in the Matter between the State and Schabir Shaik and Others: Summary of Substantial Facts in terms of Section 144(3)(a) of Act 51 of 1977. Available at: www.armsdeal-vpo.co.za.
69 H Squires, Judgment in the High Court of South Africa (Durban and Coastal Local Division) in the Matter Between The State and Schabir Shaik et al., Case no. CC27/04, 31 March 2005. Available for download from www.saflii.org.za.
70 *Ibid.*
71 'German firm in R1.2m lobby agreement', *Mail & Guardian*, 12 April 2001.
72 H Squires, Judgment in the High Court of South Africa (Durban and Coastal Local Division) in the Matter Between The State and Schabir Shaik *et al.*, Case no. CC27/04, 31 March 2005. Available for download from www.saflii.org.za.
73 *Ibid.*
74 *Ibid.*
75 'The R30m bombshell that points fingers at both Mbeki and his former Deputy: Special Investigation', *Sunday Times*, 3 August 2008.
76 *Ibid.*
77 'The spy who fingered Mbeki', *Mail & Guardian*, 8 August 2008.
78 Feinstein, *After the Party*, p 276.
79 'Presidency's guns fire at Sunday Times', *Mail & Guardian*/SAPA, 3 August 2008, and 'Arms dealer requests correction', *Cape Times*, 10 August 2008.
80 'Deputy President tried to keep arms investigation away from Heath's unit', *Cape Times*, 27 August 2003.
81 *Ibid.*
82 'Executive had power to influence arms probe', *Mail & Guardian*, 30 November 2001.
83 *Ibid.*

84 *Ibid.*

85 'Mbeki thought to have used apartheid legislation to vet investigator's report', *Mail & Guardian*, 16 November 2001.

86 'Executive had power to influence arms probe', *Mail & Guardian*, 30 November 2001.

87 'Arms deal participant fired', *Business Day*, 30 May 2002.

88 *Special Review by the Auditor-General of the Selection Process of Strategic Defence Packages for the Acquisition of Armaments at the Department of Defence*, RP161/2000, 15 September 2000, para 3.2. Available at: www.armsdeal-vpo.co.za.

89 'Heath, OSEO probing R30-b arms deal', *IOL*, 7 February 2000.

90 Baqwa launches arms deal investigation', *IOL*, 29 September 2000.

91 Feinstein, *After the Party*, p 161.

92 *Ibid*, p 165.

93 *Strategic Defence Packages: Joint Report*, Chapter 10, paragraph 10.5.4, 2001. Available at: www.info.gov.za.

94 Standing Committee on Public Accounts: *Special Review of Strategic Arms Purchases – SANDF, 30 October 2000*. Available at: www.pmg.org.za.

95 'Summary of background information on the Strategic Defence Procurement Package', issued on behalf of the Government of South Africa by the Ministers of Defence, Finance, Public Enterprises and Trade and Industry, Government Communication Information Systems, 12 January 2001. Available at: www.info.gov.za.

96 Letter from Thabo Mbeki to Judge Willem Heath, 19 January 2001. www.info.gov.za.

97 'Mbeki organogram mystery solved', *News24*, 22 January 2001.

98 'Public broadcast on the issue of the strategic defence acquisition programme', Government Communication and Information Service, 19 January 2001. www.info.gov.za.

99 Feinstein, *After the Party*, pp 176–7.

100 *Ibid.*

101 'ANC cracks whip in watchdog committee', *Sunday Independent*, 3 February 2001.

102 'Scopa "too busy" for arms probe', *News24*, 12 June 2001.

103 See *Strategic Defence Packages: Joint Report*, chapter 10, para 10.5.4, 2001. www.info.gov.za.

104 *Strategic Defence Packages: Joint Report*, chapter 14, para 14.1.25. www.info.gov.za.

105 *Ibid*, para 14.1.1.

106 T Mbeki, 'Truth stands in the way of arms deal accusers', *ANC Today*, 16 November 2001. www.anc.org.za.

107 Memo dated 3 October 2001, Subject: Printing and releasing the draft joint report, R Young Personal Archive/PAIA Requests. Used with the kind permission of Dr Richard Young.

108 Letter from Shauket Fakie to Thabo Mbeki, 4 October 2001, R Young Personal Archive/PAIA Requests. Used with the kind permission of Dr Richard Young.

109 'Directorate of Special Operations: Report on the Investigation into the Strategic Defence Packages of the South African National Defence Force', Draft Report (Part C), undated, R Young Personal Archive/PAIA Requests, used with the kind permission of Dr Richard Young.

110 'This is a story about a 4x4, one of the most powerful men in Parliament and how they got bogged down in the R43bn arms deal controversy', *Sunday Times*, 25 March 2001.

111 'In the Matter between The State and Tony Sithembiso Yengeni (Accused no 1) and Michael Joseph Worfel (Accused no 2), Accused no1's Plea of Guilty', Case no 14/09193/01, 2003. www.armsdeal-vpo.co.za.

112 'Yengeni has "72 hours to report to Pollsmoor"', IOL/SAPA, 21 August 2006.

113 'Shaik walks free', *Cape Times*, 3 March 2009.

114 'Shaik accused of assaulting journo', *SAPA/News24*, 27 February 2011.

115 'Action against Schabir Shaik welcomed', *Mail & Guardian*, 14 March 2011.

116 'Shaik gets R5m in "secret deal" with the State', *Cape Times*, 22 January 2009.

117 *Ibid.*

118 *Ibid.*

119 'Arms Deal probe "cancelled"', *Citizen*, 11 October 2010, and 'Arms Deal probe (2000–2010)', *Mail & Guardian*, 15 October 2010.

120 *Ibid.*

121 *Ibid.*

122 '2008 Estimates of National Expenditure, Vote 19: Defence', p 379. www.treasury. gov.za. Also see Holden, *Arms Deal in your pocket*, pp 26–7.

123 'Strategic Defence Packages: Joint Report', 2001. www.info.gov.za. See Chapter 9: Cost to the State and, in particular, para 9.3.1.

124 Author's calculation.

125 *Ibid.*

126 'High Court sets aside Public Protector's Oilgate report', SAPA/*Politicsweb*, 30 July 2009.

Chapter 5 Smoke, Mirrors, Emails and Tapes: The Uses and Abuses of Intelligence

1 This chapter draws on research that was conducted during the writing of P Holden and H van Vuuren, *The devil in the detail: How the Arms Deal changed everything*. Johannesburg: Jonathan Ball, 2011. The research was funded by the Institute for Security Studies, Cape Town.

2 Hutton, *Looking beneath the cloak: An analysis of intelligence governance in South Africa*, Institute for Security Studies Paper no 154. www.issafrica.org

3 See P Holden & L Segal, *Great Lives: Pivotal Moments*, Jacana: Johannesburg, 2008.

4 'Going to Goch Street', *Sunday Times* Heritage Project. www.thetimes.co.za.

5 Submission to the Truth and Reconciliation Commission by General Magnus

Malan, http://www.justice.gov.za/trc/hrvtrans/submit/malan.htm.

6 'Malan admits to setting up CCB, ordering raids', SAPA, 7 May 1997.

7 See: *Final Report of the Truth and Reconciliation Commission,* vol 2, para 377–418. www.justice.gov.za.

8 *Ibid.*

9 *Ibid.*

10 *Ibid.*

11 See *Report of the Motsuenyane Commission on the Treatment of ANC Prisoners,* 23 August 1993, South African History Archives, AL2516 (ANC Commission of Inquiry Collection).

12 See Shubin, *ANC: A View from Moscow.* Johannesburg: Jacana, p 67; and H Macmillan, 'The "Hani Memorandum" – introduced and annotated', in *Transformation,* no 69, 2009.

13 Macmillan, 'The "Hani Memorandum"', pp 111–12.

14 *Ibid.*

15 *Report of the Motsuenyane Commission on the Treatment of ANC Prisoners.*

16 *Ibid.*

17 *Ibid.*

18 *Ibid,* p 25.

19 J Sanders, *Apartheid's friends: The rise and fall of South Africa's secret service.* London: John Murray, 2006, p 293.

20 *Report of the Motsuenyane Commission on the Treatment of ANC Prisoners,* p 26.

21 See B Ketele, B Maxongo, Z Tshona, R Masango and L Mbengo (1990), 'A miscarriage of democracy', in P Trewhela (ed), *Inside Quatro.* Johannesburg: Jacana, 2009; S Ellis, 'Mbokodo: Security in the ANC Camps, 1961 – 1990', *African Affairs,* vol 93, no 371, April 1994, p 288; S Ellis and T Sechaba, *Comrades against apartheid. London: James Currey,* 1991.

22 H Marais, *South Africa: Limits to change.* Cape Town: UCT Press and London: Zed Books, 2001, p 63.

23 *Report of the Motsuenyane Commission on the Treatment of ANC Prisoners,* p 47.

24 See Ketele *et al.,* 'A miscarriage of democracy'; Ellis, 'Mbokodo: Security in the ANC Camps, 1961-1990', p 288; Ellis and Sechaba, *Comrades against apartheid.*

25 *Report of the Motsuenyane Commission on the Treatment of ANC Prisoners.*

26 See C Braam, *Operation Vula.* Johannesburg: Jacana, 2004; R Kasrils, *Armed and dangerous.* London: Heinemann, 1993; and T Jenkin, 'Talking to Vula', *Mayibuye,* May 1995–October 1995.

27 H Barrell, 'Conscripts to their age: African National Congress operational strategy, 1976-1986', DPhil Thesis, University of Oxford, 1993, postscript.

28 *Ibid.*

29 J Gordin, 'The Zuma alumni', *Politicsweb,* 12 June 2009. www.politicsweb.co.za.

30 Sanders, *Apartheid's Friends,* pp 299-300.

31 *Constitution of the Republic of South Africa,* 1996, chapter 11, para 199 (7).

32 'ANC cracks down on Mbeki rivals', *Sunday Times*, 22 April 2001.

33 'Tshwete allegations draw fire', *Business Day*, 26 April 2001, and 'The plot thickens', *Daily News*, 25 April 2001.

34 'Smoking them out', *Witness*, 28 April 2001.

35 'Tshwete allegations draw fire', *Business Day*, 26 April 2001.

36 'SA leader fights a fraying image', *New York Times*, 28 April 2001.

37 Gevisser, *Thabo Mbeki*, p 649.

38 'Attempts to destabilize the ANC', Statement by Deputy President Jacob Zuma, 3 April 2001. www.anc.org.

39 ZT Ngcakani, *Executive summary of the final report of an investigation into the operations carried out by Mr S Macozoma; Extended terms of reference report on the authenticity of the allegedly intercepted emails*, Office of the Inspector-General for Intelligence, 23 March 2006, p 13.

40 *Ibid.*

41 *Ibid.*

42 'South Africa: spies bugged opposition, Goniwe, Ramaphosa', *Sunday Independent*, 27 March 2006.

43 ZT Ngcakani, *Executive summary of the final report of an investigation into the operations carried out by Mr S Macozoma*, p 15.

44 *Ibid*, pp 19-20.

45 *Ibid.*

46 *Ibid,* part 3, pp 24–40.

47 *Ibid.*

48 *Ibid,* and 'Masetlha charged with fraud', SAPA/IOL, 11 December 2006.

49 'Kunene gets life for murder of estate agent', *Mail & Guardian*, 29 May 2009.

50 '"My dad shot me"', *Pretoria News*, 8 March 2011.

51 'State slams Masetlha's "sci-fi" story', *Pretoria News*, 12 November 2007.

52 'Hoax email case falls apart', *Mail & Guardian*, 6 March 2008, and 'Hoax email shocker', *Citizen*, 12 June 2008.

53 'Questions revived about email hoax', IOL, 23 August 2006.

54 'What the ANC hoax email report says', *Mail & Guardian*, 11 November 2008.

55 'Hoax email case falls apart', *Mail & Guardian*, 6 March 2008, and 'Hoax email shocker', *Citizen*, 12 June 2008.

56 *Ibid.*

57 'Special Browse "Mole" Consolidated Report', 7 December 2006, p 1.

58 *Ibid*, pp 6-7.

59 *Ibid.*

60 *Ibid.*

61 *Ibid*, p 9.

62 *Ibid*, pp 11-12.

63 *Ibid*, p 13.

64 I Powell, 'Smoke and mirrors', *Mail & Guardian*, 1 May 2009.

65 *Special Report of the Joint Standing Committee on Intelligence on the Special 'Browse' Mole Consolidated Report*, 27 November 2007. Available from www.pmg.org.za.

66 *Ibid*, pp 3-4.

67 'Inside the Browse "Mole" Row', *Mail & Guardian*, 3 August 2007.

68 *Ibid.*

69 *Ibid.*

70 Special Report of the Joint Standing Committee on Intelligence on the Special 'Browse' Mole Consolidated Report, 27 November 2007.

71 Powell, 'Smoke and mirrors'.

72 See *In the High Court of South Africa (Durban and Coastal Local Division) in the Matter between the State and Schabir Shaik and Others: Indictment.* www. armsdeal-vpo.co.za.

73 'Press statement by Bulelani Thandabantu Ngcuka, National Director of Public Prosecutions on the decision on whether to prosecute after the completion of the investigation against Deputy President, Mr Jacob Zuma, Schabir Shaik and others', 23 August 2003. www.armsdeal-vpo.co.za.

74 'Was Ngcuka a spy?', *City Press*, 6 September 2003.

75 *Ibid.*

76 'Spy claim just a sign of desperation', *The Star*, 12 September 2003.

77 'Mo: I went public for Zuma', *The Star*, 21 November 2003.

78 See Gevisser, *Thabo Mbeki*, pp 399-401.

79 '"I am Agent RS452"', *The Star*, 21 October 2003.

80 *Ibid.*

81 'The truth should make Ngcuka's accusers hang heads in shame', *Business Day*, 23 October 2003.

82 'Ngcuka a spy? Impossible, says Maqhubela', *Daily News*, 22 October 2003.

83 *Ibid.*

84 'Ngcuka cleared on spy charges', *Cape Times*, 20 January 2004.

85 'Statement by the National Director of Public Prosecutions on the Matter of S v Zuma and Others', 6 April 2009. www.mg.co.za.

86 *Ibid.*

87 *Ibid.*

88 'Zuma spy tapes: will anyone be prosecuted?', 9 November 2009, www.constitutionallyspeaking.co.za.

89 *Ibid.*

90 'The spy who saved Zuma', *Mail & Guardian*, 9 April 2009.

91 'Spy tapes: "Selebi Saved Zuma"', *City Press*, 23 January 2011.

92 'Zuma spy tapes not on the agenda', Timeslive, 1 February 2010.

93 'DA seeks access to spy-tapes report', *Mail & Guardian*, 24 January 2011.

94 'Mpshe "sloppy and undisciplined" – Seagroatt', www.politicsweb.co.za, 30 April 2009. See also: 'Mpshe's big Fong Kong', *Mail & Guardian*, 17 April 2009.

95 *Ibid.*

96 *Ibid.*

97 The Nicholson judgment has been much misunderstood. The central legal issue was the matter of whether the case should proceed against Jacob Zuma, based on an interpretation of whether or not Zuma should have been invited to make

representations to the National Director of Prosecutions, if a decision was made to embark on a prosecution that flowed from an earlier decision not to prosecute. This, in turn, was based on the contested claim that if a NDPP 'reviewed' an early decision not to prosecute in order to pursue a prosecution, representations from the accused should be invited. Nicholson, remarkably, found that the decision to prosecute Jacob Zuma reached by Mpshe in 2007 was a 'review' of a decision not to prosecute on the part of Bulelani Ngcuka in 2003. This despite the fact, as confirmed by the Supreme Court, that the charges brought by Mpshe were substantively new and involved considerable amounts of new evidence. The Supreme Court found that Mpshe's 2007 decision was not a review of Ngcuka's decision at all, meaning that Zuma could not contest his prosecution on this fine legal point: 'In addition, as held by the Constitutional Court, as soon as the matter had been struck from the roll by Msimang, J., the criminal proceedings were terminated and the proceedings were no longer pending. Removal of a matter from the roll aborts the trial proceedings. The effect of this is that what went before the Mpshe decision was spent and a new decision to prosecute was required. The Mpshe decision was not simply a review of the Ngcuka decision, which was no longer extant. On these facts, s179(5)(d) had, irrespective of whichever interpretation is correct, no application, and Mr. Zuma's reliance on it was misplaced.' *National Director of Public Prosecutions v. Zuma* (573/08) [2009] ZASCA (12 Jan 2009), para 75.

The findings regarding political interference were delivered in response to a request on the part of the NPA to have them struck from Zuma's affidavits as 'scandalous' and 'vexatious'. Notably, the Supreme Court of Appeal found that Nicholson, in reaching his judgment in this regard, had pronounced on facts and issues not before him, additionally admitting evidence that was hearsay. In one stinging paragraph, the Supreme Court of Appeal criticised Nicholson for delivering a judgment 'by ambush' by relying on accusations not made in any of the founding affidavits before him. In fact, the Supreme Court of Appeal argued, in relation to Zuma's political manipulation claims, that 'most of the allegations were not only irrelevant but they were gratuitous and based on suspicion and not fact ... There may well be a reason to hold that many of the allegations were vexatious and scandalous ...' *Ibid*, para 81.

98 *Ibid*, para 13.

99 *Ibid*, para 37.

100 'Statement by the National Director of Public Prosecutions on the Matter of S v Zuma and Others', 6 April 2009, available from www.mg.co.za.

101 H Squires, 'Judgment in the Matter between the State and Schabir Shaik *et al*.' Case No. CC27/04, 31 May 2005. Available at: www.armsdeal-vpo.co.za.

102 *Ibid*.

103 'Jacob Gedleyihlekisa Zuma: An extraordinary life', 5 May 2009. Now available for download from www.politicsweb.co.za.

104 Squires, 'Judgment in the Matter between the State and Schabir Shaik *et al*.' Case No. CC27/04, 31 May 2005. Available at: www.armsdeal-vpo.co.za.

105 Gordin, 'The Zuma alumni', *Politicsweb*, 12 June 2009, www.politicsweb.co.za.
106 'Moe Shaik's appointment angers opposition parties', *Mail & Guardian*, 3 October 2009.
107 *Ibid.*
108 'Mo Shaik threatened to expose Zuma foes', *Pretoria News*, 24 January 2011, and 'Cable from the US Embassy Pretoria to Washington DC, 10 September 2008. www.politicsweb.co.za.
109 'Mdluli granted bail of R20 000', *Mail & Guardian*, 21 April 2011, and 'Mdluli, co-accused granted bail', SAPA, 20 April 2011.
110 *Ibid.*
111 'Zuma plot fallout continues', *Mail & Guardian*, 6 May 2011.
112 'The game is on', *The Witness*, 16 April 2011.
113 'Sexwale vows to set his lawyer on "coup plot" peddlars', *Mail & Guardian*, 5 May 2011.
114 'Zuma plot fallout continues', *Mail & Guardian*, 6 May 2011.
115 'What the ANC said about the Zuma plot', *Mail & Guardian*, 3 June 2011.
116 'Charges to be dropped, no trial for Mdluli', *News24*, 22 February 2012, and 'Crime boss Mdluli's charges withdrawn', *News24*, 14 December 2011.
117 'Top cop "targeted" after spooking spy boss', *Mail & Guardian*, 12 February 2012.
118 'NPA rubbishes Mdluli, Breytenbach links', *Mail & Guardian*, 3 February 2012.
119 'Spooks back to their old tricks', *Mail & Guardian*, 8 April 2011.
120 'The game is on', *The Witness*, 16 April 2011.
121 *Ibid.*
122 See 'Protection of Information Bill', Republic of South Africa, as introduced in the National Assembly (proposed section 75), 5 March 2010'. www.info.gov.za.
123 *Ibid.*

Chapter 6 The Last Bastions: Judiciary, Media and Civil Society

1 M Wesson and M du Plessis, 'Fifteen years on: Central issues relating to the transformation of the South African judiciary', *South African Journal of Human Rights,* vol 24, 2008, p 190.
2 E Cameron, 'Legal chauvinism, executive-mindedness and justice – LC Steyn's impact on South African law, *South African Legal Journal*, vol 38, 1982.
3 H Corder, 'Judicial authority in a changing South Africa', *Legal Studies*, vol 24, 2004, pp 253 and 255, quoted in Wesson and Du Plessis, 'Fifteen years on', p 191.
4 Interim Constitution: South Africa, 1994, Schedule Six, Para II. www. constitutionalcourt.co.za.
5 E Christiansen, 'Adjudicating non-justiciable rights: Socio-economic rights and the South African Constitutional Court', *Columbia Human Rights L. Rev 321*, 38, 2007, p 348.

6 F Mnyongani, 'The judiciary as a site of struggle for political power: A South
   African perspective', Department of Jurisprudence, UNISA, undated, pp 6–7.
7 *Ibid.*
8 Constitution of the Republic of South Africa, 1996, Section 177(1).
9 It should not, however, be taken for granted that the entire legal system, per se, was
   considered illegitimate by the broader South African population. Stephen Ellman,
   in an oft-quoted study from 1995, noted that the judiciary and the rule of law
   retained at least a baseline level of legitimacy in the eyes of most South Africans;
   even those that had borne the brunt of the judiciary's previous infractions.
   While the reasons could be many, Ellman suggests that anti-apartheid lawyering
   indicated that the legal system, if it were correctly structured and aligned to a
   human rights discourse, could serve a useful function in guaranteeing freedoms.
   See S Ellman, 'Law and legitimacy in South Africa', *Law & Social Enquiry*, vol 20,
   no 2, 1995.
10 See Certification of the South African Constitution of the Republic of South
   Africa, CCT 23/96, 6 September 1996.
11 G Budlender, 'Transforming the judiciary: The politics of the judiciary in a
   democratic South Africa', *The South African Law Journal*, vol 122, 2005, p 715.
12 *Soobramoney v Minister of Health (Kwazulu-Natal),* Constitutional Court, Case
   Number: CCT32/97, para 8.
13 Constitution of South Africa, chapter 2 – Bill of Rights, Section 8 – Application.
   www.info.gov.za.
14 *Ibid*, sections 26, 27 and 29.www.info.gov.za.
15 *Soobramoney v Minister of Health.*
16 *Government of the Republic of South Africa & Others v Grootboom & Others,*
   Constitutional Court, case number: CCT11/00.
17 *Minister of Health & Others v Treatment Action Campaign & Others,*
   Constitutional Court, Case Number: CCT88/02.
18 M Wesson, '*Grootboom* and beyond: Reassessing the socio-economic
   jurisprudence of the South African Constitutional Court', *South African Journal
   of Human Rights*, vol 20, 2004, p 286.
19 C Steinberg, 'Can reasonableness protect the poor? A review of South Africa's
   socio-economic rights jurisprudence', *South African Law Journal*, vol 123, no 2,
   July 2006, p 269.
20 See, for example, D Bilchitz, 'Giving socio-economic rights teeth: The minimum
   core and its importance', *South African Law Journal*, vol 119, no 3, 2002.
21 *Ibid.*
22 This is not to suggest that using a minimum core approach was entirely out of the
   question, at least initially. During the Grootboom judgment, the Court suggested
   that there 'may be cases where it may be possible and appropriate to have regard to
   the content of a minimum core obligation.' In this case, the Court argued that it
   did not have the information at its disposal to determine the appropriate minimum
   core. However, by the time of the TAC judgment, the Court's decision suggested
   less willingness to adopt a minimum core approach.

23 Wesson, '*Grootboom* and beyond', p 287.

24 *Soobramoney v Minister of Health* , paras 99 (b) and 99 (c).

25 *Minister of Health & Others v Treatment Action Campaign & Others*, para 135
    (2b and c).

26 *Government of the Republic of South Africa & Others v Grootboom & Others*,
    paras 32 and 41.

27 *Minister of Health & Others v Treatment Action Campaign & Others*, paras 37
    and 38.

28 While some critical academic commentary that promotes the use of the minimum
    core has been referenced in notes above, interested readers may also benefit from
    reading a convincing and spirited rejection of the inferences of minimum core:
    K Lehman, 'In defence of the Constitutional Court: Litigating socio-economic
    rights and the myth of the minimum core', *American University International Law
    Review*, vol 22, no 1, 2006, pp 163–97.

29 Telephonic interview with Geoff Budlender, March 2012.

30 'Constitutional Court planning to "pounce" on Zuma – Mantashe', *SAPA/
    Politicsweb*, 5 July 2008.

31 President Zuma's keynote address to the Access to Justice Conference, 8 July 2011.
    www.constitutionallyspeaking.co.za.

32 'Inclusion of SCA decisions in ConCourt review "concerning"', *City Press*,
    27 March 2012.

33 Discussion document on the transformation of the judicial system and the role of
    the judiciary in the developmental South African state, Department of Justice and
    Constitutional Development, February 2012, para 5.1.2.

34 'Full interview: ANC's Mantashe lambasts judges', *Sowetan*, 18 August 2011.
    http://www.sowetanlive.co.za/news/2011/08/18/
    full-interview-ancs-mantashe-lambasts-judges.

35 Telephonic interview with Sipho Pityana, March 2012.

36 Simelane has since filed leave to appeal in the Constitutional Court.

37 *Judgment in the Supreme Court of Appeal in the Matter of Democratic Alliance v
    the President of the Republic of South Africa & Others*, case no 263/11, December
    2011, para 4. www.saflii.org.

38 *Ibid*, paras 66 and 122.

39 *Judgment in the Supreme Court of Appeal in the Matter of Democratic Alliance
    & Others v The Acting National Director of Public Prosecutions & Others*, case
    no 288/11, 20 March 2012, para 31.

40 R Teer-Tomaselli, 'The role of the public broadcaster', in E Hadland (ed),
    Changing the Fourth Estate: Essays on South African journalism. Cape Town:
    HSRC Press, 2005, p 201.

41 R Teer-Tomaselli and K Tomaselli, 'Reconstituting public service broadcasting:
    Media and democracy during transition in South Africa', Paper presented at the
    Media and Democracy Conference, University of Oslo, January 1994, p 3.
    www.hsrc.ac.za.

42 *Ibid*.

43 Community survey 2007 (rev ed), Statistical release P0301, Statistics South Africa, fig 6.15, and Community survey 2007 (Gauteng), report no 03-01-27, table GP13.

44 Community survey 2007 (rev ed), Statistical release P0301, Statistics South Africa, fig 6.15, and Community survey 2007 (Gauteng), report no 03-01-27, table GP14.

45 'SABC public broadcasting stations'. www.southafrica.info.

46 'This is the SABC', SABC undated pamphlet. www.vintagemedia.co.za.

47 J Myburgh, 'SA's daily newspapers in decline', 1 November 2011. www.themediaonline.co.za.

48 'SABC editorial policies', April 2004. www.sabc.co.za.

49 *Business Day*, 27 June 2006.

50 *Sunday Times*, 25 June 2006.

51 'SABC bans top Mbeki critics', *Sowetan*, 20 June 2006.

52 Commission of Enquiry into blacklisting and alleged related matters, Draft report, published by the *Mail & Guardian* on 14 October 2006. www.mg.co.za.

53 *Judgment in the South Gauteng High Court (Johannesburg) in the Matter between the Freedom of Expression Institute and Chair, Complaints and Compliance Committee & Others*, case number 2009/51933, 24 January 2011, para 6.

54 *Ibid*, para 14.

55 See, for example, 'SABC loses another board member', *Business Day*, 1 July 2011; and 'MMA on political interference, governance at SABC', 5 July 2011. www.themediaonline.co.za.

56 'Furore at SABC over COO appointment', *Sunday Independent*, 6 February 2012.

57 'New SABC COO failed matric (twice) – Natasha Michael', DA statement, 17 November 2011. www.politicsweb.co.za.

58 *Ibid*.

59 *Report of the Auditor-General on an Investigation at the South African Broadcasting Corporation*, September 2009, RP 237/2009, paras 1.2.4.1 and 1.2.5.1.

60 *Ibid*, para 1.2.4.3.

61 'Little progress on AG's SABC findings', *Mail & Guardian*, 6 March 2012.

62 'SABC bleeding viewers as e.TV tunes in', *TimesLive*, 18 March 2012.

63 'SABC news losing viewers due to biased coverage – NUM', Statement issued by Lesiba Seshoka, NUM spokesperson, 18 March 2012. www.politicsweb.co.za.

64 Telephonic interview with Ray Hartley, March 2012.

65 Telephonic interview with Nic Dawes, March 2012.

66 See, for example, 'How the ANC fell for Saddam's oil', *Mail & Guardian*, 6 February 2004.

67 'Public Protector back on Oilgate case', *Mail & Guardian*, 19 September 2011.

68 *Judgment in the Supreme Court of Appeal in the Matter of Public Protector v Mail and Guardian Ltd and Others*, case no 422/10, 1 June 2011, para 116.

69 Telephonic interview with Ray Hartley, March 2012.

70 'Media transformation, ownership and diversity', ANC discussion document, 2010. www.anc.org.za.

71 '70% increase in SA press complaints', *SAPA/IOL*, 11 February 2012.

72 *Ibid.*

73 Telephonic interview with Ray Hartley, March 2012.

74 *Ibid.*

75 Telephonic interview with Nic Dawes, March 2012.

Chapter 7 Ensuring Reproduction: The ANC and Its Models of Party Funding, 1994 to 2011

1 This chapter draws on research that was conducted during the writing of P Holden and H van Vuuren, *The devil in the detail: How the Arms Deal changed everything. Johannesburg:* Jonathan Ball, 2011. The research was funded by the Institute for Security Studies, Cape Town.

2 R Southall & G Wood, 'Political party funding in southern Africa', in *Funding democratisation,* ed P Burnell & A Ware. Manchester: Manchester University Press, 1998, p 211.

3 *Ibid,* p 212.

4 1994 ANC report on 'State of the Organisation' – presented at December meeting, Bloemfontein; also see Holden, *Arms Deal in your pocket.*

5 Report of the Office of the Treasurer General to the 50th National Conference of the ANC, 16–20 December 1997.

6 *Ibid.*

7 Financial report by ANC Treasurer-General, Mendi Msimang, p 1.

8 Compiled using data sourced from the Financial Report by ANC Treasurer-General Mendi Msimang, delivered at ANC 52nd National Conference, December 2007, p 6. Kindly compiled by Collette Herzenberg.

9 Financial report by ANC Treasurer-General Mendi Msimang, delivered at ANC 52nd National Conference, December 2007, p 3.

10 'Secret Taiwan fund sought friends, influence abroad', *Washington Post,* 5 April 2002. Also see T Lodge, 'Southern Africa', in *Global Corruption Report 2003,* Transparency International, p 253. www.transparency.org.

11 V Robinson and S Brummer, *SA democracy incorporated corporate fronts and political party funding,* ISS Paper 129, November 2006, p 5.

12 R Ellis, 'Political party funding in South Africa', MA dissertation, University of Cape Town, 2000, p 36.

13 'ANC's dodgy funders', *Mail & Guardian,* 21 March 2009.

14 Financial report by ANC Treasurer General, Mendi Msimang.

15 See RW Johnson, *South Africa's brave new world: The beloved country since the end of apartheid.* London: Allen Lane, 2009, p 163.

16 Statement by Ian Davidson, Democratic Alliance Chief Whip, on ANC foreign funding, 24 March 2009. Available from www.da.org.za.

17 'How not to deal with dictators', *Politicsweb,* 7 August 2008. www.politicsweb. co.za.

18 'Mandela invests Suharto with Order of Good Hope', SAPA, 22 November 1997.

19 'Secret Taiwan fund sought friends, influence abroad', *Washington Post*, 5 April
   2002. Also see T Lodge, 'Southern Africa', in *Global Corruption Report 2003*,
   Transparency International, 2003, p. 253. www.transparency.org.

20 *Ibid.*

21 *Ibid.*

22 *Ibid.*

23 *Ibid.*

24 Jovial Rantao, 'Daunting task faces newly elected treasurer-general', *The Star*,
   22 December 1997, p 13.

25 'Independent Inquiry Committee into the United Nations Oil-For-Food
   Programme', 27 October 2005, pp 9–21. www.iic-offp.org.

26 *Ibid.*

27 'Independent Inquiry Committee into the United Nations Oil-For-Food
   Programme', Chapter 2: Report on Programme Manipulation, 27 October 2005,
   p. 103. www.iic-offp.org, pp 15–27.

28 *Ibid,* see section C: Surcharges.

29 *Ibid*, Chapter 2, p 103.

30 *Ibid.*

31 *Ibid*, p 105.

32 *Ibid.*

33 *Ibid*, pp 105–8.

34 *Ibid*, p 108.

35 *Ibid*, p 109.

36 *Ibid*, p 108.

37 'Responses of Sandi Majali & Imvume Management (Proprietary) Limited to the
   Summary Provided by the IIC in Respect of the Report to be issued in regard to
   the conduct of Montega Trading (Proprietary) Limited and Imvume Management
   (Proprietary) Limited in relation to the United Nations Iraq Oil-For-Food
   Programme', in *Ibid*, p 223

38 *Ibid*, p 109.

39 'The ANC's Oilgate', *Mail & Guardian*, 3 May 2005.

40 *Ibid.*

41 *Ibid.*

42 Treasurer-General's report to the 52nd ANC National Conference held in
   Polokwane, Limpopo, 16 to 20 December 2007.

43 V Robinson and S Brummer, *SA democracy incorporated: Corporate fronts and
   political party funding*, Institute for Security Studies, Paper 129, November 2006.
   www.iss.org.za.

44 *Ibid*, p 18.

45 'Untold millions: Financing the ANC', *Financial Mail*, 19 January 2007.

46 *Report on an investigation into an allegation of improper conduct by the former
   Chairperson of the Board of Directors of Eskom Holding Limited, Mr V Moosa,
   relating to the award of a contract*, Public Protector of South Africa, Report no 30
   of 2008/2009. www.pmg.org.za .

47 Robinson and Brummer, 'SA democracy incorporated', p 19. www.iss.org.za.
48 'Breaking new ground in its industry', *www.miningweekly.com*, 2 October 2009.
49 Robinson and Brummer, 2006. 'SA Democracy Incorporated'. www.iss.org.za.
50 *Ibid.*
51 *Ibid.*
52 *Ibid.*
53 *Ibid.*
54 See www.eskom.co.za and 'Moosa in R38-billion tender conflict', *Mail & Guardian*, 8 February 2008.
55 'Chancellor House nets R50m from Eskom deal', *Mail & Guardian*, 20 April 2010.
56 'The politics of money in SA', *Mail & Guardian*, 29 October 2010.
57 'Moosa in R38-billion tender conflict', *Mail & Guardian*, 8 February 2008.
58 *Report on an investigation into an allegation of improper conduct by the former Chairperson of the Board of Directors of Eskom Holding Limited, Mr V Moosa, relating to the award of a contract*, Public Protector of South Africa, Report no 30 of 2008/2009, para. 15.5.5. www.pmg.org.za.
59 *Ibid*, para 20.2.
60 According to the potted history on the Progressive Business Forum website: www.pbf.org.za.
61 'ANC defends its "progressive forum"', *Mail & Guardian*, 19 February 2007.
62 *Ibid.*
63 'Zuma lauds ANC's relationship with business', *Times Live*, 22 September 2010.
64 'ANC defends its "progressive forum"', *Mail & Guardian*, 19 February 2007.
65 'Zuma lauds ANC's relationship with business', *Times Live*, 22 September 2010.
66 Robinson and Brummer, 2006. 'SA Democracy Incorporated', p 14. www.iss.org.za.
67 *Ibid.*
68 S Rose-Ackerman, *Corruption and government: Causes, consequences, and reform*, Chapter 8: 'Democracy and corruption: Incentives and reforms'. Cambridge: Cambridge University Press, 1999, p 133.

Chapter 8   Precarious Power: BEE and the Growth of South Africa's Black Middle Class

1 'Vavi told to "Go to hell"', *Die Burger*, 29 October 2010.
2 For an excellent discussion of how Afrikaner capital began to demand reforms of apartheid and finally prefigure the formation of the break-away Conservative Party, see D O'Meara, *Forty lost years*. Johannesburg: Ravan Press, 1997; and C Charney, 'Restructuring white politics: The transformation of the National Party', in *South African Review*, vol 1, 1983.
3 For detailed accounts of the various preliminary meetings between the ANC in exile and representatives of white business and white academics, see: M du Preez, *Pale native: Memories of a renegade reporter*, Cape Town: Zebra, 2003, and P Waldmeir, *Anatomy of a miracle*, Rutgers University Press, 1998.

4 A Butler, 'Black Economic Empowerment', Draft Paper, 2006. www.yale.edu.

5 For an account of such travails, particularly in the homeland of KwaNdebele, see: P Holden and S Mathabatha, 'The politics of resistance: 1948–1990', in P Delius (ed), *Mpumalanga: History and heritage*. Scottsville: UKZN Press, 2007.

6 *Reconstruction and Development Program*, ANC, 1994, para 4.4.6.3.

7 P Carmody, 'Between globalisation and (post) apartheid: The political economy of restructuring in South Africa', *Journal of Southern African Studies*, vol 28, no 2, June 2002, pp 256–7.

8 D Acemoglu, S Gelb & J Robinson, 'Black Economic Empowerment and economic performance in South Africa', Non-technical policy brief, National Treasury, 2007. www.treasury.gov.za.

9 Carmody, 'Between globalisation and (post) apartheid', p 264.

10 S Ponte, S Roberts and L van Sittert, 'To BEE or not to BEE?: South Africa's "Black Economic Empowerment" (BEE), corporate governance and the state in the south', Danish Institute for International Affairs Working Paper no 2006/27, 2006, p 35.

11 'BEE transaction contribution to total transaction value, 1994 – 2009' in 'Business and Labour Online' in *South Africa Survey 2009/2010*, South African Institute of Race Relations, p 63.

12 Acemoglu, Gelb & Robinson, 'Black Economic Empowerment and Economic Performance in South Africa'. www.treasury.gov.za

13 Carmody, 'Between globalisation and (post) apartheid', p 265.

14 *Ibid*.

15 For a detailed discussion as to the detail of employment equity, see R Burger and R Jafta, 'Affirmative action in South Africa: An empirical assessment of the impact on labour market outcomes', CRISE Working Paper no 76, Centre for Research on Inequality, Human Security and Ethnicity, 2010.

16 Acemoglu, Gelb and Robinson, 'Black economic empowerment and economic performance in South Africa'. www.treasury.gov.za

17 Black Economic Empowerment Commission Report, 2001. Johannesburg: Skotaville Press.

18 For a detailed brief history of the adoption of industry charters, see A Hirsch, 2005. *Season of Hope: Economic Reform under Mandela and Mbeki*. Scottsville: University of KwaZulu-Natal Press, 2005, pp 222–5.

19 Acemoglu, Gelb and Robinson, 'Black economic empowerment and economic performance in South Africa'. www.treasury.gov.za.

20 The generic BEE scorecard was first published in 'South Africa's economic transformation: A strategy for broad-based Black Economic Empowerment', Department of Trade and Industry. www.dti.gov.za.

21 T Mbeki, Speech at the Annual National Conference of the Black Management Forum, Kempton Park, 20 November 1999, www.dfa.gov.za.

22 'Welcome to the club', *Time*, 6 June 2005.

23 'Hold your nose', *The Economist*, 3 June 2010.

24 R Hall, 'A political economy of land reform in South Africa', *Review of African Political Economy*, vol 31, no 100, June 2004, p 220.

25 S Ponte and L van Sittert, 'The chimera of redistribution in post-apartheid South Africa: "Black Economic Empowerment (BEE)" in industrial fisheries', *African Affairs*, vol 106, no 424, 2007, p 438.

26 A Emery, 'Class and race domination and transformation in South Africa', *Critical Sociology*, vol 34, no 3, 2008, p 424.

27 'BEE transaction contribution to total transaction value, 1994–2009', p 63.

28 'South Africa: The new Randlords', *Time*, 17 April 2005.

29 BEE transaction contribution to total transaction value, 1994–2009', p 63.

30 BEE transaction contribution to total transaction value, 1994–2009', p 63.

31 'Crunching numbers on the JSE', *Financial Mail*, 13 October 2011, and 'JSE black directorships, 2008–2010', in 'Business and labour online', in *South Africa Survey 2009/2010*, South African Institute of Race Relations, p 63.

32 *Ibid.*

33 'Crunching numbers on the JSE', *Financial Mail*, 13 October 2011.

34 *Ibid.*

35 *Ibid.*

36 For an excellent and pithy take on Khumalo's business strategy, see J Cargill, *Trick or treat: Rethinking black empowerment.* Johannesburg: Jacana, 2010, pp 38–9.

37 A Butler, 'Consolidation first: Institutional reform priorities in the creation of a development state in South Africa', in O Edigheji (ed), *Constructing a democratic development state in South Africa.* Cape Town: HSRC Press, 2010, p 196. Note that, writing in 2011, Butler presented slightly different figures, citing R200 billion in empowerment deals and private asset value at R5tn. See: A Butler, 'Black Economic Empowerment since 1994: Diverse hopes and differentially fulfilled aspirations', in I Shapiro & K Tebeau, *After apartheid.* Virginia: University of Virginia Press, 2011, p 62.

38 Cargill, *Trick or treat: Rethinking black empowerment*, p 36.

39 *Ibid.*

40 *Ibid.*

41 *Ibid.*

42 M Mbeki, *Architects of poverty*, pp 66–8.

43 'Mvela's multi-billion rand payoff', *Mineweb*, 17 March 2009.

44 'Mvela share sale to Kazakh firm raises questions', *TimesLive*, 2 May 2010.

45 'Put profits aside for now', *Financial Mail*, 7 October 2010.

46 'ANC U-turn on mines', *Mail & Guardian*, 12 July 2009, and 'Nationalisation call a ploy to bail out business in trouble – NUM', *Business Day*, 14 October 2010.

47 For a discussion of the various methodologies deployed to date, see J Visagie & D Posel, 'A reconsideration of what and who is middle class in South Africa', Working Paper no 29, October 2011, University of KwaZulu-Natal.

48 *Ibid*, tables 4 and 5, pp 16–17.

49 R Southall, 'Political change and the black middle class in democratic South Africa', *Canadian Journal of African Studies*, vol 38, no 3, 2004, p 527.

50 *Ibid.*

51 Visagie and Posel, 'A reconsideration of what and who is middle class in South

Africa', tables 4 and 5, pp 16–17.

52 J van den Heever, 2007. 'Household debt, interest rates and insolvencies in South
    Africa', *IFC Bulletin,* no 26, 2007, figure 1.

53 *Africa Yearbook Five: Politics, economy and society south of the Sahara.* Leiden:
    Koningklijke Brill NV, p 488.

54 *Report on the indebtedness of public servants,* Public Service Commission,
    November 2007, para 4.3.1.

55 *Ibid,* para 4.3.3.

56 *Ibid,* para 4.3.1.

57 R Southall, 'Ten propositions about Black Economic Empowerment in South
    Africa', *Review of African Political Economy,* vol 34, no 111, 2007, p 75.

58 *Ibid,* p 75.

59 'Absa meets charter target with BEE deal', *Mail & Guardian,* 6 April 2004.

60 'Batho Bonke's big bonsela', *Mail & Guardian,* 12 August 2005.

61 *Ibid,* and 'The Tao of Steve and Tokyo', *Mail & Guardian,* 31 October 2005.

62 Gumede, *Thabo Mbeki and the battle for the soul of the ANC,* p 417.

63 B Turok, *From the Freedom Charter to Polokwane: The evolution of ANC
    economic policy.* Cape Town: New Agenda, 2009, p 157.

64 N Nattrass and J Seekings, 'State, business and growth in post-apartheid South
    Africa', IPPG discussion paper no 34, January 2010, p 35. www.ippg.org.uk.

65 H Bhorat and C van der Westhuizen, 'Economic growth, poverty and inequality
    in South Africa: The first decade of democracy', Paper commissioned by the
    presidency as part of fifteen-year review process, undated, p 11.

66 'Gordhan says businesses must help create South African jobs', *Bloomberg Business
    Week,* 25 February 2011.

67 Bhorat and van der Westhuizen, 'Economic growth, poverty and inequality in
    South Africa: The first decade of democracy', p 11.

68 A Bosch, J Rossouw, T Claasens and B du Plessis, 'A second look at measuring
    inequality in South Africa: a modified Gini coefficient', School of Development
    Studies, working paper no 58, September 2010. www.ukzn.ac.za.

69 'Legends of ore: The rise and fall of a venerable name in South African mining',
    New York Times, 5 February 1998.

70 T Mbeki, Nelson Mandela Memorial Lecture, University of the Witwatersrand,
    29 July 2006. www.dfa.gov.za.

71 See, for example, 'Nationalisation a call to help elite BEE, says SACP', *Business
    Day,* 28 June 2011.

72 'Vodacom: ANC's elephant hunt', *Mail & Guardian,* 25 May 2009.

Chapter 9 The One That Got Away: How Helen Zille Built a Political Fortress in Cape Town

1 This chapter was written with the kind assistance of Mersini Iakovidis.

2 ANC, *Strategy and Tactics, as amended at the 50th National Conference of the*

African National Congress, 16 December 1997. A 'Cadre Policy' resolution was passed at the conference. For details of how it is to operate see *Umrabulo* no 6 (third quarter 1999). The Democratic Alliance has provided a critique of the policy: *Power to the Party: The ANC's programme to eliminate the distinctions between party and state and extend its hegemony over civil society*, March 2000

3 R Southall, 'Opposition and democracy in South Africa', in *Democratization*, vol 8, no 1, special issue Spring 2001, p 14.

4 See, for example, Address of President Thabo Mbeki at the 90th anniversary of the African National Congress, 6 January 2002. http://www.info.gov.za/speeches/2002/020108946a1001.htm.

5 *Sowetan* Live, 9 September 2008 – 'ANC will rule until Jesus comes back'. http://www.sowetanlive.co.za/sowetan/archive/2008/09/09/anc-will-rule-until-jesus-comes-back.

6 http://www.sundaytribune.co.za/detractors-jealous-of-zuma-wit-anc-1.1022653.

7 Electoral Commission of South Africa, 2009 election report, table 36.

8 *Ibid*, table 45.

9 BBC website, 25 April 2009. http://news.bbc.co.uk/1/hi/world/africa/8017713.stm.

10 SAPA, 8 May 2009.

11 SAPA, 12 May 2009.

12 SAPA, 13 May 2009.

13 SAPA, 29 May 2009.

14 RB Beck, *The history of South Africa*. London: Greenwood Publishing Group, 2000, p 138.

15 H Suzman, *In no uncertain terms: A South African memoir*. Johannesburg: Jonathan Ball, 1993, p 47.

16 1993. *The Democratic Party Constitution & Policy – DP – Democratic Party, One Nation. One Future, Manifesto*, p 1.

17 Suzman, *In no uncertain terms*, p 58.

18 *Ibid*, p 25.

19 *Ibid*, p 181.

20 *Democratic Party Constitution & Policy*, p 1.

21 Suzman, *In no uncertain terms*, p 287.

22 J Bloom, *Out of step: Life-story of a politician – Politics and religion in a world at war*. Norwood: Jack Bloom, 2005, p 50.

23 Reports of the Independent Electoral Commission of South Africa. The 2011 local election vote is not directly comparable with the national elections of the previous years, but the percentage share of vote is broadly indicative of DA support.

24 *Report of the Independent Electoral Commission of South Africa, National and Provincial Elections, 2 June 1999*, p 75.

25 J Daniel and R Southall, *Zunami: The 2009 South African elections*. Johannesburg: Jacana, 2009, p 133.

26 A Lemon, 'The implications for opposition parties of South Africa's 2009 general election', Paper for presentation at the 'Democratization in Africa' conference, Leeds University, 4–5 December 2009, p 4.

27 *Ibid*, p 78.
28 Tony Leon, *On the contrary: Leading the opposition in a democratic South Africa.* Johannesburg: Jonathan Ball, 2008, p 542.
29 *Ibid*, pp 559–74 gives a lengthy explanation for the split. See also: http://www.iol. co.za/news/politics/western-cape-political-circus-is-over-1.210476.
30 Daniel and Southall, *Zunami: The 2009 South African Elections*, p 134.
31 Report of the Independent Electoral Commission of South Africa, National and Provincial Elections, 14 April 2004, p 60.
32 DA – Our history. http://www.da.org.za/about. htm?action=view-page&category=383.
33 http://www.bbc.co.uk/news/world-africa-10981635.
34 Daniel & Southall, *Zunami: The 2009 South African elections*, p 137.
35 *Ibid*, p 143.
36 SAPA, 9 February 2011. http://mg.co.za/ article/2011-02-09-opposition-party-shenanigans-ruinous-for-democracy/.
37 L Schlemmer, April – July 2008. *Weight and counterweight: Analysis of the results of a political opinion survey on party support patterns and inter-party cooperation.* http://www.politicsweb.co.za/politicsweb/action/media/ downloadFile?media_fileid=1099.
38 *Ibid*, p 11.
39 *Ibid*.
40 http://www.da.org.za/newsroom.htm?action=view-news-item&id=9252.
41 http://www.timeslive.co.za/specialreports/elections2011/article1070004.ece/ Zuma-and-Malema-creating-divisions-Zille.
42 http://www.timeslive.co.za/Politics/article1078449.ece/ Malema-refuses-debate-with-tea-girl-Mazibuko.
43 http://www.iol.co.za/news/anc-feathers-ruffled-1.1072014.
44 SAPA, 19 May 2011.
45 *Times* (Johannesburg), 25 May 2011.
46 *Cape Times*, 25 May 2011.
47 P Berkowitz, *Daily Maverick*, 25 May 2011. http://dailymaverick.co.za/ article/2011-05-25-analysis-what-anc-decline-a-different-view.
48 Cosatu press release, 3 December 2010.
49 http://www.da.org.za/about.htm?action=view-page&category=386.
50 http://www.anc.org.za/show.php?include=docs/misc/2010/anc.html (accessed 26 February 2011).
51 http://www.news24.com/SouthAfrica/News/Minister-defends-welfare-system-20100223 (accessed 26 February 2011).
52 South African Institute of Race Relations. http://moneyweb.co.za/mw/view/mw/ en/page292681?oid=527279&sn=2009+Detail+no+image&pid=287226 (accessed 26 February 2011).
53 https://docs.google.com/viewer?a=v&pid=explorer&chrome=true&srcid=0B_-slGu8-FTxYmEoOTE1ZmYtZmNjOSooOGRkLTk2NmUtM2E1ZGQ2OTZlNm E4&hl=en (accessed 26 February 2011).

54 Lemon, 'The implications for opposition parties of South Africa's 2009 general election', p 10.

55 Statistics South Africa, Community Survey 2007, table 3.3.

56 *Ibid.*

57 Mohamed Adhikari, Not white enough, not black enough; Racial identity in the South African coloured community, Ohio University Press, 2005, p 10.

58 Zwelethu Jolobe, 'The Democratic Alliance: Consolidating the official opposition', in Southall and Daniel (eds), *Zunami: The 2009 South African Election*, p 145.

59 Lemon, 'The implications for opposition parties of South Africa's 2009 general election'.

60 *Ibid*, p 12.

61 Jolobe, 'The Democratic Alliance: Consolidating the official opposition', p 145.

62 *Ibid.*

63 http://www.globalratings.net/attachment_view.php?aa_id=101, vol 12, no 3, March 2009. Global Credit Rating, African edition.

64 Empowerdex (2009) Service Delivery Index. http://www.empowerdex.com/Portals/5/docs/munidex_report_final.pdf.

65 http://www.moneyweb.co.za/mw/view/mw/en/page295025?oid=559856&sn=2009+Detail.

66 Basic Services Publication, Department of Cooperative Governance and Traditional Affairs, ISBN: 978-0-620-45326-4.

67 *Cape Argus*, 24 November 2010. http://www.iol.co.za/news/south-africa/western-cape/cape-is-sa-s-best-performer-by-far-1.876247?showComments=true.

68 The DA's performance is not uniformly good, nor is the ANC's uniformly bad. A recent survey found that the ANC's service delivery in Saldanha Bay had been excellent, while the DA had performed poorly in Theewaterskloof municipality in Caledon. http://www.timeslive.co.za/sundaytimes/article1066606.ece/Municipal-finance-meltdown.

69 *Mail & Guardian*, 2 December 2010. http://www.mg.co.za/article/2010-12-02-mantashe-anc-is-a-cinderella-party.

70 *Mail & Guardian*, 3 December 2010. http://www.mg.co.za/article/2010-12-03-municipal-poll-jitters-for-the-anc.

71 *Mail & Guardian*, 2 December 2010. http://www.mg.co.za/article/2010-12-02-mantashe-anc-is-a-cinderella-party.

72 News24, 12 February 2011. http://www.news24.com/SouthAfrica/Politics/Marius-Fransman-to-take-on-Helen-Zille-20110212.

73 *Ibid.*

74 Cosatu press release, 3 December 2010.

75 http://www.politicsweb.co.za/politicsweb/view/politicsweb/en/page71656?oid=180321&sn=Detail.

76 Judgment of Justice Erasmus, Western Cape High Court, Case No: 21332/10, 29 April 2011.

77 http://www.politicsweb.co.za/politicsweb/view/politicsweb/en/page71656?oid=168833&sn=Detail (accessed 27 February 2011).

78 SAPA, 25 May 2010.

79 *Ibid.*

80 http://www.mg.co.za/article/2010-05-25-cape-town-at-crossroads-over-toilets.

81 SAPA, 31 May 2010.

82 http://sjc.org.za/2010/06/sahrc-finds-city-violated-makhaza-residents-right-dignity.

83 Judgment of Justice Erasmus, para 29. http://www.politicsweb.co.za/politicsweb/
    view/politicsweb/en/page71656?oid=233509&sn=Detail&pid=71616.

84 SAPA, 29 April 2011.

85 SAPA, 21 September 2010.

86 *Ibid.*

87 SAPA, 28 September 2010.

88 http://mg.co.za/article/2010-10-07-rights-commission-slams-zilles-wild-claim/.

89 SAPA, 7 October 2010.

90 http://mg.co.za/article/2011-05-16-moqhaka-municipality-violated-right-to-human-
    dignity/.

91 SAPA, 14 May 2011.

92 'Battle for Cape township voters', *Business Day*, 28 January 2011. http://www.
    businessday.co.za/articles/Content.aspx?id=132737.

93 http://writingrights.org/2010/05/27/the-toilets-the-da-and-the-anc-youth-league/.

94 *Ibid.*

95 Politicsweb, 19 December 2011. phttp://www.politicsweb.co.za/politicsweb/view/
    politicsweb/en/page71654?oid=272371&sn=Detail&pid=71616.

96 *Times* (Johannesburg), 29 December 2011. http://www.iol.co.za/news/politics/
    zille-jibe-sparks-new-twitter-war-1.1205691.

97 http://www.iol.co.za/dailynews/news/outrage-at-zille-s-refugee-comment-1.1261770

98 http://mg.co.za/article/2011-05-03-slinging-mud-the-week-that-sa-politics-got-
    dirty/.

99 http://www.politicsweb.co.za/politicsweb/view/politicsweb/en/page71656?oid=2378
    03&sn=Detail&pid=71616

100 http://www.businessday.co.za/Articles/Content.aspx?id=143480

Chapter 10 Crime, Corruption and Connections

1 This chapter was written with the kind assistance of Richard McLaverty

2 The charges against Mdluli were subsequently withdrawn.

3 Institute for Security Studies, *Early manifestations of organised crime in South
   Africa,* ISS Monograph 28, 1998.

4 RW Johnson, *South Africa's brave new world.* London: Allen Lane, 2009, pp 27 ff.

5 N Motlana, quoted in Clive Glaser, *Students, tsotsis and the Congress Youth
   League; Youth organisation on the Rand in the 1940's and 1950's,* University of the
   Witwatersrand, History Workshop, 9–14 February, 1987.

6 C Glaser, *When are we going to fight? Tsotsis, youth politics and the PAC of the
   Witwatersrand during the 1950's and early 1960's,* University of the Witwatersrand,

History Workshop, 9–14 February, 1987.

7 *Ibid*, p 22.

8 Johnson, *South Africa's Brave New World*, pp 27 ff.

9 For a much fuller exposition of Modise's role in the torture and killing of ANC mutineers in camps in Angola, see P Trewhela, *Inside Quatro: Uncovering the exile history of the ANC and SWAPO.* Johannesburg: Jacana, 2009.

10 *Ibid*, p 31.

11 *Ibid.*

12 S Ellis and T Sechaba, *Comrades against apartheid: The ANC and South African Communist Party in exile.* London: James Currey, 1992, p 130. They go on to quote reports of ANC leaders living the high life and making free with the wives of ANC members, who felt helpless to complain, p 192.

13 P Gastrow, *Organised crime in South Africa: An assessment of its nature and origins,* Institute for Security Studies, no 28, August 1998.

14 *Ibid.*

15 D Pinnock, *The Brotherhoods: Street gangs and state control in Cape Town.* Cape Town: David Philip, 1984.

16 *Ibid*, p 5.

17 Gastrow, *Organised crime in South Africa.*

18 C Gould and P Folb, *Project Coast: Apartheid's chemical and biological warfare programme.* Cape Town: United Nations Institute for Disarmament Research and Centre for Conflict Resolution, 2002, p 126.

19 *Ibid.*

20 *Ibid,* p 127. The supplies were destroyed in 1993, just before the end of apartheid.

21 Gastrow, *Organised crime in South Africa.*

22 *Ibid.*

23 H van Vuuren, *Apartheid grand corruption: A report prepared by civil society in terms of a resolution of the Second National Anti-Corruption Summit for presentation at the National Anti-Corruption Forum,* May 2006. Pretoria: Institute for Security Studies.

24 *Ibid*, p 3.

25 T Bell and D Ntsebeza, *Unfinished business.* London: Verso, 2003, p 7 details the role of the furnaces. *Noseweek* no 132 says that the burning of documents was given the code name 'Operation Masada'.

26 Van Vuuren, *Apartheid grand corruption*, p 16.

27 *Ibid*, p 53. Note: the figure is in rands at 2005 values.

28 *Ibid*, p 49.

29 *Ibid*, pp 32–5.

30 *Ibid*, p 45.

31 *Ibid*, p 43.

32 *Ibid*, p 5.

33 http://www.thoughtleader.co.za/amabhungane/2010/04/23/selebi-case/.

34 *Mail & Guardian*, 4 October 2005.

35 *Mercury*, 5 October 2005.

36 Barry Sergeant, *Brett Kebble: the inside story.* Cape Town: Zebra, 2006, p 9.

37 *Guardian*, 7 October 2007. http://www.guardian.co.uk/news/2005/oct/07/ guardianobituaries.southafrica.

38 Sergeant, *Brett Kebble: the inside story* p 90.

39 *Ibid*, p 103.

40 *Ibid*, p 24.

41 *Ibid*, p 9.

42 SAPA, 25 January 2003.

43 *Noseweek*, no 55, April 2004.

44 *Mail & Guardian*, 28 September 2005. http://www.mg.co.za/ article/2005-09-28-kebble-killing-was-pure-assassination.

45 *Noseweek*, no 55, April 2004.

46 *Mail & Guardian*, 24 October 2008. http://mg.co.za/ article/2008-10-24-youth-leagues-dirtymoney-deals.

47 Sergeant, *Brett Kebble: the inside story*, p 13. In his last known interview, Kebble allegedly named those he believed were attempting to prevent Jacob Zuma becoming the next president of South Africa. Liesl Göttert interviewed Kebble for a documentary four-part documentary, *The Zuma Media Trial*, which has never been broadcast. She said Kebble was 'the only one with the guts to say what he thought on camera.' She went on to become Zuma's spin-doctor. http://www.iol. co.za/news/politics/mining-magnate-named-zuma-plotters-on-film-1.254840.

48 *Sunday Times* (Johannesburg), 11 March 2007.http://www.timeslive.co.za/ sundaytimes/article85955.ece.

49 *Ibid*.

50 *Sunday Times* (Johannesburg), 2 October 2005. http://www.timeslive.co.za/ sundaytimes/article74121.ece.

51 *Noseweek*, no 63, December 2004.

52 Sergeant, *Brett Kebble: the inside story*, p 24.

53 M Wiener, *Killing Kebble: An underworld exposed*. Johannesburg: Pan Macmillan, 2011, p 104.

54 *Mail & Guardian* editorial, quoted in *Noseweek*, no 86, December 2006.

55 D Klatzow, *Steeped in blood: The life and times of a forensic scientist*. Cape Town: Zebra, 2010, p 236.

56 Klatzow, *Steeped in blood*, pp 235–6.

57 The state v Norbert Glenn Agliotti, South Gauteng High Court, Johannesburg, case number SS 154/2009, 25 November 2010, p 32, para 46.

58 *Ibid*, p 37, para 59.

59 *Ibid*, p 42, para 61.

60 *Ibid*, p 152, para 298.

61o *Ibid*, p 24, para 24.

62 A Basson, *Finish & klaar: Selebi's fall from Interpol to the underworld*. Cape Town: Tafelberg, 2010, p 5.

63 *Ibid*, pp 30 ff.

64 http://www.interpol.int/Public/ICPO/PressReleases/PR2004/PR200433.asp.

65 Basson, *Finish & klaar*, p 4.

66 The state v Norbert Glenn Agliotti, South Gauteng High Court, Johannesburg, case number SS 154/2009. Date: 25/11/2010, p 98, para 173.2.

67 *Ibid*, p 25. Selebi is appealing against the judgment.

68 *Ibid*, p 82, para 151.15. Kebble's butler, Andrew Minaar, put the sum higher (p 96, para 168), telling the court that R15 million was involved and that shortly before his death Kebble had discussed how he might get it back.

69 State versus Jacob Sello Selebi, Judgment by Justice J Joffe, South Gauteng High Court, Case 25/09, para 154. http://www.saflii.org/za/cases/ZAGPJHC/2010/53. html.

70 Basson, *Finish & klaar*, p 272.

71 *Mail & Guardian*, 26 May 2006. http://www.mg.co.za/ article/2006-05-26-jackie-selebis-shady-kebble-links.

72 J Irish-Qhobosheane, *Gentlemen or villains, thugs or heroes? The social economy of crime in South Afric*a. Pretoria: South African Institute for International Affairs, 2007. Between 2005 and 2007, the police investigated 13 679 cases of commercial crime. Only 23 per cent of cases were referred to court, 47 per cent of which resulted in successful convictions.

73 *Business Day*, 16 October 2007. It was estimated that 72 per cent of companies had been affected by these crimes, compared to 43 per cent globally – an increase of 110 per cent since 2005. South Africa was estimated to have lost more than R600 million to economic crime in the preceding two years.

74 Adriaan Basson, *Finish & klaar,* p 191.

75 Klatzow, *Steeped in blood*, p 237.

76 Wiener, *Killing Kebble*, p 374.

77 Klatzow, *Steeped in blood*, p 239.

78 See Transparency International Corruption Perception Index, 1995, 2010 and 2011. http://www.transparency.org/policy_research/surveys_indices/cpi.

79 TNS survey, 10 January 2012. http://www.politicsweb.co.za/politicsweb/view/ politicsweb/en/page71619?oid=274466&sn=Detail.

80 Editorial, *Noseweek*, no 145, 1 November 2011.

81 'Cwele sentenced to 12 years, will appeal'. http://www.timeslive.co.za/local/ article1053767.ece/Sheryl-Cwele-sentenced-to-12-years-in-jail.

82 She is appealing against her conviction.

83 *Sunday Independent*, 9 May 2011. http://www.iol.co.za/sundayindependent/ president-knew-about-sheryl-1.1066360.

84 http://www.r2k.org.za/updates/131-right2know-demands-answers-from-president-zuma-on-cwele-drug-conviction.

85 Mr Cwele subsequently divorced his wife. SAPA, 15 September, 2011.

86 These findings were released by the Institute for Security Studies when it launched the 'Who owns what database', which is part of the Institute's corruption and governance programme. *Business Report*, 5 August 2011.

87 'Zuma incorporated', *Mail & Guardian*, 19 March 2011. http://mg.co.za/ article/2010-03-19-zuma-incorporated.

88 'Mozambique's 'Mr "Guebusiness"', *Mail & Guardian*, 6 January 2012. http:// mg.co.za/article/2012-01-06-mozambiques-mr-guebusiness/.

89 'Congo president cancels block agreements with Tullow', *Oil and Gas Journal,*

25 June 2010. http://www.ogj.com/articles/2010/06/congo-president-cancels.html.

90 SAPA, 29 August 2011.

91 Business Live, 13 September 2011. http://www.businesslive.co.za/ southafrica/2011/09/13/zuma-rejects-scrutiny-of-family-business-interests.

92 'Zuma Jnr link in iron war', *Mail & Guardian*, 16 April 2010. http://mg.co.za/ article/2010-04-16-zuma-jr-link-in-iron-war.

93 'ICT "forged Kumba application"', miningmx, 26 April 2011. http://www. miningmx.com/news/markets/ICT-forged-Kumba-application.htm

94 *Times* (Johannesburg), 2 March 2011. http://www.iol.co.za/news/politics/ gupta-and-zuma-s-son-meet-cosatu-1.1034586

95 Author's interviews for a BBC programme, April 2011. http://www.bbc.co.uk/ iplayer/episode/b01ot6lp/Crossing_Continents_South_Africa/.

96 *Ibid.*

97 Interview with SA FM live, 14 July 2007. http://www.auroraempowerment.com/ news.html.

98 'Shandong visit could be Aurora's last chance', *Times* (Johannesburg), 15 May 2011. http://www.timeslive.co.za/business/article1068951.ece/ Shandong-visit-could-be-Auroras-last-chance.

99 'Zuma Inc hits skids', *Times* (Johannesburg), 29 May 2011. http://www.timeslive. co.za/business/article1090195.ece/Zuma-Inc-hits-skids.

100 SAPA, 28 April 2011.

101 *Times* (Johannesburg), 17 October 2010.

102 *Financial Mail*, 12 August 2010.

103 *Business Day*, 4 November 2011. http://www.businessday.co.za/articles/Content. aspx?id=157846.

104 *Sunday Independent*, 8 April 2012

105 M Nicol, Z Gubeni and L Makgamathe, *Overflows and outages: Mismanagement of utilities in two cities.* in Brown, S. (ed) *Economic Transformation Audit: Money and Morality,* Cape Town: Institute for Justice and Reconciliation, 2006, p 99.

106 Survey by the *Financial Mail*, quoted by Allister Sparks, *Witness*, 20 February 2008. http://www.witness.co.za/index.php?showcontent&global[_id]=4019.

107 P van Hoof (ed), *The state of local governance in South Africa from a citizen perspective.* Pretoria: Idasa, April 2011, p 7.

108 *Ibid*, p 32.

109 *Ibid*, p 36.

110 D Atkinson, 'Taking to the streets: Has developmental local government failed in South Africa?' in *State of the Nation: South Africa 2007*. Cape Town: HSRC Press, 2007, p 66.

111 J Hirsch, *Community protests in South Africa: Trends, analysis and explanations*, Community Law Centre, August 2010; Jelani Karamoko, *Community protests in South Africa: Trends, analysis and explanations*, Community Law Centre, July 2011. There were 8.73 protests a month in 2007, 9.83 in 2008, 19.18 in 2009 and 16.33 in the first half of 2010. After this the number of clashes declined (to

11.08 per month – possibly because of the World Cup celebrations), a trend that continued in the early months of 2011, when there were 8.08 incidents a month. But the research points to increasing violence involving larger numbers of participants.

112 Karamoko, *Community protests in South Africa*, p 35.

113 P Gastrow, *Organised crime in South Africa*.

114 *Ibid.*

115 P Williams, 'Transnational organised crime and national and international security: A global assessment', in V Gamba (ed), *Society under siege: Crime, violence and illegal weapons,* TCP Series, vol 1. Halfway House: Institute for Security Studies, September 1997, pp 19–23.

116 M Shaw, 'State responses to organised crime in South Africa', *Transnational organised crime*, vol 3, no 2, Summer 1997, p 3.

117 Institute for Security Studies, Enhancing regional responses against organised crime (EROC) project, 'Towards more effective responses to organised crime in Southern Africa: South Africa and Lesotho', unpublished report, p 4.

118 *Ibid.*

119 *Ibid*, p 11.

120 *Ibid*, p 25.

121 P Gastrow, 'Main trends in the development of South Africa's organised crime', Halfway House: Institute for Security Studies, *African Security Review*, vol 8, no 6, 1999.

122 *Ibid.*

123 *Ibid.*

124 'Russia linked to arms and drugs in South Africa', World Justice Information Network (WJIN) News, 25 November 1998.

125 *Ibid.*

126 *Guardian,* 5 April 2012 http://www.guardian.co.uk/world/2012/apr/05/ viktor-bout-sentenced-25-years-prison.

127 *Ibid.*

128 *Ibid.*

129 SAPA, 1 September 2011.

130 South African Institute of Security Studies, *Organising against organised rhino poaching,* 24 May 2010. http://www.issafrica.org/iss_today.php?ID=955.

131 *Mail & Guardian,* 15 September 2011. http://mg.co.za/ article/2011-09-15-accused-rhino-poaching-kingpin-denied-bail.

132 *Mail & Guardian*, 22 July 2011. http://mg.co.za/ article/2011-07-22-poachers-prostitutes-and-profit.

133 For background see 'Men of Honor', *Africa Confidential*, vol 40, no 3, 5 February 1999.

134 'Palazzolo case wasted the court's time', *Weekend Argus,* 14 March 2003.

135 'Men of Honor', *Africa Confidential*.

136 'State applies to have Palazzolo bail withdrawn', *Daily Dispatch,* 7 March 2000.

137 'Palazzolo: The mobster from Burgersdorp, *Mail & Guardian,* 19 November 1999.

138 'Nats were in bed with Mafia boss', *Mail & Guardian,* 5 February 1999.

139 'Dispatch readers first to hear of Palazzolo', *Daily Dispatch*, 15 October 1998.

140 'Palazzolo: The mobster from Burgersdorp', *Mail & Guardian* 19 November 1999.

141 'Top SA spy linked to Vito Palazzolo', *Mail & Guardian*, 1 January 2002.

142 Palazzolo v Minister of Justice and Constitutional Development and Others (4731/2010) [2010] ZAWCHC 422 (14 June 2010). http://www.saflii.org/za/cases/ZAWCHC/2010/422.html.

143 'Department of Justice accused of bias against Palazzolo', *Cape Times*, 19 May 2010.

144 Associated Press 31 March 2012, Bankok Post, 9 April 2011. http://www.bangkokpost.com/news/crimes/288025/thai-police-do-a-job-on-italian-mafioso.

145 Statement of the ANC National Working Committee, 1 December 1998: 'The NWC discussed and adopted a document on the ANC deployment strategy. The deployment strategy will provide broad guidelines for deployment of ANC cadres to all areas which the movement regards as crucial for the transformation project. The deployment strategy will ensure that the movement deploys its cadres in accordance with their knowledge, skills, abilities and experience. A deployment committee headed by ANC deputy president Jacob Zuma has been established and will advise the National Executive Committee on all matters of deployment.'

146 *Herald*, 9 December 2011. http://www.peherald.com/news/article/3975.

147 D Atkinson, Taking to the streets: Has developmental local government failed in South Africa, *State of the Nation 2007*, Cape Town, HSCR, p 66.

148 ANC, National General Council Document, Transformation of State and Governance, July 2010.

149 SAPA, 14 September 2011.

150 Cosatu-SACP joint statement on fighting corruption and tenderpreneurship, 7 April 2011

151 Cosatu Secretary-General Zwelinzima Vavi's message of solidarity to the SACP at a rally to celebrate the SACP's 90th anniversary, 31 July 2011. http://www.cosatu.org.za/show.php?ID=5253

152 *Business Day*, 20 September 2011.

153 Financial Action Task Force, *Mutual evaluation report anti-money laundering and combating the financing of terrorism*, 26 February 2009.

154 Country report to the 11th United Nations Congress on Crime prevention and criminal justice, parts 1 and 2.

155 *Ibid*, part 2, p 18. The report's message was somewhat undermined by the front cover of the publication, featuring a smiling picture of South Africa's representative – the National Commissioner of the South African Police, Jackie Selebi. The man who was telling the UN of his country's achievements in fighting organised crime would just a few years later be convicted of corruption and found to have had links with just such crime syndicates.

156 National Prosecuting Authority (NPA) Annual Report 2006/2007.

157 *The Khampepe Commission of Inquiry Report*, February 2006, p 6.

158 *Ibid*, p 8.

159 Prince Mashele, *The Khampepe Commission: The future of the Scorpions at stake*, Institute for Security Studies Occasional Paper 126, June 2006.

160 Democratic Alliance, The case for retaining the Scorpions, February 2008. www.da.org.za/docs/6647/Scorpions_document.pdf.

161 *National Prosecuting Authority (NPA) Annual Report 2008/2009*. The value of goods seized fell from over R4 billion in 2007/2008 to just R35 million in 2008/2007.

162 Constitutional Court of South Africa, Case CCT 48/10 [2011] ZACC 6, 17 March 2011. The court ruled that: 'Chapter 6A of the South African Police Service Act 68 of 1995 is inconsistent with Constitution and invalid to the extent that it fails to secure an adequate degree of independence for the Directorate for Priority Crime Investigation.'

163 *Ibid*, para 236.

164 T Ndebele, K Lebone and F Cronje, *Broken blue line: The involvement of the South African Police Force in serious and violent crime in South Africa*. A research paper by the Unit for Risk Analysis, South African Institute of Race Relations, 14 February 2011. The authors analysed statistics from the official Independent Complaint Directorate's report for 2008/09. In that period, 387 police assaults were reported to the Directorate, yet only six officers were officially prosecuted, a success rate of just 1.58 per cent.

165 Financial Action Task Force, *Mutual evaluation report anti-money laundering and combating the financing of terrorism*, p 79.

166 'In 2002/03, 47 per cent (225 cases) of those investigated for financial misconduct were discharged, but this figure fell to 11 per cent in 2008/09. An increasing number of guilty employees receive a final written warning as a disciplinary step, while 23 per cent receive a combination of sanctions.' *Implementing the Public Finance Management Act in South Africa: How Far Are We?* Idasa 2012, p 26.

167 Meeting between the President and coordinating ministers: Justice Crime prevention and Security (jcps) cluster: outcome 3: progress report, p 15.

168 Author's interview, April 2011.

169 Statement issued by the Presidency, 24 October 2011.

170 *Business Day*, 25 October 2011.

171 OECD Directorate for Financial and Enterprise Affairs, South Africa: phase 2 report on the application of the convention on combating bribery of foreign public officials in international business transactions and the 2009 recommendation for further combating bribery of foreign public officials in international business transactions, p 9.

172 Cosatu CEC political discussion paper, September 2010. http://www.cosatu.org.za/list.php?type=Discussion.

173 *Pretoria News*, 7 December 2011. http://www.iol.co.za/news/special-features/the-zuma-era/state-used-to-fight-zuma-foes-1.1193649.

174 MB Makiwane and DOD Chimere-Dan (eds), *The people matter: The state of the population in the Eastern Cape*, Research and Population Unit, Eastern Cape Department of Social Development, 2010, pp 15-16; W Punt, *Case story: Eastern*

Cape – *Introduction of regional anticorruption programmes.*
www.unglobalcompact.org/docs/issues_doc/7.7/.../BAC_2D.3.pd..

175 ANC statement on its list of candidates for legislatures, 13 February 1999.
http://www.anc.org.za/show.php?id=8137.

176 *Mail & Guardian*, 15 January 2007.

177 SAPA, 22 May 2001. This included Transport Minister Dullah Omar, ANC
national spokesman Smuts Ngonyama and Deputy Home Affairs Minister
Charles Nqakula.

178 For example, police corruption has also been found to play a role in vehicle
hijackings, either through police collusion with hijackers or bribes taken by the
traffic department for licensing and re-registration of stolen vehicles. It has also
been argued that police and private security companies play an integral part in
cash-in-transit robberies, see J Irish-Qhobosheane and N Moshe. 'Modern day
pirates on South African roads: Cash-in-transit networks in South Africa', in
Irish-Qhobosheane, *Gentlemen or villains, thugs or heroes? The social economy
of crime in South Africa,* Pretoria: South African Institute for International
Affairs, 2007.

179 Author's interview, April 2011.

180 Institute for Security Studies, *Enhancing regional responses against organised
crime,* p 85.

Chapter 11   Sharing the Beloved Country: Land Reform Since 1994

1 *Sol Plaatje: selected writings,* ed B Willan. Athens, Ohio: Ohio University press,
1997, p 186.

2 L Platzky and C Walker, *The surplus people: Forced removals in South Africa.*
Johannesburg: Ravan Press, 1985, quoted in M Wegerif, B Russell and I Grundling,
Still searching for security: the reality of farm dweller evictions in South Africa,
Nkuzi Development Association and Social Surveys, December 2005, p 28.

3 Department of Rural Development and Land Reform, Strategic Plan, 2011-2014,
p 40.

4 Department of Rural Development and Land Reform, Annual Report, 2009-2010,
p 27.

5 African National Congress, 1994. *The Reconstruction and Development
Programme: A Policy Framework.* Johannesburg: Umanyano Publications,
paragraph 2.4.1.

6 C Walker. *Landmarked: Land claims and land restitution in South Africa.*
Johannesburg: Jacana Press and Athens, OH: Ohio University Press, 2008, p 43,
quoted in D Atkinson, 'Breaking down barriers: Policy gaps and new options in
South African land reform', in J Daniel, P Naidoo, D Pillay and R Southall (eds),
New South Africa Review. Johannesburg: Wits University Press, 2011.

7 *Report of the Committee of Inquiry into Farm Attacks, 31 July 2003,* p 434.
http://www.issafrica.org/CJM/farmrep/index.htm.

8 *Business Day*, 1 July 2011. http://www.businessday.co.za/articles/Content. aspx?id=147345.

9 MC Lyne and MAG Darroch, *Land redistribution in South Africa: Past performance and future policy*, BASIS CRSP Research Paper, Department of Agricultural and Applied Economics, University of Wisconsin-Madison, 2003.

10 Statement issued by the Freedom Front Plus, 15 February 2012. http://www. politicsweb.co.za/politicsweb/view/politicsweb/en/page71656?oid=280327&sn=De tail&pid=71656.

11 Address by President Jacob Zuma in response to the debate on the State of the Nation Address, National Assembly, Cape Town, 16 February 2012.

12 J Koch, *The food security policy context in South Africa*, International Policy Centre for Inclusive Growth, 2011. Others put the number of African and coloured farmers much higher, at 2.5 million households. See M Alber, *Exploring Statistics South Africa's National Household Surveys as a source of information about food security and subsistence agriculture*, Centre for Poverty Employment and Growth, HSRC, March 2009.

13 Author's interview, 12 July 2011.

14 B Cousins, 'Agrarian reform and the 'two economies': transforming South Africa's countryside', in L Ntsebeza and R Hall, *The Land Question in South Africa*. Cape Town: HSRC Press, p 230.

15 ANC Youth League 24th National Congress: Political Report, 16 June 2011, Gallagher Estates, Midrand. http://www.ancyl.org.za/show.php?id=8036.

16 Message by Oliver Tambo to the National Executive Committee of the African National Congress on the 73rd anniversary of ANC, 'Render South Africa ungovernable!' 8 January 1985. http://www.anc.org.za/show. php?id=4460&t=ES%20Reddy.

17 TAU SA statement, 22 June 2011, *Should farmers stay or go?* http://www.tlu.co.za/.

18 http://afrikaner-genocide-achives.blogspot.com/2011/02/farm-murders-victim-names-1994-2011_10.html.

19 *Report of the Committee of Inquiry into Farm Attacks*, 31 July 2003, p 418. http://www.issafrica.org/CJM/farmrep/index.htm. Some of these would have been considered political by the Truth and Reconciliation Commission, since they were carried out before 1991 and may have been a response to the PAC's call for members to attack farms to acquire arms and food.

20 http://news.bbc.co.uk/1/hi/world/africa/4492953.stm.

21 http://news.bbc.co.uk/1/hi/world/africa/7574362.stm.

22 Josee Koch, *The food security policy context in South Africa*, International Policy Centre for Inclusive Growth, 2011, p 26.

23 *Ibid*.

24 Sam Moyo, 'The land question in southern Africa: a comparative review', in L Ntsebeza and R Hall, *The Land Question in South Africa*, p 66.

25 N Andrew and P Jacobs. *Nourishing the soil for rural poverty: South Africa's unchanging land relations*. Cape Town: HSRC, 2009. They point to the problems of defining the rural areas, saying: 'One of the points of controversy today

is naturally who and what is rural and what is urban; one of the most visible measures of change are the migrations to rural towns and peripheries of large cities, which are unable to absorb them as part of either the formal or informal economies. Together with plant closings, particularly the mines, this has provoked some reverse migration and has accentuated pressures on limited available land.'

26 P Jacobs, *Agricultural Market Reforms and the Rural Poor in South Africa*, PLAAS Poverty Workshop 2009, March 2009.

27 Statistics SA, *Agricultural Surveys 2008 and 2009* (Preliminary), 23 June 2011, p 4.

28 M Wegerif, B Russell and I Grundling, *Still searching for security: The reality of farm dweller evictions in South Africa*, Nkuzi Development Association and Social Surveys, December 2005, p 185.

29 'The Nkuzi figures do not accord with census data, which showed a rise in the African population on commercial farms, but eviction survey researchers, who investigated this anomaly, argued that there might have been mistakes in Statistics South Africa's classification of enumerator areas, and therefore in overall figures. Nevertheless, the scale of evictions and displacement are enormous, and are even higher than the 1.1m black people who were forcibly removed from white farms between 1960 and 1983, at the height of apartheid. It is possible that the Nkuzi figures are too high.'

Alison Todes *et al*, 'Contemporary South African urbanisation dynamics', Paper for UNU-WIDER Conference: 'Beyond the tipping point. African development in an urban world', Cape Town, June 2008, p 7.

30 Ibid, p 187.

31 *Ibid*, p 88.

32 http://www.info.gov.za/gazette/acts/1996/a3-96.htm.

33 A du Toit and F Ally, *The externalisation and casualisation of farm labour in Western Cape horticulture*, Centre for Legal Studies, University of the Western Cape, Research Report 16, December 2003.

34 http://mg.co.za/article/2011-01-07-farmers-slam-tougher-land-law.

35 Economy diagnostic report, National Planning Commission, 9 June 2011, Centre for Poverty Employment and Growth, HSRC, p 13.

36 M Alber, *Exploring Statistics: South Africa's National Household Surveys as a source of information about food security and subsistence agriculture*, Centre for Poverty Employment and Growth, HSRC, March 2009, p 42.

37 Statistics SA, Rural Survey, June 1999.

38 MB Makiwane and DOD Chimere-Dan (eds), *The people matter: The state of the population in the Eastern Cape,* Research and Population Unit, Eastern Cape Department of Social Development, 2010, pp 15–16.

39 *State of local government in South Africa overview report*, National State of Local Government Assessments Working Documents, COGTA 2009, p 77.

40 Atkinson, *Breaking down barriers: Policy gaps and new options in South African land reform*, in *New South African Review 1*, p 374.

41 *South Africa: Land reform programme unsustainable*, IRIN News, 2 September 2009.http://www.irinnews.org/Report.aspx?ReportId=85974.

42 Atkinson, *Breaking down barriers,* p 366.

43 *Ibid*, p 366.

44 *Ibid*, p 367.

45 SAPA, 2 February 2007.

46 *Sunday Times*, 28 February 2009.

47 See Atkinson, *Breaking down barriers*, p 370.

48 Transcript of Economic Sectors and Employment cluster briefing presented by Gugile Nkwinti, Minister of Rural Development and Land Reform and Naledi Pandor, Minister of Science and Technology at Imbizo Media Centre, Cape Town, 2 March 2010.http://www.politicsweb.co.za/politicsweb/view/politicsweb/en/page71656?oid=164364&sn=Detail.

49 E Lahiff, 'Land reform in South Africa', in H Binswanger-Kkhize, C Bourguignon and R van den Brink et al (eds), *Agricultural Land Redistribution*. Washington: World Bank, 2009, p 176.

50 Hans P. Binswanger-Mkhize *Land redistribution for agricultural development: Case studies in three provinces*. Cape Town: HSRC, October 2003.

51 E Lahiff, *Land redistribution in South Africa: Progress to date*, Programme for Land and Agrarian Studies, University of the Western Cape, 17 December 2008.

52 Agence France Presse, 31 August 2011. http://www.news24.com/SouthAfrica/Politics/Black-farmers-selling-land-back-to-whites-20110831.

53 Department of Rural Development and Land Reform, Green Paper on Land Reform, 2011, pp 5-6.

54 Agence France Presse, 31 August 2011.

55 *Times* (Johannesburg), 2 September 2011. http://www.iol.co.za/business/business-news/land-reform-proposals-under-attack-1.1129918

56 Agence France Presse, 31 August 2011.

57 SAPA, 2 September 2011.

58 Draft Green Paper on Land Reform: The DA critique, 12 September 2011. http://www.politicsweb.co.za/politicsweb/view/politicsweb/en/page71654?oid=255688&sn=Detail.

59 http://www.thedailymaverick.co.za/article/2011-07-20-analysis-valuing-land-the-next-frontier.

60 City Press, 10 July 2011.

61 P Kumar, 'Zimbabwe: Good economic genes stunted by politics', blog, 2 May 2011. http://blogs.worldbank.org/africacan/zimbabwe-good-economic-genes-stunted-by-politics.

62 *Special Report: FAO/WFP Crops and food supply assessment mission to Zimbabwe*, 29 May 2002.

63 *Ibid*.

64 BM Sims, *The politics of land in Zimbabwe*. Pretoria: Idasa, 30 May 2011. http://www.idasa.org/our_work/programme/states_in_transition/.

65 Human Rights Watch, *Fast track land reform in Zimbabwe*, vol 14, no 1, March 2002, p 26.

66 *Special Report, FAO/WFP Crop and Food supply Assessment Mission to Zimbabwe*, 29 May 2002.

67 FEWSNET report, 17 July 2002.

68 FEWSNET report, 23 December 2002.

69 FAO/WFP Special alert, number 307 Zimbabwe, 28 April 2000.

70 FEWSNET report, 23 December 2002.

71 S Pazvakavambwa and V Hungwe, 'Land Redistribution in Zimbabwe', in *Agricultural Land Redistribution*, ed H Binswanger-Kkhize, C Bourguignon and R van den Brink et al, p 156.

72 *Special Report, FAO/WFP: Crop and Food Security Assessment Mission to Zimbabwe*, 9 August 2010.

73 *Ibid.*

74 Phone interview with author and email, 17 July 2011. Many white farmers simply left the country, taking up farming in neighbouring countries. As a result, tobacco production in Tanzania, Zambia and Malawi have boomed. http://www.tobaccofarmquarterly.com/home.php?id=119&cid=4&article_id=10136.

75 *Ibid.*

76 Author's interviews, November 2011.

77 *Ibid.*

78 SAPA, 19 November 2010.

79 http://www.capegateway.gov.za/eng/your_gov/3150/speeches/2010/jul/202385.

80 SAPA, 19 November 2010.

81 K Sartorius and J Kirsten, *Contracts and contract farming as potential mechanisms to improve market access for black farmers in South Africa*, School of Accountancy, University of the Witwatersrand and Department of Agricultural Economics, Extension and Rural Development, University of Pretoria, February 2006.

82 E Lahiff, 'Land reform in South Africa: Progress to date', Paper presented at 'Land Redistribution: Towards a Common Vision, Regional Course, Southern Africa, 9–13 July 2007'.

83 *Independent* (London), 3 September 2011.

Chapter 12 Rumbles and Rifts: Service Delivery Protests

1 L Thompson and N Nleya, *Community activism and protest in Khayelitsha, Cape Town*, African Centre For Citizenship & Democracy (Accede), 2010, p 5.

2 'Catapults against stun grenades', *The Witness*, 15 April 2011.

3 The concept of 'repertoires' of protest is more fully explored in the seminal *The smoke that calls: Insurgent citizenship, collective violence and the struggle for a place in the New South Africa*, Centre for the Study of Violence and Reconciliation, July 2011.

4 J Karamoko, 'Community protests in South Africa: Trends, analysis and explanations', *Local Democracy, Peace & Human Security*, 2011, p 7.

5 'Gauteng overtakes W Cape in municipal productivity – Municipal IQ', *Politicsweb*, 6 December 2011.

6   Karamoko, 'Community Protests in South Africa, pp 1–2.

7   *Ibid*, pp 12–13.

8   P Alexander, 'Rebellion of the poor: South Africa's service delivery protest – a Preliminary analysis', *Review of African Political Economy*, vol. 37, no 123, 2010, pp 26–7.

9   Minister of Police reply to question no 194, Internal Question Paper no 2, 19 April 2010, available from www.pmg.org.za.

10 *Ibid*, para (d).

11 *Ibid*, para (e).

12 'Service delivery protests decline', *Business Report*, 10 October 2011.

13 In December 2011, for example, Jacob Zuma made waves by placing five Limpopo departments under national administration, citing frequent and persistent governance problems. Critics have responded claiming that the move was predicated on the desire to undercut the support of anti-Zuma factions in the province, although these claims have struggled against the fact that governance indicators from the province remain poor.

14 'Service delivery protests decline', *Business Report*, 10 October 2011.

15 Municipal IQ presentation to City of Johannesburg, 30 August 2011. www.municipaliq.co.za.

16 National Assembly, written reply to question no 2516, Minister of Human Settlements, 14 October 2010. Available from www.pmg.org.za.

17 Statistics SA, General Household Survey 2010, publication number P0318, p 21. www.statssa.gov.za.

18 D Malzbender, 'Domestic electricity provision in democratic South Africa', Paper for Nordic Africa Institute's conflicting forms of citizenship programme, September 2005, p 9.

19 Statistics SA, General Household Survey 2010, p 4. www.statssa.gov.za.

20 *Ibid*, p 5.

21 *Ibid*, p 20.

22 D Atkinson, 'Taking to the streets: Has developmental local government failed in South Africa?' in *State of the Nation: South Africa 2007*. Pretoria: HSRC Press, 2007, p 60.

23 General Household Survey, 2010, Statistics SA, publication number P0318, p 4. www.statssa.gov.za.

24 'Crack team for KZN housing projects', *The Mercury*, 4 March 2011.

25 T Gurr, *Why men rebel,* Princeton: Princeton University Press, 1970, p 24.

26 See, for example, N Nleya, L Thompson, C Tapscott, L Piper and M Esau, 'Reconsidering the origins of protest in South Africa: Some lessons from Cape Town and Pietermaritzburg', *Africanus*, vol 41, no 1, 2011, p 26; and K Allan and K Heese, 'Understanding why service delivery protests take place and who is to blame'. www.municipaliq.co.za.

27 R Dowse and J Hughes, *Political sociology*. Great Britain: John Wesley and Sons, 1986; and P Lupsha, 'Explanation of political violence: Some psychological theories versus indignation', in *Politics & Society*, vol 2, no 1, 1971.

28 General Household Survey, 2010, Statistics SA, publication number P0318, fig 17.
    www.statssa.gov.za.

29 *Ibid.*

30 *The smoke that calls,* p 19.

31 *Ibid,* p 19.

32 Karamoko, 'Community protests in South Africa', p 8.

33 *Consolidated general report on local government audit outcomes 2009–10,*
    Auditor-General's Office, RP 92/2011, p 2.

34 Atkinson, 'Taking to the streets', p 62.

35 *Ibid,* p 61.

36 *Ibid.*

37 See, for example, L Marais, Z Matebesi, M Mthombeni, L Botes and D van
    Rooyen, 'Municipal unrest in the Free State (South Africa): A new form of social
    movement?' in *Politeia,* vol 27, no 2, 2008, p 65.

38 Quoted in V Naidoo and P Jackson, 'Reviewing South Africa's efforts to combat
    corruption in its bureaucracy: 1994–2009', in P Jackson, J Muzondidya, V
    Naidoo, M Ndletyana and M Sithole, *South African governance in review: Anti-
    corruption, local government, traditional leadership.* Pretoria: HSRC Press, 2009,
    p 8.

39 Atkinson, 'Taking to the streets', p 62.

40 *The smoke that calls,* p 20.

41 *Ibid.*

42 This account is drawn from *The Smoke that Calls.*

43 N Nleya, 'Linking service delivery and protest in South Africa: An exploration of
    evidence from Khayelitsha', *Africanus,* vol 41, no 1, 2011, p 10.

Conclusion: So Who Does Rule South Africa?

1 NR Mandela, *Long walk to freedom.* Boston: Little Brown, 1994, pp 85–6.

2 'Facing down the new authoritarians', *Mail & Guardian,* 23 December 2010.
   http://uk.mg40.mail.yahoo.com/author/contact/nic-dawes.

3 Hein Marais, *South Africa pushed to the limit: the political economy of change.*
   London: Zed Press, 2011, p 144.

4 'Ngoako Ramatlhodi: ANC's fatal concessions', *Times* (Johannesburg),
   1 September 2011. http://www.timeslive.co.za/opinion/commentary/2011/09/01/
   the-big-read-anc-s-fatal-concessions.

Acknowledgements

Our grateful thanks to Chris Bulford, Nic Dawes, Nick Erickson, Stephen Ellis, Andrew Feinstein, Hermann Giliomee, Raymond Hartley, Annette Hübschle, Martin Nicol, Sipho Pityana, Zina Rohan, Chris Saunders, Colette Schulz-Herzenberg, Wolfgang Thomas, Stanley Uys, Hennie van Vuuren, Sue de Villiers, and Mandy Wiener, for their various contributions.

Thanks to Mersini Iakovidis for her research on Chapter 9: The One That Got Away: How Helen Zille Built a Political Fortress in Cape Town, and to Richard McLaverty for his research on Chapter 10: Crime, Corruption and Connections.

Thanks to Jeremy Boraine for his encouragement and patience, and Frances Perryer for her careful editing.

To our friends and family, who have been an endless source of inspiration and encouragement. To Gill Black for her endless support, love and criticism, and to Mia Allers for enduring yet another book with love and understanding.

INDEX